ROBERT EMMET AND THE R

Robert Emmet and the Rebellion of 1798

Ruán O'Donnell

University of Limerick

IRISH ACADEMIC PRESS

DUBLIN • PORTLAND, OR

First published in 2003 by
IRISH ACADEMIC PRESS
44 Northumberland Road, Dublin 4, Ireland

and in the United States of America by
IRISH ACADEMIC PRESS
c/o ISBS, 920 N.E. 58th Avenue, Suite 300, Portland
Oregon 97213–3786

Website: www.iap.ie

© Ruán O'Donnell 2003

British Library Cataloguing in Publication Data

A catalogue record of this book is available from the British Library.
ISBN 0–7165–2788–X (cloth)
ISBN 0–7165–2789–8

Library of Congress Cataloging-in-Publication Data

A catalog record of this book is available from the Library of Congress.

Cover design by Susan Waine shows Emmet depicted as
Washington, and the Parliament House by James Malton
(courtesy of the National Library of Ireland).

Typeset in 11 pt on 13 pt Sabon
by Carrigboy Typesetting Services, County Cork
Printed by ßetaprint Ltd., Dublin

*For Emmet Donnelly and family of Ballymurphy,
Belfast, in hope for the future.*

Contents

LIST OF ILLUSTRATIONS   viii

ACKNOWLEDGEMENTS   ix

PREFACE   x

Chapter One
Early Life and Education   1

Chapter Two
The United Irishmen   28

Chapter Three
Dublin in the Great Rebellion of 1798   80

Chapter Four
Revival and Crisis, 1799   122

Chapter Five
Emmet Abroad, 1800–1802   162

NOTES   205

INDEX   263

Illustrations

1 'A new plan of Dublin'
2 The Emmet family home
3 Thomas Addis Emmet
4 Henry Grattan
5 Archibald Hamilton Rowan
6 Thomas Moore
7 Theobald Wolfe Tone
8 John Sheares
9 William James MacNeven
10 William Sampson
11 Robert Emmet
12 Symbols of the United Irishmen
13 Emmet's notes on Locke
14 John Fitzgibbon, Lord Clare
15 Edward Hudson
16 Moira House by William Brocas
17 Lord Edward Fitzgerald
18 The Trinity College expulsions
19 Dublin Castle Proclamation
20 Dublin rebels in Wexford
21 Joseph Holt
22 Henry Charles Sirr by T. Martyn
23 James Hope by William Charles Nixon
24 Edward Cooke
25 Listing for Philip Long from *Wilson's Dublin Directory*, 1803
26 Michael Dwyer by George Petrie
27 Insurgents
28 Fort George, Scotland
29 William Corbett
30 Arthur O'Connor
31 Samuel Neilson
32 Napper Tandy
33 Philip Yorke, Earl Hardwicke

Acknowledgements

I would like to thank the following friends, colleagues and relatives for their encouragement: John Logan, Bernadette Whelan, Padraig Lenihan, Eoin Devereux, John O'Brennan, Catherine Lawless, Tom Bartlett, Liam Chambers, John O'Connor, Brian O'Clerigh, David N. Doyle, Peter Moore, Kevin Whelan, Angus Mitchell, Jim Smyth, Bobby Ballagh, Jimmy Kelly, Daire Keogh, Breandan Mac Suibhne, Richard Roche, Bob and Lesley Reece, Iain McCalman, Jon Manley, Frank Cass, John P. Waters, John and Anne Nolan, Henry and Mary Cairns, Shay and Mary Courtney, Bernard Browne, Stephen Leslie, Eddy Vickery, Peter Gifford, David Granville, Joe Jamison, Joe O'Hara, Tony Tracy, Sean Goff, Anne-Marie Whitaker, Leo and Rosy Fitzgerald, Padraig O'Mathuna, Gay Clery, Sean Sherwin, Diarmuid Coogan, Brendan O'Donoghue, Colette O'Flaherty, Brian McNally, Michael O'Flanagan, Michael O Doibhilin, Lorcan Collins, James McGuire, Jim Quinn, Fintan Lane, Sylvie Kleinman, Gerry McGeough, Joanna Finegan, Owen Rodgers, Perry McIntyre, Gerry Long, Catriona Crowe, Jack Hyland, Jim and Geraldine Donnelly, Robert Dowds, Sally Shiels, William O'Brien, Daphne and Olive Kirwan, Austin and Kay Kirwan, Jimmy and Fiona O'Donnell, Terry, Stephanie, Conor, Eoin and Kieran Dardis, Maurice and Christine Kirwan, Al Kirwan, Rory and Patsy Buckley, Niall and Ashley Hughes, Sighle and Caomhin Buckley, Aoife and Cameron Clotworthy, Al, June and Conor O'Donnell, Melissa and Peter O'Faherty, Maeve, Ruairi, Fiachra, Cormac and Saoirse O'Donnell, John Bowman and my late friend Jonathan Philbin Bowman.

Preface

Robert Emmet, one of the best-known names in Irish history, has no major biography. This is due in no small part to the absence of his private papers, which has stymied efforts to account for large gaps in his short life of twenty-five years. Other than several innocuous letters to Sarah Curran, no sizeable cache of Emmet's correspondence has been found. Fundamental details such as his place of birth and the date of his induction into the revolutionary Society of United Irishmen cannot be ascertained with certainty. While Emmet died too young to contemplate drafting his memoirs, the fact that the location of his grave site was deliberately concealed from his contemporaries suggests that many significant omissions from the documentary record were far from circumstantial. This is symptomatic of the intensity of Emmet's clandestine political activity between 1796 and 1803, the entire span of his adult years.[1]

As a youth Emmet cultivated the skill of writing in different styles, avoided signing his name and used codes and invisible ink to disguise his intentions. His known aliases include Ellis, Hewitt and Cunningham and several patriotic poems written by him were attributed to 'Trebor', the reverse of his christian name. There were probably many more. What little remains of Emmet's acknowledged writings, therefore, cannot be taken at face value. The short account of the Rising of 1803 written by him on the eve of his execution is suspect as it passed into the hands of his enemies when the cause of the United Irishmen was not yet lost. Given his highly developed penchant for subterfuge, a counter-intelligence dimension to the document cannot be discounted. It certainly contained claims that were untrue and omitted details which would have revealed the full scope of the conspiracy. Sentiments expressed so powerfully by Emmet in his speech from the dock on 19 September 1803, arguably the most famous speech in modern Irish history, are almost invariably taken out of context. Assessing his role in the United Irishmen is further complicated by the lack of an authoritative biography setting down his formative political experiences and objectives.[2]

The events of 23 July 1803, 'Emmet's Rebellion', have proved exceptionally difficult to untangle. Government officials Alexander

Marsden, William Wickham, General Henry Edward Fox and Earl Hardwicke (Philip Yorke) produced incompatible reports on the subject, attesting to the confusion which reigned that night. The controversy stirred up by the Rising of 1803 in the imperial parliament in London ensured that the standard problems of subjectivism and contradictory testimony were compounded by the ulterior personal concerns of commentators. A bitter conflict of interest emerged in Ireland between the civil administrators in Dublin Castle and the military authorities at Army Headquarters. This reverberated in Westminster in the form of a gulf between liberal Whigs and Conservatives. Hardwicke commented privately in February 1804: 'the circumstances of the unfortunate insurrection in Dublin are very imperfectly, if at all known' and that the 'anxiety' of politicians 'to avert all discussion has been too apparent'.[3] Uncertainty surrounds the basic sequence of incidents during the Rising and no sufficiently detailed and analysed account of the upheaval has yet appeared. Under the circumstances, it is not surprising that Emmet's intentions remain a matter for debate.

It may have been to respect his brother's perceived final wishes that Thomas Addis Emmet, the towering republican influence on his short political career, neglected to set down a potentially definitive perspective. Self-reproach probably stayed his hand in view of the dismal manner in which their joint venture terminated in Dublin. Robert Emmet had returned to Ireland from the safety of Paris in October 1802 to advance the agenda of the senior republican leadership coterie adhering to Addis Emmet. Failure brought the younger Emmet to the scaffold and the elder to permanent exile in the United States. Family sources attested that even when safe in New York from the reach of his enemies Addis Emmet 'was never known in after life to have made a voluntary reference to his brother Robert'.[4]

The fate of Emmet also haunted Thomas Moore, a near neighbour and companion from childhood. Moore wrote a biography of a United Irishman he once glimpsed at a distance on Grafton Street, Lord Edward Fitzgerald, in preference to the student radical with whom he conversed and conspired in 1797–98. The poet's subsumed apologia for his own United Irish days was interspersed with passages in which Emmet was warmly recollected as a youth. If Moore's veiled characterisation of Emmet as 'The Minstrel Boy' fuelled his friend's popularity in the nineteenth century, it was only to the detriment of the factual record. Moore had published items on the story of Emmet and Curran as early as 1807 which made no explicit reference to their inspiration. Guilt played its part in this silence. Moore narrowly survived the April 1798 crackdown which ended Emmet's formal education at Trinity College and progressed to the haven of Bermuda in the same year his young companion was executed. Deprived of the lost biographies of Moore and Addis Emmet, historians have struggled to interpret the anecdotal snippets relayed by other contemporaries such as Thomas Cloney, Walter Cox, Miles Byrne, James Hope, Anne Devlin, William Drennan and Valentine Lawless.[5]

That Emmet was the pre-eminent conspirator in Ireland in 1803 is beyond question, although his interaction with Thomas Russell, Thomas Addis Emmet, William Dowdall, Philip Long and William MacNeven is evidence of a far more serious conspiracy than indicated by the skirmishes in Dublin's south city. In fact, the uprising planned by Emmet's staff in Dublin never took place and they took pains to ensure that various contingencies were cancelled when disaster seemed inevitable. Neither Emmet nor his leading associates should be judged on the basis of the clashes of 23 July 1803. The fighting was, nonetheless, intense and deadly, marking one of the few occasions when Irish insurgents combated regular soldiers on the streets of the national capital. Although long misrepresented as a free-ranging outburst by a leaderless and drunken rabble, there is compelling evidence pointing to a high degree of localised deliberation and determination. Respected mid-level United Irish leaders held and defended the administrative heart of the capital after Emmet's officers had departed the scene. They won a series of tactical victories in skirmishes which only proved pyrrhic when they failed to ignite a massive revolt. That the United Irishmen were capable of achieving even temporary ascendancy in a time of war with France and in a city garrisoned by 4,000 troops warrants greater consideration than hitherto extended. While Emmet's seemingly immortal fame is not without foundation it rests on the wrong pillars. This contextualised biography offers an opportunity to reassess Emmet's influence in its proper historical framework, Ireland in the revolutionary decade of 1793–1803.

CHAPTER ONE

Early Life and Education

Robert Emmet's ancestors, the Emmotts of Emmott Hall, Colne, Lancashire, arrived in Ireland from England in the early 1600s. While no genealogical line had been traced between the Emmets and Emmotts, the coat of arms granted to the English branch was identical to that displayed by Robert Emmet's family over a hundred years later. By the eighteenth century the Irish Emmetts were established in counties Tipperary, Limerick, Waterford and Kildare and had inter-married with many landed families in Munster and Leinster. Christopher Emmett of Tipperary town, grandfather of Robert Emmet, was an eminent doctor who owned a 150-acre estate at Crossayle near Cappawhite.[1] He married Rebecca Temple in February 1727, grand-daughter of Sir Thomas Temple, and quickly had two sons, Thomas and Robert. The younger boy, Robert, was born in Tipperary on 29 November 1729 and became the father of the eponymous revolu-tionary. As a young man, Robert Emmet senior studied medicine at the Royal Academy of Sciences in Montpellier University, France. On receiving his MD around 1750, he travelled on the Continent before returning to Ireland and setting up practice in Cork city. He was apparently the first of the Munster Emmetts to drop the second 't' from his surname. Dr Robert Emmet spent the early years of his medical career producing *Tentamina Medica, de Mensium Fluxu et de Curatione Morborum Cephalicorum*, a gynaecological text pub-lished in 1753. He joined the Board of Cork's Charitable Infirmary and worked there in often trying conditions until April 1770. He was described by an acquaintance as being 'a man of venerable appear-ance, grave deportment, impressive manner, and easy, unaffected politeness in conversation and address'.[2]

It was during his time in Cork city that Dr Emmet encountered Elizabeth 'Betty' Mason of Ballydowney (Kerry), whom he married on 16 November 1760. This widened the social connections of the Emmets to include the Spring-Rices of west Limerick, the Powers of Elton Grove, Kerry, and other families with roots in the south and west of Ireland. Kerry links were maintained throughout Dr Emmet's life and in January 1802 his leasehold property at Knockenna was bequeathed to his eldest surviving son, Thomas Addis Emmet. Marriage brought several properties under Dr Emmet's control from which he attempted to derive income. Two substantial mountain farms at Dooneny and Derreenvealnaslee, eight miles from Bantry, were advertised by him for lease in December 1766. The main family home was at Hammond's Marsh in Cork city and they kept a villa at Cottage.[3]

In 1769 the Emmets moved to a new house built for them on Dunscombe's Marsh not long before an unexpected offer to Dr Emmet of appointment as State Physician. Securing the most senior medical post in Ireland required the urgent payment of £1,000, which Dr Emmet could not raise without selling some of his many houses and farms. On 1 January 1770 he put the properties at Dunscombe's Marsh, Inchigeela, Cottage and Dooneny on the market. This generated an insufficient sum and by 22 January a small Killarney estate he had acquired by purchase was also advertised for lease or sale. While the disposal of these assets was being arranged, the family rented a house in George's Street, Cork, where they remained until late April 1770.[4]

Dr Emmet's appointment as State Physician was arranged through the agency of his relative on his maternal side, Lord George Grenville Nugent Temple, later 1st Marquis of Buckingham. Under his patronage, Emmet obtained the office on 28 February 1770 for £1,000, the equivalent of one year's salary. The money was paid to the widow of Dr Robert Robinson, the previous incumbent, who had held the position since 1753.[5] Dr Emmet's duties in Dublin commenced on 6 March 1770 and included governorship of Saint Patrick's Hospital for the Insane, Ireland's first institute of the kind which had been founded in 1745 by Dean Swift. Emmet was also Physician and Treasurer at Saint Patrick's, for which he was paid £400 per annum in addition to his salary as State Physician. In 1772 his status in the medical establishment was further exalted when he became Licentiate in Physic at the College of Physicians in Dublin. These lucrative and responsible appointments required frequent attendance in the capital, where the family moved before the close of 1770.[6]

The Emmets took up residence in the Kildare Street end of Molesworth Street, no. 35, within sight of the city seat of the Duke of Leinster, Ireland's premier titled family. The Duke was the brother of Lord Edward Fitzgerald, leader of the United Irishmen in May 1798, and was also a cousin of English Whig leader Charles James

Fox. There were then three children in the Emmet family: Christopher Temple and Thomas Addis, born in Cork in 1761 and 1764 respectively, and Mary Anne, born in Dublin in 1773 after the deaths of numerous infant siblings from smallpox and typhoid. Smallpox, a virulent and often deadly disease which ravaged all classes, also claimed Dr Emmet's only brother, Thomas, at his Tipperary home in June 1758. The Emmets lived in Molesworth Street until 1776 or early 1777 when they moved to St Stephen's Green West, beside the College of Surgeons. Relocation testified to the family's secure financial position and brought them into an expanding and increasingly fashionable quarter of Georgian Dublin. The La Touches, borough patrons and founders of the Bank of Ireland, purchased three houses around the Green. The magnate Lansdowne and Meath families also moved into the district while the famous Thomas 'Buck' Whaley lived at no. 86 until his death in 1800. The new Emmet home was much larger than their first city property and was close to the Houses of Parliament at College Green, Trinity College and Dublin Castle, the seat of the Viceroy's executive.[7]

The house purchased by the Emmets, demolished in the 1980s, stood at the corner of Glover's Alley and Stephen's Green West. It may have been briefly used by Dr Emmet for office space convenient to the College of Surgeons rather than as the principal family home. The building was re-fronted and divided into two addresses shortly after occupation by the Emmets and was re-addressed as numbers 109–110. Dr Emmet retained no. 109, while, by 1794, Thomas Addis Emmet and his wife, Jane Patten, lived next door. The numbers were changed once again to 124 and 125 respectively after the Emmet's sold up. In the 1790s Dr Emmet bought no. 2 Palace Street, a house built in 1766, and other city properties, which were leased to tenants.[8]

CHILDHOOD

Robert Emmet was born on 4 March 1778, Ash Wednesday, and baptised six days later in St Peter's and Kevin's Church, Aungier Street. He was the fourth successive child named in honour of his father between 1774 and 1778 and the only one to survive the early stages of infancy. The 'Robert Emett [sic], late of Stephen's Green' buried in St Peter's on 2 September 1777 was very probably the last of these sickly children. His burial from the Stephen's Green address establishes that the future United Irish leader, born six months later, was also delivered in that house rather than in Molesworth Street.[9]

Although physically slight from birth, Emmet's constitution proved sufficiently robust to withstand the dangers which threatened children of his generation and his family more than most. He survived small-pox infection with only minor facial scarring. This must have provided solace to his parents, who had endured the harrowing deaths of at least thirteen children whose names and dates were entered in the family Bible. Their distracted state of mind may be discerned from the fact that one child, Henry, born and deceased in 1762, was inadvertently omitted from the otherwise comprehensive Bible list. An intelligent, artistic and active boy, Robert Emmet was fondly recalled by his collateral descendants in America as having a 'precocious' tempera-ment. It may be presumed that the circumstances of his birth, marking the culmination of his mother's seventeenth and final pregnancy, allowed the infant a degree of latitude denied to his elder brothers and sister.[10]

The early manifestation of Emmet's considerable mental ability led to his being sent to Oswald's School in Dopping Court off Golden Lane at a young age. Past pupils included James Tandy, son of city radical Napper Tandy and an alleged associate of Emmet in 1803, and also Henry Charles Sirr, who in August of that year arrested Emmet on charges of high treason. The school was run by the Edwards brothers and was renowned for its teaching of mathematics, a subject in which Emmet excelled when at Trinity. It seems, however, that his equally impressive verbal and language proficiency was partly attained at home. Family tradition claimed that 'Latin and French were the languages commonly used . . . Irish being spoken to the servants, and English seldom used, except in social life'. One suspects that this assertion owed something to the family biographer's interest in reviving the Irish language, although it was indeed widely spoken by servants in late eighteenth-century Dublin.[11]

Emmet's time at Oswald's, while reputedly successful in academic terms, may not have been entirely positive. He was soon transferred the short distance from Golden Lane to Samuel Whyte's highly regarded English Grammar School located from 1758 at 75 (later 79) Grafton Street.[12] Whyte had taught the playwright Richard Brinsley Sheridan and his personal interest in drama extended to bringing his students to perform in Crow Street Theatre. Sheridan, for his part, was notably active in the Westminster parliamentary debates sparked by the Rising of 1803. Whyte edited the *The Shamrock, or, Hibernian Cresses* in 1772 and published further volumes of patriotic poetry in 1792, 1795 and 1800. The strong educational ethos promoted by

Whyte, therefore, reinforced the liberal, pro-reform and nationalist tenor of Emmet's home life.[13]

Thomas Moore, amongst Emmet's closest friends, became acquainted with the man he helped immortalise in poetry and song when attending Whyte's academy. As the pair were also contemporaries at Trinity College, the comparatively long duration of their relationship was unique. Another childhood friend of Emmet's, Archibald Douglas, nephew of Sir Edward Crosbie and a Church of Ireland minister in adulthood, informed the historian Madden in 1842 that Emmet 'almost lived in our house'.[14] Emmet was also on very friendly terms as a boy with his Kerry cousin St John Mason, who was a frequent visitor to Stephen's Green. Another relative, John Patten, lived in the house after the marriage of his sister to Addis Emmet in 1792. Although four years older that Robert, Patten became one of the most reliable commentators on his life. Moore, Patten and St John Mason shared Robert Emmet's political opinions when in their teens and became United Irishmen as adults. Douglas did not and this distancing may have hastened their amicable parting of ways in the 1790s.[15]

While the personalities and events of Emmet's early years are not documented in sufficient detail to assess their impact on his later political endeavours, the vibrant social life of his home resonated with formative influences. The vigorous intellectual environment at Stephen's Green had long preceded his birth and continued throughout the politically turbulent 1780s and 1790s. A key event for the Emmet family was the American War of Independence which – from 1775 – pitted the British army against thirteen of King George III's North American colonies attempting to sever their ties with the Empire. The war impinged directly on the Emmet household shortly after the Declaration of Independence in 1776 disposed their wealthy New England relatives to become refugees. The Temples, the family of Dr Emmet's mother and his chief patron, were not entirely unsympathetic to the American Patriot cause yet felt ill-at-ease with the proposed total separation of the new republic from Britain. Their sentiments were undoubtedly sharpened by the fact that Mrs Harriet Temple was the daughter of William Shirley of Roxbury, former Governor of Massachusetts and Commander-in-Chief of British forces in the colonies. On witnessing the Battle of Bunker Hill, Robert Temple, brother of Sir John Temple, settled his affairs in Boston and New York and brought his wife and three daughters to live with the Emmets in Dublin. Many American loyalists left the Boston area in March 1776 never to return. The Temples were obliged to forfeit much of their American property by returning to Ireland, for which they were compensated by the Government.[16]

The Temples stayed at Stephen's Green for eighteen months, during which time the American War which occasioned their presence must have been frequently discussed. Dr Emmet and Christopher Temple Emmet were amongst many in Ireland who supported the perspective of the insurgents. The origins and implications of the conflict had repercussions in Ireland arising from personal and business contacts, as well as the common issue of colonial status. The crisis provided the Irish 'Patriot' interest adhering to Henry Grattan and Henry Flood in Dublin's House of Commons with the opportunity to bring pressure to bear on Westminster in support of parliamentary reform. Increased legislative autonomy for the Irish parliament at College Green was sought and ultimately obtained. Grattan was acquainted with Dr Emmet and described him as a man 'with a pill and a plan. He would kill the patient who would take one, and ruin the country that would listen to the other'. They evidently did not always see eye-to-eye on political matters.[17]

The bargaining power of the Irish Patriots derived in the main from British dependence on Irish revenue and manpower. Concessions from Westminster were also encouraged by the perceived militancy of the Volunteer corps raised in 1778–79 to inhibit French invaders from exploiting the army's overseas commitments. The Volunteers came to represent the threat of the unilateral, armed assertion of Irish independence, a scenario implied by their leaders at a series of Conventions in 1782–83. One of the first fruits of the imbroglio was the commencement of the formal dismantling of the oppressive and sectarian penal laws with the passing of the Relief Bill of 1778. This palliative measure was capped by the repeal of Poyning's Law in May 1782, which enabled the Irish parliament to enact most categories of legislation without automatic referral of bills to London for ratification. College Green gained much greater control of an economy that had hitherto been subject to trade restrictions by the British parliament. Dr Emmet's Tipperary friend Richard Pennefather was the Colonel of the Cashel Volunteers at their zenith in June 1783 and was often entertained in Stephen's Green. The family had a home on Dublin's Merrion Square. Edward Moore, another Tipperary Volunteer Colonel and Grand Juryman, was later politically involved with Addis Emmet and, in March 1782, went further than Pennefather in advocating the repeal of Poyning's Law.[18] On 12 July 1784, Lisburn MP William Todd Jones urged the Belfast Volunteers to maintain 'a desire and duty to liberate the Catholics'. The Pennefathers ultimately supported the Government in 1798 and 1803 whereas Todd Jones, a United Irishman, was implicated in the conspiracy fomented by Robert Emmet.[19]

The 1780s were an increasingly profitable, stable and confident period for the socially privileged classes to which the Emmets belonged. Dr Emmet resigned his governorship of St Patrick's Hospital and received a valuable piece of silver plate on 3 February 1783 in recognition of his long service. He remained the institution's Treasurer and Physician and was the recipient of increased patronage from Dublin Castle after 15 September 1782 when his relative, George Grenville Nugent Temple, the 2nd Earl Temple, became Lord Lieutenant. As viceregal physician, Emmet administered to the de facto head of the Irish executive, a connection which granted the Emmets access to the thoughts of the British and Irish ruling elite. One of the many ironies of this promotion was that Dr Emmet was required to preserve the health of the same monarch during trips to Ireland whom his sons were later committed to overthrowing. The sudden death of the Lord Lieutenant, Charles, Duke of Rutland, in late October 1787 paved the way for Temple's return to the viceroyalty on 16 December 1787 for a rare second term. He was then known as Marquis of Buckingham and commenced a tumultuous tenure in Dublin Castle that was notorious for extravagance, nepotism and the corruption of the press. Dr Emmet, when stepping back from certain medical offices in the late 1780s, was said to have 'continued to practise, though not in the first line, yet with considerable celebrity'.[20]

Dr Emmet was passionately interested in politics and expressed his views in print on occasion. A contemporary claimed that Emmet, 'though always remarkable for giving his opinion freely respecting men, measures, and the conduct of political affairs in general . . . has never been suspected of any tendency to assist at treasonable or seditious cabals'.[21] He surrounded himself with like-minded liberals for whom the advance of 1782 had served to encourage demands for even greater reforms of the political system. One of his associates, Dublin politician Sir Edward Newenham, a fellow governor of the Foundling Hospital, chaired a pro-reform meeting at the Weaver's Hall on 11 October 1784 and joined a committee 'to consider of and adopt the most effectual and constitutional means to obtain a Parliamentary Reform'.[22] He was derided by Sir Jonah Barrington for his persistent efforts to correspond with a wary George Washington and his habit of intimating with 'significant nods that he knew vastly more than he thought proper to communicate'.[23] Newenham met the younger members of the Emmet family when dining at their home.

Bonds between the Emmet and Temple families were strengthened in September 1784 when Christopher Temple Emmet married his second cousin, Anne Western Temple, daughter of John Temple. They were the eldest children in their respective families and were first acquainted when Anne stayed with the Emmets on returning from America. The Temples continued to be near neighbours after purchasing a house on Stephen's Green, a factor that evidently facilitated the intimacy which developed between the pair. Dr Emmet became the guardian of Anne's two unmarried sisters on the death of their father. Deemed an exceptionally gifted youth, Christopher had graduated as Bachelor of Arts (BA) from Trinity College Dublin in 1780 and was admitted to the Bar in 1781. He commenced work on the Munster Circuit where he had many relatives and family friends, particularly in Cork, Tipperary and Kerry. In 1786 his means were such as to move with his wife and daughter Catherine ('Kitty'), born in April 1785, into their own home at no. 25 York Street.[24]

Temple Emmet's socially advantageous marriage enhanced his prospects in legal circles in which his renowned oratorical skills had marked him as a rising figure. He was a member of the elite St Patrick's Society when the distinguished barrister John Philpot Curran was Prior between 1779 and 1785. Appointment as King's Counsel in 1787 and being called to the Inner Bar also boded well for Temple Emmet's prospects of eventually reaching high office. Such hopes were dashed in February 1788 when he took gravely ill attending the spring assizes in Munster, probably yet another Emmet family victim of smallpox. Temple Emmet died within two days of collapsing and on 9 March 1788 was buried alongside the remains of his Dublin relatives in St Peter's, Aungier Street. The tragedy of this premature death, accentuated by the high career expectations held for him by contemporaries, cast a pall over the surviving Emmets.[25]

Robert Emmet was at the impressionable age of ten when his eldest brother died. While this must have come as a tremendous shock to him the most discernible and surprising reaction was that of Thomas Addis Emmet, who had recently completed medical studies in Edinburgh. Addis Emmet's education had commenced in Mr Kerr's school, which Temple Emmet had attended a few years earlier. On being prepared for Trinity by Mr Hales, Addis Emmet entered college in 1781 and graduated BA two years later. In 1783 he proceeded to Edinburgh University to take his MD and immersed himself in student life to the extent that he was simultaneously president of five societies.[26] Addis Emmet graduated in late 1784 but was content to remain at Edinburgh for a short period to perfect his medical skills before going to Guy's Hospital, London, to study surgery with Dr Babington. While constructively detained in England, Dr Robert Emmet used his considerable influence with Marquis Buckingham in Dublin to have Addis Emmet's name added to the patent of the State Physicianship; a great career in medicine for his son was thereby virtually assured. In 1785 'T.A. Emmet MD' was listed as a state officer in the *Irish Directory*, which noted in its entry for 1787 that he was abroad. Addis Emmet had embarked on a European excursion with George Knox, Lord Northland's son, which brought him to Switzerland, France, Germany and Italy visiting medical centres. He was in Paris in the spring of 1788 when word reached him of the death of his brother.[27]

In what must have seemed an impetuous, if not unsound, course of action, Addis Emmet abandoned all thoughts of practising medicine and returned to Dublin via London to train as a barrister. While rising to become Attorney General of New York State in 1812, his dramatic retreat from medicine exchanged the highly promising career path mapped for him by his father for that pursued by his deceased sibling. Addis Emmet's son Robert, when President of the Repeal Association of New York in 1841, informed Madden that this change of direction was the will of Dr Emmet. Yet, there was no evidence of reluctance and the possibility of duress was discounted by Addis Emmet's confidante William Murphy. On receiving his Bachelor of Laws in November 1788, Addis Emmet returned to London to read law at the Temple on the advice of his Edinburgh University friend Sir James Mackintosh. He re-encountered William Conyngham Plunket at the Inns of Court, an 'intimate' from their Trinity days, who, when a parliamentarian in 1798, advocated the harsh treatment of United Irish prisoners. Plunket prosecuted Robert Emmet in September 1803 with a zeal which earned the enmity of Irish nationalists.[28]

THOMAS ADDIS EMMET

A secondary and fateful outcome of Christopher's death was Addis Emmet's meeting at the Temple with another expatriate aspirant lawyer, Theobald Wolfe Tone. That they became firm friends may be inferred from Tone's comment in his 'Memoirs' that they had shared 'from the very commencement of our acquaintance, a coincidence of sentiment, a harmony of feelings'.[29] In 1796 Tone rated Addis Emmet and his Cork friend Thomas Russell as being above all his other associates. Addis Emmet, for his part, unreservedly expressed his 'esteem and love' for Tone under more poignant circumstances two years later. The meeting of Addis Emmet and Tone came at one of the most portentous junctures in modern history when the shockwaves of the French Revolution of July 1789 were reshaping the political landscape of Europe. That the Revolution seemed certain to reverberate much further changed the world view and ambitions of both men. Tone was central to this emergent radicalism in Ireland in 1790–91 and, within a few years, had drawn both surviving Emmet brothers into the maelstrom of revolutionary politics.[30]

On completing his legal training in London, Addis Emmet returned to Dublin in early 1790 and was called to the Irish Bar the following May during the Michaelmas term. Dublin was gripped that month by a general election which saw the return of Henry Grattan and Henry Fitzgerald, brother of the Duke of Leinster, ahead of conservative candidates John Exshaw and Henry Gore Sankey. The reformers were boosted by the unpopularity of the Buckingham viceroyalty and by fissures in the Castle bloc, which had arisen during the regency crisis of the previous year when George III temporarily succumbed to the afflictions of mental illness. Napper Tandy, a long-serving radical republican and former Volunteer commander, helped to organise the strong showing of the pro-reform vote. Progress made in other parts of the country indicated that the stagnation which had stifled Irish liberals in the late 1780s was abating. Another power broker, master sweep William Horish, emerged as a respected city United Irishman in 1798 and remained so at the time Robert Emmet assumed a command role in the movement.[31]

Dr William Drennan observed a Dublin city procession and hustings on 3 May 1790 in which his acquaintance Dr Emmet, a fellow licentiate at the College of Physicians, engaged Grattan in a memorable exchange. Having obtained Grattan's assurances that he was indeed a reformer, in front of a crowd of 1,400 supporters, the doctor urged him to satisfy the demands of those 'enlisted' in his 'party' by obtaining 'proper representation' of the people in parliament. Twelve-year-old Robert Emmet junior, 'a fine boy', had accompanied his father to the meeting and amazed Grattan by reciting a short essay on liberty which Drennan had written.[32] Guided by his father's growing enthusiasm for reform politics, the younger Emmet composed 'Erin's Call' around this time, which contained the prophetic lines 'Brothers,

march, march on to glory. In your country's cause unite'. Dr Emmet
was also an avid amateur poet whose penchant for patriotic themes
influenced the writings of both Christopher Temple and Robert,
Thomas Addis Emmet reputedly wrote excellent Latin verse and
Mary Anne's views on the Act of Union were published in 1799.[33]

Tone had followed Addis Emmet back to Dublin by late 1790
where he abandoned a legal career in favour of political activism.
Dublin was then animated by reports of the French republic which
were widely discussed in the intellectually charged environs of the
Emmet household. The destruction of a despotic *ancien régime* by
popular upheaval was startling enough but that it had been effected
by Catholics was also significant given the prevailing sectarian attitudes of the Irish 'Protestant Ascendancy'. Irish liberals and reformers
were impressed by the progressive sentiments of the French revolutionaries and by their capacity to replace a corrupt monarchy with
democratic government. French notions of citizenship, freedom of
worship and the abolition of tithes were popular in Ireland where
rural unrest had grown steadily in organisation and scope since the
agrarian insurgency of the Munster Whiteboys in the early 1760s.
Those interested in channelling popular discord towards specific
political ends in the 1790s were encouraged by the celebrations of the
first two anniversaries of the French Revolution in Dublin and
Belfast. Among those enthused by the spectacle were Samuel Neilson
and Revd William Steel Dickson, both of whom liaised with Robert
Emmet when a United Irishman.[34]

Drennan became a visitor to Stephen's Green after May 1790
where he encountered the recently returned Addis Emmet, whose
own political awakening was in train. The Belfast man had preceded
Addis Emmet at Edinburgh University in 1778 and was acquainted
with Dr Emmet from their joint medical duties in Dublin. Drennan
became distantly related to the family when Addis Emmet married
Jane Patten in St Mary's Church, Mary Street, on 11 June 1791.
Sarah Colville, sister-in-law of Jane Patten's mother, was the friend
and cousin of Martha McTier (née Drennan) of Belfast. Martha was
William Drennan's sister and the person who kept him regularly
informed of the activities of the radical families of their acquaintance
in the north, such as the Simms, McTiers, Browns and Neilsons. Dr
Drennan evidently flirted with Mary Anne Emmet in the mid-1790s
and numbered the man she married in 1799, Robert Holmes,
amongst his closest friends. By marriage and association, therefore,
the Emmets of Dublin developed strong links with the men who

formed the ideological backbone of Irish republicanism in the early 1790s.[35]

Jane Patten was the twenty-year-old daughter of Revd John Patten of Annerville, the Presbyterian Minister of Clonmel, Tipperary, until his death in 1787. Her uncle, William Colville, was governor of the Bank of Ireland (in which Dr Emmet was a major investor) and guardian of her considerable dowry of £2,000. The marriage of Jane to Addis Emmet evidently suggested the partition of the Stephen's Green household into two separately fronted addresses, one of which was inhabited by the new couple and their guests by 1794 at the latest. The romance developed quickly and, while news of their engagement was public knowledge in Ireland from December 1790, it came as a surprise to Addis Emmet's friends in England and Scotland. Following closely in the footsteps of his lamented and distinguished brother, Addis Emmet elected to practise on the Munster Circuit. He obtained a reputation as a defence lawyer, an occupation which earned him £500 per annum. Addis Emmet also assumed control of the family's sprawling legal affairs and dealt with the Tipperary-based lawyer Richard Sadlier in matters of inheritance. His first son, born on 9 September 1792, was named Robert, a gesture which must have pleased both Dr Emmet and his younger brother. The couple had six children by 1798.[36]

The publication of *Reflections on the Revolution in France* in November 1790, Edmund Burke's denunciation of events in Paris, precipitated an intense debate in Ireland when challenged by Tom Paine's *Rights of Man*. The ferment caused by this controversy evidently moved Addis Emmet to become openly political alongside Wolfe Tone and his circle. Tone had joined the Grattanite Whig Club in 1790 to debate such themes but tired of its inertia and moderation and formed his own more radical discussion group in Trinity College. This forum attracted Addis Emmet and Drennan, leading to their contact with Samuel Neilson and ex-army officer Thomas Russell who had seen action in India. Tone, Drennan and Russell became regular dinner guests of the Emmets as their coterie defined an increasingly coherent republican agenda, which resulted in the founding of the Society of United Irishmen within months. Drennan dined with the newlyweds Thomas and Jane Emmet in June 1791, at which time the approach of the second anniversary of the French Revolution offered symbolic opportunities for radicals.[37]

The crux of the programme advanced by Tone was a political alliance between northern Presbyterian dissenters and the disaffected

Catholic population, the two most oppressed elements in Irish society. Support from Church of Ireland liberals and members of the Whig tradition was also anticipated as it had been present in some degree from the outset. William Todd Jones, a wealthy Protestant from Lurgan, Armagh, was one of the most prolific and determined pamphleteers in favour of Catholic civil rights. Antrim Presbyterian Revd William Steel Dickson had also sermonised in favour of this objective since the days of the Volunteers.[38] That this project might well flourish was suggested by the huge procession in Dublin city on 14 July 1791 which passed close to the Emmet home on Stephen's Green and continued down Grafton Street and Dame Street to the Royal Exchange. Dr Emmet's friend Sir Edward Newenham was a central figure in organising this pro-French, pro-Polish and pro-American demonstration. Several elaborate 'transparent lanthorns [sic]' were displayed bearing reform slogans such as: 'WE DO NOT REJOICE BECAUSE WE ARE SLAVES, BUT BECAUSE FRENCHMEN ARE FREE.'[39]

On the same day Tone sent a document to Neilson's Belfast associates entitled 'Declaration and Resolutions of the Society of United Irishmen of Belfast', which decried the lack of representative government in Ireland and condemned the Dublin Castle executive. The stated objective of the proposed organisation was to effect the 'equal representation of all the people in Parliament', essentially the inauguration in Ireland of American- or French-style democracy.[40] Seeking to abolish the Establishment's institutionalised sectarianism was tantamount to advocating a constitutional revolution in Ireland, a path which had led to bloody conflict on both sides of the Atlantic in the previous decade. The United Irishmen hoped to forestall similar strife by convincing College Green to embrace the new popular politics. Tone went to Belfast where discussions with Presbyterian leaders led to the founding on 14 October 1791 of the Society of United Irishmen. A second club convened at the Eagle Tavern, Eustace Street, Dublin on 9 November under Napper Tandy's chairmanship.

UNITED IRISHMEN

The United Irishmen were by far the most significant middle-class reformist agency in Ireland. Formed as a lobbying group pledged to unite 'Catholic, Protestant and Dissenter' in the cause of radical parliamentary reform, success entailed the inversion of the political system in the face of inevitable conservative reaction. This was a mammoth task of propaganda, persuasion and mobilisation inside and outside parliament. Crucially, defending a fledgling democracy in Ireland from a Westminster backlash was deemed to require a much clearer delineation of Irish sovereignty than contained in College Green's 'Constitution of 1782'. United Irish objectives shifted the emphasis from 'Protestant Nationalism' to the new ideology of Republican democracy adapted to Irish circumstances. Tone addressed this delicate issue in a letter to Russell in which he acknowledged that attaining United Irish objectives necessitated the 'separation' of Ireland from Britain. Nobody close to the United Irish movement, as Addis Emmet was from the outset, could fail to understand that this was inherently seditious.[41]

Addis Emmet was on the fringes of the Dublin branch of the United Irishmen from its earliest days and, on occasion, acted as chairman of its proceedings. His advisory and direct input was valued by Tone who described him as 'a man completely after my own heart, of a great and comprehensive mind; of the warmest and sincerest affection for his friends; and of a firm and steady adherence to his principles'. Tone claimed his friend would 'sacrifice his life' in defence of his political integrity.[42] In the event, Tone and Robert Emmet became the martyred heroes whereas Addis Emmet ultimately prospered. The emergence of the United Irishmen in 1791 introduced a powerful new dynamic into the city household in which the younger Emmet was raised. His boyhood days elapsed as the United Irishmen matured. Members of the Dublin society under Dublin Castle surveillance in December 1791 included Walter Byrne, Anthony Perry, Thomas Reynolds, Thomas Bacon, James Moore, William Todd Jones, Robert Dillon, Mathew Dowling, William John MacNeven and many others whose lives intersected with the younger Emmet's by 1803.[43]

While political discussions at Stephen's Green may have passed over Robert Emmet's head, just 13 in 1791, or have been held out of his earshot, there is evidence to suggest that their general import influenced his intellectual development. The themes of Emmet's juvenilia and his sentiments as reported by contemporaries attest to his early consciousness of the basic agenda of reform politics. That he learned and publicly recited Drennan's essay in 1790 was an astonishing feat which accrued from his living in a house where political discourse had been aired from the time of his birth. It must be assumed that Robert followed the affairs of his surviving brother with great interest and enjoyed his father's tacit approval in sympathising with the radical position. The arch-conservative Lord Redesdale caustically remarked in December 1803 that Emmet had been 'educated by his father and brother in the wild principles of modern philosophy'. By his mid-teens it was apparent that Emmet wished to second the efforts of his brother, which is precisely what he did between 1796 and 1803.[44]

Robert Emmet was an insatiably curious youth given to conducting difficult and dangerous experiments, possibly inspired by his brother's papers on the use and properties of medicinal chemicals, which he wrote in Edinburgh. Access to chemicals presented no problem in the home of two trained doctors and Robert Emmet's solid grounding in mathematics equipped him to explore complex scientific problems. Accidental poisoning nearly cost him his life when John Patten, staying in the house as a guest of Addis Emmet, left him unaided during a particularly involved experiment. On realising that he had inadvertently ingested a corrosive and poisonous substance which had been smeared on his fingers, Emmet, around fourteen years old, took the drastic measure of eating chalk. Remarkably, when stricken with severe stomach pains, he had calmly informed himself of this remedy by looking up a medical textbook and then broke into the family stables at the rear of the house to obtain the chalk. It never occurred to him that waking his father and elder brother might have been wise. He reputedly cut a sorrowful and ashen figure at breakfast the following morning.[45]

An important if indirect step in the radicalisation of the Emmets occurred in July 1792 when Wolfe Tone was appointed agent to the restructured Catholic Committee under the auspices of John Keogh and Thomas Braughall. Richard McCormick, Theobald McKenna and William Todd Jones were also deeply involved and had their pro-reform writings published by Patrick Byrne of Grafton Street.[46] Keogh was recalled by Addis Emmet as a 'ready as well as able orator' who, with Braughall, had recently displaced the moderate adherents of Kerry leader Lord Kenmare. They were motivated and rendered increasingly militant by the paltry concessions of the Relief Act of 1792. A silent influx of United Irishmen transformed the Committee into a front organisation for republicans of all religious backgrounds. Their controlling hand was seen in the newly aggressive assertion of the rights of the downtrodden majority faith. Petitioning in support of a Catholic Convention in December 1792 offered tens of thousands their first opportunity to express themselves politically. Convention agitation challenged the fiction that the national parliament represented the population it maintained unenfranchised.[47]

Addis Emmet was apparently not involved in the Committee's routine activities until Tone introduced him to its Convention organisers on 15 October 1792. They were greatly impressed by his bearing and supportive comments, just as Tone had anticipated. He was, Tone wrote, 'the best of all the friends to Catholic emancipation, always excepting Mr Hutton. Worth two of [Whitley] Stokes, and ten of [Peter] Burrowes, and a hundred of Drennan'. This light-hearted slight on Drennan arose from the northerner's obsessive fear of the restrictive hand of socially conservative Catholics if in a position to overwhelm the pioneering republicans. Drennan was consequently supplanted in Committee affairs by the more enthusiastic Addis Emmet, a man who considered radical Catholics William MacNeven and Valentine Lawless close friends and was not afraid to reach out to plebeian elements for support. Addis Emmet was further connected to this clique by Mathew Dowling, an ex-Volunteer lawyer associate and agent for Lawless' Kildare estate.[48]

Addis Emmet assisted Tone from October 1792 in drafting replies to Grand Jury resolutions which had condemned the mooted Convention. 'Citizen Emmet's paper' on the political benefits and legitimacy of Catholic mobilisation was greeted with 'unanimous approbation' when read to the Convention subcommittee on 27 October.[49] A strong writer, Addis Emmet was commissioned to produce populist addresses when Drennan's style was 'deemed too florid and refined for the people'. He moved rapidly from assisting the Convention towards affirming his deepening convictions in other, more overt political groups. By December 1792 Addis Emmet was a member of the Association of the Friends of the Constitution, Liberty and Peace, an organisation headed by the Duke of Leinster (Henry Fitzgerald). Having by then facilitated the Association's contact with the kindred United Irishmen, Addis Emmet was the principal architect of their absorption into the larger body. He also began to blend his private political life with his new public career in a manner that courted controversy.[50]

Napper Tandy, inaugural secretary of the Dublin United Irishmen, provided Addis Emmet with his first high profile trial as a barrister in November 1792. Addis Emmet had assisted Tandy, Archibald Hamilton Rowan, Oliver Bond and others in the plan to re-found a Volunteer-style 'National Guard' in the autumn of 1792 and linked its failure to excite popular support to the weakness of republicanism in the capital at that time. The irrepressible Tandy was no stranger to legal proceedings, to which he proved remarkably resilient. Addis Emmet aided United Irish barristers Leonard MacNally (aka McNally) and Simon Butler in pressing a bold assertion advanced by Mathew Dowling in June 1792. Dowling, also a United Irishman with Defender links, had argued that Lord Lieutenant Westmoreland and the Privy Council had illegitimately offered a reward for Tandy's arrest. By November Tandy was a fugitive from sedition charges in Louth and had also evaded a warrant to appear at the bar of the House of Commons arising from a challenge he had delivered to Solicitor-General John Toler. Toler, as Judge Norbury, sentenced Robert Emmet to death in September 1803.[51]

Ignoring the discomforting absence of their client, Tandy's lawyers argued on 26 November 1792 that a proclamation issued by the viceroy and Privy Council could not be upheld by an Irish court if its authority rested on letters patent granted under the great seal of Great Britain rather than the great seal of Ireland. This had potentially far reaching repercussions for British administration in Ireland. Addis Emmet pressed this point forcefully and created an uproar by claiming 'that there has been no legal viceroy in Ireland for the last six hundred years'.[52] This permitted subversive interpretation and may have helped elicit an admission that the viceroy could be sued. Proceedings were abruptly terminated by the Attorney-General when warned of the danger, possibly by MacNally, who was later a secret ally of the Castle. The Privy Council's warrant was subsequently quashed and the delighted United Irishmen arranged publication of the trial transcript in December 1792. Its editors toned down Emmet's comments in places, perhaps fearing that the unexpurgated version would incur excessive Dublin Castle interest in a man whom the informer Thomas Collins identified as one of their members.[53]

The meteoric rise of Addis Emmet in city radicalism led to a predictable and premeditated proposal by Drennan and Rowan on 4 December that he be formally invited to join the United Irishmen. He had, it seems, been poised to fully enter into their activities for some time and 'Counsellor Emmett' was sworn into the Dublin society ten days later. On signing the roll of members, Emmet introduced three delegates from the Carrick and Dromard districts of Tipperary and thus revealed his role in encouraging the spread of the United Irishmen in Munster. The men were very probably known to him from trips to his ancestral homes in the south and his work on the province's assize circuit. This suggests that he had encouraged the early showing of reformers in Tipperary where, at Clonmel and Nenagh, some of the first United Irish societies had been founded

outside Dublin, Belfast and Cork.[54] Addis Emmet, moreover, maintained a deep interest in Tipperary politics throughout the 1790s. One
of his correspondents, Moore of Mooresfort, was a former Colonel
of Tipperary Volunteers who, when a Grand Juryman, advocated the
repeal of Poyning's Law in March 1782 and the abolition of the tithe
during the Rightboy disturbances of June 1786.[55]

No sooner had Addis Emmet nailed his colours to the republican
mast than he was obliged to stress on 23 December 1792 that the
United Irishmen 'would never countenance any mode of resistance
but what should be perfectly legal'.[56] Whether this reflected the
barrister's genuine inner convictions was a matter of debate amongst
his contemporaries and at variance with Tone's private observations.
The context for this legally prudent remark was the prosecution of
Archibald Hamilton Rowan arising from the suppression of the
National Guard, as well as the vehement criticism by conservatives of
the Catholic Convention which met at the Tailor's Hall. The United
Irishmen, for the first time, were under pressure from the political
and legal establishment, which soon ensnared many of their leaders
in prosecutions for seditious libel and high treason. Given this
looming crisis and his previous statements, it must have seemed
incongruous that Addis Emmet argued on 4 January 1793 that the
United Irishmen should 'leave to itself the expediency of resorting
to arms if necessity required the measure'. Few within the society
believed that this decisive moment had come and Addis Emmet
instead applied himself to heading the subcommittee on parliamentary reform.[57]

Addis Emmet's belligerent comments, nevertheless, were made at a
sensitive juncture. On 2 January an estimated 700 Defenders had
massed north of Dublin at Dunleer and threatened a servant of the
Speaker of the House of Commons as well as a King's Messenger.
Freeman's Journal claimed: 'it is all the despicable frenzy of the
moment in the lower classes, whose minds have been disturbed by
Tom Paine's six-penny edition, dispersed gratis through the country
by Whigs of the capital, and who have taken up weapons, agreeable
to the call of the United Irishmen . . . a blast of faction, that the
power of the laws, and executive justice, will soon put down'. The
'show trials' of July 1793 were one of the sequels to unrest in the
Naul at which time Joseph Corbally was sentenced to transportation
for acting as a 'sergeant'. When awaiting his fate in Kilmainham,
Corbally was pressed to accuse Rowan and Tandy of leading the
Defenders, charges which once more endangered Emmet's associates.[58]

Laying the groundwork for the Convention offered the United Irishmen a legal means to advance Catholic mobilisation to the extent that inter-communal and inter-class alliances could be fostered with northern Presbyterians. The Convention's address to the King requested effective relief measures and deputed a delegation to present him with a massive petition. Their reception in London in early January 1793 was coloured by British intentions to declare war on France, a decision which became public knowledge on 7 February. War altered the context of the Tailor's Hall submission in both positive and negative ways and exerted a profound influence on United Irish objectives. Addis Emmet condemned the conflict as 'madness and wickedness' and alluded to the possibility that it might lead in Ireland to 'joining the arms of France'.[59]

Although keen to permit Catholics to bear arms so that untapped Irish manpower resources might be enlisted, Westminster balked at granting emancipation lest the vehement opposition of the landed Ascendancy towards this measure rendered them unmanageable in times of crisis. The main concession of the Relief Act of 1793, therefore, was the enfranchisement of all forty-shilling freeholders in the county elections which forwarded two MPs each to parliament. Property-qualified voting rights were a largely symbolic gesture given that they were heavily outnumbered by non-county MPs in the House of Commons. Many of the Commons borough and corporation seats were in the gift of members of the veto-wielding House of Lords, which was dominated by conservatives and oligarchs. A more practical aspect of the 1793 Act was the voiding of bans preventing Catholic participation in the professions, magistracy and corporations. This moved a small minority of Catholics with mercantile capital and land holdings closer towards state interests. It also opened Trinity College to much greater non-Protestant enrolment in 1794, a factor which differentiated Robert Emmet's student days from those of his brothers. Members of the Catholic Keogh, McLaughlin and Farrell families shared his time at college, youths whose fathers belonged to the circles in which Addis Emmet was by then a major figure.

The imperviousness of the Irish Parliament to the machinations of non-Protestant members of the electorate aroused a variety of responses. It was hoped, on the one hand, that the influential Catholics heading the Convention would be mollified and that conservatives would accept such disquieting developments as being in the best interests of the country. This proved illusory. The United Irishmen and Catholic Committee were offended by the continued refusal to recognise what they insisted were fundamental birthrights and were incensed by the vitriolic language used by those opposed to any further dismantling of the penal laws. Also problematic was the presentation of the Relief Act of 1793 as the final word on Catholic agitation for the foreseeable future and certainly as long as the war against France continued.[60]

The Establishment side-stepped the invidious position it had been placed in by the Patriots and Volunteers during the American War by raising a militia that was firmly under its control. Officers were chosen by Dublin Castle rather than being popularly acclaimed and led a uniformed, full-time and trained militia subject to central military command and law. The United Irishmen, having failed in their efforts to reconstitute the Volunteers in Dublin, were denied access to the new militia, over which there could be little hope of exerting decisive influence. The loss of the most effective means of making political capital was underlined by a prohibition on conventions. This prevented the holding of public forums such as had met at Tailor's Hall. The outlets for legal protest were, therefore, drastically reduced. Praising the politics of the enemy French Directory also became far more difficult, particularly when the exigencies of the Revolutionary Wars resulted in the 'Terror'. The future looked bleak for the United Irishmen.[61]

Addis Emmet was active in Dublin politics throughout 1793 when not employed on the Munster Circuit where the deteriorating security situation generated an increasing number of sedition cases. Perhaps emboldened by his early success with Tandy, Addis Emmet defended the Paine-ite ex-priest-turned-deist Denis Driscoll on charges of seditious libel at Cork assizes in September 1793. Temporarily preserved by Addis Emmet, the inveterate Driscoll, editor of the anti-government *Cork Gazette*, was not imprisoned until the following year for libelling the king. The paper was described by Isaac Heron of the rival *Waterford Gazette* as a 'wicked' publication. This was Addis Emmet's most notable appearance since he secured the acquittal in Tralee five months earlier of Lieutenant Carr of the 40th Regiment for killing one O'Connell in a duel. His Cork outing, however, occurred against a more disturbed backdrop of quasi-revolutionary violence in Munster. Braving the hostility of Cork's sizeable loyalist community, Addis Emmet was once more successful in a political case. This added to his reputation as a practitioner of law whilst safeguarding a client whose opinions agreed very much with his own. On 8 November 1793 Addis Emmet was elected president of the Dublin Society of United Irishmen in place of the imprisoned Rowan.[62]

Government attempts to implement the Militia Act in the summer of 1793 aroused the most concerted anti-state violence in living memory. Conscription was opposed by the 'Defenders', who had evolved from the narrow base of sectional conflict in 1780s Armagh into a popular, Jacobin-style revolutionary organisation. Although initially strong in rural towns of south Ulster, north Leinster and Dublin city, the prospect of French invaders overthrowing the Irish political system helped spread the federated Defender lodges throughout the country. This unprecedented surge in disaffection created a popular dynamic which Tone, Addis Emmet and, later, Robert Emmet wished to fashion into the vanguard of an Irish revolution. Resisting the raising of the Militia gave the otherwise inchoate and sprawling Defenders a defining national issue which presaged their emergence as the first mass-based seditious organisation in Irish history.[63]

The Defenders had first come to the attention of the United Irishmen in mid-1792 when Tone, Russell, Tandy and others attempted to convince their leaders in south Ulster to refrain from large-scale arms raiding. They feared a premature rising and the instigation of coercion likely to destroy the political programme of the United Irishmen along with Defenderism. Yet, several leading United Irishmen were also high-ranking Defenders, indicating that there were those in the republican movement who countenanced, if not favoured, revolutionary means. Connections between the socially elite, legal and public United Irish radicals and plebeian, illegal and clandestine Defender paramilitaries became a matter of public record in December 1792 when Tandy was arrested for swearing the Defender oath at Castlebellingham, Louth. War with France, to which the Defenders looked for military deliverance, focused Dublin Castle attention on city activists like Addis Emmet, whose defence of Driscoll protected an agitator linked to Defenderism.[64]

Anti-militia protests by the Defenders resulted in hundreds of deaths in the summer of 1793. Kerry, Limerick, Roscommon, Wexford, Down, Meath, Cavan, Sligo and Fermanagh were amongst the worst affected, although few parts of the country were entirely untouched. Cork jails contained over 200 Defender prisoners in early 1794, many of whom were brought to trial on the Munster Circuit on which Addis Emmet was employed. The worst of the disturbances abated by 1794 owing to militarisation of afflicted districts and the eventual embodiment of the regiments by volunteers and balloted conscripts. The legacy of the 1793 riots, however, was still keenly felt and United Irishmen were obliged to tread with extreme caution as their profile and prospects waned.[65] The trial of Rowan in January 1794 was part of a sustained attempt by the government to hinder their recovery. Rowan invited Addis Emmet to defend him on charges arising from the Tandy case of November 1792 but he deferred to the far more experienced Curran. Addis Emmet's authorship in January 1794 of 'a sensible, popular introduction' to a United Irish document 'printed on a single sheet for the purpose of hanging up in cabins' indicates that his decision was not symptomatic of personal political unease.[66]

These months of turmoil coincided with an important transition in Robert Emmet's education. Having outgrown Whyte's Academy, he was sent to a Camden Street school where Revd Lewis prepared him to enter Trinity. This was no onerous task for a student of Emmet's uncommon abilities and he commenced university studies on 7 October 1793 when still in his fifteenth year. Emmet was assigned Revd Richard Graves as his tutor, a junior fellow at Trinity and a member of the Royal Irish Academy's literature committee. Already proficient in Latin and French, Emmet was a very strong student from the outset. His serious-minded and near-obsessive approach to academic work is indicated by the copious margin notes he inscribed on the books he owned as a young man. He was in every respect the brilliant scion of a brilliant family and was expected to match the high achievements of Christopher and Thomas. That this did not occur was due in no small part to the crackdown on the United Irishmen in 1795 and the ill effects this caused his family. One harbinger of trouble was the near coincidence of Robert Emmet's commencement with the departure of loyalist student Oliver Fry of Frybrook (Roscommon) to defend his family's Boyle property from the Defenders. In July 1803 Fry commanded the Limerick Brigade of artillery which protected the town from United Irishmen Emmet had encouraged to act.[67]

The possibility of pitting Irish disaffection against British interests encouraged the French Directory to establish contact with the United Irishmen in 1794. The most important emissary, Revd William Jackson, an Anglican clergyman and employee of the feared Committee for Public Safety, met Tone in Dublin in April 1794. An offer of French military aid in assisting a revolution in Ireland was accepted by Tone, who could see no other means of advancing the United Irish cause. His decision exposed him to well-grounded allegations of treason when Jackson, under close surveillance since passing through England, was seized by the authorities in Palace Street, Dublin, on 28 April. Clear-cut proof of sedition provided the government with the pretext they had long sought to proscribe the United Irishmen. They were banned on 24 May 1794, splitting the movement definitively into estranged revolutionary and constitutional wings.[68]

Drennan, Rowan and others perceived to be moderating voices within the United Irish leadership distanced themselves from the Society of United Irishmen in 1794 and Tone made preparations to go into exile in America. Addis Emmet was importuned to do likewise and, warned of impending danger to his person some weeks prior to the suppression, was reputedly 'panic struck' at its materialisation.[69] If so he quickly steadied his nerves and on 7 May 1794 addressed a letter to 'My dear F' which firmly rejected a suggestion that he 'withdraw from the Society of U[nited] I[rishmen]'. Internal evidence indicates that the cryptic correspondent had been friendly with both Christopher Temple Emmet and Addis Emmet, despite his sinister allusions to treason and 'professional emolument' in previous contacts.[70] The most likely candidate for authorship of the items was an occasional Dublin Castle correspondent who years later signed himself 'F' in letters concerning Robert Emmet. One of these letters was endorsed 'secret information Fullar', a careless security slip by its recipient. This may have referred to Corkman James Fuller, who entered Trinity College in March 1777 when Temple Emmet was enrolled. He would certainly have possessed the necessary city, college and personal contacts to aid the authorities in the manner chosen by 'F'.[71]

Addis Emmet's reply to 'F' in 1794 contradicted the claim that the United Irishmen had any seditious intent, a necessary disavowal, whilst refusing to repudiate either his political actions or the society's objectives. From 24 May, however, he had no alternative but to step back from a public position of leadership. An undated document written shortly after this exchange by the spy Collins conveyed a very different sense of Addis Emmet's opinions when expressed verbally amongst friends. Collins placed the barrister's name at the head of an extensive list of United Irishmen and noted: 'has often declared that a revolution only can save Ireland'.[72] Something of this inner steel had been in evidence on 18 May when Addis Emmet acted as a second in a duel fought outside Enniskerry at the Scalp, Co. Wicklow. Beauchamp Bagenal Harvey, who in May/June 1798 was Commander-in-Chief of the Wexford insurgents, fought Dublin loyalist Ambrose Harding Giffard. The ostensible cause of the duel was Giffard's accusation that the United Irishmen had incited sectarian unrest in the north of Ireland. Backed by Addis Emmet, Harvey risked his life to defend the honour of the society.[73]

On 25 June 1794 Addis Emmet facilitated the acquittal of Drennan on nine sedition charges. Critical to the defence was 'Wright's evidence brought forward by [Addis] Emmet' which was utilized by Curran in his typically withering cross-examination of the main prosecution witness, William Carey.[74] Surgeon Thomas Wright of Great Ship Street had been secretary to the United Irishmen of Dublin in September 1792 and was friendly with both Drennan and Addis Emmet. He was suspected of being an infiltrator by several colleagues but probably in error given his militant conduct in the Rebellion of 1798 and his failure to mention such service when forced to give information in May 1799. Described by Collins as a 'fire-brand' in mid-1794, Wright attended Curran during his illness of October 1794 and remained on good terms with Drennan two years later when his marriage underwent difficulties. Wright returned to prominence during the Rebellion of 1798 and evidently sponsored Robert Emmet's entry into the United Irish leadership in the city. Victory in the June 1794 trial ensured that Drennan's name was not added to those of Tone, Jackson, Reynolds and Rowan against whom grand jury bills of indictment for high treason were brought the following day. Even though the indictments were subsequently suspended in all cases except for Jackson's, Drennan's clean escape gave him the breathing space he required to reconsider the dangerous path he was being taken along by his politics.[75]

Addis Emmet proceeded with caution in political matters in late 1794 yet was prepared to act as a front for men who deemed it advantageous to remain in the wings. One such person was William Rowan, Crosbie's election agent in Derry, who enlisted Addis Emmet to place an 'Address to the clergy of the county of Derry' in the *Dublin Evening Post* on 4 and 5 December 1794.[76] The notice was duly published. The arrival of the liberal Earl Fitzwilliam in Dublin as Viceroy in January 1795, however, raised hopes that the Duke of Portland's Whig coalition in England might re-address the reform issue in Ireland. Remarkably, the Earl's efforts to improve the status of Irish Catholics and Presbyterians resulted in his recall to London in March owing to the ill feeling generated against him in Westminster by the disgruntled conservative office-holders he had ousted from Dublin Castle. This delivered a body blow to the reinvigorated Catholic Committee and was viewed by Addis Emmet and MacNeven as a factor which impelled the United Irishmen towards fomenting revolution. In place of the progressive Fitzwilliam, Dublin Castle received Earl Camden, an ardent champion of the Ascendancy.[77]

REPRESSION

On 10 May 1795 the United Irishmen adopted a new constitution designed to incorporate Defender lodges where they existed and to recruit elsewhere. This secret, oath-bound body was intended to function as an auxiliary army in support of French invaders, and they adhered to democratic principles by electing leaders every three months at parish, barony and county level. The process advanced rapidly in Dublin, where the Defenders were strongly represented in the iron foundries of the north city and in the silk weaving communities of the Liberties. The Defenders continued to organise, however, and their increasing lateral cohesion assisted United Irish organisers tasked with bringing them into a hierarchical system. In late August Justice John Bell and Phibsborough loyalists arrested seven men from Artane and Coolock who had been sworn 'to be faithful to the French and true to the Defenders'. The two emissaries responsible were found in possession of printed copies of the Defender oath and were trying to 'carry on a correspondence between the different bodies of Defenders'.[78] Provincial-level command was the highest to which United Irishmen could be advanced by voting and the highly secret business of this tier was controlled by a Supreme or Executive Directory in Dublin. Addis Emmet belonged to this national-level command in January 1797, as did Robert Emmet two years later. Proselytising in 1795–96 benefited from disaffection arising from the collapse of the reform effort and the evidence of the implacable hostility of the hard-line Camden administration.[79]

Injustices were highlighted in Armagh, where magistrates inflicted seemingly arbitrary punishments on Defenders yet reacted with notable leniency towards the Peep of Day Boy (Orange Order) offenders who terrorised Catholic communities. It appeared as if the conservative magistracy had grasped the political utility of promoting anti-Catholic intimidation that had its roots in economic factors. Army Commander-in-Chief Lieutenant-General Lord Carhampton had crushed Defenderism in Sligo, Mayo, Leitrim and Roscommon in 1795 by the illegal, summary deportation to the fleet of over 1,000 untried suspects yet did nothing to protect the beleaguered Catholics streaming out of Armagh as refugees. This blatant injustice disposed MPs Arthur O'Connor and Lord Edward Fitzgerald to join the United Irishmen and to conspire with the French to overthrow the government. Fitzgerald's frequent visits to Addis Emmet at Stephen's Green supports Tone's contention that his barrister friend, while comparatively moderate, was au fait with United Irish revolutionary plans. When examined before the Secret Committee in August 1798 Addis Emmet admitted that he 'knew Lord Edward right well, and have done a great deal of business with him'. He had also dealt with Fitzgerald's brother, the Duke of Leinster, in the more temperate times of 1792. This intimacy explains in part the ease with which Robert Emmet was accepted into the confidence of Fitzgerald's former assistants in 1798–1803.[80]

Much in demand for his solid track record in court, Addis Emmet's earnings in 1795 reached the healthy sum of £750 per annum. Financial security did not act as a brake on his political life with which his legal career frequently intersected. Addis Emmet and William Sampson appeared for Defender suspects at the Dublin 'show trials' of late 1795 when they protected men who professed politics very similar to their own. Addis Emmet recalled: 'The evidence on [sic] those trials shewed [sic] that the views of the Catholics of that rank of life, in and near the metropolis, though they had never yet heard of the United System, were perfectly conformable to those of the northern republicans. This coincidence determined the latter to open a communication which should pave the way for the extention [sic] of their own organization.'[81] It was presumably in the hope of highlighting this opportunity that Addis Emmet made the sensational decision of swearing the United Irish oath in open court and extolling its merits. His gesture violated several proscriptions on illegal oaths; scores of Dubliners had been transported to the fleets of the Royal Navy and to 'Botany Bay' (New South Wales, Australia) on presumption of having done just this in 1795–97.[82]

In the year granted to Tone to settle his affairs in Ireland before going into exile, the United Irishmen were exposed to the Fitzwilliam crisis, the dragooning of Connacht and the reconstitution of their organisation as a revolutionary movement. Difficulties arising from the trial and suicide of Revd Jackson in April 1795 obliged Tone to finalise his travel plans. Before leaving Ireland Tone visited his associates in the Dublin area and in early-to-mid May called to Rathfarnham to see Addis Emmet, who had leased or purchased a country home and an office in the area. Tone wrote:

> A short time before my departure, my friend [Thomas] Russell being in town, he and I walked out together to Rathfarnham to see [Thomas Addis] Emmet, who has a charming villa there. He showed us a little study, of an elliptical form, which he was building at the bottom of the

lawn and which he said he would consecrate to our meetings if ever we lived to see our country emancipated.

Emmet joined the pair on the return journey to Dublin and it was then that Tone claimed they discussed his intention to quit America for Paris to 'apply . . . for the assistance of France, to enable us to assert our independence . . . this plan met with the warmest approbation and support from both Russell and Emmet'. Addis Emmet, therefore, was in agreement with the strategy of effecting revolution in Ireland with French military aid. It was later to become apparent that his main reservation was whether large-scale French assistance was commensurate with long-term Irish interests. The question of scale was a pragmatic one informed by the often repressive conduct of the French in occupied territories. In 1795 Addis Emmet may have feared that such ascendancy might be exploited in Ireland, a stance which undoubtedly affected the outlook and decisions taken by Robert Emmet the following year.[83]

Tone left Dublin for Belfast on 20 May 1795 and took ship with his family for Philadelphia on 13 June. Prior to embarking on the *Cincinnatus* he rekindled his friendship with Samuel Neilson, Charles Teeling and Henry Joy McCracken. At Cave Hill Tone, Neilson and McCracken rededicated themselves to 'breaking the connection with England', an objective attempted by force of arms in 1798 and 1803. The flurry of organisational activity which preceded the 1795 consultations gave rise to Tone's confident and far-reaching assertion that he could speak 'for the catholics, for the dissenters and for the Defenders'.[84] Possibly no other United Irishman was then justified in making such a claim. Addis Emmet had an inkling of what was planned and on learning of Tone's imminent departure from Simon Maguire, a Dublin United Irish merchant at Bachelor's Walk, he wrote a final letter to his 'dear friend'. Tone was urged to keep up their correspondence which, Addis Emmet noted, would be 'useful . . . for regulating my future settlement in life'.[85]

CHAPTER TWO

The United Irishmen

Robert Emmet's transition from the elite academies of his boyhood to the challenges of student life at Trinity College Dublin was highly successful. In the summer of 1795 he was one of twenty-four students to win premiums from the College's quarterly exams. This distinction, if anything, underestimated his academic prowess. His flair for chemistry and mathematics, while hardly latent given his home experiences, became fully apparent when attending Trinity. Another talent, oratory, first blossomed during his college years. His contributions to the Historical Society in 1798 were vividly recalled by Thomas Moore and other peers as being of remarkable quality in terms of content and delivery. These performances offered glimpses of the verve displayed by Emmet in his speech from the dock in 1803.[1]

Moore commenced studies eight months after Emmet, when just 14, and left the most complete account of his contemporary's time at college. Near neighbours in the city, both youths were the Dublin-born sons of Kerry parents. Moore recalled Emmet's ardent patriotism and fascination with scientific knowledge, one of many interests fostered at home by caring and indulgent parents, which re-emerged in the last years of his life. In his biography of another notable United Irishman, Lord Edward Fitzgerald, Moore stated:

> were I to number, indeed, the men, among all I have ever known, who appeared to me to combine, in the greatest degree, pure moral worth with intellectual power, I should, among the highest of the few, place Robert Emmet. Wholly free from the follies and frailties of youth . . . the pursuit of science, in which he eminently distinguished himself, seemed, at this time, the only object that at all divided his thoughts with that enthusiasm for Irish freedom which in him was an [sic] hereditary as well as national feeling.[2]

Emmet's extra-curricular activities at Trinity emulated those of his deceased brother, Christopher Temple Emmet. This would have pleased his parents who had marvelled in their eldest son's natural abilities only to see them cruelly extinguished when he was in his prime. Temple Emmet had dabbled in poetry as a youth, selections of which merited posthumous publication in 1789 and 1803. It was, however, in his stellar performances in Trinity's Historical Society that he truly excelled. Robert Emmet entered this difficult ground with much to prove and performed admirably. Ultimately, the younger Emmet lived to exceed his brother's poetical accomplishments and possibly also surpassed his reputation for learned eloquence at Trinity. The political dimension to his student days proved his undoing.[3]

In hindsight it was clear to Robert Emmet's associates that his greatest qualities and vulnerabilities were displayed during the debates hosted by the Debating Society and the more renowned Historical Society. Formed in 1770, the Historical Society declined in popularity in the late 1780s but was revived as the Junior Historical Society in April 1792, not long before Emmet's commencement at Trinity. As a freshman in late 1794, he attended the group's highly structured proceedings in the Exhibition Room, the period when it ran foul of the Board of Fellows, who feared the encroachment of republicanism. In 1794 opposition to the attendance of Wolfe Tone, who had been the Society's auditor in 1785, and of Peter Burrowes, led to increased scrutiny by Revd George Millar and the enforcement of a ban on non-student membership. John Sheares, a future United Irish leader with whom Emmet had much in common, also witnessed this controversy. In 1794 and 1795 Emmet observed the debates of the senior students who dominated the Society whilst continuing his undergraduate studies of classical poetry and ancient history. He drew upon this newfound knowledge with great effect when honing his oratorical skills in 1798. The country, meanwhile, was plunged into a state of flux, which exploded in the Rebellion of 1798.[4]

Army reserve camps were established outside Dublin, Belfast, Cork and other likely sites of invasion in 1795–96 to deter foreign intervention and to inhibit domestic agitation. Draconian Indemnity and Insurrection Acts were passed in late 1796 which retrospectively protected state agents from prosecution for their illegal actions in Connacht. More importantly, the new laws provided a methodology for managing future counter-insurgent operations and declaring martial law. The Insurrection Act's 'idle and disorderly' clause was designed to circumvent the cumbersome civil legal apparatus by sending suspects directly to the Fleet. Any two magistrates could summarily transport a suspect in a district in which martial law had been declared. The theoretical right to appeal at the assizes was negated by the practice of keeping such men in the *Thomas* and other prison tenders off the coast. Curfews could be imposed under the Insurrection Act along with such intrusions as arbitrary house searches and the requisition of goods. As before, the French war provided the main context in which the rise of republicanism was viewed in Dublin Castle and Westminster.[5]

Defending the Irish coastline required the Royal Navy blockade of French Atlantic ports, raids on their facilities and winning important victories at Cape St Vincent and Camperdown (Texel). Yet invasion remained a threat as it was widely held in Dublin and London that a major French landing in Ireland could not be repulsed. From September 1796 the poor prospects of maintaining law and order in the countryside inspired the raising of a massive force of loyalist auxiliaries. In October 1796 the officers of the yeomanry corps were gazetted, with units of thirty to sixty men generally mounted and commanded by conservative magistrates and lesser gentry. The ultra-loyalist Orange Order was permitted to penetrate the yeomanry, militia and the army in a bid to impede republican infiltration.

For supporters of Government the unthinkable almost happened in late December 1796 when a large French fleet confounded British intelligence assessments and naval defences by mooring in Bantry Bay, County Cork. The 12,000 French army regulars under General Lazare Hoche would very probably have made short work of the inexperienced Crown forces in Ireland had they been able to push inland but unusually severe weather conditions scattered their fleet before landings were effected. Tone, on board the *Indomptable*, was bitterly disappointed at the reverse, if consoled by the fact that his fellow United Irishmen would take heart from the demonstrated commitment of their allies. The Castle put a brave face on the reprieve whilst aware that the crisis abated owing to natural factors over which they had no control. The ability of the French Directory to assist the United Irishmen and the likelihood that they would return in better weather demanded immediate action.[6]

The tantalising failure of Bantry Bay proved that the central plank of United Irish strategy was feasible and this realisation spurred massive growth of the organisation in Ulster and further afield. An Ulster Directory was formed to oversee the extension of the organisation throughout the province and to stimulate parallel growth in Leinster. Henry Joy McCracken, Fr James Coigley, William Putnam McCabe, James Hope, Richard Dry and the Teeling brothers,

Bartholomew, George and Charles, worked unceasingly towards this end. Preliminary efforts had been made by Hope in mid-1796 to liaise with the republicans of the capital, many of whom had standing in the lateral and comparatively diffuse Defender groups. In late 1796, with no constitutional alternative in sight and the last vestiges of the pro-reform lobby subject to unrelenting pressure from a deeply conservative regime, the invasion crisis may well have been the catalyst for the wholehearted engagement of the Emmet brothers in the United Irishmen.

Addis Emmet, although prominent throughout the legal phase of the Society's existence, may have deferred his decision to pursue the revolutionary strategy adopted by the United Irishmen in May 1795 until the following year. Tone had received his friends' assurances of support in the summer of 1795 yet hesitated when adding Addis Emmet's name to a list of contacts he prepared in Paris on 10 April 1796 for the use of an emissary named Aherne. The 'quare' recorded beside Addis Emmet's name presumably reflected doubts as to his backing for the magnitude of the proposed French military commitment. Information on this matter may well have been communicated to Paris, where Tone had arrived three months before.[7] An informer based in France the following year turned this assessment on its head by claiming that Addis Emmet was 'the bloodiest man in the world'.[8]

Of crucial importance to Addis Emmet's advancement to the highest levels of the republican movement were his connections with all major cliques within the broad United Irish leadership. He was well respected by the Catholic Committee element dominated by William MacNeven, Richard McCormick and John Keogh while still personally friendly with the rump of the reformist tendency in which William Drennan and Hamilton Rowan held sway until 1794. Moreover, Addis Emmet was sufficiently committed to radicalising the general population to appeal to both the conspiratorial Neilson/McCracken group in Belfast and their militant Dublin-based allies, Oliver Bond, Henry Jackson, Mathew Dowling, Richard Dry and John and Henry Sheares. While frequently at odds with Arthur O'Connor in the 1800s, Addis Emmet considered Lord Edward Fitzgerald, a near neighbour and the only permanent member of the Leinster executive from January 1797 to May 1798, a close friend and political colleague. The myriad Emmet family links with the Fitzgerald nexus in Dublin was possibly the most important single factor in the subsequent rise of Robert Emmet through the ranks of the United Irishmen in Dublin.[9]

CITY RADICALISM

If Addis Emmet was reticent with regard to the direction taken by the United Irishmen after their suppression in mid-1794, it is highly probable that his opinion was binding on his younger brother, with whom great trust and brotherly intimacy existed. Crucially, this situation had been all but dispelled by the end of 1796 when Addis Emmet joined Bond, MacNeven, McCormick, Jackson, O'Connor and Fitzgerald at the head of an organisation planning a French-supported revolution in Ireland. Fitzgerald and O'Connor had also crossed the threshold of subversion in the early months of 1796 to add their combined talents, social status and militancy to the highest levels of the conspiracy. Madden ascertained that O'Connor had unsuccessfully pressed Addis Emmet to join the Executive Directory in 1796 and that this only transpired in February 1797 when O'Connor's temporary imprisonment opened a vacancy. In August 1798 Addis Emmet stated before his peers and without contradiction that he had been a member of the Directory from January 1797 to May 1797 and then from December 1797 until his arrest in March 1798. No explanation was given by Emmet for the seven-month hiatus in his leadership role which may simply have arisen from the rotation of members within the society's elite at the prescribed three-monthly elections.[10]

More certain is that the Directory was divided into a camp consisting of Arthur O'Connor, Fitzgerald and Jackson, which welcomed as much French military aid as could be secured, and another adhering to Addis Emmet, MacNeven and McCormick, which believed that the United Irishmen should be the primary agent of change. They looked to the precedent of the American War where French financial and moral assistance was provided to the rebels while their military support remained largely offshore. Both factions accepted that the French Directory would play a major role in Ireland. MacNeven stated that they 'wished through the cooperation of a respectable French force, to exclude the barbarity of a purely civil war'.[11] When Fitzgerald and O'Connor tentatively raised the possibility of an Ulster-centred rising without waiting for the French in late 1797, it was Addis Emmet and MacNeven who refused on the ground that they were too weak to prevail. While long-standing fault lines between the two main factions broadened in the early 1800s, the salient point in 1797 revolved around the nature of French military support rather than the propriety of fomenting revolution in Ireland.

Both elements comprised committed republican separatists who envisaged the United Irishmen directly engaging the British military with the assistance of the French.[12]

Their task was not only to obtain French backing but to complete the national organisation and link its paramilitary potential to the proliferating societies of Dublin city. Metropolitan committees claimed 4,420 members in April 1797 due to the exertions of 'Citizen' Miles Duigenan of 68 Grafton Street, a grocer, money-lender and wine and spirit merchant, as well as Richard Dry of Weaver's Square, Mathew Dowling, Thomas Warren, James Dixon of Old Kilmainham and other radical urban organisers with Defender credentials.[13] By then the funerals of popular United Irishmen, such as that of Duigenan's associate and fellow grocer Edward Dunn on 3 April 1797, had been seized upon as opportunities to openly mass their forces in marshalled parades. Freestanding republican clubs such as the Philanthropic Society, Telegraphic Society, the Strugglers and Athenian Society were rapidly subsumed by United Irish command structures. Sympathetic masonic lodges, illegal proto-trade-union 'combinations' and the remnants of independent Defender groups which thrived in the manufacturing sectors of the city were also absorbed. New fronts, such as the Donnybrook Hurlers, were created to radicalise and recruit targeted elements. This process brought pre-formed cliques of like-minded radicals into the broader United Irish system. Such groupings were to prove extremely important in May/June 1798 when martial law threatened the cohesion and ideological integrity of the democratic superstructure by forcing the Directory to devolve its authority to mid-level activists.

Duigenan, according to the English informer John Bird (aka Smith), joined the recently formed 'military department' and 'military committee' to prepare contingencies for 'the capture of Dublin'.[14] In the spring of 1797 Duigenan claimed:

> as soon as the inhabitants of Dublin were ready to revolt, notice was to be given to the six [sic, four] adjoining counties, within three hours march, to send in four thousand men each . . . 12,000 of whom were to assist the citizens of Dublin against their internal enemies; the remaining 12,000 to keep off the soldiers in the country from assisting those in the town.

With minor modifications this strategy remained the basic plan of the United Irishmen until 1803.[15] It is likely that Walter 'Watty' Cox of Abbey Street, gunsmith and armourer of the Commissioners of the

Revenue, played a major role in Duigenan's affairs. A delegate of the fluid Executive Committee of Dublin apprised the Ulster Directory which met in Armagh on 10 May 1797 that they 'had now laid a plan to take Dublin, Chapelizod [artillery barracks] and the Camp [at Loughlinstown], and to seize the executive government'. Elements of this coup d'état model were attempted by Robert Emmet in July 1803.[16]

Duigenan found it difficult to restrain his subordinates who demanded immediate action in 1797. Many had presumably cut their teeth when Defenders in clashes with the military, as well as in the trade-related city riots of the early 1790s. The grievances of the Earl of Carhampton's excesses in Connacht were two years old in 1797 yet sufficiently fresh in the minds of Dublin republicans to inspire a plot to assassinate him at his Luttrellstown estate. James Dunn and Patrick Carty were allegedly selected to kill the former Commander-in-Chief on 14 May 1797, although the real details were obscured in a morass of supposition and denial surrounding their trial. Duigenan was implicated in the conspiracy and arrested on 24 May 1797, just as a massive drive was underway in Leinster to accelerate the recruit-ment of the men required to carry out the seizure of Dublin. Lord Edward Fitzgerald and Arthur O'Connor took an increasingly hands-on approach to fulfilling this task and assembled a team of assistants who commanded disproportionate influence in the Society. This function was delegated some years later to Robert Emmet, whom Duigenan almost certainly encountered in 1802–3.[17]

EMMET AND MOORE

Robert Emmet touched upon such developments in a Trinity debate attended by Thomas Moore. Many students in attendance must have wondered how the unfolding political crisis would affect their lives, families and careers. Emmet told the Historical Society: 'when a people advancing rapidly in civilisation and knowledge of their right, look back after a long lapse of years, and perceive how far their government has lagged behind them what then, I ask, is to be done by them in such a case? What but pull the government up to the people?'[18] Emmet envisaged a personal role in effecting this juncture and became a United Irishman. The date of Robert Emmet's induction remains a point of speculation owing to the apparent absence of extant private papers and eyewitness testimony. Madden, who interviewed many of his closest associates, believed that Emmet joined in the period between the Bantry Bay crisis of December 1796 and the early months of 1798, by which time he had 'adopted its principles'. A spy known as 'Jones' was more specific and potentially authoritative in claiming that Emmet's participation in the United Irish conspiracy commenced in December 1796 when they were both at Trinity.[19]

The Trinity informer and possible witness stated that the first cell of United Irishmen in the College, as opposed to informal gatherings of individual members, consisted of '[Robert] Emmett [sic], Corbet[t], [Mc]Loughlin, O'Gorman' and Michael Farrell who were all sworn 'immediately before the arrival of Hoche's fleet in [December 17]96'.[20] This seems reasonable given Emmet's exposure to the inner workings of republicanism and his attainment of the right to apply for membership on turning 18. Adult responsibility had been granted to the younger Emmet by his father in July 1796 when he acted as witness to a family property lease. A point of interest is the allegation that Emmet did not require the highly positive news from Bantry Bay to make his commitment. The concurrent gravitation of Addis Emmet towards the United Irish Directory in the closing months of 1796 and his acknowledged assumption of an executive position in January 1797 was another major, if not critical, factor. While Robert Emmet's youth and inexperience probably limited his contribution to the wider movement at first, his characteristic dynamism and revolutionary acumen soon earned him respect.[21]

The identity of the intelligent and careful informant 'Jones' has eluded detection although there are grounds for believing that he was John Egan, son of Dublin chemist Sylvester Egan. His entry to Trinity as a scholar in 1795 was an early Catholic success story in a once for-bidding environment. Egan graduated BA two years later and stayed on for further studies. A self-confessed United Irishman, Egan certainly assisted the authorities in their April 1798 investigations into College subversion and re-encountered Emmet in 1802 when he was part of an Irish touring party which fell in with the young radical in Paris. This time frame corresponds with the range of information furnished by 'Jones' in 1803, even if the informant included incompatible biographical data which may have been intended to complicate his identification by enemies, a technique used by MacNally, Collins, Turner and other professional agents. There are, furthermore, details pertaining to Egan's life which indicate that he was indeed the well-placed Trinity informer.[22]

If Egan's information is reliable, it seems that Addis Emmet and Thomas Corbett recruited several members of the Historical Society to form the nucleus of the College's undergraduate United Irishmen cell in December 1796. The new men reputedly received the oath of membership from William MacNeven, 'who waited on them' for the purpose. MacNeven was a conspicuously prominent master of ceremonies whose presence would have signified the importance placed on the 'collegians'. Trinity lecturer and moderate republican Whitley Stokes, a friend of Addis Emmet and MacNeven, may have been consulted but was evidently not closely involved. William Corbett, younger brother of Thomas and a student in 1796–97, was deeply engaged. The elder Corbett was lieutenant of the College yeomanry corps and William its sergeant, positions of authority which gave them a deep reach into the ostensibly loyal student population. Robert Emmet, Michael Farrell of Ballymahon (Longford) and James Thomas Flinn of Dublin were apparently chosen to direct the new grouping and presumably used their knowledge of their peers to select suitable persons for induction.[23] Michael Farrell, three years older than Emmet and from a Catholic background, entered Trinity in November 1794, where he became 'very intimate with young [Robert] Emmet'. The implication of Addis Emmet as one of the main initiators of the infiltration establishes that he had absolute confidence in his brother's capabilities. Their seditious partnership flourished until 1803.[24]

By 1797 Robert Emmet's charisma and leadership qualities had developed to the point that he made a strong impression on those he encountered, an important attribute for an organiser of sedition and propaganda. In his often disingenuous memoirs written many years after the events described, Valentine Lawless claimed to have been 'familiarly acquainted' with 'both the Emmetts [sic], and with M[ac]Nevin [sic], [Oliver] Bond, and [William] Sampson' in 1797. Lawless, a leading United Irishman in Britain in 1797–99, recalled Robert Emmet as 'a mere boy, but full of talent, enthusiasm, and kind feeling'. Emmet was the contemporary, friend and co-conspirator of Lawless' relative, John Lawless, who had also entered Trinity in 1794. The paths of the Lawless and Emmet families, distantly related through the Colvilles, were destined to cross under different circumstances over the following years in both Dublin and Paris.[25]

John Locke's *The Origin, Extent and End of Civil Government* was one of many works of history, poetry and philosophy read by Robert Emmet when at Trinity. His personal copy is covered with two distinct sets of marginal notes, one of which, as Kevin Whelan noted, pertained to the book's philosophic content. The other revealed Emmet's familiarity with William Godwin's *An Enquiry Concerning Political Justice*, first published in 1793, indicating that Emmet had re-read Locke for its political content. Godwin's argument that Governments alienated and corrupted their people was a viewpoint of which Emmet needed little convincing. He clearly identified with the Enlightenment writings which underpinned the United Irish agenda as perceived and advanced by his brother. In the 1790s Godwin, Locke and Voltaire were exploited by republican propagandists who mass distributed excerpts from inaccessible and expensive books in pamphlet form. These compilations, along with Tom Paine's *The Rights of Man*, reached a huge non-traditional readership in 1795–98 and contributed greatly to Addis Emmet's objective of 'making every man a politician'.[26]

The Armagh 'outrages' proved the extreme partiality of Camden's administration whereas the dragooning of Ulster from March 1797 confirmed the worst fears of moderates Earl Moira, Lord Charlemont and Sir Laurence Parsons. Lieutenant-General Gerard Lake was ordered by Camden to take 'decisive measures' to recover firearms from known and prospective enemies and, under the cloak of martial law, permitted his troops to run amok. The revamped Insurrection Act of February 1797 stipulated the punishment of transportation for those found out of doors after curfew or who were deemed to have sworn illegal oaths. Administering the United Irish 'test' became a capital offence.[27] The Earl of Leinster and the Earl of Bellamont, his relative, resigned their colonelcies of militia regiments in protest at the orders.[28] On 14 October 1797 Antrim's William Orr of Farranshane became the first man executed for swearing others into the United Irishmen and an instant martyr figure. Prison tenders moored in Belfast Lough and Derry's Lough Foyle received hundreds of detainees flushed out by the 'flying camps' of dragoons, yeomen and infantry. They descended on suspected communities to arrest and flog and sometimes to burn houses and shoot their inhabitants.[29] Antrim and Down bore the brunt of the crackdown although Derry, Tyrone, Monaghan, Louth and Armagh were also badly affected in the spring and early summer of 1797. A July 1797 raid carried out by the Welsh 'Ancient Britons' resulted in the firing of thirty dwellings in Ballynahinch, Dromore and Hillsborough. The Bantry Bay emergency silenced many who had previously opposed summary justice.[30]

Even as their grass roots were being assailed and terrorised, United Irish expectations of mass defections from the militia to the French during an invasion were severely undermined by the execution in

May 1797 of four Monaghan militiamen found guilty of sedition and shot in Blaris Camp outside Belfast.[31] Courts martial in army camps around the country and in Dublin's Phoenix Park may not have fatally weakened republican influence in the military but their cumulative effect obliged the Irish Directory to place greater reliance on the French dimension. The shooting of two Kildare militiamen in Phoenix Park in June 1797 caused a sensation in a city which dreaded Jacobin infiltration and probably spurred the resignation of many of the less resolute United Irishmen. The government's show of strength had previously concentrated the minds of Dublin republicans in April 1797, when six carriage loads of their Ulster comrades arrived in the city as prisoners. They included Dubliner Thomas Dry, brother of Richard, who had fled to Belfast to avoid an indictment for high treason.[32] These prominent northerners were detained in Kilmainham and Newgate, where they formed the nucleus of the 'state prisoners', a category which extended to Addis Emmet within a year. Chief Secretary Thomas Pelham remarked in May that 'in Dublin the spirit is down. We no longer hear either of insurrection or assassination. At the same time I believe that an invasion would produce both.'[33]

Pelham, as usual, was mistaken regarding the morale of the United Irishmen. A close-knit grouping of long-standing members attached to Oliver Bond of 9 and 13 Lower Bridge Street and his son-in-law, Henry Jackson of 159–60 Church Street, were busy supervising the perfection of the military format in Dublin and its extension elsewhere. Bond hailed from Donegal and Derry and his connections with the militants of Belfast in east Ulster – and Neilson in particular – preserved something of the dynamism of northern politics in the capital when their more exposed leadership was imprisoned. Neilson's other Dublin associates, Richard and Thomas Dry and the late Edward Dunn of Dorset Street, had also been involved with Duigenan in bringing Leinster up to the level of organisation attained in the north. This, in the first instance, entailed incorporating the Defenders, to whom they had previously offered leadership. Jackson, for his part, a major iron founder and United Irish armourer in Church Street and Clonskeagh, had in October 1794 backed calls from John Sheares and Thomas Wright to restructure the Society as a hierarchy of revolutionary cells. This had met with resistance in 1794 but, by early 1797, was essential to the survival of the republican organisation outside Ulster. On 5 June 1797 Jackson hosted a meeting at Church Street attended by his employee John McCann and northerners Alexander Lowry and Bartholomew Teeling, who stayed in Aungier

Street on this occasion. They agreed a 'plan of insurrection' with McCann and other city delegates, which did not go forward owing to dissension in Ulster and divisions in the Dublin leadership. A short-term effect of the dragooning of Ulster, therefore, was the enhanced emphasis on organising in Leinster. It was agreed that the northern counties would have to be left to their own devices until the military relented.[34]

With the assent of Neilson and Teeling, experienced full-time activists such as William Putnam McCabe of Belfast, James Hope of Templepatrick, William Miness of Saintfield and William Metcalfe of Antrim became available to oversee the adoption of the United Irish format in strategic counties. This took place in tandem with refinements to the command structure of the city societies, which were re-organised under four district committees within the obsolete police divisions: Workhouse and Stephen's Green to the south of the Liffey and Rotunda and Barrack to the north of the river. Wicklow, Meath, Kildare and Dublin County were prioritised for organisation in the spring of 1797, although considerable progress was also made in Carlow, Wexford, Waterford and beyond. Baronial and county committees came into being, which made possible the formation of the Leinster Provincial Directory and transitional bodies in Munster and Connacht. On 27 August the principal Dublin city committee ordered its constituents to 'be new modelled immediately', that is to reduce their cell size from thirty-six to a more manageable and discreet twelve. Temperance and prudence were strongly encouraged.[35] By late 1797, the elected members of the Leinster committee, together with those of the pre-existing Ulster body, dominated the national United Irish leadership and would do so until the advent of the Rebellion. Admiral Duncan's defeat of an Ireland-bound Franco-Dutch fleet at Camperdown (Texel) on 11 October 1797 represented a setback but also reaffirmed French willingness to venture their resources.[36] An informer claimed the following month: 'in the city of Dublin, county and vicinity, there are twenty-two organised regiments [of United Irishmen] ready to turn out on any occasion, but much want of arms'.[37]

Addis Emmet, one of those responsible for the rapid accretion of United Irish strength in 1797, would have been keenly aware that he and his confederates were engaged in a race against time with the government. The transfer of military flying camps from Ulster to the midlands and to the south raised the spectre of unprecedented and rigorous challenges to the nascent provincial networks. Martial law was declared in four Leinster counties in May 1797 where arms raiding, illegal assemblies and attacks on magistrates had flared. This pattern continued throughout the summer and autumn months as more and more baronies and counties were militarised under the Insurrection Act. Murder, rapine and summary transportation became common occurrences and the ravages of the Ulster crackdown were rivalled in Westmeath where almost 500 homes were burned by the Wicklow militia in the summer months of 1797.

CRISIS

At this low point of fortune French army successes in the Italian states offered hope of salvation as the young Napoleon Bonaparte routed the Austrian forces of occupation in 1797. The United Irishmen then had few options of which the French were not a central part. A unilateral rising was out of the question owing to their lack of firearms, and the only token defence which could be offered to Castle repression ahead of an invasion was in the realm of propaganda. Skirmishing with state forces, as the Defenders had with such enthusiasm and human cost in 1793, was likely to incur immediate disasters given that the military were alert and deployed in all critical sectors by mid-1797. The army, furthermore, was being directed towards suspected elements by locally-based yeomanry auxiliaries and ultra-conservative magistrates.

Highlighting extra-judicial state terrorism for the purposes of United Irish propaganda and recruitment encouraged Addis Emmet to contribute articles to the *Press* newspaper as 'Montanus'. He simultaneously began to withhold his services from high profile legal political cases. Edited by Arthur O'Connor and reputedly sponsored by Addis Emmet, Valentine Lawless and Lord Edward Fitzgerald, the emphatically republican *Press* replaced Samuel Neilson's vandalised *Northern Star* in September 1797 as the main organ of the United Irishmen.[38] Walter Cox's extreme *Union Star* and Roger O'Connor's even more ephemeral Cork-produced *Harp of Erin* fulfilled the same brief in 1797–98, but it was the *Press* which most accurately reflected the mood and interests of the United Irish leadership prior to March 1798.[39] Addis Emmet wrote for the same forum in which Arthur O'Connor, Sampson, Russell, Drennan and John Sheares published their incisive diatribes against the Establishment's coercion policy and conservatism. One of its later backers was Westmeath United Irishman William Dowdall, a man of means and member of the Donnybrook Hurlers, with whom Robert Emmet had very close dealings in 1802–3. It was in the pages of the *Press* that the political activism of Addis Emmet and Robert Emmet verifiably converged for the first time under the shield of assumed identities.[40]

Robert Emmet's imperceptible gravitation towards radicalism could not have surprised anyone familiar with his family background. More than most United Irishmen, he had been exposed to a diverse range of expert political opinion when living at home, flowing from the extensive social circle maintained by his father. The friends of Dr Emmet, no stranger to controversy, included Judge Chamberlain and Baron George, who tried capital sedition cases in the late 1790s and possessed first-hand experience of the difficult assizes of 1796. Lord Pennefather, Judge Pennefather and Charles Kendal Bushe called to Stephen's Green and Lady Anne Fitzgerald was reputedly a 'constant visitor'. Suffolk-born Sir Edward Newenham was another well-informed regular at the family table, as was Revd Walter Blake Kirwan, curate of St Nicholas Without. Kirwan was a renowned Jesuit-trained orator and convert from Galway who gave charity sermons in St Peter's, Aungier Street. Patriots and Whigs of all hues aired their views in Stephen's Green and, owing to their senior status in politics and the law, had much greater insight into the genuine state of the country than was reflected by the Castle press. Munster, particularly Cork and Tipperary associations, were a common thread between many of the guests, which provided a stimulating countervailing context for Robert Emmet in relation to his brother's distinctly radical oeuvre.[41]

Dr Emmet and Addis Emmet also welcomed Tone's friends Peter Burrowes and John Philpot Curran to Stephen's Green, men whom Robert Emmet had independently encountered as an adolescent at Trinity debates in 1794. Guests of Addis Emmet during this period included Thomas Russell, when free of his commitments as librarian of Belfast's Linen Hall Library, Lord Edward Fitzgerald, Dr William MacNeven, Arthur O'Connor and probably also 'Captain' John Sweetman, a substantial porter brewer and neighbour.[42] All were prime movers in the United Irish Directory and played vital roles in the lives of the distinguished Emmet brothers. Social calls may well have been the primary reason for many of the visits, although political meetings were secretly held in the house after the suppression of the Society in 1794. John Patten, a United Irishman and an occasional lodger in the home during the 1790s, claimed that Robert Emmet was present at several gatherings in the house prior to 1798. These were probably held in his brother's quarters. What, if any, connections existed between such illicit transactions and those convened under Robert Emmet's authority within the precincts of Trinity is open to question.[43]

While the consultations at Stephen's Green were clearly not the high-level discussions in which his elder brother participated in Bond's house during the same period, Robert Emmet, by his mere presence, had committed an offence for which hundreds had been transported to the Fleet. That he was not simply a trusted observer of illegal proceedings is established by his acceptance of three separate commissions to design seals for the use of the Leinster United Irishmen. One was allegedly inspired by Drennan's poetic vision of 'Erin'. All were completed to the approbation of the Society and one was engraved on an emerald which Sir John Temple had obtained in India and presented to Dr Emmet. This extravagant refinement required the consent of Addis Emmet, to whom the emerald had been presented and who presumably requested that it be made given that he retained ownership of the cherished seal for the rest of his life. The younger Emmet's impressive artistic skills around this time extended to sculpting pieces of non-political themes. He reputedly carved a marble bas-relief of Neptune and Nereids in a grotto-like arched recess erected on the grounds of the family's Milltown retreat.[44]

Robert Emmet, therefore, was an active Dublin United Irishman with the approval of his brother in 1796–98. This long-term commitment accounts in part for his otherwise surprising promotion to the Directory by January 1799. No extant evidence indicates a role for Emmet in the pre-Rebellion 'military' wing directed by the subcommittee controlled by Fitzgerald and O'Connor, yet it may be significant that this was the side of the movement in which he operated in 1799. Fitzgerald's advisers included Philip Long, Walter Cox and William Cole, all of whom were implicated in the Rising of 1803. Agents such as William Putnam McCabe, James Hope, John Palmer junior and Mathew Doyle, future adherents of Robert Emmet, extrapolated a paramilitary command structure from its civil precursor in 1797–98. They were assisted by Miles Duigenan – once he was freed from prison in December 1797 – and by several others, whose evasion of Castle scrutiny rendered them virtually anonymous. Secretaries and treasurers of simple societies and those advanced to baronial and county committees were transformed into 'sergeants', 'captains' and 'colonels' in order to function within a military chain of command alongside the French. Contingencies were planned and personnel armed and trained. Pike-drilling and arms raids were common in the countryside but less so in the teeming confines of Dublin city. Emmet's talents were, in any case, better suited to political agitation and making preparations to receive the continental allies of the United Irishmen.[45]

Trinity College in the early months of 1798, while still a place of study and reflection, was by no means immune from the side effects of the gathering storm. Four students had been admonished in July 1796 for attending political meetings outside college and the Fellows were alert to the possibility of greater dangers. Dozens of under-graduates and a prominent lecturer, Dr Whitley Stokes, were United Irishmen, while his colleague Robert Coombs evidently dropped out of the Society after its 1794 proscription. As republicans, active or otherwise, they were secretly committed to overthrowing the elite social and political framework of which they had availed. Hereditary privilege and the sectarian rubric which sustained the Irish gov-ernment were slated for abolition. Unfortunately, Moore's published recollections of Emmet and Trinity in 1798 are vitiated by his desire to minimise his own association with the United Irishmen. Moore played a major, if inadvertent, part in sparking the suppression of college radicalism, which presaged the end of his friend's educational pursuits. His sense of guilt arising from this may explain why Moore in later life wrote a biography of Lord Edward Fitzgerald, rather than of his equally famous close friend, Robert Emmet.[46]

Several of Emmet's United Irish colleagues at Trinity were the sons of men who called to Stephen's Green to visit his brother and father and were probably known to him prior to attending university. They included Cork-born Richard Curran, 23 in 1798 and the eldest son of the famous barrister John Philpot Curran. The younger Curran, who was detained in England on treason charges during the Rebellion, was also the 'friend and private secretary' of Valentine Lawless, an Emmet family associate held in the Tower of London from 8 May 1799 to March 1801. Richard Curran evidently intro-duced Robert Emmet to his sister, Sarah, the one known romance of his life. From 1790 the Currans kept a country house, The Priory, located off Grange Road, Rathfarnham, which was close to David La Touche's Marley estate. The Curran children may well have visited the second home of Addis Emmet, which was also in the neighbourhood.[47]

John Keogh junior, son of the Catholic Committee leader, was a year behind Robert Emmet at Trinity and just eighteen when implicated in seditious activities in April 1798. His fifteen-year-old brother George was expelled at that time after a spirited display in the face of his inquisitors. The Keoghs re-encountered Emmet in their Mount Jerome (Harold's Cross) home in October 1802 when, as a more senior United Irishman, Emmet called to enlist their father's support for his planned uprising. The spy 'Jones' identified John Keogh as one of Emmet's associates in College along with St John Mason, who was Emmet's first cousin, John Lawless and Edward Hudson. Hudson, the cousin and tenant of the eponymous Cork-born Grafton Street dentist, was an intimate of both Emmet and Thomas Moore. He interested the pair in the revival of Irish music spearheaded by Edward Bunting in 1796 with the publication of his *Collection of Ancient Irish Music*. Bunting, in turn, had been aided by Thomas Russell and the McCracken family of Belfast. As Moore lived to play a notable role in furthering this United Irish-supported project, it is appropriate that eight of the twelve airs used in his first edition of *Irish Melodies* had been collected by Bunting. Dacre Hamilton, another Trinity student, was a discreet young man who came to the notice of the authorities through his friendship with Emmet.[48]

Which, if any, of these youths were active in the United Irish Society of which Emmet was secretary in Trinity in 1798 is unknown, but from August 1797 this position ordinarily stemmed from being elected by the majority of twelve sworn members. The other three secretaries were William Corbett, Peter McLaughlin and James Thomas Flinn, whom Lord Clare alleged comprised 'a superior Committee'. It is inconceivable that the doctrinaire and democratic United Irishmen would have permitted the Trinity coterie to disregard the structures laid down in their constitution. The Trinity cells paid weekly subscriptions of 6d a week, as did all other formally constituted United Irish societies.[49] If properly affiliated with the city organisation, the Trinity societies would have come under the control of the district or baronial committee of the Stephen's Green Division. This administrative detail had a bearing on Robert Emmet's rise through the ranks during the Rebellion of 1798.[50]

Standing in the quarterly elections which filled simple society officerships required being known and respected by one's republican peers. Robert Emmet's return as secretary or treasurer prior to April 1798 confirmed his popularity in the circle he had helped create and offered leadership. Victory entitled the officer to represent his cell on a committee composed of ten such figures. This may have opened a formal channel of communication between the Trinity group and high-ranking city United Irishmen which Emmet's impeccable private connections had independently facilitated. 'Jones' contended that the bridging of this organisational gap had occurred in late 1797 when Robert Emmet and Michael Farrell liaised with the city and national leadership through Addis Emmet, Arthur O'Connor and John Chambers. They conferred in 5 Abbey Street, the home of Chambers, a bookseller, printer and stationer.[51] A point of corroboration may be that O'Connor and Chambers were indeed on the Leinster Executive from September to November 1797, sitting together for the first and last time in that capacity. Emmet and Farrell were apparently 'empowered to administer oaths & to communicate with the different societies in town'. Their comrade Flinn was preoccupied in his own right with 'aiding the organization on the Quays' close to his lodgings with his brother.[52] The arrangement described by 'Jones' evidently superseded the use of one Reilly to report between the 'collegians' and the baronial-level committees of the capital.[53]

Personal associations between Trinity and senior United Irish figures were also much in evidence: a Down-based brother of student Richard Caldwell was on that county's ruling committee in January 1798 and another was active in the capital and Michael Farrell, moreover, was an elected colonel of Longford United Irishmen by the following spring.[54] It was understood by one Trinity informer that Emmet, William Corbett, Martin Farrell, Michael Farrell, Thomas Bennett of Cork and one Butler of Dame Street headed the 'committee for the College assassins'. This was probably the military cadre of the United Irishmen in the university. The same informer elsewhere attributed this role to Emmet, the two Corbetts and the Farrells, who were reputedly 'appointed to lead in the risings then expected'.[55] Michael Farrell attended at least one United Irish meeting in the city in the mid-1790s with Whitley Stokes and Major James Plunkett, not to mention Bond, MacNeven, Jackson and Wright. Such company would have facilitated the Longford man's interest in the armed wing of the organisation.[56] William Corbett's extra-curricular activities prior to the Rebellion included his attendance of meetings in Francis Street chapel with several Trinity activists who supported Catholic emancipation. Edward 'Ned' Kennedy of New Street, step-brother of Wexford republican Miles Byrne of Monaseed, attended the gathering in April 1795 and told him that Thomas Street lawyer Edward Lewins had spoken with great effect. Kennedy further claimed that 'the presence too of the students from Trinity College was hailed with rapturous applause'. Lewins, Thomas Braughall's nephew, was soon afterwards sent to France to establish a United Irish embassy, which was revived after the Rebellion by Robert Emmet and Malachy Delaney.[57]

Emmet found it impossible to completely conceal his double life at Trinity and would have been compromised from the outset by the public profile of his elder brother. To some extent, the younger Emmet resigned himself to an acceptable level of risk and hid from the Castle in plain sight. Revd Dr Arthur Chichester Macartney provided Madden with details of Emmet's fateful speech in early 1798 on the theme of free speech and good government. This contentious motion was apparently chosen by mischievous associates in order to play to Emmet's academic strengths whilst placing him in a quandary on political grounds. Although strictly prohibited under the Society's rules from making explicit allusions to contemporary politics, Emmet's comments on tyranny in ancient Greece and Rome led to a forthright exchange with the respondent, the highly experienced debater Thomas Lefroy. Moore claimed that Fellows were obliged to attend debates at which Emmet spoke 'to neutralize the impressions of his fervid eloquence', particularly after his debut in the senior society in his last year at college. Indeed, ex-Historical Society champion and barrister James Geraghty returned to the scene of his own student exploits to oppose, and ultimately undermine, its rising star. Emmet's thinly disguised exposition of classical precedents for what was taking place in Ireland in January/February 1798 evidently hit their mark without violating the Society's rules.[58]

Macartney, son of a prominent Antrim yeomanry captain and magistrate, was impressed by the skill and logic of Emmet's speeches but amazed when the Dubliner did not relent in the face of Lefroy's lengthy retort. Unusually and unwisely, Emmet offered a strong defence of his position on that occasion against the objections raised by the conservative visitor. This bold and perhaps overconfident stance broadcast the depth of Emmet's convictions, an act reminiscent of the 1795 court appearance in which Addis Emmet had all but dared the authorities to prosecute him for swearing the United Irish oath. Whether family background was the decisive or merely a contributory factor in forming Robert Emmet's intense political opinions is open to question. That his home life disposed him to articulate controversial views in public, however imprudently, evinces the charged environment in which he had been raised and was living in 1798.[59] Revd Thomas Elrington, later Provost of Trinity, recalled Emmet's appearance with malign clarity five years after instructing him in mathematics. According to Elrington, Emmet had: 'an ugly, sour countenance; small eyes, but not near-sighted; a dirty brownish complexion; at a distance looks as if somewhat marked with the small pox; about five feet six inches high; rather thin than fat, but not of an emaciated figure – on the contrary, somewhat broad made; walks briskly, but does not swing his arms'.[60] This ungenerous description illustrates the disquiet caused by Emmet's presence in Trinity in the months preceding the Rebellion. Members of the Hammond family, who knew the Emmets, insisted that he was closer to six feet tall. He was, furthermore, short-sighted.

While few details of Emmet's seditious activities outside Trinity in early 1798 can be documented, it stands to reason that his youth, notwithstanding the entrée offered by his brother, militated against high-level involvement. His formal contribution to United Irish affairs was apparently split between the socially elite Trinity cells and similar activity inside his Stephen's Green home. He was far more than a nominal member of an illegal organisation and, along with his friend Thomas Moore, contributed patriotic poetry to the *Press* in 1797–98. Discerning Emmet's material from that of others, not least from Moore's – with whom collaboration was possible, is complicated by the use of pen-names by all writers. The prudence of this was underlined in November 1797 when Peter Finnerty of Church Lane, nominal proprietor of the *Press*, was prosecuted for libel arising from an item on the William Orr case.[61] The unfortunate Finnerty was 'double bolted, as well as hand cuffed' when hauled off to the New Prison (Newgate) on Green Street by jailer Tresham Gregg. He was subsequently pilloried.[62]

Anecdotal, family and documentary evidence points to Emmet's authorship of five politically themed poems between October 1797 and March 1799, of which 'Arbour Hill' is the best known. Madden was assisted in collecting some of the rarer pieces by their custodian, Mary Anne McCracken, who possessed unique manuscript versions written in invisible ink. Emmet's first published poem, 'The London Pride and Shamrock', appeared in the *Press* on 21 October 1797 and was signed 'Trebor', the reverse spelling of his christian name. John Sheares, a more frequent contributor, shared Cork and Trinity links with Emmet, and also had an elder brother prominent in both the United Irishmen and the Bar. The last known composition of John Sheares was an impassioned call to arms which closely resembled in language and tone that issued by Emmet and Philip Long five years later. It was Moore's early writing, however, that most affected Emmet's well-being in the spring of 1798.[63]

The first published essay acknowledged by the prolific Moore was 'Extract from a poem in imitation of Ossian', which appeared in the *Press* on 19 October 1797. Moore never admitted that the piece had already appeared in the final issue of the vandalised *Northern Star* in May 1797, a fact which undermined his disavowal in later life of serious political purpose when a young man. Literary merit aside, its subsumed radical content was sufficiently obscured by its pseudo-Ossianic style as to enable it to pass without notice in the *Press*. This was not the case with Moore's second effort. His address 'To the students of Trinity College', published on 2 December 1797, was viewed in the context of the November expulsion of two United Irish students: Arthur Ardagh of Tipperary and David Power of Cork.[64]

A more guarded approach from Moore might have been suggested by the fall-out of the episode of which the highlight was a duel between Ardagh and Macartney. Unlike Moore's literary foray into the affair, the meeting passed off harmlessly and Macartney survived several more contests with those who blamed him for the disgrace of Power and Ardagh. Many years later loyalist student William Blacker confirmed that Macartney had indeed divulged information on the Trinity United Irishmen which he had received from a Belfast friend, a well-placed spy named Macartney and one Scully as student informers in 1798. No explicit proof of Macartney's loyalism would have been required by Emmet's friends, who knew that the northerner's brother had led the yeomanry patrol which arrested William Orr at Milltown, Antrim, on 17 September 1796. The Macartneys, furthermore, kept their city home on Stephen's Green where intermittent social contact with their famous Emmet neighbours was highly likely.[65]

'Sophister', as Moore styled himself on his second political outing, reassured *Press* readers that there were many in Trinity College willing to assume the responsibilities of the ousted Power and Ardagh. Unfortunately, the repercussions of throwing down the gauntlet to the Board of Fellows in this manner were such that Moore could avoid but the more vulnerable and disfavoured Robert Emmet could not. While Clare student Nicholas Purcell O'Gorman was expelled for criticising the Board's handing of the affair, Emmet had a few months' grace before the matter was thoroughly investigated by Lord Chancellor Fitzgibbon (Lord Clare) and Dr Patrick Duigenan. This was an uneasy lull for him as events proved that he had anticipated their April 1798 'Visitation'. O'Gorman, furthermore, had been one of the original members of the Trinity United Irish leadership to which Emmet belonged. Tensions were rising within the College and in February 1798 unidentified persons pelted the windows of 27 Library Square as loyalist students convened inside.[66]

Thomas Addis Emmet left no record of his brother's first steps into subversion and was exceptionally busy when they occurred. In late 1797 the United Irish leadership retained the services of many of Addis Emmet's closest legal colleagues, most notably Curran, who frequently defended political prisoners. Curran's fees were subvented by an illegal monthly, later weekly, subscription of six pence paid by all United Irishmen to their treasurers. United Irishmen dominated the pool of barristers which assisted Curran in 1797–98, including Sampson, Dowling, MacNally and Henry Sheares. That Addis Emmet was conspicuously absent from most panels in political cases was due to an 'understanding' he had reached with other members of the United Irish leadership in 1797. This permitted him to shun the legal limelight in order to disguise the true extent of his commitment. More than most, Addis Emmet's conduct in court trod the fine line between professional and personal advocacy.[67]

An exception to this policy was made on 10 October 1797 when he appeared at the Court of King's Bench on behalf of twelve men freed from a Belfast artillery barracks to stand trial under a writ of habeas corpus. They had originally been due to appear at the Antrim assizes in April 1797 but the collapse of so many important political cases prompted Marcus Beresford to return them to custody in Belfast without bringing them before the judges. John Pollock had advised General Lake against flaunting the law in such a manner only to be criticised for his ignorance of the state's agenda and its best interests.[68] The position of the prisoners was successfully advocated in Dublin by Addis Emmet, who lambasted Lake and Belfast commander Colonel Lucius Barber for detaining untried suspects in harsh conditions. Barber was also held responsible by the United Irishmen for the Blaris Moore executions of four Monaghan militiamen. Addis Emmet availed of a technicality in the Belfast case that, even under martial law, a barracks was not a prison and was, therefore, unsuitable for holding men arrested on the basis of a warrant from the Chief Secretary. A far bolder step was Addis Emmet's rebuke of the government and the judiciary for not using their 'venerable authority in favour of insulted law'. Parts of the speech were printed in the *Press* to raise the ire of its readers.[69]

Also provocative, if more discreet, was a letter sent by Addis Emmet to Pollock on 5 December 1797. He accused the senior Crown legal advisor and one-time reform advocate of an improper 'connection' with the *Hibernian Telegraph*. Stung by this, Pollock replied immediately from his Jervis Street lodgings to deny the insinuation. Pollock further claimed that 'the present system of those prints excites my abhorrence & disgust. The sole object . . . of all the publick [sic] prints is to procure National Confusion or individual assassination, or to heap personal slander & calumny on the objects of their resentment'.[70] The implication that Addis Emmet had similarly calumniated Pollock angered a powerful enemy who secretly handled United Irish double agents Leonard MacNally and Samuel Turner. Addis Emmet also continued circulating draft proposals for constitutional reform to trusted associates, presumably post-revolutionary forms of Government. One 'D', possibly Dowling or Dowdall, advised that '500 is perhaps too large an assembly – after a certain amount wisdom does not accumulate in the same ratio' as membership. D, moreover, believed that Addis Emmet had not gone far enough regarding the status of the churches and should 'take away from the clergy of every religion every pretext for intermeddling with politics'.[71]

One of the last cases undertaken by Addis Emmet in Ireland commenced at the Dublin Commission of Oyer and Terminer on 16 January 1798. He then assisted Curran in defending men suspected of plotting to kill Lord Carhampton. The *Union Star* had insulted the former army commander by referring to him by his surname, 'LUTTRELL', and describing him as the 'sanguinary journeyman' of William Pitt.[72] Patrick Finney, the main defendant, was a Dublin yeoman and prominent south city United Irishman. He faced the capital charge of high treason defined as 'compassing and imagining the death of the King, and adhering to his enemies'. Fortunately for Finney, the credibility of the main prosecution witness, Jemmy O'Brien, collapsed under Curran's searing cross-examination. O'Brien, a former United Irishman from Stradbally, Queen's County, was a much-reviled member of Town Major Henry Charles Sirr's staff of police agents in Dublin Castle and destined to be executed for murder. Judge Chamberlain, who had taken part in the Drennan trial in 1794 and knew the Emmets socially, directed the bailing of sixteen of the defendants on 19 January 1798.[73] Over twenty south city United Irishmen were soon released arising from the victory leading to the lighting of celebratory bonfires in the Liberties at the Coombe and Jordan's Alley. Chamberlain's attitude may have been adversely affected had he been privy to intelligence that Addis Emmet, Fitzgerald, Jackson, Sampson and others had adjourned on the eve of the Finney trial from a United Irish meeting at Hearn's in the Corn Market and reconvened in Bond's on Bridge Street.[74]

The Finney verdict solidified the reputation of Addis Emmet as a stalwart of grass-roots urban republicanism, a distinction shared by Bond, Jackson, McCormick and, later, by Robert Emmet. Less obvious was his hand in drafting an internal United Irish document in mid-January which criticized Camden's speech on the re-opening of parliament. Finney was subjected to a personal surety of £200 but might well have been executed for organising city United Irishmen at the Sheaf of Wheat pub on Thomas Street in April 1797. He regarded himself as something of a marked man and migrated to London for four years, where he remained politically active in the city's large Irish community. His decision to return to Ireland to participate in the Rising of 1803 may have owed something to his perceived indebtedness to the Emmet family. By the same token, Finney's close relationship and social connections with south city United Irish leaders Patrick McCabe, Jonathan Gray and Owen Kirwan could well have helped bind them to the 1803 conspiracy in which they also featured prominently.[75]

Addis Emmet's hatred of Carhampton was almost palpable, not so much from his conduct in court during the Finney trial but from the pen of 'Montanus' in the pages of the *Press* on 23 November 1797. The letter addressed by 'Montanus' to 'satanides', as Carhampton was referred to, slated the general's 'crusade against the peasantry of Ireland' and accused him of superintending 'the establishment of martial law; perhaps to complete the annexation of this island to Great Britain, as a conquered and enslaved province, under the plausible name and form of an [sic] Union'. By issuing a death threat in the form of a mock epitaph for the general, depicted as having been executed and gibbeted for the 'parricide of the country that gave him birth', Addis Emmet publicly, yet furtively, crossed into the realm of those he defended at the Commission. The depths of this dichotomy between raw private anger and dutiful courtroom persona may explain the difficulty Addis Emmet experienced in taking such cases.[76]

The repressive legal and political climate continued to deteriorate in the months ahead, leaving the United Irish leaders with less and less room to manoeuvre. Isolated and often casual acts of violence in the city attuned loyalists to the growing presence of the United Irishmen in their midst and, perhaps, the inability of the anonymous republican leadership to control their adherents. On 11 January 1798 yeomen were warned to be 'on their guard in walking the streets of Dublin at night' after an assault on a private on South George's Street. During the following week the body of a Fermanagh militiaman was pulled from the Liffey and an Antrim militiaman was found dead near the Royal Barracks with hammer wounds to the head. On the 13th two off-duty King's County militiamen bayoneted one Thompson to death on Strand Street. Later that month John Allen allegedly participated in the killing of a loyalist named Kelly outside Astley's Theatre on Kevin Street. Offence had been taken at Kelly's insistence that 'God save the King' be played after the performance, despite the vocal objections of United Irishmen in the audience. Republicans correctly believed men were paid to make loyal declarations in public and this mercenary dimension may have increased their hostility towards Kelly and one Murphy. This undisciplined attack evidently boosted Allen's status with the rank-and-file city men and rendered his influence useful to Robert Emmet in 1803.[77] Allen, a woollen draper who lived at 80 Francis Street, was acquainted with Lord Edward Fitzgerald, who sent him out of the country to avoid the repercussions of the Kevin Street incident. He was also required to assist Arthur O'Connor in a delicate mission in England and was evidently trusted in such matters due to his membership of the Donnybrook Hurlers.[78] Addis Emmet may have had a particular interest in Allen's fate given that he and Fitzgerald dined with Francis Magan and others just two days before O'Connor left for England on the same mission.[79]

Private McDermott of the Royal Artillery may have increased public anger towards soldiers on 3 February 1798 by shooting dead the pregnant wife of Bryan Maguire when she refused to sell him more beer.[80] There was clearly a problem in Dublin with the boorish and violent behaviour of soldiers who were permitted to commit depredations in baronies under martial law yet obliged to observe the Articles of War and general military practice elsewhere. The Antrim, King's County and Cavan militia boasted hundreds of sworn United Irishmen in the Dublin area whilst being the main instrument of counter-insurgency in several south Leinster garrisons. Militarisation bore some fruit in the form of confiscated weaponry and prisoners but only at the expense of discipline. Lieutenant-General Sir Peter Craig, commander of the Eastern District, issued a General Order to the garrison on 26 February 1798 respecting the 'very disgraceful frequency of Courts-martial'. General Craig instituted tighter controls of troops based in Dublin who left their quarters after hours and of army patrols assisting the Revenue Officers.[81]

Thomas Addis Emmet and Lord Edward Fitzgerald were summoned before the Court of King's Bench on 12 February 1798 to account for the non-appearance for questioning of Arthur O'Connor, for whom they had posted bail. A heated exchange with Crown Solicitor Thomas Kemmis and Attorney General John Toler followed as Addis Emmet tried to explain O'Connor's highly suspicious absence. O'Connor, it was claimed, had notified Dublin Castle of his intention to travel to England on personal business and had not been informed of the intention to bring him to trial in February. The Drumcondra spy Thomas Boyle had informed Edward Cooke in late January that O'Connor had gone to London and it may be that the proceedings were permitted to proceed regardless to incriminate him still further in treasonous activities. The Court was eventually persuaded by Addis Emmet to set a later date for O'Connor's appearance, but compelling and damning reasons for his absence became apparent to all in the interim.[82]

On 28 February 1798 O'Connor and four other United Irishmen were arrested at Margate on the south coast of England as they illegally sought passage to France. Fr James Coigley, the best known of the other detainees, was an indefatigable Armagh priest with Defender connections. Coigley had previously visited England and France on republican business and was known in Dublin Castle as a revolutionary of great ability. He reputedly inducted Valentine Lawless into the United Irishmen and knew Kilmainham militant James Dixon. The Irish group at Margate included John Binns, a leading figure in British republican circles, John Allen and Jeremiah O'Leary. Binns and Allen were important members of the Emmet conspiracy five years later whereas O'Leary was a low-ranking United Irishman who dropped out of sight. The purpose of their 1798 trip, sanctioned by the Directory in Dublin, was to urge an invasion of Ireland at the earliest possible moment. Addis Emmet and Fitzgerald would have been fully briefed of this mission when they attempted to deflect the interest of the Court of King's Bench with regard to O'Connor's whereabouts. Instead of sailing to France, the emissaries were committed to the Tower of London on 6 March, by which time the implications of their arrest were being digested in Dublin Castle.[83] It came to light in 1803 that Fitzgerald's assistant Walter Cox had twice travelled to England in 1798 on behalf of the United Irishmen and attempted to spring O'Connor on 'the day he was tried' at Maidstone.[84]

The Castle played its trump card against the United Irishmen on 12 March 1798, which had been gifted to them by Thomas Reynolds of Kilrea, Kildare. Reynolds, just promoted to the Kildare County Committee, approached the authorities in consequence of his fears that the strategy adopted by the republican leadership would bring ruin to the country.[85] This was a calculated act of betrayal that Reynolds believed was in the public interest. He had called to Leinster House to visit his relative Lord Edward Fitzgerald on 11 March and learned of plans to run French arms, munitions and soldiers into a southern Irish port. Reynolds recalled Fitzgerald musing that 'Wexford might do: that it would be unsuspected'. Other secrets were disclosed in consequence of his rise through the organisation, including a reliable survey of its elected and unelected men of influence.[86]

Reynolds was not privy to one vital aspect of United Irish plans, their strategy for seizing and holding the capital when the French landed. Fitzgerald had drafted a pragmatic and far sighted document by early March concerning the tactics to be used by irregulars under his command when fighting regular troops in built up areas. He knew from his own training that military doctrine was designed with open field contests in mind and required officers to be 'very cautious of bringing the best-disciplined troops into a large city'. Fitzgerald estimated that Dublin's widest street would permit a body of 1,000 soldiers to present a front of just sixty men capable of opening fire. Moreover, room had to be allowed on each flank for the firing line to fall back in formation as their comrades simultaneously reloaded and moved into position at timed intervals. Fitzgerald believed: 'if the sixty men in front rank were defeated, the whole body, however numerous, are unable to assist, and immediately become a small mob in uniform'. The army's rate of fire would collapse to virtually nil as soon as the rebels broke into their midst either through their frontage or from their sides. Flanks were particularly vulnerable in cities due to the availability of lanes and alternate communication routes to their opponents. In a melee situation it was obvious that a socket bayonet mounted on a musket would be no match for a stronger and heavier pike blade fixed to an eight foot shaft. In fact, the disparity in thrust and reach meant that pikemen advancing shoulder to shoulder and in depth formed a phalanx which neither cavalry nor infantry were likely to break at close quarters. Irregulars were also favoured by their superior numbers which would permit the manning and exploitation of vantages overlooking their adversaries. Fitzgerald envisaged 'showers of bricks, coping stones & which may be at hand' falling on the soldiers, as he understood had occurred in Paris during the French Revolution. At the same time rebels would block surrounding streets with barricades of carts, doors and hogsheads to impede the army's ability to rally and redeploy. The importance of morale and leadership were highlighted by Fitzgerald, both of which were critical in motivating a mass of untested insurgents to sustain the heavy casualties they would inevitably endure when closing with a well trained and better equipped enemy. Also noteworthy were Fitzgerald's comments on the 'broken roads, or enclosed fields, in a country like ours, covered with innumerable and continued intersections of ditches and hedges, every one of which are an advantage to an irregular body'. Not mentioned in the Leinster House draft was his intention to use signal rockets to coordinate the interaction of rural and urban revolutionaries, and his theories regarding special equipment such as grappling irons, chain barriers and ladders to isolate and capture strategic objectives in the capital.[87]

A well-informed source claimed several years later that Cox had made a valuable input into the Fitzgerald plan. He was certainly regarded as 'an officer under' Fitzgerald and was presented with an inscribed copy of 'Gen[era]l Dundas's Military book' by the Dublin leader. The depth of Cox's role in United Irish affairs eluded the authorities which wrongly assumed from his family's association with Lord Carhampton and token disclosures in the Castle after December 1797 that little of note was withheld in 1798.[88] The Fitzgerald document also bore a striking similarity to passages of Philip Long's July 1803 address to the 'Citizens of Dublin' in which the United Irishmen were urged to make 'each street . . . a defile; and each House a Battery'. Long, a former army officer in Naples, may also have assisted in tactical planning in the capital in 1797–98.[89]

ARRESTS

Information channelled by Reynolds to William Cope enabled Major Sirr to raid Oliver Bond's house in 9 Lower Bridge Street on the 12th while a meeting of the Leinster Provincial Committee was in session.[90] Sirr's men arrested everyone in attendance and in one fell swoop detained most of the Leinster leadership. Important United Irish documents were found in the room and several were recovered in the possession of delegates. The Wexford representatives had delayed in the nearby Brazen Head pub long enough to hear the commotion across the street and slipped away with incriminating papers which would have proved the strength of the organisation in their native county. Dublin delegate Thomas Traynor, a spirit merchant and ship owner from 4 Poolbeg Street, was less fortunate but managed to consume his illegal documents. The arrival of Sirr's party was, nonetheless, an exceptionally serious blow to the conspirators. The loss of Bond alone was highly significant in view of his sterling reputation in the manufacturing classes of Ulster and Dublin. John Beresford, Chief Commissioner of Revenue, rejoiced that the raid had produced the first written proof of the United Irishmen's 'treasonable designs and actions'.[91] Items in the handwriting of John McCann, Henry Jackson's bookkeeper and the Secretary of the Leinster Directory, made sobering reading for loyalists. McCann's notes revealed that Dublin city claimed 2,177 United Irishmen, with a further 3,010 in the county, estimates which referred only to those in paramilitary cells that had been restructured during the previous month.[92]

Members of the Executive Directory and such known associates as had been absent from Bond's house were slated for arrest at home and in their workplaces. Thomas Addis Emmet, Henry Jackson, William MacNeven, John Sweetman and William Sampson were all detained in separate raids on the 12th.[93] Richard McCormick apparently anticipated arrest and fled the city. The crackdown netted the bulk of the Dublin-based United Irish leadership and, of the top-ranking men with military authority left at large, only Fitzgerald managed to evade arrest by nightfall of 13 March. He had been out of his Leinster House rooms when the military called with Alderman Oliver Carleton, although a search of his quarters uncovered seditious letters sent to him by Arthur O'Connor and Fr Coigley. Also found was the draft in Fitzgerald's handwriting described as 'the plan of attack of the city of Dublin . . . a well-designed one'. This document, in modified form, was the basis of the coup d'état strategy of Robert Emmet and Philip Long in July 1803. Fitzgerald was forced into hiding in March 1798 with a price of £1,000 on his head and developed the conspiracy with the aid of northerners Samuel Neilson, who lived on Donegall Street, and William Putnam McCabe. Neilson was not long released from Kilmainham and McCabe was extraordinarily difficult to pin down.[94]

Alderman William Alexander arrested Thomas Addis Emmet at his Stephen's Green home on the 12th in front of his wife and children. Robert Emmet may have stood witness as soldiers were deployed around their house with fixed bayonets to ensure that no escape was possible while his brother and family papers were secured. The size of the operation may be gauged from the fact that over thirty soldiers led by Captain Atkinson had been sent to detain Sweetman. An informer, probably MacNally, had alerted the authorities to the existence of the emerald seal designed by Robert Emmet in Stephen's Green, but this splendid prize, valuable in terms of its intrinsic worth and as a piece of evidence, was not recovered. It transpired that it had been concealed on the person of Jane Emmet, whose coolness when faced by the aggressive raiding party safeguarded her husband, as well as her young brother-in-law. The raiding party spent from 12.00 to 3.00 a.m. searching the building and collecting family documentation. Alexander took possession of legal papers, correspondence, receipts, hand bills and sundry, mostly innocuous items. This bundle formed the basis of a file in the Castle, to which was added letters seized from Addis Emmet when in prison in Ireland. The raid was the first of several on the house over the following months.[95]

There seemed to be a degree of confusion regarding Addis Emmet's treatment as he was first held in the Castle only to be sent home under guard after a short period. He was committed to Kilmainham the following day to be reunited with colleagues sent directly to the county prison from the Castle on the 14th. Given that 'Counsellor Emmett' had been listed for arrest by Camden two days earlier, it is apparent that his status in the United Irishmen had been strongly suspected, if not positively ascertained. In addition to his statements in court, unfavourable inferences would have been drawn from the presence of Addis Emmet and Lord Edward Fitzgerald at the late February funeral of William Kane, a barber who had been executed for sedition.[96] The authorities may have expected specific information regarding Emmet's many acts of treason to come to light during the preliminary interrogation of his associates in the Castle. If so, they were disappointed. Another possibility was that his respite from the damp cells of Kilmainham was a stratagem designed to convince those processed through the Castle that he had agreed to cooperate in the treason trials likely to commence in the immediate future. In fact, hard evidence of treason was only obtained against a few prisoners and not one of the suspects agreed to support the comparatively limited insights of Reynolds in court.[97]

Jane Emmet again showed uncommon spirit during the early days of Addis Emmet's confinement by overstaying a visit and hiding under his prison bed. Her presence in this small cell came to the notice of the chief jailer after several days but she cleverly exploited a regulation forbidding the use of force to evict her against her will.

Addis Emmet's reputation as a lawyer may have stayed the hand of those prepared to risk contravening this loophole. As matters stood, no charges had been brought against him and the prospect of his release to seek legal redress could not have been discounted. Voluntarily exiting the prison at any time, however, entitled the authorities to refuse Jane Emmet readmission and to disbar her from future visits. With this absolute stricture in mind, she shared her husband's ordeal for a year, only once contriving to visit their sick child in Stephen's Green with the aid of a sympathetic jailer's wife who allowed her access through the guard's residence.[98]

Robert Emmet was presumably shocked by the physical threat hanging over his brother after 12 March. The weakness of the government's case against him was not immediately apparent and a treason trial seemed likely. The bizarre circumstances of his sister-in-law's absence from Stephen's Green whilst her young children remained with him at home would have served as a constant reminder of the reverses sustained by the family. More than most, Emmet would have realised the magnitude of the setback inflicted on United Irish plans by the arrests, a cause in which he had already taken great risks and invested profound hopes for the future. Contact with the imprisoned men was initially restricted and he would have been very unwise to enter a prison without guarantees that he would be permitted to leave. Addis Emmet was reputedly held in 'close confinement' for a time in March 1798 and was forbidden to see anyone. Solitary, in practice, meant that the political prisoners were held two to a cell and prevented from communicating with each other.[99]

In March the younger Emmet had reason to consider the precariousness of his own position. The house in which he resided, attended illegal committees and had written seditious compositions had been overrun by soldiers fixated by the ultimate prospect of executing his brother for high treason. One of many documents taken away by Alexander was an unsigned address to the United Irishmen, which Robert Emmet was subsequently understood to have written four days previously. It urged restraint in the face of the 'illegal and unconstitutional measures . . . employed to force you into insurrection . . . when the members of a most corrupt and infamous Administration are earnestly hoping, and anxiously watching, for the first appearance of Rebellion'.[100] This recalled the difficulty faced by Miles Duigenan the previous year when the city United Irishmen demanded the right to fight back. Forty men evidently did just this on 16 March 1798 when they killed Daniel Carroll near the intersection of the Rathmines and Rathfarnham roads. Carroll resisted their attempt to raid the home of his employer, Charles Farren, Deputy Clerk of the Pleas in the Court of Exchequer and a reputed Orangeman.[101]

The purpose of Emmet's address was to calm the clamour for action, which was again building within the movement, but its closing remark that 'a time will come when you shall sleep no more' hinted that rebellion was fast approaching. Had positive evidence of his United Irish activity been recovered on 12 March there is little doubt that he too would have been jailed by nightfall. If the Alexander raid was not warning enough, John Stockdale's Abbey Street *Press* printing offices, which had received Emmet's first writings submitted for publication, were raided on 13 March. The last edition of the paper was then impounded and the United Irishmen all but silenced in consequence. Given the fate of the *Northern Star* this did not come as a complete surprise. Indeed, Stockdale had been brought before the House of Lords some weeks earlier to answer questions regarding republican propaganda. His duties were afterwards performed by William Dowdall, one-time secretary to the Whig Club and a future close ally of Robert Emmet.[102]

Attending Trinity would never be the same for Emmet, particularly as his College acquaintance Edward Hudson had been amongst those detained from Bond's. Emmet must have realised that students and staff who had formed adverse opinions of him during his recent debating outings would be vindicated in their suspicions of his United Irish connections. Their increased hostility could be taken for granted and their palpable wariness was confirmed when Thomas Moore's tutor, Robert Phipps, called to visit Moore's parents. Phipps, an assistant lecturer in Greek and College censor, 'confidentially and strenuously' advised the Moores that their son 'should avoid being seen so much in public with Robert Emmet . . . and that there were circumstances which rendered it highly imprudent'. This explicit warning had to be taken seriously in the light of the revelations concerning the prominence in seditious activities of Hudson, Moore's music mentor and his own declarations in Francis Street chapel during the Fitzwilliam crisis. The poet's memoirs omit mention of whether he passed on word of this tip-off to Emmet.[103]

While Emmet put a brave face on matters in Trinity and attempted to continue his studies, the examination of documents captured at Bond's established that the United Irish conspiracy had mushroomed in scale to 280,000 sworn adherents by the end of February 1798. Ulster republicans, the Castle learned, enumerated their strength at

110,990 men, an impressive total given the events of the previous year. There were evidently 100,634 men in Munster, where comparatively little headway had been made in identifying leadership cadres and recovering weaponry. Limerick and Cork were consequently heavily garrisoned by May. It was also discovered that United Irish enrolments closer to Dublin had reached 10,865 members in Kildare, 11,689 in Queen's County (Laois), 9,414 in Carlow and 14,000 in both Meath and Wicklow. The Dublin organisation in the city and county sectors continued to grow and represented a major threat to Irish security in the event of a French invasion.[104]

Even though coercion regulations limited the amount of gunpowder available for purchase by the United Irishmen and made it more difficult for them to buy or steal firearms, the widespread felling of young ash trees testified to the large-scale manufacture of pikes. Nocturnal assemblages for pike-drilling and intimidating loyalists remained common and fatal attacks on magistrates and state's witnesses were stepped up. On 28 March 1798 the Pennefathers of Newpark, friends of the Emmets in more peaceful times, were to the fore of an armed clash at Tubberadora, Tipperary. Colonel Pennefather led the Cashel yeoman cavalry to assist the Louth militia in confronting a 500-strong body of insurgents gathered at Holycross. Three rebels were killed and twenty-one taken prisoner. The Dublin Castle triumvirate of Lord Lieutenant Camden, Chief Secretary Lord Castlereagh and Undersecretary Edward Cooke decided in late March that the army should not be restrained if the United Irishmen were to be contained.[105]

April 1798 proved the most challenging month yet experienced by the Leinster United Irishmen as the tempo of militarisation was stepped up. Recourse was made to 'freequarters', in which soldiers were billeted in disaffected communities to commandeer resources and conscript labour without compensation. Areas in Ulster in which martial law had already been declared were deluged by hardened veterans of counter-insurgency and all major garrisons were reinforced. In Kildare, Wicklow, Carlow and Wexford heightened levels of coercion were visited on the population. In addition to house-burning and summary transportation, random flogging of suspects on wooden triangles and the use of such devices as the 'pitch cap' and 'picket' were used to extort confessions. Pikes were recovered in their thousands but the torture and execution of United Irishmen in Athy, Naas, Ballitore, Bray, Carnew, Dunlavin, Newtownmountkennedy, Enniscorthy, Gorey and other south Leinster towns in the spring of

1798 marked the magistrates, yeomanry corps and military units involved for revenge attacks during the Rebellion. Moreover, the appearance of hundreds of untried men marched to the city in chains for deportation to the Fleet from Dublin Bay was greatly resented by their urban comrades.[106] News that trees had been felled on Alderman Lundy Foote's Rathfarnham property on 2 April brought the conspiracy much closer to Government than simultaneously disseminated reports that 200 ash, larch and elm plants had disappeared in Westmeath.[107]

Excesses were rarer in the capital although attacks on suspected informers and soldiers became more common, especially in the south city. On 26 March a man denounced on Thomas Street as a prosecution witness at Naas assizes was severely beaten, slashed with knives and dragged by the heels to Coal Quay as if to be thrown in the Liffey. He was instead dashed off the pavement and left for dead in Charles Street. Another suspected informer was stoned by a crowd in the Lower Coombe on 2 April and badly injured in a second attack on Patrick Street some hours later.[108] Violent clashes became weekly occurrences as the United Irishmen of the Barrack, Workhouse, Rotunda and Stephen's Green divisions built up their strength and unofficially retaliated against the forces of the Crown. Major Sirr's men were freed in April from the formality of obtaining warrants to enter houses, and confrontations ensued during arms searches. Justice William Bellingham Swan and the Revenue Corps of yeomen seized five United Irishmen at John Cusack's pub in Ely Place on 4 April. This resulted in charges being laid for sedition, as well as the illegal sale of spirits. Intensive yeomanry patrols were mounted to warn the 'incendiaries . . . that there is the closest watch upon their anarchical movements'.[109] An alarmed Lord Shannon observed 'a monstrous crowd' that quickly gathered at Temple Lane on 10 April just after Lieutenant Blaney Winslow of the Fermanagh militia killed a prisoner, allegedly in a drunken rage. A larger military patrol arrived in time to prevent a riot by onlookers. Shannon felt 'things look as bad as possible, and his Excellency [Camden is] very undecided, where vigour and decision are so necessary'. As news of the extension of martial law to parts of Wexford and Kilkenny reached the city, the Castle Guard began keeping members of the public and suspected 'crops' – United Irishmen ('croppies') – out of the complex.[110] It was undoubtedly a matter of an embarrassment that Thomas Traynor, one of the Bond detainees, escaped from the Castle that week. Moreover, when the 'seditious vicinity' of Traynor's home was searched on 6

April, it was discovered that the United Irishmen had responded to the loss of the *Press* by publishing and openly selling pamphlets on Poolbeg Street such as *Union and Freedom*.[111]

Trinity student William Fitton, with whom Emmet had also attended Whyte's Academy, was arrested around this time for possession of a geology hammer. Fitton was no assassin, although the proliferating accounts of armed actions in the Dublin area engendered a climate of uncertainty. Concerned loyalists for whom membership of the yeomanry and watchmen was either unappealing or disallowed instituted vigilante patrols in the parish of St Mark. Emmet would have been acutely aware of the dangers of convening United Irish meetings in his home and presumably either destroyed or concealed documents connecting him to sedition. The decisiveness with which Emmet acted during the official examination into United Irish activity in Trinity College on 19–22 April 1798 suggests that he was well prepared for the event. A less than wholehearted response from the student body in February to news that they were to present a loyal address to the Lord Lieutenant may have suggested caution. It was hardly surprising that the reluctance of many students to formally proclaim their support for the Camden administration would lead to an investigation of their political allegiances.[112]

THE VISITATION

Lord Chancellor Fitzgibbon, who was Vice-Chancellor of the University, commenced his three-day 'Visitation' on 19 April, aided by his ultra-conservative associate Dr Patrick Duigenan. Fitzgibbon told Shannon that he would 'root the new doctrines out of the College'.[113] Students, teachers and administrators were questioned under oath in the Dining Hall in order to flush out those responsible for submitting two anti-government articles to the *Press*, a journal decried by Fitzgibbon for having 'scattered the seeds of rebellion more thick and extensively than any other machine'. Other seditious documents had also come to light in the College during the course of the month.[114] One of the offending *Press* articles had been written by Thomas Moore, whose academic career was protected by his use of a nom de plume and the silence of his friends. Moore was by no means the sole object of the investigation and Fitzgibbon and Duigenan clearly relished the opportunity of conducting a trawling operation in which Catholics and students from pro-reform families were implicated. The only lecturer compromised, Dr Stokes, friend of Addis Emmet, Tone,

McCormick and Sampson, was suspended from his post for three years.[115]

The proceedings in the Dining Hall were closely observed by William Blacker, who was drawn into an argument with Stokes on the illegal presence of Orange societies in the College. Blacker, along with members of other northern loyalist families, had founded lodges in Trinity in late 1796 on returning from the summer break in counties disturbed by the rise of the United Irishmen. He recalled: 'A student of the House named [John] Egan was the first called up and being sworn deposed to being one of the College Society of United Irishmen – stated when their meetings had been held and implicated a number of the lads as fellow traitors. He was a low vulgar wretch.'[116] This was a pre-meditated act on Egan's part given his overtures to students on the periphery of republican activities in Trinity ahead of the Visitation. Another witness of the proceedings noted how 'E[gan]' attempted to engage him in a 'confidential communication' pleading that he had been 'deeply compromised, and in hourly expectation of being arrested'. It was later alleged that Egan had been 'a principal agent' in collecting information ahead of the arrival of Fitzgibbon and Duigenan. This was the role Egan seemingly resumed in the guise of 'Jones' when he ran into his erstwhile companion Robert Emmet in France in 1802.[117]

Emmet realised in April 1798 that his extra-curricular activities would be closely looked into owing to the notoriety of his jailed brother. Compliance with the examiners was not an option and, if privy to the substance of the warning given to Moore by Phipps, Emmet may have suspected that he had been betrayed by an informer. He attempted to avoid almost inevitable expulsion for non-cooperation with the enquiry by requesting that the Board of Fellows remove his name from the student enrolment. This brought an abrupt end to Emmet's formal education and, with it, all hope of progressing to a professional career in the footsteps of his brother, father and grandfather. Significantly, this was precisely the course also taken by his close associate Michael Farrell, presumably after discussion with Emmet. Graves, Emmet's tutor, appeared before the investigators on 20 April to mount an ineffectual defence of his student's integrity, if not also to safeguard his own reputation. This drew further attention to Emmet's evasiveness.[118]

An account by Bishop Young, revised by Fitzgibbon, noted that Graves had 'made some observations relative to Emmett [sic] who long since wished to have taken his name off the College books, but had been dissuaded by Mr Graves his tutor'. Evidence of Emmet's foresight then prompted a revealing outburst from Fitzgibbon, who evidently discerned a challenge to his authority in the absent Dubliner's defiance. The Vice Chancellor told Graves: 'I have been for some time in possession of everything that has been going forward in the College – and I know that Emmett [sic] is one of the most active & wicked members of [the] society of U[nited] I[rishmen] – and I did desire [the] Provost not to suffer any person whatever to take his name off the College Books, that I might bring him & others of his association to punishment – We will now call Mr Emmett [sic] – & if he does not appear, we will expel him – and I will take care to communicate due information of this to the heads of houses [i.e. universities] of England & Scotland.'[119]

Emmet, of course, did not appear, and his actions had predictable consequences. His name was added to the list of students barred from the College for offering dissent or for having been denounced as United Irishmen. At one point over fifty students had been under threat of expulsion until a pragmatic shift in Fitzgibbon's line of questioning forestalled such an embarrassing prospect. This was not unexpected as Fitzgibbon knew on the 19th that thirty students had refused to be examined and that sixteen more had already confessed to being United Irishmen.[120] Uncovering and punishing so many disloyal students in the midst of Ireland's future clerical and professional elite would have been counterproductive. Affairs in Trinity teetered on the brink of a political own goal notwithstanding the hastily reduced scope of Fitzgibbon's crackdown. City United Irishmen were said to have viewed the disclosure of their influence with 'the youth of the country' as 'their masterstroke'.[121]

Outright dissent at the Visitation had to be dealt with harshly if the exercise was to be meaningful. Emmet's friend Dacre Hamilton was one of several youths dismissed for declining to answer questions when summoned to the Dining Hall. Moore, surprisingly, managed to remain at Trinity despite his initial efforts to avoid taking the oath by repeatedly refusing to hold the swearing Bible. He eventually relented and weakly denied an interest in politics, an exceptionally unconvincing declaration under the circumstances but one which satisfied his exasperated interrogators. Important United Irishmen evaded detection, not least Richard Caldwell of Ballymoney, who left Trinity of his own volition prior to the Rebellion and reappeared as a colonel of Down insurgents in June 1798.[122]

Longford's Michael Farrell also refused to meet the inquisitors of the Visitation in the same manner as followed by his Dublin comrade.

Graves claimed: 'the disturbed state in the part of the country in which he is, prevents his attendance', to which Fitzgibbon retorted: 'If I had not reason to suspect that a considerable part of the disturbance of that county might be traced to him, I might perhaps be induced to excuse him – but as I know that he acted as a secretary to the United Irishmen I must insist on his appearance.' Fitzgibbon must also have been aware that Farrell had acted in concert with Emmet in withdrawing from College.[123]

A disastrous outcome was virtually unavoidable insofar as Emmet was concerned, possibly much worse than expulsion. Fitzgibbon and Duigenan gleaned information from fearful and compliant students who correctly named him as the secretary of one of the university's four United Irish societies. This, if anything, underestimated his involvement in student radicalism, yet was more than enough to open the way for prosecution. Dealings between Phipps and the Moore family strongly suggests that Macartney, Blacker, Scully, Egan or some other voluble student had linked Emmet's name to sedition ahead of the Chancellor's descent on the College. This scenario was all but stated by Fitzgibbon when questioning Graves. Certain students were apparently earmarked for close attention while others, like Moore, were permitted to shrive themselves in front of their peers of what could be represented as immature political dabbling. In the final analysis, Emmet was fortunate to avoid prosecution in March/April 1798 and had made a prescient choice in writing to the Board of Fellows.[124]

The enforced, if technically voluntary, resignation from college, coming so soon after his brother's imprisonment, added to tensions in the Emmet household. It was perhaps to palliate the dismal implications of these events that Emmet had conferred with his father and showed him a draft of the letter he later submitted to the Board. Emmet may also have told his father that Graves had strongly advised against this course. John Patten recalled Dr Emmet's 'entire approbation' of his son's mature handling of a difficult situation.[125] This must have been very difficult. One son had died in his prime, another was in prison and the third would never fulfil the great promise of his talents in the professions. Robert Emmet had been 'intended for the bar' after his Trinity BA and had investigated studying at King's Inns but there was no longer a viable path to this end in either Ireland or Britain from 19 April 1798.[126]

How Emmet occupied himself in the month between his departure from Trinity and the onset of the Rebellion in May 1798 is unknown. Evidence indicating that he spent the early weeks expecting arrest may well account for the missing details. Drennan, when writing to his sister in Belfast on 23 April 1798, noted that Emmet might accompany John Browne to the northern port. Browne's family were Belfast bankers on good terms with the Drennans and he was also friendly in Dublin with Thomas Moore. Browne carried messages which Drennan dared not entrust to the heavily scrutinised postal system. Even though Browne had been obliged to leave college for political reasons, Drennan prudently made no explicit reference to his predicament when observing: 'Nineteen students have been expelled . . . It is said that those who were suspected as United Irishmen do not choose to appear for fear of a farther prosecution . . . Browne will tell you all and perhaps young Emmet if he accompanies him. He is a wonderful orator, though so modest and diffident in company.' Drennan's high opinion of Emmet is important, as is the implication that he and Browne dared not 'appear' in Dublin.[127] The two ex-students were firm friends and their names were jointly raised in April 1799 when both were once again suspected of sedition.[128]

Moving to Belfast or embarking at its docks for Britain was not the safest of options for United Irish fugitives in the last week of April 1798. Even so, it may have seemed a route to comparative safety given rumours in Dublin that a warrant was 'out for young Robert Emmet'. Drennan was sufficiently disturbed by the persistence of this story as to call to Stephen's Green to confer with Emmet's parents. His concerns could not have been allayed by finding the once bustling house in which he had spent so many evenings strangely deserted. Robert Emmet clearly wished to avoid being seen in public and may have laid low in the family's country house near Milltown. Casino House was located on a thirteen-acre estate at the corner of Bird Avenue, off the Dundrum road. It was unlikely that Emmet would have encountered loyalists who knew him in that area, although the family's nearest neighbour was none other than Alderman John Exshaw whose defeat in the Dublin election of 1790 was due in no small part to Dr Emmet's Grattanite friends. Local associates included the republican Jackson family – iron and brass founders at Clonskeagh and Church Street, Dublin – who owned a country house at Roebuck.[129]

Under the circumstances, it is unlikely that Emmet persevered in attending the public gallery in parliament where he had once observed debates on the political crisis. A role in the preparation of the Dublin city United Irishmen for insurrection was not out of the question given Emmet's at least tangential association with its central figure, Lord Edward Fitzgerald. He also had a close relationship with a newly prominent activist, John Lawless, his twenty-three-year-old comrade from Trinity. Lawless' relative, Valentine Lawless, was a lifelong friend of Addis Emmet and a senior United Irishman. While no details of such pre-Rebellion activity are extant concerning Robert Emmet, his sudden prominence at command level by January 1799 reflects a significant deepening of involvement in 1798. Indeed, the fact that he was being sought for questioning before the Rebellion may well account for his heightened security-consciousness.[130]

THE ONSET OF REBELLION

The arrests of 12 March 1798 forced the rump United Irish leadership to reconsider their policy. The loss of weapons and personnel under martial law in Leinster had raised the issue of launching a mass uprising without the assistance of French troops, just as the dragooning of Ulster had put the question on the agenda the previous year. In early 1798 the United Irishmen possessed a large, if poorly armed, national organisation. After the arrests at Bond's, the Sheares brothers moved much closer towards the centre of the conspiracy. They argued in April/May 1798 that disaffected militiamen based at Lehaunstown Camp outside Bray could be relied upon to rise en masse in support of the United Irishmen. Their associate John Lawless, another recent addition to the reduced Directory, presumably agreed. His relative, surgeon William Lawless of French Street and Shankhill, had visited the camp with the Sheares brothers and Sampson in 1797–8 to distribute propaganda. Events at Bond's accentuated Fitzgerald's influence in military planning, which took a major step forward during the months of April with the election of colonels in the city and county. He was aided by Samuel Neilson, who returned to Dublin after a period in hiding with Henry Jackson's brothers at Creeve and Cremone, Monaghan. It does not appear, however, that an adjutant-general was appointed in Dublin and this probably reflected the logistical problems posed by the increasingly severe security climate in the capital.[131] Weapons were lost during the first week of May in Howth, Coolock and Clontarf in the northern coastal suburbs which were increasingly difficult to replace.[132]

While by no means uncritically endorsed by Fitzgerald and Neilson, the Lehaunstown plan proposed by the Sheares brothers and Lawless offered a rationale for rising without the French. Foreign military aid had hitherto been deemed essential to the success of the United Irish effort and moves towards unilateralism were, therefore, highly contentious. The extreme pressure being brought to bear on the movement by the summary transportation of suspects, random floggings and house-burnings, however, threatened its destruction or enfeeblement before the arrival of their allies. City United Irish committees were busy in mid-to-late April 1798 electing officers to serve for the following three-month terms. These promotions, as matters transpired, were of leaders who were *in situ* when the Rebellion commenced. On 19 April Fitzgerald's military subcommittee issued 'instructions' to subordinates of the Leinster Provincial Committee as if to reassure its officers that a higher command had regrouped.[133] A spy reported that

> Military organization has been adopted in the city and some battalions are already formed & officers appointed, there are two in the Rotunda division & one in the Barrack [division]. It has been sent down in the report to form the committee that they have succeeded in obtaining twelve men of the first military talents and experience that have been in actual service.[134]

Major Sirr may have disrupted a simple society election in the last days of April when he raided a gathering of eleven men at Widow Magrath's tavern on Rogerson's Quay.[135]

The rate of United Irish expansion in the city, while not spectacular after March, was surprisingly steady. Edward Rattigan, who evidently assumed some of the imprisoned John McCann's duties, noted that the Workhouse Division had 1,095 members in sixty-six societies, while the Barrack had 1,595 in sixty-nine and the Rotunda 1,327 in seventy-three. The strength of Emmet's Green Division was incorrectly enumerated as just 403 men in twenty-six societies, a clerical anomaly which probably resulted from a failure to submit the proper returns for assessment. The Green Division's paper shortfall, however, was one of the few obvious signs of disruption in an organisation that continued to raise funds from lotteries, appoint officers, train its members and increase its complement from 2,177 in March to an underestimated 4,420 in May. Another internal source claimed 8,597 city rebels in April.[136]

Preparations intensified in May given that more and more physical evidence of an approaching calamity accumulated in the capital. Buck, a Pembroke Court silversmith and sergeant of United Irishmen, drilled pikemen of the Green Division on 22 April between Harold's

Cross and Dolphin's Barn. They possibly used pikes forged by Kilmore of Camac Place and reputedly had access to 2,500 such weapons. A cache of 350 pike handles was uncovered by Sirr's men in Bridgefoot Street on 8 May and Lieutenant Stewart of the Derry militia was stabbed by one Stringer during a search of Sweetman's brewery at 23 Francis Court, Francis Street. Pikes were found by Alderman Alexander on Sackville Street and others by Lord Charles Stanley Monck in the south county villages of Dundrum and Milltown.[137]

Camden expressed surprise on 11 May at the 'very alarming number of pikes . . . secreted in Dublin which can only be for the purpose of insurrection'. It was also discouraging that the United Irishmen of the city environs were sufficiently confident to plant a 'tree of liberty' in Finglas notwithstanding the more frequent army and yeomanry patrols. Moreover, Alexander's arrest of suspects in Thomas Street and Smithfield retrieved a fresh item of United Irish propaganda concerning Downpatrick-born spy Edward John Newell, who was missing and presumed dead. The recovery of five cannons on 11 May by Sirr, Swan and Ryan in a North King Street yard, also sent a ripple of fear through the Establishment, even though the guns probably belonged to a defunct Volunteer unit and were never in the hands of the United Irishmen.[138] In response, yeomanry activity was stepped up to display the strength of Irish loyalism and to encourage the timid to resist the United Irishmen. Monck, one of several north Wicklow yeomanry officers to hold a commission of the peace for Dublin, had caused offence by bringing the Powerscourt corps as far as Milltown on the 9th, an act interpreted as a slight on the honour of local units and magistrates. His gesture was reciprocated five days later when Alderman Exshaw's Stephen's Green Division of yeomanry rode to Enniskerry and Powerscourt to conduct a 'sham battle' and camp overnight.[139] The city yeomanry contained seven cavalry and thirteen less prestigious infantry corps in comparison with one infantry and thirteen cavalry in the county where mobility was far more important.[140]

Sirr came close to capturing Lord Edward Fitzgerald on the 17th and loosing his life in the process. Fitzgerald left James Moore's home at 124 Thomas Street, where his assistant and lodger, Patrick Gallagher, worked as a clerk, and headed for Francis Magan's house at 20 Usher's Island. Magan was a newly qualified barrister and double agent who warned Major Sirr that the United Irish leader would pass through Watling Street. Magan, who had only been advanced to the Dublin City Committee earlier that day, began to channel high-grade information to the Castle through 'Sham Squire' Francis Higgins, editor of the *Freeman's Journal*. With Miss Moore on his arm, Fitzgerald was shepherded into the street by Gallagher, William Putnam McCabe and John Palmer junior of 12 Cutpurse Row, all of whom had worked unceasingly to prepare United Irish paramilitary structures since the early months of 1797. Gallagher, a colonel of the United Irishmen, also liaised closely with the Westmeath network through John McManus of Kilbeggan. On sighting Sirr and hearing his challenge, Gallagher and McCabe produced pistols which they snapped at his head. Both misfired. Gallagher then stabbed the prostrate Major no less than seven times but without effect as Sirr had taken the precaution of wearing his chain mail vest. Sirr's dagger, on the other hand, cut into Gallagher's calf, causing a bloody injury. Fitzgerald escaped in the confusion to Thomas Street and the trail went cold for two days.[141]

Magan's treachery compromised a part of the city much favoured by Fitzgerald. Amongst those known to have sheltered him in the area were the Bretts of 2 and the McLaughlins of 13 Usher's Island. John Keogh of Mount Jerome had previously chaired republican meetings in McLaughlin's house and both men were suspected of membership of the post-Rebellion United Irish Directory. Moira House, the Dublin residence of the English Whig leader and United Irish sympathiser Earl Moira, was also in the vicinity. Lady Pamela, Fitzgerald's wife, was Moira's guest in the mansion in mid-May where she probably received fleeting visits from her fugitive husband. Moira generally lived in England or on his Irish estate at Ballynahinch in Down, where a major battle was fought in June 1798. Access to Moira's substantial city home stemmed from his support for radical political change and also from his status as a senior British freemason. Many, if not most, United Irish emissaries were freemasons and McCabe, Gallagher and others relied heavily on the craft's traditions of recognition, secrecy and sanctuary.[142]

A raid on 18 May by Justice Drury on two smiths in a laneway forge off Thomas Street found no evidence of illegal activity despite his men inflicting 'bodily pain' on one of the suspects.[143] At length, it was discovered that pike heads had been passed into an adjacent building through a camouflaged hole in the dividing wall. Drury committed the pair to the Castle but had angered local sympathisers in a republican stronghold where it was alleged 'every third house was a public house'. A daring rescue attempt was mounted in

Skinner's Row which, although unsuccessful, confirmed the escalating trend of violent opposition to state agents in the capital. Drury's actions at this time were probably recalled by many Dublin rebels who shot at him in the Coombe during the Rising of 1803.[144]

United Irishmen meeting in James's Gate tannery on the 18th had a narrow escape that afternoon when warned by the intrepid Miss Moore that the military party which stormed her house on Thomas Street was on its way. The delegates rapidly exited into Watling Street, leaving papers and other incriminating paraphernalia behind. Moore's role was suspected by the soldiers who ran into her outside Nicholas Roe's distillery at 33 Pimlico. On being recognised as the daughter of the suspected harbourer they had just visited, she was slashed across her shoulders with a bayonet. This was allegedly observed by a rebel gunman who shot and killed her attacker from a vantage at the corner of Crane Lane. The Francis Street house of John Cormick, a reputed colonel of city United Irishmen, was occupied by the military on the basis of the correct assumption that William Lawless had recently brought Fitzgerald to stay there. Fitzgerald also used the home of Dr Henry Kennedy at 13 Aungier Street, Thomas Moore's neighbour, and that of Mrs Dillon in Portobello on the Rathmines Road.[145]

Martial law was formally declared in Dublin city and county on 18 May 1798 following a special meeting at the Sessions House of twenty-two magistrates who petitioned the Lord Lieutenant to extend the Insurrection Act. From that day the constant patrolling of the yeomanry and posting of sentries on the Liffey and canal bridges brought an air of menace to daily life in the capital. Preparations were made to fit iron gates, in storage for over a month, to all the main bridges. This was intended to increase the efficiency of the curfew and impede illegal traffic. Richard Farrell, a twenty-two-year-old Catholic student at Trinity, believed that coercion was unnecessary. He wrote on the 18th: 'the city of Dublin never presented such a face of tranquillity in the ordinary times of peace . . . it *was a dead calm* such as often precedes a storm . . . all was mirth & gaiety nothing portending danger was to be seen in the countenances of those who were in a manner dancing blindfold on the very verge of an awful precipice'.[146]

Nicholas Murphy's house at 153 Thomas Street, one of several main hideaways used by Fitzgerald, was raided on the 19th by Sirr, Justice Swan and Captain Thomas Ryan. Neilson had exited the building after dinner an hour before, leaving a door unsecured through which the raiding party entered. Sirr's team seized the most wanted man in Ireland after a vicious struggle in which Swan was injured and Ryan, a Wexford Orangeman, expired from multiple stab wounds inflicted by Fitzgerald. Their assailant was mortally wounded by Swan's double-barrelled pistol and a single shot from Sirr but clung grimly to life until 4 June. Fitzgerald's usefulness to the United Irishmen, however, had ended with his seizure.[147] News of the disaster quickly permeated Dublin society. Farrell was going to the Castle later that day when he found 'its avenues guarded & no body permitted to pass'. A sentry acknowledged that 'there was a prisoner then under examination' but it was some hours later before Fitzgerald's name was mentioned. By the following morning 'the public mind seemed much agitated . . . some expressed great grief . . . [a] few open joy but most were serious, the yeomanry were reviewed in different quarters of the town & paraded the streets in great number'.[148]

A Dublin county colonel, Felix Rourke of Rathcoole, was briefly and incorrectly blamed by the United Irishmen for indiscretions which led to Fitzgerald's detention. Neilson was also unfairly reproached whereas Magan's treachery went unsuspected for several decades. Edward Rattigan, an elected colonel of United Irishmen, and William Lawless, attempted to rescue their leader as he was being hurried towards the Castle on the 19th. Rattigan and Lawless were together on Queen Street when they learned of Fitzgerald's detention and quickly outfitted a rescue party with weapons taken from Catherine Street watch house. Ironically, the guns had been placed by the Castle under Rattigan's control for peacekeeping duties. Thus diverted, they failed to intercept Sirr's group before they reached their destination, a manoeuvre undertaken with extreme caution in the light of Drury's experiences the previous day. The butchers of Patrick Street market also obtained pikes from Garden Lane, Hanover Lane and Carsman Hall but not in time to effect their end. McCabe was arrested on Watling Street shortly afterwards and, not for the first or last time, managed to bluff his way out of prison before anyone ascertained his identity. It was not then noticed that his pistol was the match of one found in Murphy's house which was commandeered as an auxiliary barracks to punish its owner. Another of Fitzgerald's weapons was used by Gallagher at Blackmore Hill and in the Wicklow mountains during the Rebellion.[149]

Fitzgerald was an irreplaceable loss owing to his unique status and military expertise. He could hardly have been detained at a more critical time having only just fixed the date of the national rising for 24 May, later changed by Neilson to the 23rd. This decision, presumably, had brought county Dublin leaders such as Rourke to the capital, a man who with Edward Farrell and James Rose was said to have 'organized the county of Dublin in 1798'.[150] It must also have been debated by Fitzgerald's regional ex-army associates in Dublin: Major James Plunkett (Connacht), Colonel Lumm (Leinster) and Hervey Mountmorency Morres (Munster). Senior emissaries had been dispatched from the city to warn the provincial networks to hold themselves in readiness and certain designated adjutant generals, such as Garret Byrne of Ballymanus, Wicklow, were briefed in the capital. Fitzgerald was reputedly on the point of leaving the city for Kildare when captured and Magan believed he intended to 'erect his rebel standard at the Hill of Tara'.[151] It is by no means certain that all high-level United Irish committees received or understood this message, a factor which may explain the inconsistent responses of rural rebel forces on the night of the 23rd. A case in point may be the 1,342 United Irishmen in the Coolock area who received the oath of allegiance from John Beresford on the 23rd when they were supposed to be preparing to fight. The transmission of messages was generally more straightforward in the inner city, although matters were not helped in this regard by the launch of the most concerted arms search yet seen on the day selected by Neilson to rise.[152]

The basic strategy envisaged by Neilson, following Fitzgerald's plan, was for an internal city revolt after dark supported by an inrush of reinforcements from adjacent parts of county Dublin, Wicklow, Kildare and Meath. This was to be seconded in the outlying counties of Leinster and throughout Ireland by a staggered wave of diversionary attacks to pin down the military and threaten road access to the capital.[153] In Ulster, the second most important strategic sector, a meeting of the Provincial Directory at William Campbell's Inn in Armagh was attended by delegates from Louth, Derry, Tyrone, Antrim, Down, Donegal and Armagh who appointed Henry Joy McCracken and Robert Hunter to devise a specific plan of action. It was understood on 29 May that 'Dublin [was] to rise & seize on the Ex[ecutive] Government, & the mail coaches were to be burnt for a signal of [sic] the whole kingdom to act'. This proposed lag in armed actions was mirrored by an unintentional and critical delay in communications which meant that the Leinster segment had faltered before the Ulstermen were prepared to turn out.[154]

United Irish plans had been plunged into disarray when efforts to restore the weakened chain of command failed owing to the continuous pressure. The arrest of John and Henry Sheares on 21 May, who were less influential than they had been some weeks before, must have demoralised those who still favoured the Lehaunstown mass defection option. Their colleague William Lawless was also actively sought by Major Sirr, and Patrick Byrne, the bookseller who had introduced the Sheares brothers to their nemesis, Captain John Warneford Armstrong, was detained on the 22nd. Byrne was the main publisher and seller of radical material in Dublin and his seizure would have affected many who used his premises at 108 Grafton Street as a type of salon. The Lehaunstown conspiracy and design on the artillery barracks at Chapelizod were known to the authorities on the 21st, when an insurrection was expected within '48 hours'.[155] Consternation greeted the recovery and publication on 22 May of an address to 'the people' written by John Sheares which exhorted them to 'rise, and to shed the blood of tyrants'. This frightened loyalists and probably unsettled those who had looked to Sheares and Lawless for leadership. News of the death sentence imposed on Fr James Coigley at Maidstone on the 21st was also received at this sensitive time. His past dealings with the urban Defenders and the Church Street/Pill Lane grouping of Bond, Jackson and Duigenan would have caused many Dubliners to reflect on his fate. Whatever satisfaction may have been derived from the providential acquittal of Arthur O'Connor, Allen, O'Leary and Binns was tempered by the realisation that they were in no position to assist with the impending events in Ireland.[156]

To many observers it seemed that anarchy was creeping into the heart of the capital, an impression bolstered by the frequency with which frustrated and ill-disciplined United Irish elements clashed with government forces. The discovery of pikes in Rattigan's lumber yard in 2 Bridgefoot Street (aka Dirty Lane) and a raid on Richard McCormick's house, 9 Mark's Alley, was answered by the firing of shots at troops in nearby Meath market. Rattigan's yard was razed and his domestic furniture burned in the street when documents listing the numerical strength and equipment of the city United Irishmen were found in his house.[157] The south city Liberties were saturated with troops and yeomen on the 22nd who reputedly flogged 'some unfortunate wretches in order to extort confessions' and 'burned any house in which they found concealed arms'. Philip Long, a mid-ranking United Irishman and Crow Street merchant, reminded the victims of this reign of terror when attempting to mobilise insurgents five years later.[158]

Fears of more serious city disturbances prompted the positioning of cannons outside Kilmainham and Newgate in mid-May 1798, a precaution meant to ensure that no Bastille would fall in Dublin to trigger revolution. This was a prescient decision as Neilson established a pike dump convenient to Kilmainham prison in a field owned by his associate James Dixon.[159] Flogging triangles were erected in the Castle yard where the prodigious use of the cat-o'-nine-tails produced more suspects and more arms finds. For the first time, counter-insurgent excesses, which had become a fact of life in many parts of rural Leinster and Munster, were apparent to residents of the metropolis. Exposure to state violence polarised the citizens of the capital and left everyone psychologically if not physically vulnerable. Farrell was coming from the Four Courts on 22 May with a Mayo companion, Thomas Moore, when a soldier noticed that the country-man sported a cropped hairstyle. This was sufficient provocation for the redcoat to grab the walking stick of a passing stroller in order to beat the defenceless Moore. Farrell was resigned to such behaviour and noted: 'one hour of the night a man was liable to be forcibly cropped [by the United Irishmen], the next he run the risk of being grossly abused by the military & having his head crowned with a pitch cap'.[160] No further pretence of normality could be presented by the government to interested parties in London and Paris. The Privy Council took the initiative that day of offering rewards of £300 for Neilson, McCormick, Chambers, Rattigan, Surgeon Lawless, Thomas Trevor [sic, Traynor], John Cormick and Michael Reynolds of Naas.[161] The Council also approved a major arms recovery operation on the 23rd with the result that 'all the streets of the city' were 'blockaded by the yeomen' for much of the day. House raids, burnings, floggings and arrests, therefore, assailed the capital's United Irish infra-structure at the very moment they required freedom of movement and association.[162]

An attack on Newgate to free its political prisoners was being considered by Neilson on 23 May when he was spotted reconnoitring the prison and arrested by Tresham Gregg. Word of a threat to Newgate and to Kilmainham had been leaked to Higgins by Fr Peter Moran of Francis Street chapel.[163] Neilson had planned to muster his men in Eccles Street and infiltrate a rescue squad over the prison walls while a larger party under Thomas Seagrave distracted the guards by opening fire on them from James Halpin's distillery at the corner of Petticoat Lane. The Belfast man had feigned drunkenness on moving through Little Britain Street to allay suspicions of his designs but did not outwit the alert, if not forewarned, Gregg. The Englishman grabbed Neilson's arm to prevent him firing his pistol and succeeded in knocking the powder necessary to discharge the weapon out of its pan. The commotion was such that the first guard to join the fray clubbed Gregg's head in error. Gregg and a Newgate corporal eventually overpowered Neilson, after which the northerner received numerous minor wounds from his agitated and exultant captors. This was a further critical reverse as Neilson had only just briefed fifteen city and Dublin county commanders in a house in Church Lane on the specifics of the uprising. Southwell McClune of the Rotunda Division was amongst those present, who later distinguished himself as a fighting leader in the Rebellion. Other consultations took place around the city under the noses of the confused authorities. Watty Cox recalled that around 9.00 p.m. on the night of 23 May 'a very busy and extensive range of preparation took place in Dublin and its vicinity', including a meeting of senior figures in Abbey Street. This may have been the group who waited in vain for Neilson's final instructions until midnight. Cox, an associate of Duigenan, had been an advisor to Fitzgerald for over a year and was very well informed of United Irish affairs in the city.[164] He admitted to a confidant that he 'had put up more than 1000 men' and was appointed 'adjutant General' of a city district in 1798.[165]

MOBILISATION

As night fell, hundreds of United Irishmen in Dublin left their homes and retrieved weapons from concealed hides. Many, reputedly 3,000, entered the north city while another large group assembled on Clontarf Strand. A sizeable faction obtained equipment from a secret depot on Eccles Street, probably the men Neilson and Seagrave had hoped to command, and reports reached the Castle of the unimpeded distribution of two cart-loads of pikes in the south city. The rebels were immediately rendered conspicuous by their bulky and threatening armaments as they moved towards pre-designated rallying sites to organise fighting groups. Rebel companies under McMahon and Quinn, a veteran of the American army, were ordered to muster at the 'Old Bridge' before heading out of the city via Dolphin's Barn to link up with south and west county Dublin forces.[166] The Green Division had received rudimentary training in the area during the spring and possibly practised the manoeuvres expected of them in May. This flurry of activity naturally attracted loyalist attention in a city where many government supporters lived next door to their ideological opponents. Emmet minimised the risk of premature discovery five years later by locating arms dumps in close proximity to rallying points and tactical objectives. On 23 May 1798 numerous accounts of unusual crowd behaviour reached the Castle and, while no clear picture of United Irish intentions emerged, the weight of evidence pointed to an imminent revolt.[167]

A timely intelligence breakthrough from the Sproule/Lees network alerted the garrison to the threat of the rising within an hour of its commencement. This confirmed a report delivered to the Custom House by the informer Boyle and accorded with the prediction of the Magan/Higgins partnership. City yeomen took up positions on Smithfield, Newmarket, the Barley fields and other locations which had been identified as insurgent mobilisation sites after 10.00 p.m. The sight of uniformed yeomen cavalrymen in Smithfield and elsewhere convinced the rebels that their plans had been betrayed. Insurgents who gathered in their hundreds in Bride's Alley mill yard and outside the city at Sandymount found their officers absent, presumably the men who spent a further two hours waiting for Neilson. With no alternate contingency they had little option but to discard their incriminating weaponry and return home. This was not accomplished without incident and the Attorneys, Barrack and Lawyers corps were involved in minor clashes with small groups of rebels around Smithfield. Sir John Macartney, captain of the Attorneys Cavalry, investigated suspicious bands of men in Greek Street and Pill Lane while other elements of the unit shot at rebels fleeing over rooftops to Church Street. A self-confessed insurgent captain named Ryan and several of his subordinates were taken prisoner and admitted that they had been due to receive orders from Neilson.[168] One Taker of Lower Fitzwilliam Street was more fortunate. Having stolen his employer's guns and gone towards the 'place of rendezvous' he ran straight into a military patrol. Taker managed to explain his way out of the situation by pretending that he was bringing Mr Beatty's arms to him in Trinity College. Queen Street resident Captain J. Medlicott of the Rotunda Cavalry had a narrow escape when approaching armed rebels in Eccles Street. An unidentified insurgent 'snapped a pistol' at the officer without effect before melting away.[169]

A loyalist who prepared to defend his sister's house on Buckingham Street claimed: 'The streets were silent and deserted; no sound was heard but the measured tread of the different yeomanry corps taking up their appointed stations . . . more than once, in the still, calm night, I thought I heard the undulating buzz and sound of a crowd, and the regular tread of a mass of men marching, but all else was awfully still'.[170] An estimated 500 pikes were found in Bridgefoot Street the following morning and an intact horde was uncovered in St Michan's burial ground on Church Street. Rooney, a Newmarket brewer, had also sent ammunition in beer casks to an 'ale house a little above Rathfarnham' for the use of supporting rural rebels. It was further reported by MacNally that four cart-loads of arms had been sent into the Dublin and Wicklow mountains, possibly those later borne by the citymen who went to the insurgent bases that ringed the capital.[171] Fires from the mountain camps of Wicklow refugees and rebels had been visible in the city for several days and Sir Richard Musgrave was not alone in assuming that manipulation of their flames on the night of the 23rd was a method of signalling between rebel groups. Lord Shannon informed his son

> whipping goes on at a great rate, and by proper flagellation, quantities of arms have been given up; but the cat-o'nine-tails is laid on with uncommon severity. The town is in one uproar, the streets so crowded that one walks with difficulty. We have had a most providential escape here. It was more than an even bet that the rebels had prevailed, nor is the attack considered as over yet, but I should think the steps that have been taken and the discoveries that have been made will prevent the intended general rising.[172]

Fighting, notwithstanding the city collapse, had broken out on the outskirts of the capital. Clashes at Swords, Saggart, Dunshaughlin and Balbriggan were the most dramatic actions of north Dublin rebels during the first days of the Rebellion. They also succeeded in stopping the Belfast mails at Santry and the Westmeath coach in Lucan. To the south and west of the city a series of skirmishes were fought at Fox and Geese Common and Crumlin by around 500 rebels who had left the mountains above Rathfarnham under yeomanry infiltrators Ledwich, Wade, James Byrne, Edward Keogh and David Keely (aka Kelly). They battled loyalist yeoman and Fifth Dragoons on their way to join forces near Clondalkin with Dubliners moving towards them, such as those led by Francis McMahon. At the Ponds (Nutgrove) outside Rathfarnham a 'great concourse of rebels armed with muskets, pikes and pistols' guarded two cart-loads of weapons and waited for news from the city. Rebel officers may have hoped to catch sight of the signal rockets Fitzgerald intended to use, if not flames and smoke billowing from the ruins of Dublin Castle. Their men included around seventy of David La Touche's Marley estate workers and were heard to shout, 'Liberty, and no King!' Bennett of the Rathfarnham

Cavalry, whose corps had unwisely moved to Harold's Cross, informed Musgrave: 'the rebels in great numbers were risen, and were in the road and in the adjacent fields as he went to Dublin. In the city, particularly in the suburbs, [there were] . . . a great number of rebels with pikes, in the gate-ways, alleys and stable lanes, waiting the beat of their drums, and the approach of rebel columns from the country'. It was later ascertained that a squad of insurgents armed with muskets lay in ambush in New Street to shoot the Rathfarnham corps if they proceeded into the city.[173]

Most of the rebel groups that assembled in the greater Dublin area did not skirmish owing to the indecision caused by the initial failure of the citymen. Insurgents who rallied at Dalkey, Blackrock, Tallaght, Rathcoole, Ringsend, Lusk, Artane, Clontarf and elsewhere either dispersed on learning of events in the capital or quickly made their way to the major insurgent camps established at Blackmore Hill above Blessington (Wicklow) and at Tara Hill in Meath. Occupying and defending high ground positions around the city may well have been an agreed contingency. By a quirk of fate, the spy MacNally was staying in Rathfarnham, where it was believed on the 24th that the rebels who had threatened the village had gone into Kildare. Many insurgents, however, quickly lost their martial spirit and accepted the conditional pardons on offer from nervous army officers. Considerable numbers also sneaked back to their homes undetected and the Dalkey United Irishmen were apparently persuaded to do so by a revenue officer named Sherwood. Heavy fighting, nevertheless, had commenced in Kildare amidst rumours that Dublin had fallen into rebel hands.[174]

CHAPTER THREE

Dublin in the Great Rebellion of 1798

The Rebellion that broke out on 23 May 1798 was not the irresistible national uprising supported by the French army which Robert Emmet had fomented in Trinity College, Stephen's Green and in the *Press*. He had argued strongly against an unassisted rising in the unpublished 'address' written just prior to the March arrests. This was also the official position of the United Irish leadership when Addis Emmet, MacNeven, O'Connor and Bond were at liberty, but much had changed by mid-May when the decision to press on without foreign aid was reluctantly taken. Robert Emmet may have seen the logic of the strategy agreed by Fitzgerald and Neilson in view of the steady erosion of United Irish cohesion in the provinces. In mid-May a collapse of the republican organisation in the capital was also threatened. As events proved five years later, Emmet was prepared to jettison carefully laid plans if circumstances demanded immediate action. In many respects, the Rebellion of 1798 and Rising of 1803 were contingencies which lost all resemblance to what had been planned within hours of commencement.[1]

Emmet's movements cannot be pinpointed at the time the 1798 Rebellion commenced. He may have been lying low at either Stephen's Green or Casino when the dramatic scenes got underway. Although on the periphery of the leadership, he had little proven involvement with purely military preparations outside the College and may not have known of the planned revolt until a late stage. Given his rank and profile, word may well have reached him of what was intended after Neilson's briefings had primed city officers. There is, however, evidence which indicates that Emmet attended one of these conferences. A spy claimed that, whereas Michael Farrell of the Trinity cells had been ordered to Longford 'before the 23d of May', Emmet received his 'instructions . . . at Chambers'. It is unclear whether this referred to the opening night of the Rebellion or its final preparations. The information may concern the meeting mentioned by Cox and attended by McClune in Abbey Street, in or near the building where Chambers had frequently debriefed the two student leaders until mid-March. Farrell certainly attempted to rouse the rebels of Longford, Westmeath and Cavan in late May and could only have received authorisation to do so between 19 and 23 May. The elusive Emmet, therefore, may well have been one of several hundred Dubliners who stirred from a city home on the 23rd and returned without being arrested.[2]

As darkness approached, army deployments around Government buildings at College Green and on Dame Street signalled that something serious was afoot. Alderman Thomas Fleming feared the approach of militia defectors from Lehaunstown Camp and posted the reliable Cork militia with their two battalion guns on the north side of Stephen's Green to hold them off. The subsequent defection of hundreds of militiamen, including scores of the King's County militia suborned by the Sheares brothers and others, proved that this scenario was not entirely fanciful.[3] On 23 May, however, proactive counter-insurgency and yet another shift in United Irish strategy combined to ensure that Fleming's precautions were superfluous.[4] The Grange (Rathfarnham) rebels who approached Crumlin did so in the belief that 1,800 rebels would simultaneously 'beset Laughlinstown [sic] camp', but if such a body actually stirred they did not initiate a diversionary attack.[5] The 1,500 United Irishmen of Emmet's Green Division were comparatively quiet in their home sector on the 23rd and never brought their approximately 500 muskets and 2,500 pikes to bear in the neighbourhood. Yet, in the months ahead they were almost as dynamic as the Workhouse Division, with whom they shared the burden of the fighting. If Emmet wended his way through familiar back streets towards a compromised rallying point, no record of the event survives and little of his activity after April 1798 can be documented. The Rebellion of 1798, nonetheless, was of central importance to his plans five years later when he was the principal strategist of the United Irishmen. The lessons of 1798 were then reflected in terms of tactics, objectives and personnel. The Rising of 1803, as envisaged by Emmet's faction, was in many respects the logical development of an insurrectionary strategy shaped by hard-won experience.[6]

While no fighter in Wicklow or Wexford in 1798 – unlike many of his Dublin comrades – Emmet was fully engaged in the city's United Irish organisation. Working behind the scenes boosted his stature in the movement and rendered him a credible figure to the veterans destined to play critical roles in the plot of 1803. Like Emmet, Malachy Delaney, Felix Rourke, Nicholas Gray, Michael Dwyer, Patrick McCabe, Miles Byrne, Mathew Doyle and Michael Quigley did not spring from obscurity to prominence in the spring of 1803. Emmet was attached to a core of Dublin militants who had been placed in a quandary by the outbreak of a faltering and unpredictable rebellion. Insurgent attacks on west Wicklow, Kildare and Meath garrisons on 23–24 May made some headway without securing the major victories necessary for widespread mobilisation. Furthermore, the hard-pressed military abandoned parts of Kildare rather than suffer defeat and withstood the most threatening foray of the United Irishmen towards the capital at Kilcullen Bridge. The rebels ran into the well-armed New Romney Fencible Light Dragoons and were reputedly 'killed in such numbers as to cover the streets with their bodies'. This rearguard prevented the numerous Kildaremen from entering the city suburbs as was evidently the allotted role of particular columns. Crucially, communication and command difficulties ensured that no major rebel actions occurred in Munster or Connacht. Ulster United Irish leaders also prevaricated and by 25 May it was apparent that no national insurrection was pending. Inactivity in the regions destroyed the viability of the Fitzgerald/Neilson strategy by ceding the initiative to the more decisive and better-equipped army. This produced further reactive contingencies by rebel committees in Dublin city and in the field. An immediate concern was that the Leinster men who had taken arms on 23–6 May could not expect assistance from southern Ulster and north Munster in the form of reinforcement or diversionary activities. They would instead have to rely on local resources in a partially mobilised zone when facing inevitable state counter-attacks.[7]

MARTIAL LAW IN DUBLIN

Fleming, the excitable and bigoted Lord Mayor of Dublin, attempted to restore order in the capital on the 24th by issuing a proclamation requiring the registration of arms. Persons found with unlicensed weapons were threatened with conscription into the Royal Navy. Householders were directed to place lists of their families and tenants on their front doors so that troops and yeomen policing the curfew could isolate malefactors. Walter Cox was one of the first to safeguard his life by depositing twenty-seven firearms in the Castle which had been commissioned by the Board of Ordnance.[8] Cox's apparent contrition on the 24th secured him a cell in Kilmainham rather than an appearance on a Liffey gallows. Fleming's document drew its real strength from another issued on the same day by Lieutenant General Gerard Lake which explained that Lord Camden had invested him with 'full powers to PUT DOWN THE REBELLION and to PUNISH REBELS in the most summary manner, according to martial law'. Given the excesses which attended Lake's anti-insurgent drive in Ulster the previous year none could have doubted his determination to enforce the 9.00 p.m. to 5.00 a.m. curfew. Lake's orders to take no prisoners ensured that many early battles of the Rebellion where characterised by slaughter and the summary execution of wounded rebels. In excess of 100 untried rebel prisoners detained prior to the outbreak were put to death in cold blood at Ballymore Eustace, Dunlavin and Carnew during the first week of the insurrection.[9] Richard Farrell heard Lake's proclamation being read in the Castle yard and watched as Thomas Braughall, the respected associate of Thomas Addis Emmet and John Keogh, was taken from Castlereagh's office to Kilmainham.[10]

Rebellion also brought unfamiliar sights of horror to Dublin city which were intended to terrorise the disaffected population while reassuring loyalists that matters were under control. Two of the rebel leaders captured after the clash at Fox and Geese Common, Ledwich and Wade of Ballyboden (Rathfarnham), were hanged on Queen's Bridge on 26 May after a perfunctory court martial in College Green the previous day. Magnanimity was unlikely given that the panel which tried them included Lord Roden who, backed by the Fifth Dragoons, had fought against the defendants and brought the bodies of two of their associates to the Castle yard for display. Another Rathfarnham leader, Edward Keogh of Whitehall, had been severely wounded in the same action and was respited in unusual circumstances in the Castle. An offer of £2,000 bail by Keogh's father for his son's release was supported by Jonah Barrington, the erratic MP, duellist and barrister who was related to Wexford United Irishmen Bagenal Harvey and Mathew Keogh.[11]

Edward Keogh's south Dublin comrades were amongst the first thrown into the notorious 'Croppies Hole' where many other United Irishmen were soon buried amongst the rubbish of the Royal Barracks. The waste pit was located in the narrow strip of land between the main entrance of the Barracks and the north bank of the Liffey. Mutilated bodies of three men were left exposed to the elements in Barrack Street with their harmless pikes tied to their bodies. They had been killed near Clondalkin on the 23rd by a patrol headed by

Lieutenant Colonel John Finlay MP of the Dublin County militia, who in 1803 had cause to regret his calculated act of derision. Carroll, the Fingal rebel leader who captured Westphalstown House on the 23rd, was hanged on Church Street Bridge (aka Old Bridge) three days later and tossed into the putrid ditch on the riverside. His men had been challenged on their march to Tara Hill by Major King's company of the Fermanagh Militia and the Swords Cavalry. The military had rushed to intercept the rebels from a house-burning mission at Ballyboghill. It was alleged that Carroll's corpse joined those of several lamplighters who had endeavoured to keep the city in darkness when the Rebellion began. This tactic was used with considerable effect by Emmet's followers in July 1803 and Braughall was suspected in 1798 of stockpiling oil lamps in his 7 Eccles Street cellars for the use of city rebels. While captured insurgents Adams and Fox were executed inside the Provost prison before being thrown into the nearby 'Croppies Hole', most of those executed in May had been hanged from public lamp-posts. This crude method of execution was also employed in Cork, Limerick, Waterford and other rural centres. Dubliners were put to death and allegedly dismembered at the Liffey corner of Bridgefoot Street, a location convenient to the bridges and what became known as 'Croppy's Acre'.[12]

By 1 June the flyblown corpse of Private Raymond of the St Sepulchre yeomanry was confronting those who needed to cross the Old Bridge, as was one Fennell. Raymond was executed for plotting to clear the way for rebels to pass from the mountains through the section of Dolphin's Barn guarded by his corps. As a perceived traitor in the eyes of loyalists he was liable to endure the full weight of exemplary justice. Dr John Esmonde's body was also ritually desecrated on 14 June on Carlisle Bridge, although subjected to the additional dishonour of having his lieutenant's yeomanry overcoat turned inside out. This mark of disgrace alluded to his defection from the Clane Cavalry to the Kildare rebel forces during the attack on Prosperous on 23 May. Emmet may not have seen the decaying bodies of rebel officers strung up on the river crossings but he was sufficiently moved by the brutal symbolism of Croppy's Acre to write 'Arbour Hill' on the subject in March 1799. By then Mathew Tone, Bartholomew Teeling and other members of leading republican families known to his were interred at the site. Another casualty familiar to the Emmets, ex-Volunteer commander Thomas Bacon, a reputed colonel of the Green Division, was arrested in a hackney coach on 2 June when disguised as a woman and executed two days later on Carlisle Bridge.[13]

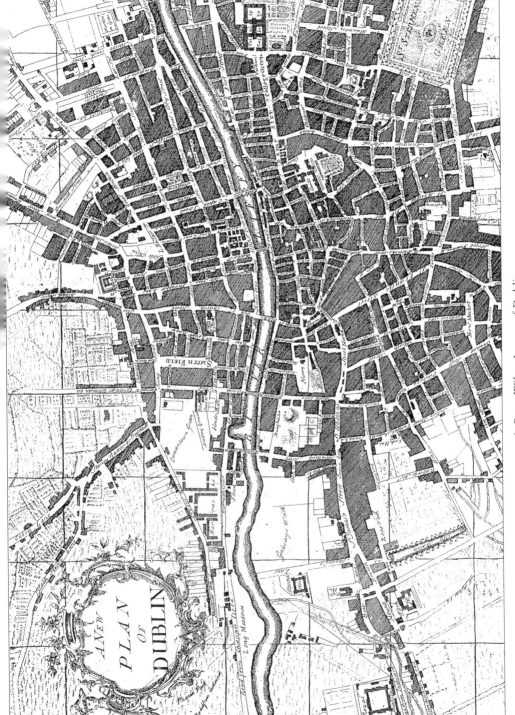

1 Peter Wilson's map of Dublin

2 The Emmet family home (on the right)

3 Thomas Addis Emmet
(courtesy of the National
Library of Ireland)

4 Henry Grattan

5 Archibald Hamilton Rowan

6 Thomas Moore

7 Theobald Wolfe Tone

8 John Sheares

9 William James MacNeven

10 William Sampson

11 Robert Emmet

12 Symbols of the United Irishmen

Reasons, why one Man may lawfully do harm to another, which is that we call *Punishment*. In transgref-
fing the Law of Nature, the Offender declares him-
felf to live by another Rule than that of Reafon and
common Equity, which is that meafure God has fet
to the Actions of Men, for their mutual Security;
and fo he becomes dangerous to Mankind, the Tie,
which is to fecure them from Injury and Violence,
being flighted and broken by him. Which being a
Trefpafs againft the whole Species, and the Peace and
Safety of it, provided for by the Law of Nature, every
Man upon this Score, by the Right he hath to pre-
ferve Mankind in general, may reftrain, or, where it
is neceffary, deftroy things noxious to them, and fo
may bring fuch Evil on any one, who hath transgref-
fed that Law, as may make him repent the doing of
it, and thereby deter him, and, by his Example,
others, from doing the like Mifchief. And in this
Cafe, and upon this Ground, *every Man hath a Right
to punifh the Offender, and be Executioner of the Law
of Nature.*

§ 9. I doubt not but this will feem a very ftrange
Doctrine to fome Men: But before they condemn it,
I defire them to refolve me, by what Right any Prince
or State can put to death or *punifh an Alien,* for any
Crime he commits in their Country? 'Tis certain
their Laws, by virtue of any Sanction they receive
from the promulgated Will of the Legiflative, reach
not a Stranger: They fpeak not to him, nor, if they
did, is he bound to hearken to them. The legiflative Authority, by which they are in Force over the
Subjects of that Commonwealth, hath no Power over
him. Thofe who have the fupreme Power of making
Laws in *England, France,* or *Holland,* are to an *Indian*
but like the reft of the World, Men without Authority: And therefore, if by the Law of Nature, every
Man hath not a Power to punifh Offences againft it,
as he foberly judges the Cafe to require, I fee not
how

14 John Fitzgibbon, Lord Clare

15 Edward Hudson

16 Moira House by William Brocas (courtesy of the National Library of Ireland)

17 Lord Edward Fitzgerald

One of the last sounds heard by the dying Fitzgerald on the night of 3–4 June was a warning shot fired by a sentry outside Newgate to deter a crowd from cutting down the hanged body of John Clinch of Rathcoole. Yeomen had gathered to jeer the condemned man while others present were moved by his fate. Clinch had been a prominent United Irishman in the Rathcoole district and a lieutenant in the town's yeoman infantry. Fitzgerald, agitated by this commotion and deep in the throes of delirium, exclaimed: 'Dear Ireland! I die for you! My country, you will be free!'[14]

The deliberate severity of the crackdown was illustrated by a circular from the Lord Mayor dated 26 May, packaged as 'A CAUTION, lest the innocent should suffer for the guilty'. It warned that the streets should be kept 'as clear as possible' after dark so that the garrison could more readily discern and punish illegal practices.[15] A strange display took place in Great Britain Street on the north side of the city where three drummers 'marched abreast with scourges in their hands practising the art of whipping and were apparently perfect adepts. The eldest was not more than fourteen the youngest about twelve. Their emulation had its effect on all who saw them and fear only in the spectators prevented vengeance.' This exhibition may have been inspired by the theft of firearms from a local resident named Finney and the knowledge that a district committee met regularly in Great Britain Street. Something of a vicious circle developed in which those fearing courts martial and flogging were driven from their homes with little option other than joining the rebels gathering in the woods, bogs and mountains of south Leinster.[16] Labourers and porters from Thomas Street were known to have taken part in the first clashes of the Rebellion and it was to discourage others from following their example that a house in Carter's Alley off Townsend Street was burned when pikes were found inside. This also happened to the home of a deceased Tallaght rebel leader named Byrne which was torched on the 27th, presumably that of the James Byrne who had acted in concert with the Rathfarnham rebels. Miles Duigenan's home was subsequently razed and those of Braughall, Nicholas Murphy and the Kilmainham leader James Dixon occupied by soldiers. United Irishmen were informed by the *Freeman's Journal* that the consequences of insurrection 'will not terminate with their own lives but that the summary and signal justice will pour down posthumous inflictions' on their families.[17]

Yeomen were encouraged to take such forthright means by their brigade-major, William Sandys, who was subsequently praised for his 'execution of the very unpleasant duty' by his superiors in the Castle.[18] Its effect on the population was more difficult to gauge. MacNally noted: the 'common people consider themselves as betrayed or abandoned by those of the more respectable orders' but feared that the 'great severity' of the military created 'sullen, silent rancour and revenge will be a consequence. It would astonish you to hear the vindictive language and better curses of the carmen on this subject. Executions are now considered martyrdoms and when the processions for an execution commences, those within doors to whose knowledge it comes go to prayers.'[19]

SUCCESS AND FAILURE IN LEINSTER

Hundreds of south county Dubliners who presumed that all was lost availed of the chance to swear the oath of allegiance before Justice Frederick Drury at Kilgobbin, Dundrum and Churchtown on 27–9 May. Six hundred received the oath at Sandymount from Alderman Thomas Truelock and the Blackrock Association at the same time and the famously corrupt Justice John Winder tendered the oath in Harold's Cross. John Beresford was under no illusion that those who came forward to proclaim their change of heart could be trusted. He noted: 'many who took protections one day were killed or taken in arms the next'.[20] The Finglas area rebels retained sufficient pikes to fill 'several cartloads' and hid them so well that they were not uncovered until November.[21] All was not lost in May, however, and the establishment of several large insurgent camps in Kildare and the Dublin and Wicklow mountains brought considerable swathes of territory within striking distance of the capital under rebel control. Government confidence of weathering the storm, though, was boosted by holding Hacketstown on the Carlow/Wicklow border on the 25th and the infliction of up to 500 casualties on the insurgents who assaulted Carlow town. Furthermore, the arrival of reinforcements from Belfast on 25–6 May freed up troops for a decisive attack on the main camp of the Meath rebels on Tara Hill. Two companies of Reay Fencible Highlanders had lost their baggage to rebel attack near rebel-occupied Dunshaughlin on the 25th, but after a night billeted on Sackville Street avenged this affront at Tara the following day. James McNally, a United Irish smuggler, emissary and quartermaster from Lusk, was bringing cannon to the rebel forces encamped at Tara when he learned of their defeat. The Meath and Fingal men had expected substantial reinforcements from Westmeath, Louth, Cavan and Monaghan. This did not occur and loyalists were relieved that the rebels they expected to advance on the city from Lucan, Howth and Rathfarnham in the last days of May did not come. The many setbacks suffered by the United Irishmen were offset in part by their resolute defence of Rathangan in Kildare and the first stirrings of unrest in north and east Wexford.[22]

The annihilation of a company of the North Cork militia at Oulart Hill on 27 May represented a stunning victory for the Wexford rebels whose momentum yielded Enniscorthy the following day. Their prowess confounded military conventions which rated irregulars exceptionally poor fighters; neither massed troops in the field nor defended urban centres were afterwards considered totally secure. The Kildare rising then appeared to be petering out as it had in Meath and Carlow and may have done so within days were it not for the massacre of 350 unarmed rebels attempting to surrender at the Gibbet Rath (Curragh) on 29 May. Soldiers arriving from Limerick under Major-General Sir James Duff, finally released by their nervous north Munster commander, Sir James Stewart, committed a major tactical blunder by massacring their helpless opponents. Undefeated rebel concentrations in Kildare were instantly renewed in their militancy and retreated into mountains and bogs where troops dared not follow. Men from King's County and Westmeath joined their raiding activities while Kildare rebels from the Naas area continued to mass at Blackmore Hill overlooking Blessington. This stand-off prolonged the struggle in Leinster as, by simply remaining under arms near the capital, the Kildaremen prevented the rushing of much-needed reinforcements to Wexford and south Wicklow where matters had begun to favour the insurgents.[23]

A heavy rebel defeat at Newtownmountkennedy on 30 May prevented the large north Wicklow organisation turning out on the scale witnessed in Wexford, although thousands of United Irishmen from the district migrated to the principal fighting fronts. Access to Wexford, where the county town was abandoned to the insurgents without a contest that day, was virtually unimpeded due to government weakness in the mountains. Moreover, the temporary clearance of Blackmore Hill by the military on the 31st proved a hollow victory which simply drove thousands of Kildare, Wicklow and Dublin rebels deeper into the road-less highlands of Wicklow. As the fighters of the embryonic 'Wexford Republic' consolidated their victories, an economically ruinous guerrilla campaign began in Wicklow, Kildare and King's County. The logistics of subsistence led to the devastation of loyalist-owned livestock in rebel-controlled districts, but there was more purpose to their actions than was immediately apparent. Camps sited in the mountainous chain extending from Rathfarnham to Blessington became the launching pads for a planned attack on the metropolis. Extending these strategic centres of localised strength from the south and west of Dublin to the midlands, and also to Louth in the north, occupied the Dublin United Irishmen until mid-July.[24]

The possibility of migrating to the battle zones from the capital was largely dependent on the government's ability to man an effective cordon. This was bolstered by the erection of the long-planned gates and palisades on the Liffey bridges, which were theoretically guarded night and day by the yeomanry and military. Whereas urban geography, demography and infrastructure stymied illicit movements to and from the north of the city this was not so much the case to the west and south, where the gravest threat had materialised. Even though bridges and major road routes to southern Leinster were generally patrolled, travel between the city and the mountains via Dolphin's Barn, Harold's Cross and Rathfarnham remained relatively unhindered throughout the Rebellion.[25]

By the end of May 1798 the district-level committees with responsibility for the Dublin city United Irishmen weighed the merits of committing their followers to the rebel armies against the alternative of remaining in place to facilitate their anticipated convergence on the capital. Decision-making was complicated by the failure to appoint an undisputed adjutant-general to dictate policy, a factor exacerbated by the flight and arrests of senior United Irish personnel, which drained the small pool of colonels elected in April. Of the known elected city colonels Thomas Bacon was inactive and about to be executed while Miles Duigenan and Andrew Kearney were arrested on 28 May. Mathew Dowling was seized with his brother on the 30th and Francis McMahon, Edward Rattigan, Patrick Gallagher, Southwell McClune, Thomas Seagrave and John Doyle were either in or on their way to the Dublin and Wicklow mountains. Of the remaining reputed city colonels John Cormick was abroad, Henry Baird and Hampden Evans kept a low profile if not in hiding and Nicholas Gray was already active in Wexford. Essentially, most of the surviving elected senior officers of the military wing departed the city to fight. They were supported in their endeavours by the remnants of the military subcommittee of the Leinster Directory and their associates from the civil/political side of the republican movement. To a remarkable degree, those who had been rejected in the April colonelcy elections assisted the successful candidates by providing logistic support for the fighting groups they led in the countryside.[26] Suspicions of United Irish activism in the city evidently induced Mayor Fleming and High Constable Dawson to search cellars under the parliament buildings at College Green 'lest gunpowder or any other combustibles should have been laid there by the rebels'. Guards were placed on all public buildings to prevent arson attacks and assassination attempts on state officials and the Pigeon House hotel was transformed into the armed redoubt it remained in 1803.[27]

Colonel Francis McMahon of Aungier Street was one of the first Dublin city commanders to enter the fray. McMahon, 'a low set' prosperous attorney, inherited the practice of C. M. McMahon, an admitted solicitor in Chancery in 1794 and an attorney of the King's Bench, Common Pleas and Exchequer. Colonel McMahon had been under close surveillance by Castle agents for over a week prior to the Rebellion and was known to have met his subordinates on 17 May 1798. When the city uprising imploded on 23 May, McMahon mustered his followers at Old Bridge, off old Church Street, and went towards Clondalkin. They fell in, as was probably intended, with rebel forces coming from Rathfarnham and Tallaght and clashed with the military at Fox and Geese. This manoeuvre may well have been in accordance with pre-Rebellion orders to mass Green and Workhouse Division rebels in support of a flanking attack through the poorly guarded western approaches by their county-based comrades. It is evident that a proposal to use the Green Division in an attack on Trinity College and the Bank had been discarded and the oft-debated strategy of targeting key buildings may never have found favour with the city colonels. McMahon's attempted rendezvous to the south-west of the capital failed owing to a series of bruising encounters with mounted enemies between Rathfarnham and Crumlin. He returned to Aungier Street uninjured and determined to fight on. Other Dublin and north Wicklow units fell back upon Tara Hill and Blackmore Hill, two of several easily defended high-ground sites that were vacated within a week.[28]

EMMET AND THE GREEN DIVISION

At 10.00 a.m. on 25 May, when it was apparent that no city rising was imminent, McMahon left for the mountains with seventy men. He may have first gone to Donnybrook to borrow a horse from a calendar maker named Dillon, evidently Patrick Dillon who was 'implicated in 98 and 1803'.[29] McMahon urged rebel leaders in the camps of south Dubliners and Wicklowmen above Rathfarnham to mount an immediate assault on the capital. His contacts awaited his return at the head of 1,500 insurgents, one of whom may well have been Robert Emmet. A colonel elected in the Green Division would have almost certainly known Emmet given that he was a member of the republican electorate for two years and had lived his whole life in the neighbourhood. Casual encounters with the McMahons were also highly likely given that James McMahon of 43 Aungier Street was churchwarden of St Peter and St Kevin's Church, which the Emmets attended in the 1790s. This man was acquainted with Thomas Addis Emmet from their joint attendance at United Irish meetings in the early 1790s and was described by the terse Thomas Collins as 'James McMahon Aungier Street Jacobin'.[30]

A verifiable connection between Robert Emmet and the militants was provided by Surgeon Thomas Wright of Great Ship Street who regularly supplied McMahon's faction with money and war material. Wright had served as an army medical officer during the American War and was a licentiate of the Royal College of Surgeons. He was a founder member of the Dublin United Irishmen and if not always trusted was described as an 'ingenious and able man'. Wright was an elected captain in the city organisation in May 1798 and wielded far greater authority than this rank indicated.[31] It is unclear when he first cooperated with Robert Emmet and in what manner, although pre-Rebellion liaison is probable given that Wright had assisted Addis Emmet in the defence of Drennan in July 1794. Wright's dealings with the younger Emmet in 1798 were informed by his knowledge that he had been 'at the head of the young men who were expelled [from] the college'. John Lawless, already in the United Irish inner circle, could also have vouched for Emmet in this regard.[32] Wright hosted meetings in his home attended by Philip Long and Emmet's cousin John Patten, both of whom were implicated in the Rising of 1803.[33]

Colonel McMahon's command swelled to over 200 men by late June and operated from time to time with north Wicklow rebels attached to Joseph Holt of Mullinaveigue (Roundwood), who was later regarded as a rebel general. Between late May and mid-June the followers of Holt and McMahon frequently camped in the Ballinascorney/ Bohernabreena area, close to the home of Holt's brother Thomas and where Robert Emmet sought refuge in July 1803. Support of local United Irish networks was also available, presumably from Quinstown captain John Simpson, who came to the attention of city-based spies.

The Dublin contingent led by McMahon contained distinct elements headed by captain Nugent, a Cuffe Street baker and probable head of the committee which met at Blake's Inn on Thomas Street, and Captain Doyle. He may have been the John Doyle of Plunket Street, an innkeeper who held a colonelcy in the Green Division and, as such, would also have been known to Emmet. Doyle was certainly involved with Emmet's agents in the summer of 1803.[34] A third officer, Fitzpatrick, was 'a captain . . . [who] organised the company of men' under McMahon in the city and led them into the mountains in mid-June 1798. This may have been John Fitzpatrick Jeffrey, a relative and lodger of Richard McCormick, who remained an active combatant until September 1798.[35] He was the connection between McMahon and ex-Liberty Ranger yeoman Nicholas Gray, a Wexford-born lawyer with the status of 'colonel' in a 'Rebel Regiment in Dublin'.[36] Gray certainly knew Emmet in early 1803 and was expected to feature prominently in the rising planned for that year. The American veteran Quinn was a fourth captain under McMahon and reputedly his 'coadjutor and friend'.[37]

Colonel Felix Rourke, former permanent sergeant of the Rathcoole yeoman infantry, was a County Dublin United Irish leader whose path crossed Robert Emmet's between 1798 and 1803. Rourke led scores of County Dubliners to Blackmore Hill on 23–4 May and after the dispersal of the camp pressed southwards through Wicklow to south Wexford. Rourke's contact with Lord Edward Fitzgerald and description of Samuel Neilson as his 'valued friend' evidences his own significant role in pre-Rebellion preparations. His brother Charles was a United Irish captain in the city and proprietor of the Yellow Bottle (aka Golden Bottle), a 138 Thomas Street pub frequented by United Irishmen from Kildare. The Rourkes were closely connected to John Mathews of Tallaght Hill and undoubtedly to other west county commanders with whom they fought at Hacketstown and elsewhere. Present alongside the Rourkes at Blackmore Hill in the first days of the Rebellion was Edward Rattigan, a proclaimed fugitive from 23 May, who had quit his hiding place with Dillon of Donnybrook. Rattigan and Rourke commanded several hundred men and maintained close contact with the city committees throughout the Rebellion.[38]

Such liaisons indicate that the actions of the fielded Dublin insurgents were endorsed by those who had assumed responsibility for the national United Irish organisation. Leadership devolved on several groups which met in and around Thomas Street. The coteries attached to Wright, Thomas Seagrave, Charles O'Hara senior, John and Patrick Power and Thomas Houston were especially influential. James Moore, the ironmonger who harboured Lord Edward Fitzgerald at 124 Thomas Street, was also part of this clique and apparently the first to solicit the services of the Augustinian emissary Fr John Martin of Drogheda. Moore's employee, Patrick Gallagher, went to Blackmore Hill and later carried messages between various United Irish groupings. O'Hara of High Street, former secretary of the city United Irishmen and a member from 1792 along with early acolytes Wright, Seagrave, Moore and Bacon, replaced Neilson as the main military strategist in the city. He knew both James and Napper Tandy and considered Wright his 'intimate friend' in late 1800.[39] O'Hara was also acquainted with Patrick McCabe, a Francis Street publican who evaded prosecution for his part in the Rebellion and went on to play a leading role in the Rising of 1803.[40] Houston was evidently the Thomas Houston freed from Belfast's artillery barracks in late 1797, a release arising from the case in which Addis Emmet upheld the validity of a writ of habeas corpus at the Court of King's Bench. If so, Houston shared his Antrim background with O'Hara, his profession with Surgeon Wright and United Irish pedigree with all he conspired with in Thomas Street in June 1798. His apparent association with Oliver Bond underlines the exalted status of the Donegal man alongside Lord Edward Fitzgerald's adherents in city republicanism.[41] The Houstons of Dublin were cambric merchants at 33 Merchants Quay, near neighbours of William and John Orr who were muslin manufacturers and merchants at no. 8. The Orrs had known and very probably traded with Bond, whose warehouse was situated around the corner at 13 Bridge Street. The brothers assisted in the spread of the United Irishmen to west Wicklow in early 1797 where they had a major cloth factory at Stratford-on-Slaney. This operation employed scores of fugitive Ulster republicans and was used as a base by Putnam McCabe and James Hope when organising in south Leinster. It was no coincidence that the first representatives of Wicklow's embryonic County Committee were Ulster-born delegates from west Wicklow and Arklow who met in Dublin prior to December 1797. The striking fact that the Orrs, Bond, Houston and O'Hara were all northern United Irishmen points to their co-conspiracy and the Dublin directed practice of exploiting pre-existing rural cadres of allies in the spring of 1797.[42]

This clique, the de facto District Committee of the Workhouse Division, functioned as a substitute leadership for their imprisoned and absent superiors. O'Hara provided a connection with the military subcommittee and its pre-Rebellion activists; Gallagher, Palmer,

Farrell and Putnam McCabe were certainly utilised and already familiar with key figures in the province. The Power brothers corresponded with rebels in the Wicklow mountains and made the Cherry Tree pub available as a hospital for senior figures. Fearing infiltration, the Workhouse militants fell back on longstanding political associations which, bolstered by trade and friendship, had withstood months of aggressive probing by the authorities. They functioned as a higher committee yet probably rarely convened under one roof. It proved more efficient to sit in smaller groups which met simultaneously in several locations and then compared notes. Emissaries were frequently sent to the fighting units in south Leinster to encourage strategies which had been suggested by their overview of the general situation in the thirty-two counties and from abroad. Tight control of mobilised forces was obviously impossible, although practical help in the form of arranging recruits, munitions, medical aid and intelligence was provided by the city network throughout 1798. Wright supplied several Dublin officers active in Wicklow, as did Dillon, who concealed Rattigan in his attic from 19 to 23 May and knew McMahon. The scale of their endeavour may be inferred from Wright's admission to having used his medical skills to treat 'above five hundred men' injured in the fighting.[43]

Wright was a verifiable common denominator between Robert Emmet and McMahon et al. Emmet's role in such affairs is uncertain and may have entailed no more than assisting in the raising of funds needed to equip the fighting rebels and to provide for their dependents. Wright, for one, must have been saddened by the execution of his colleague and neighbour Thomas Bacon whose widow, Eliza, continued to run the family's tailoring business at 8 Great Ship Street. Bacon was hanged from a lamp-post on Carlisle Bridge. One of McMahon's junior officers was the 'friend' of Samuel Sproule, who kept the Castle informed of their intentions through John Lees of the Post Office. Sproule had confirmed the date and time of the Rebellion and Peter Leech (aka Leach), one of several agents, was a junior emissary of the Dublin County Committee. While Emmet's name did not feature in Sproule's extant reports this did not signify inaction given the considerable yet secretive nature of rear echelon activities. Emmet's associates Lyndon Bolton, Henry Baird and Hugh O'Hanlon all managed to evade detection despite operating at mid-level in the Dublin United Irishmen during the Rebellion. His security-consciousness and self-discipline, very much in evidence in 1799, may also have shielded his identity from informers.[44]

Dublin rebels driven from Blackmore Hill on 31 May were present at Carrickbyrne and Corbett Hill camps, Wexford, on 4–5 June 1798, just prior to the major insurgent attack on New Ross. Commissary John Brennan of Castlehaystown, later transported to New South Wales, issued supplies to Dublin county and city men commanded by Colonel Southwell McClune of Abbey Street and 'captains' Felix Rourke and Quirke. They were probably aligned with John Colclough's section of the rebel army that declined to participate in the Battle of New Ross owing to their dissatisfaction with the cavalier attitude of their nominal commander-in-chief, Bagenal Harvey. The main rebel attack was led by Thomas Cloney of Moneyhore who, like Nicholas Gray, Harvey's assistant, cooperated very closely with Emmet in 1803. McMahon's faction awaited progress in Wexford and remained in the camps of south Dublin and north Wicklow, around which heavy skirmishing was common.[45]

Dubliners also fought in detachments with the north Wexford rebel army and helped ambush and inflict heavy losses on Colonel Walpole's army column at Tubberneering on 4 June. The repulse of Walpole's corps and death of its commander, Camden's aide-de-camp, shocked the cabinet in Dublin, which was also called upon to import emergency supplies of flour from Liverpool. Shannon claimed that 'it was given as a unanimous opinion that unless a large army was with utmost expedition sent here from England, the *kingdom* is gone'.[46] Rebel leaders in the city planned for victory as Dublin veterans of Tubberneering, a numerically minor component of the whole, were committed to the crucial Battle of Arklow five days later. One Hughes, linked to a committee which met at Behan's on Bath Street, narrowly survived being carried towards government lines at Arklow on a startled horse. He returned to the city 'to see what can be done . . . & to send more friends to Wexford'. Sproule informed his Castle contacts that the 'late successes' of the rebels in Wexford had drawn 'the wavering to join them . . . Kelly [of Bath Street] is gone'. Beaghan, a vinegar merchant at 21 Cork Street, also departed. This option was discussed by a Townsend Street committee on the 4th and in Pill Lane two days later when those in attendance anticipated the imminent return of their comrades to attack the Castle with thousands of Wexford, Wicklow, Carlow and Kildare rebels. Small groups of city insurgents met in suburban Rathmines and Rathgar pubs before heading into the mountains together while other intact United Irish companies waited patiently for the opportunity to turn out in force. By 8 June a circular urging mobilisation was passing from society to society and its effectiveness may be gauged from the fact that twenty-one Thomas Street rebels survived to acknowledge taking part in the fighting. They soon learned that Antrim insurgents under Henry Joy McCracken and Down men under Henry Munro had attempted an Ulster-wide revolt on the 6th that stalled within days of its early promise.[47]

The battle which devastated Arklow on 9 June settled the fortunes of the north Wexford forces and decided the outcome of the Rebellion. An over-confident Fr Michael Murphy of Ballycanew (Wexford) informed Thomas Houston that 'great events are ripening. In a few days we shall meet [in Dublin] . . . We shall have an army of brave republicans, one hundred thousand [strong], with fourteen pieces of cannon, on Tuesday before Dublin . . . You will rise with a proportionate force.' This forecast envisaged the capture of Major-General Sir Francis Needham's artillery at Arklow and raising the inhabitants of east Wicklow and south Dublin en masse. A separate communication from Wexford suggested rallying at Tara Hill in Meath. It was not to be. Murphy was killed by cannon fire late in the struggle for the town where a 15,000-strong rebel army was repulsed with heavy losses after a five-hour battle. Colonels Edward Fitzgerald of Newpark, Anthony Perry of Inch and William 'Billy' Byrne of Ballymanus (Wicklow) withdrew to reconsider their position. The importance of the battle may be inferred from the fact that Needham's garrison of approximately 1,400 men included the bulk of the reserves from Lehaunstown Camp and amounted to almost half the total available to defend Dublin. The horses and carriage of Francis Higgins were amongst those commandeered in the city to rush the Durham fencibles to Arklow.[48]

This reverse greatly surprised the Thomas Street leaders, who had dispatched Fr John Martin to coordinate a city assault planned for 12 June. Martin left Rathfarnham on or around 6 June and visited rebel camps close to Ballinascorney where he conferred with McMahon, Holt, Nugent and Doyle. McMahon's faction remained close to the capital in anticipation of the final push and their presence helped inhibit the transfer of troops to Wexford. On 11 June the retention of soldiers in the capital seemed justified when Fr Martin divulged his mission after being captured near Rathdrum on the road to Wexford. The authorities discovered that he had been to Roundwood, Kilbride and Newcastle, as well as to parts of Meath, to hasten the proposed attempt on Dublin. Threats of summary execution disposed Fr Martin to reveal the hitherto unsuspected role of the Thomas Street men, including their efforts on two occasions to stimulate unrest in Meath. This interview may have led to adverse repercussions for the Moore and Murphy families, who were already known to have harboured Lord Edward Fitzgerald. Nicholas Murphy was certainly sent to a prison tender, freeing the soldiers who occupied his house to expropriate his assets without interference. The detention and flight of other committeemen badly damaged the provisional command echelon in the south city.[49]

Defeat at Arklow threw United Irish strategy into disarray and in mid-June north Wicklow leaders looked to their city-based comrades for clarification of their role. Holt informed a city contact that he would 'not act without orders from the executive', an acknowledgement that a loose chain of command had been restored based around the lateral coalition of south city committees. It is significant that the decisions of the unelected proxy leadership in Dublin were respected by authoritative rebel officers in the field. Indeed, this evidently occurred to a far greater extent than hitherto entertained. That insurgent bodies in Antrim, Down, Wicklow, Wexford, Kildare and King's County all centralised forces on high ground or defendable terrain in mid-June points to their adherence to a general practice, if not a specific strategy, which had been suggested by emissaries from Dublin. Holt's north Wicklowmen, meanwhile, left their camp at Clohogue to raid dozens of loyalist houses off the Roundwood to Glendalough road on the 14th, including Lord Mayor Fleming's country retreat at Diamond Hill. Holt had worked under Fleming in the 1780s when a city constable. Fr Christopher Lowe of Derrylossary was credited with saving many Wicklow homes from destruction, although it may be pertinent that he was a United Irishman and had just received a letter of introduction from Rathfarnham's suspected rebel priest, Fr Ledwich, to the Thomas Street envoy Fr John Martin. While the role of Catholic clergy in 1798 was greatly overstated by loyalist historians it seems that they were important in shoring up United Irish communications in the early months of the Rebellion.[50]

The Clohogue raids received much newspaper coverage in Dublin and clearly troubled the military, which had devised no stratagem to enable their firepower to be brought to bear against the mountain rebels. It is also significant that Revd Philip Roche, Bagenal Harvey's replacement as nominal commander-in-chief of Wexford rebels, issued orders on 19 June for the concentration of the disparate elements camped at Kilcavan, Foulksmill and Mountpleasant at Vinegar Hill (Enniscorthy). Roche overruled the objections of Perry and the majority of the more combat-experienced north Wexford and south Wicklow leaders, who favoured an immediate march to Rathdrum ahead of a descent on the capital from the Rathfarnham area. This too points to a consciously coordinated strategy which may have been influenced by information imparted by the clerical emissaries of the Dublin committees. The rebels in Wexford certainly became more proactive. Garret Byrne of Ballymanus, adjutant-general elect for Wicklow, may well have played a part in this as he quit his hiding place in the capital in time to join the insurgents near Vinegar Hill on the 21st. Byrne immediately supplanted other Wicklow leaders in Wexford, not least his brother William and Colonel Mathew Doyle. Significantly, Edward Fitzgerald of Newpark, Wexford's chosen adjutant-general, also became far more visible at this time. Both men could only have attained their seniority in conjunction with Lord Edward Fitzgerald's circle and their rise to prominence in late June reflected a willingness of more junior figures to respect their rank. While 'councils of war' convened by rebel officers to agree policy in the field remained in operation, Fitzgerald and Byrne were notably influential with north Wexford and Wicklow United Irishmen. This streamlined the hitherto defective decision-making capacity of the insurgent forces in south Leinster.[51]

The need for advice from a centralised and informed support network was heightened by news of the defeat of Ulster rebels at Ballynahinch, Down, on 12–13 June. This disaster ruled out the manifestation of a decisive rebel threat to the capital from the north. McCracken and Munro had delayed at Ballynahinch to rally stragglers from Antrim and Down and to receive reinforcements from other northern sectors. Arranging such assistance may explain the presence in Derry of Patrick Gallagher, an assistant to the military committee in Dublin. He was arrested by yeomen in north-western Ulster on 17 June 1798 in possession of suspicious letters from his brother John, another city resident who had known Fitzgerald. Dublin committeemen realised that time was not on their side owing to the disembarkation of large numbers of troops from England and Wales in mid-June and the arrival of many more in Belfast from Scotland. Their only chance was a major, preferably simultaneous, resurgence in several counties leading to decisive victories and the mass mobilisation of dormant manpower this would have permitted. Major-General Nugent's counter-attack at Ballynahinch unexpectedly wrong-footed the vital Ulstermen, just as William Aylmer's Kildaremen at Timahoe, on the fringes of the Bog of Allen, were drawn into a premature clash at Ovidstown on the 19th by Brigadier General Francis Grose.[52]

Alymer had obtained the aid of King's County rebels and his agents were agitating in Meath when their forced defence of Ovidstown disrupted the main body of 4,000 men. He assumed the role of Kildare's adjutant-general and viewed his actions as a constituent of a broad effort linking the inner counties of Leinster. It is very likely that this attempted revitalisation produced the first major stirring in Westmeath on 17 June where 3,000 rebels attacked Kilbeggan until driven back by the Seventh Dragoons for the loss of 120–300 men. Gallagher, arrested on the same day in Ulster, had been in close contact with Kilbeggan's colonel John McManus and may well have delivered a message from Dublin which had bearing on the timing of the sudden uprising. McManus, like Gallagher, was close to William Putnam McCabe and had striven to maintain contact with the city leadership. He did so again in 1803. Defeat in the field in June 1798, however, stalled the momentum essential for the escalation of the Rebellion.[53]

It was obviously a point of concern to Dublin United Irishmen that skirmishing rather than battles had taken place in the midlands and the west remained strangely passive. No insurgent victory was likely if the French did not arrive in force, and the ability of the outstanding factions to maintain themselves in remote areas was far from certain. In defensive mode, McMahon established a new camp in the second week of June at Whelp Rock, an inaccessible part of the mountains above Blessington. This became one of the refuges of the remaining Leinster insurgents who ravaged loyalist interests in the district. Rebel ammunition difficulties were alleviated in mid-June by the dispatch of small quantities of cartridges from city sympathisers which complemented stocks donated by locally-based disaffected militiamen and yeomen. This, again, was the type of practical help which Robert Emmet was in a position to furnish: a powder mill supplied by his associate Wright was used to granulate home-made gunpowder at Whelp Rock. Patrick Campbell of Fleet Street supplemented this stock with a seventy-pound batch of powder smuggled out of the city to Holt.[54]

Underground armourers, emissaries and committeemen braved the horrors of confinement in Beresford's Riding School on Marlborough Street, the Provost prison and the Royal Exchange, where scores of suspected United Irishmen were mistreated by city yeomen and magistrates. From the first days of the Rebellion it was reported that 'Hell born miscreants' were being flogged in the old Custom House barracks.[55] The upper yard of Dublin Castle became popularly known as 'Devil's Half Acre', a chilling phrase resonant of what took place within its confines. Similarly, the Liffey crossing at Bridge Street, where decomposing bodies were displayed, was unofficially referred to as 'Bloody Bridge', a name applied in earlier times and revived in 1798. One of the auxiliary barracks was fitted up for the administration of punishment in 27 Stephen's Green (Kerry House), later the Shelbourne Hotel, on the opposite side of the square to that occupied by the Emmets. Michael Masterson received 200 lashes in the 'Riding House' and Master Sweep William Horish was badly flogged, though not deterred by the experience. Much was made of Horish's coerced allegation that the rebels intended to burn the Parliament buildings and Dublin Castle. He was suspected of having previously started a blaze in the old Parliament House during a 1792 debate on taxing spirits.[56] James Glindon, an 'eminent butcher' at Coles Lane, was reputedly 'dragged from his house . . . tied up to a post in Godfrey's guard house on Summer-hill, where he was so torn by whips, that he scarcely was able to leave his apartment for more than a year'.[57] Many others were seized off the streets for interrogation by state agents indemnified for their actions by martial law. The practice was so widespread that Cornwallis issued orders on 4 July 1798 that 'no corporal punishment shall in further be inflicted on any person but by the sentence of a Court Martial. And the General officers are to issue the strictest possible injunctions to all under their command for the prevention of that practice.'[58]

In addition to the floggings, hundreds of Leinstermen were dispatched without trial to the overcrowded prison tenders moored in Dublin Bay and seventy-nine of McManus' Westmeath rebels arrested in Tubber Pond on 7 June by the Roxborough Dragoons were sent to the vessels. Luke Doyle of Lucan, a journeyman shoemaker, was put on board the *Alexandria* by the Phoenix Park Rangers on 31 July 'on suspicion' of sedition and Peter Gaffney of Cork Street, a parchment manufacturer, was embarked for using improper language when intoxicated in Dolphin's Barn. He joined Wexfordian William Darcy who was subsequently freed and took part in the Rising of 1803.[59] Tenders in Dublin Bay during the summer and autumn of 1798 included the *William and Mary, Columbine, Brunskill, John and Esther* and *Lively*. While their capacity and seaworthiness differed, the *Princess Charlotte* held 282 men off Cork in July 1798, 70 per cent of whom were discovered upon investigation to have been improperly committed.[60] For all intents and purposes, the tenders were used to intern suspected men, including those who had received conditional pardons, and to facilitate their planned deportation to the Fleet. Fear of mass breakouts and fever epidemics, as well as the desirability of frustrating rebel movements, inspired orders issued on 12 June requiring all vessels on the Liffey to moor near the North Wall.[61]

It was not until mid-June that Camden felt confident enough to allow large numbers of troops to leave the Dublin area and attempt the recovery of Wexford and south Wicklow from rebel hands. This was predicated on the arrival of the 100th Regiment and other long-awaited reinforcements from Britain and the Channel Islands whose presence was required before the garrison of the capital was weakened. While no significant Dublin insurgent forces were engaged in Wexford in the battle of Vinegar Hill on 21 June 1798 the consequences of the defeat were very serious in that the largest rebel army was driven from its chosen ground by a heavy artillery bombardment and infantry assaults. An error in timing by Major-General Needham enabled the vast majority to escape the Enniscorthy area, but they departed the county in two major bodies which were unlikely to prevail again when faced with government troops in the open field. The group headed by Fr John Murphy and Thomas Cloney went south to Kilkenny and Queen's Co. where its arrival failed to ignite the popular response anticipated. This, too, forecast doom for the revivalist contingency favoured by the Dublin committees and the militants. The second group, under Perry, Fitzgerald of Newpark and Byrne of Ballymanus, temporarily joined forces with the north Wicklowmen of Holt and his Dublin associates.

Dublin rebels were prominent during the second battle of Hacketstown on 25 June on the Wicklow/Carlow border. Fitzgerald and Byrne had pressed into Wicklow to evade Lake's army and to obtain much needed munitions in Hacketstown. The various Dublin factions in Wicklow were concentrated for the first time and bolstered by 400 men sent from the city after the 17th. McMahon had two horses shot under him at Hacketstown when directing the men under his command and Mathews of Tallaght Hill lost many followers. Dublin colonels Rattigan, Rourke and Burke of Skerries were also in action alongside captains Nicholas Lyons, a Skinner's Row silver-smith named Fitzgerald who was a private in the Rotunda Division and O'Neil of Francis Street. Hugh O'Hanlon was also present when the Rathfarnham rebels stormed the army's stone barracks with pikes, torches and some firearms. They made little headway without the cannon required to breach such defences and suffered heavy casualties in a failed attempt to burn the defenders out of their barracks. Hacketstown was reduced to uninhabitable wreckage and was abandoned by its garrison once the rebels had withdrawn.[62]

Most of the Dublin units left the main body near Donard and returned towards their native county while those which pressed on bypassed Blessington and approached the Wexford border. The Dublin contingent sent some of their wounded as far north as Lusk for recuperation but McClune, suffering from a painful stomach wound, remained in Wicklow. He had recently sent a request to Dublin for ammunition and reinforcements which was circulated amongst the coffee houses and rebel pubs of the south city. A new camp had been formed at Mount Pelier Hill to which rebels from Stillorgan, Blackrock, Mount Merrion and Booterstown had been summoned on 20 to 22 June. Such rapid and confusing movements created consternation in the capital where it was incorrectly stated that the fortified estate of Powerscourt and the strategic village of Rathfarnham had been destroyed. Both might well have met the fate of Hacketstown had not the rebel commanders decided on an alternative plan. At 2.00 a.m. on 24 June 1798 Major-General William Myers rallied over 700 yeomen at St Stephen's Green drawn from the Lawyers and Attorney's Cavalry, the Loyal Dublin Cavalry and the Rotunda Cavalry. They were supported by yeoman infantry of the Merchant's, St Stephen's Green, Lawyers and Attorney's and College corps in addition to a small detachment of the Fermanagh militia. Many of the units had been active in Dublin county for several weeks, not least Alderman Jenkins and the Stephen's Green Cavalry, which had seized pike handles in Milltown and Donnybrook in late May.[63]

The assemblage of the 24th may have been observed by Emmet from his home. He knew many of the loyalists and nominal supporters of Government engaged in the manoeuvre. Drennan's friend Robert Holmes, who secretly married Mary Anne Emmet in September 1799, had resigned from the Lawyers and Attorneys corps. General Myers marched via Rathfarnham and Stepaside to Enniskerry where they were joined by a further 200 city yeomen. They pitched camp near Roundwood and cautiously patrolled the Rathdrum area until 26 June when urgently recalled to Dublin by the incoming Lord Lieutenant Marquis Cornwallis. The new Viceroy was a Lieutenant General in the army and displaced the unpopular Lake as Commander-in-Chief. Cornwallis opposed the deployment of city yeomen outside the capital and was unsettled by the proliferating reports of large rebel bodies within twenty miles of the seat of Government. He acted without delay to reduce the numbers of courts martial sitting in Dublin and took a firm hand in ensuring that reasonable standards of evidence were maintained in their subsequent proceedings.[64]

It was not appreciated at the time that a major effort to re-open a front north of Dublin was in progress. On 24 June 'a meeting of the insurgents, convened by the authority of the Dublin Directory of United Irishmen' was held at the Fishpond, near Lisnawilly, County Louth. Dundalk United Irishmen Thomas Warren and Anthony McKeown hosted the gathering of leaders who attended from Monaghan, Armagh, Louth, Meath and Cavan. Westmeath and Cavan insurgents under McManus and one Reilly were also active at this time, often acting in concert with Longford men under Emmet's comrade Michael Farrell. Several hundred rebels intended attacking Dundalk barracks at night only to run foul of atrocious weather and the vigilance of the forewarned garrison. Warren and McKeown survived the crackdown which followed and escaped to Chester in England. The Dundalk area was a sector where Napper Tandy's friend Thomas Markey (aka Markham) had influence and where the Byrnes of Mullinahack (Dublin), a family of United Irish merchants, had extensive political and trade connections. The Fishpond reverse confirmed a new home truth to the city leaders, one already suggested by the recent experiences in Kilbeggan, Castlecomer and Ovidstown: fresh uprisings were unlikely to occur in hitherto passive or suppressed sectors without French assistance, even if large bodies of veteran fighters came into their midst. Furthermore, it was evident that the army was determined to attack rebel concentrations wherever artillery could be deployed.[65] On the positive side, the rout of a cavalry patrol on the Wicklow/Wexford border at Ballyellis on 30 June, showed that mobile rebel columns were still highly effective if skilfully commanded on chosen terrain. Almost fifty of the hated Ancient Britons and Fifth Dragoon Guards were killed for no rebel fatalities, a stunning victory which steeled a hard core of insurgents to keep fighting.[66]

The dual impact of the government's overwhelming military superiority and a generous amnesty programme introduced by Cornwallis fatally eroded rebel fighting strength in the first days of July. This was greatly accelerated on 4–5 July when a disappointing clash at Ballygullen hastened the declining Wexford rebellion towards an abrupt halt. The vast majority of active insurgents accepted liberal surrender terms under which they received immunity from prosecution in return for surrendering their arms and swearing an oath of allegiance. Many stashed their guns and placed their greased pikes in the thatch. Rumours of imminent French assistance in late July, a United Irish revival in Ulster and mass defections from the military were sufficient to sustain a militant minority. They were actively assisted by the Dublin leaders who in early July predicted the arrival of the French by the end of the month. Once again agents within the rump factions in Wicklow reported widespread expectations that an augmented insurgent army would 'pour into Dublin' from Whelp Rock and Tallaght.[67]

THE LATE REBELLION

A spate of arrests in Dublin in early July 1798 convinced many informed commentators that a major build-up of rebel forces was taking place in the nearby mountains just as their principal concentrations were melting away elsewhere. Two women seized in Camden Street on 8 July were discovered bringing salt sacks filled with gunpowder and musket balls to the rebels. A twenty-four man 'committee' rounded up at Summerhill was strongly suspected of liaising with the mountain bands at Whelp Rock and it was common knowledge that guides known as 'express boys' were bringing groups of citymen into the hills. On 9 July Captain George La Touche's Rathfarnham yeoman cavalry and Captain John Beresford junior's Dublin County Cavalry (First troop, aka 'Beresford Cavalry') intercepted fourteen men carrying munitions to the mountains. Three were shot, four hanged on the Rathfarnham Road and the remainder taken to the city. Other rebel parties from Milltown, Ballybrack, Rathfarnham, Loughlinstown, Tallaght, Kilgobbin, Rathmichael and Palmerstown reached the rebel camps in safety. These were the men upon whom Emmet and his allies were reliant in 1803.[68]

On 10 July 1798 William Hartigan, President of the Royal College of Surgeons in Ireland and a man given to carrying a pair of kittens around the city, noted that 'almost all the labourers in the environs of Dublin, and a great number of servants, absented themselves the night before last, in consequence of a requisition to join the rebel camp'. While Hartigan's assessment may have been somewhat jaundiced from the vantage of his Anne Street home, its coinciding with the discovery of large arms caches in Back Lane, Dolphin's Barn and a dung heap at Arbour Hill ensured that such opinions could not be discounted.[69] Dolphin's Barn was one of the main routes to the mountains and was consequently a convenient place to store arms. By 10 July new rebel camps had been established on Sorrel Hill,

Castlekelly, Raheen and Ballynahowa as staging points for Whelp Rock. Their secondary role was as forward bases from which an attack on Dublin could be mounted from the south. Others were reported at Ratoath and Rush, leading to suspicions that the rebels were again attempting to encircle the capital. Sproule ventured that the plan was to draw the garrison out of the city to render it more vulnerable for an attack planned for the 13th or 14th. He speculated that the rebels wanted to free the state prisoners, 'chiefly Bond whom they say if they had to send to the north that whole quarter of the Kingdom would rise'.[70] This plan was also allegedly discussed by 'some thousands' who gathered at Dunboyne and sent word of their deliberations to Power of Thomas Street. Higgins informed Cooke of the insurgent 'desire to know whether the numbers sworn to their cause will come out to aid them! or if they will instantly and fairly assist them if they shall attack the city'.[71] Richard Turner of 20 Earl Street, a veteran Church of Ireland radical and associate of James Hope, was one of those who took to the mountains where he encountered Dublin colonels Rourke, McClune, Rattigan and Thompson and Wicklow's Joseph Holt. Fresh men took the places of those slipping away to take advantage of the amnesty held out by the generals at the insistence of Cornwallis.[72]

An aggressive recruiting drive from Whelp Rock into Kildare and Meath on 8 July demonstrated the potential threat posed by the mountain camps. Most of the Dubliners, some of whom were newly mobilised, accompanied the main force on this last-ditch effort but 200 men attached to McMahon's faction remained in the Dublin mountains. McMahon's disinterest in schemes that fell short of a direct assault on the capital may have explained this stance, although the retention of a Dublin corps on the south of the city may have been considered desirable for tactical reasons. A 'camp of the friends of Ireland' was established the following week within reach of Blackrock, where disaffected members of the King's County militia hoped to defect on the 17th, a plan which ended in their court martial.[73] Another sizeable force of Wicklow and Wexford men under Michael Dwyer and Miles Byrne remained in Glenmalure and the Seven Churches (Glendalough) while their comrades entered the midlands. Dwyer and Byrne were amongst the most important supporters of Emmet in 1803. As before, it was hoped that an arc of positions could be formed around Dublin to intimidate the government and hinder their communications. They certainly succeeded in engendering a siege mentality amongst Dublin loyalists. Elements of the Dublin rebels believed that their columns would 'meet [Major] McDermot[t] and his party in [th]e North', a reference to the Fingal associates of Miles Duigenan and Lord Edward Fitzgerald who were also apparently known to Garret Byrne. Great hopes were entertained of William Aylmer's Kildaremen at Timahoe who tightened security in the vicinity of their camps at this time by issuing safe conduct passes to accredited emissaries from Dublin.[74]

The first disappointment of the expedition was the realisation that Aylmer and the other Kildare leaders based at Timahoe, reeling from their losses at Ovidstown and Fox's Hill, were tentatively engaged in negotiations to surrender. Aylmer had evidently abandoned plans to liaise with a rising in Queen's County prior to the 24th. The few Kildare rebels who joined the column on 9–14 July did not exceed those lost by attrition and desertion. An unexpected check then occurred at Clonard on the Meath/Kildare border on the 11th when a small yeoman garrison barricaded into Tyrrell's fortified house and several smaller outposts held off thousands of rebels. Dublin units were heavily committed to the assault with Rourke, Rattigan and Thomas Markey in the thick of the action. Markey, from Seaside, Dundalk, was a senior leader in north county Dublin who had probably fought at Westphalstown and Tara Hill in Meath. Given that Markey was reputedly a 'principal United Irishman' it may be that his followers had remained in their home area with McDermott until the chance arose to fight alongside the stronger rebel forces based in the Dublin and Wicklow mountains.[75] The attack crumbled when it proved impossible to penetrate Clonard's defences. The rebels reluctantly called off their effort when British cavalry and artillery reinforcements from Kinnegad threatened to inflict massive losses.[76]

Rebel weakness and exhaustion was exposed the following day during heavy skirmishing at Ryndville Hill (Knockderig), which deepened the acrimony arising from command disagreements. The bulk of the insurgent gunmen were absent foraging when the camp was attacked. In desperation Joseph Holt resorted to indiscriminate house-burning to cover the hasty retreat of the rebels with a smoke-screen, a tactic they had used with mixed results at Arklow and Hacketstown. Many Dubliners departed the diminished column of survivors and went home while the bulk of the dejected Kildaremen returned with Edward Fitzgerald to Timahoe. They were admitted to Aylmer's negotiations with Major-General Richard Wilford. The faction at Timahoe numbered Kildare officers Michael Quigley and Hugh Ware of Rathcoffey, Tyrone-born Bernard Duggan and Bryan

McDermott of Hodgestown, all of whom conspired with Emmet in 1802–3. The rump forces of Byrne and Perry struggled northwards to another costly defeat at Knightstown Bog on 14 July 1798 and a final clash at Ballyboghill, County Dublin. They found it impossible to shake off the cavalry which shadowed them across the low lands and had no answer to the cannon fire with which they were plied when standing their ground on unstable and high terrain. Pockets of rebels were dispersed as far north as Ardee in Louth and in the Navan district of Meath from whence some may have ventured the previous week. By 18 July a provisional agreement with Major-General Wilford at Sallins laid the basis for the surrender of most of the outstanding Wexford, Wicklow and Kildare officers in Dublin Castle on the 21st.[77]

Dublin magistrate William James observed rebel veterans coming into the city 'in groups of three and four – all unarmed and appear like savages with long beards, little clothes and appeared half starved'.[78] He seemingly pitied rather than feared the survivors, although the discomfort of city loyalists was evident from a letter sent to Lord Sheffield the following week by John Foster, a key figure in the discredited Camden viceroyalty. Foster wrote:

> The rebellion still continues and approaches nearer the city. About 15,000 were together near Blessington . . . The western or Connaught mail has not passed these two days; the Munster, twice plundered within this week, is now guarded by 30 Dragoons and 30 foot in gingles . . . No effectual attempt to dislodge the rebels from the confines of the metropolis . . . the mail coach from the north was seized near the Man of War by the rebels, together with the mail coach from Dublin . . . This shows the determination of the devils in pursuing their plan of surrounding the metropolis. It is now completely encircled. They began at the sea, near Wicklow, thence round by Naas, and so to Kilcock. Last night they had a strong camp near Ratoath.[79]

An emissary named Shaw was sent to Wexford prior to the 14th 'to keep up the spirits of the insurgents with promise & assurance of immediate assistance from France'. Such encouragement had not worked for Fr John Murphy and Miles Byrne when they went from Vinegar Hill into Kilkenny and Queen's Co. and had failed again when Byrne, Perry and Fitzgerald broke into the midlands.[80] This was apparent to the Marquis of Buckingham on the 23rd, who had no equivocation in announcing that 'the rebel cordon round Dublin has been entirely broken'. The United Irishmen required a new strategy which offered, at the very least, the chance to fight another day.[81]

EMMET AND THE STATE PRISONERS

Government efforts to avoid a drawn-out mopping-up operation in Leinster, costly in human life as well as to the already damaged economy, engaged Robert Emmet in his most important known activity as a United Irishman during the Rebellion. While successive proclamations had held out clemency to rebels who surrendered weapons and swore the oath of allegiance, little could be done to neutralise those determined to fight on in the woods and mountains. It was estimated that 600,000 had been 'engaged in treason' for whom it was 'prudent to open a door'. Appealing to their leaders via the imprisoned top-ranking United Irishmen offered a solution to this and other difficulties. The politically contentious and legally problematic issue of the state prisoners was central to the scheme.[82]

The fate of Thomas Addis Emmet and almost eighty other state prisoners was largely determined by the lack of evidence to convict them of high treason. Of those arrested on 12 March, Bond, William Michael Byrne of Wicklow and John McCann of Dublin were vulnerable owing to the recovery of seditious documents on their persons. Neilson, incriminated by his actions outside Newgate two weeks later, also anticipated capital conviction. Physical evidence would not have been an impediment to many more prosecutions if those who had sworn depositions were willing to appear in court. This, however, was not the case. Thomas Reynolds imposed strict limits on his services to Government while Leonard MacNally, John Hughes and Samuel Turner refused to testify in treason trials. An exception was Captain John Warneford Armstrong of the King's County militia, at no time a United Irishman, whose clear-cut evidence convicted the unwary Sheares brothers, whom he had befriended. Cornwallis later remarked in private correspondence that the other high-ranking United Irish prisoners 'were only proved to be traitors by their own confessions'.[83] In view of the complications in securing convictions, acquittal was probable in most cases. This scenario could not be countenanced by loyalist opinion after the carnage of the summer and the ongoing French threat. Treason trials, moreover, excited considerable unrest in Dublin and added fresh security fears of a breakout or violent rescue to the considerable financial burden of imprisoning Kilmainham's 'Reg[imen]t of Traitors'. Indefinite confinement was also out of the question as there were political and legal grounds for restoring habeas corpus in Ireland before 1799, not least paving the way for the Act of Union. The discharge of the most capable political prisoners was only a matter of time unless an accommodation could be reached.[84] The government would then have to be content with executing prisoners within the remit of courts martial; combatant rebel officers such as John Storey of Belfast, a printer and McCracken associate capitally convicted on 30 June.[85]

Concern that mid-level activists like Storey would die while Addis Emmet and the upper leadership escaped made the Executive receptive to the terms of a pact mediated by veteran Whig MP for Coleraine Francis Dobbs on 24–26 July 1798. Edward Cooke authorised Dobbs to press ahead with a deal after the execution of Byrne on 25 July outside Green Street courthouse. Dobbs, an eccentric former governor of North Carolina, barrister and a millenarian, was on good terms with many of those imprisoned and found that they had been shocked by the executions of Byrne, McCann and the Sheares brothers between 14 and 26 July. In return for respiting Bond's capital conviction and permitting all state prisoners to emigrate, the United Irishmen agreed to furnish the government with details of their conspiracy. It was understood that they would use their influence to encourage the acceptance of the Amnesty Act in the parts of the country where insurgents were determined to keep fighting. Dublin loyalists hoped that revelations from the prisoners would unmask 'men in high situation' in Ireland and Britain, although the Castle was privately satisfied that the simple admission of guilt by the prisoners, their implicit contrition and support for the amnesty programme would suffice.[86] Cornwallis presented the deal to the Home Office as 'a most favourable opportunity of sending almost every dangerous man out of this country'.[87]

Securing the deal required the backing of scores of imprisoned United Irishmen, who had to consider their respective positions with utmost caution. Most were aware that their ambiguous legal status was the only real bargaining chip they possessed. Addis Emmet, prior to consenting to answer questions in College Green, was apprised by a Crown solicitor that 'there were no legal grounds discovered' to prefer a bill of indictment against him on charges of high treason.[88] Nevertheless, Addis Emmet signed a pact which was deemed to be in the best interests of the United Irishmen and definitely so in the cases of Bond and Neilson. On 26 July Arthur O'Connor and a small group who had quibbled with the terms outlined by Dobbs made their participation contingent on a guarantee that 'the place of their banishment should neither be Botany Bay nor any part of the world to which convicts are sent'. This established that the prisoners – who had risked their lives for ideological motives – would not accept the stigma of criminalisation. Granting this precondition bolstered the attractiveness of the deal as the signatories assumed that they would be permitted to emigrate to the United States or to other neutral countries where they would be free to regroup.[89]

A second concession was that the United Irishmen would not be required to name third parties, either during questioning in College Green or in the written account of the conspiracy they agreed to produce for the government. Fitzgibbon and Duigenan had previously adopted this position when questioning Robert Emmet's associates in Trinity College in April 1798. Fitzgibbon, trusted by ultra-loyalists, again signalled that this strategy was warranted under the circumstances.[90] Consequently, when examined before the Secret Committee of the House of Lords in early August, Addis Emmet, O'Connor and MacNeven saw no reason to reveal United Irish business of which the authorities appeared ignorant. Calculated responses to explicit queries came as no surprise to the Castle, which doubted that intelligence of 'real value beyond what we know' could be obtained. Agreeing this strategy by 26 July, however, involved intensive deliberations between a large group of prisoners who were divided between three prisons and into various factions. There was also considerable time pressure given that the respected Bond was under imminent sentence of death.[91]

Robert Emmet's employment as a 'messenger and confidential agent' between the state prisoners and the government at this fraught juncture indicates that he enjoyed a reputation for reliability.[92] He reputedly visited Kilmainham, Newgate and the Bridewell to relate the positions of the various groups to each other. Emmet would have been on first name terms with many of the prisoners and a known entity to all given the stature of his elder brother. Arthur O'Connor, who spoke for the Bridewell group, was in a difficult position as Neilson alleged that the Corkman's prevarication in signing the compact, a stance also taken by Roger O'Connor and William Dowdall, had resulted in the execution of William Michael Byrne. Unstated by Neilson, if undoubtedly assumed by many, was an assumption that O'Connor's self-serving behaviour when on trial at Maidstone in May had helped send Fr. Coigley to the gallows. Emmet had to choose his words very carefully in view of such undercurrents. He presumably conferred with Dobbs on the progress made and possibly also in secret with William Sampson, who operated behind the scenes. It later transpired that Emmet was the most effective United Irish emissary engaged in this task given that their main lawyer at this time, MacNally, was in the pay of the government. Addis Emmet may have entrusted his brother with instructions for the ad hoc Directory in the city which he knew could be accessed by him through Lawless and Wright. Illicit private letters were certainly exchanged by the leaders in different prisons, which the authorities impounded whenever they were discovered in cell searches. The imprisoned leaders eventually reached a common position and communicated their acceptance of terms to Dobbs. Addis Emmet, Arthur O'Connor and MacNeven were taken to Dublin Castle on 29 July to meet Castlereagh, Fitzgibbon and Cooke and formally accept the revised terms of the Dobbs pact.[93]

The charged circumstances under which Robert Emmet departed from Trinity ensured that he could not be complacent about his own legal status, even if there was no apparent intention to pursue him on charges of United Irish membership. His engagement in the July negotiations was bound to draw negative attention from informed loyalists and Emmet may, in this respect, have benefitted from the truce-like arrangement which the Castle honoured in order to facilitate the implementation of the pact. William Putnam McCabe, notorious in Castle circles, and his associate, James Farrell, a Waterford man who worked as a clerk in Parliament Street, were permitted to travel armed into the Wicklow mountains. It was hoped that they could convince rebel commanders Holt and Dwyer to avail of the amnesty proclamation. United Irish leaders were technically ineligible for clemency but could, under certain circumstances, negotiate personal terms with senior army officers. The state prisoners had clearly received sanction for this deal and were supported by Dobbs, who also visited Major-General John Moore's camp in west Wicklow in late August. Dwyer and his men, who were camped out in the rugged valley of Imaal, rejected McCabe's request, as did Holt, who may not have met the delegates in person before they returned to the city from Bray. The emissaries were fortunate to evade arrest in Quinn's Hotel, Bray, when they found themselves in the company of an ill-informed loyalist who was on their trail although unaware of their identities.[94]

Charles Broderick, Bishop of Kilmore and a member of the Middleton family, informed a London friend: 'the traitors . . . pardoned on the condition of banishment have sent themselves to work in earnest by means of emissaries accredited by them to tranquillize the country, and I really believe you may look forward with confidence to the complete subjection of the rebels: I do not say to a restoration of harmony and confidence, but to a quiet which is to arise from their feeling that they have not the power to do anything effective against the Government . . . in this country disappointed and mortified men, and those who do not look beyond the circumstances of the present moment, or to the future arrangement of the country, are enraged at the measures of lenity . . . do not expect that you will ever secure the affection of the people of Ireland (I mean the multitude) to British Government, in any shape that has ever been tried'.[95] Broderick was evidently cognizant that an Act of Union was the planned sequel to the clemency initiative and appreciated that the reforms were inextricably linked. The government's intention to reach definitive solutions, however, ensured that the drive against the general United Irish community of Dublin city was unrelenting. This served to placate the 'mortified' politicians who lived in the capital while threatening the outstanding, as well as imprisoned, republican cadres. Sirr detained yet another mid-ranking figure on the North Circular Road on 19 July when there were 'daily executions' in the city.[96] One Hynes, reputedly the 'Rebel Commissary General' of Dublin, was taken into custody where it was hoped he would reveal the locations of arms and ammunition dumps.[97]

Contrary to Cooke's expectations, the extension of surrender terms to Holt and Dwyer proved ineffective. Much greater success was met with in regard to the west Dublin factions, whose leaders agreed to meet General Ralph Dundas at Kilcullen on 7 August 1798. Felix and Charles Rourke, Bartholomew Mahon and Nicholas Lyons surrendered to Dundas believing that they would be granted the same terms of self-exile granted to the state prisoners.[98] The Rourke group was amenable to the Dobbs proposals. Rattigan independently approached a high-ranking officer within a day of the Kilcullen breakthrough and sought admission to the pact. McClune, Burke and others also complied and reappeared in the city by the autumn. Thomas Markey was evidently arrested, given his court martial in Dundalk and subsequent offer to emigrate to America in December. By 1801 he was an officer in the Irish Legion of the French army. McMahon was the only major Dublin faction leader who decided to fight on in the mountains. The reduction of Dublin forces was a matter of some relief to the Castle which responded to an uprising scare in the city on 4 August 1798 by mobilising the yeomanry and forcing the Warwickshire Regiment to sleep in their uniforms. Several 'committees' were also raided, and although nothing of a seditious nature was uncovered Sirr's men were unconvinced by their possession of pardons and claims 'that they only meet for innocent recreation'.[99] Vigilance had to be maintained, as evidenced by the discovery and prompt execution of a rebel spy in Lehaunstown army camp on 2 August.[100]

The short written 'memoir' produced on 4 August 1798 by MacNeven, O'Connor and Addis Emmet, although deemed 'insolent' for its defiant tone and criticism of the Irish Executive, was welcomed for confirming information already known to the Castle. The trio and Neilson appeared at College Green between 7 and 11 August before the Secret Committee of the House of Lords to answer questions regarding the origins of the United Irishmen and their links with France.[101] The Duke of Portland informed the King on the 11th that the 'narrative' was remarkable in that 'so much reserve has been used & so much arrogance & insolence have [sic] been manifested'. The duke went so far as to imply that the 'lenity' towards it authors had been 'misapplied' but that the resolve of Cornwallis to 'take other methods of getting to the bottom of the rebellion' would ultimately vindicate the compromise entered into with the state prisoners. An edited version of the interviews was appended to the published report of the Secret Committee before the end of August which, in conjunction with misleading press reports of their revelations, disposed the United Irishmen to respond outside official channels.[102]

A letter signed by Addis Emmet, O'Connor and MacNeven appeared in both *Hibernian Journal* and *Saunder's Newsletter* on the 27th repudiating Castle intimations that they had incriminated associates in their dealings with the Secret Committee. This caused a furore in the conservative press, particularly in the pages of *Faulkner's Dublin Journal* on 28 August and 8 September 1798. The publication of the letter led to the immediate solitary confinement of its authors and the confiscation of their papers. They were fortunate that Castlereagh resisted demands in the Commons that they be excluded from the indemnity offered to the state prisoners.[103] Amongst the documents taken was a manuscript history of Ireland that Addis Emmet had been working on, presumably an early draft of the chapter entitled 'Part of an essay towards the history of Ireland' which appeared in *Pieces of Irish History* in 1807. Writing to the press addressed the fears of undetected United Irishmen whose support the leadership expected to call upon when their fortunes improved.[104]

THE FRENCH EXPEDITION

From 22 August 1798 it seemed that just such a favourable opportunity was imminent with the arrival off Mayo of the vanguard of a large French expeditionary force. That General Jean Joseph Humbert's 1,100 men would be defeated before they could be reinforced from France could not have been foreseen. In this context, the public reassurances of good faith by the Kilmainham leaders to their grass roots on the 27th intimated that the pact was nothing more than a short-term stratagem. The United Irishmen remained in business.[105] On hearing of the Mayo landings the state prisoners in Kilmainham gathered and gave three cheers. The brief and spectacular march of the French in the west, marked by rebel-assisted victories at Killala, Castlebar and Cloone by 5 September, sent a tremor through the Establishment, which watched as its numerically superior forces were defeated. The Connacht Republic came into being but could not survive in the absence of substantial additional French assistance and major United Irish uprisings. The prospect of both was voided at Ballinamuck on 8 September by the containment of the main Franco-Irish column.[106]

The invasion crisis occasioned a meeting of United Irish officers in Kevin Street in late August 1798 attended by Thomas Wright, Hugh O'Hanlon, Henry Baird and one Thompson. O'Hanlon and Thompson had fought with Holt and were sufficiently experienced to assess what could and could not be achieved in late August. That three, if not four, of these men conspired with Emmet by January 1799 at the latest signifies the depth of his involvement in city republicanism. The Kevin Street meeting considered plans to attack Dublin Castle, the Pigeon House and other strategic government buildings to alleviate pressure on the French, but 'nothing was agreed on'. Wright confirmed in May 1799 that an attempt had been made to replace the imprisoned Directory around the nucleus of the Kevin Street coterie and that Robert Emmet was a participant. Three Ulstermen apparently responded to an overture in connection with this initiative and Emmet, although delayed, came in time to ensure that 'some business was done'.[107] When questioned in the Castle in 1799, Wright claimed to have been absent when Emmet joined the company, although this may have been a ploy to withhold information regarding an important fugitive. His aversion to naming names displeased his interrogators. Another old conspirator, John Cusack of Ely Place, had evidently recovered from Major Swan's malign attention in April and was one of those 'determined to avail . . . of the opportunity' created by the French in August 1798.[108]

The meeting attended by Emmet evidently occurred prior to the defeat of the French expedition when coordinated activity on the east coast was again desirable. He was one of few trusted United Irishmen with recent access to the state prisoners and must have benefited from Wright's positive attention. A specific reason for enlisting Emmet's support for military planning was his authority as a 'collegian' in the Green Division. This assumed heightened significance arising from the fact that one of its colonels, Francis McMahon, was the only city leader of stature under arms when the French arrived. Certainly, on 26 August Wexford United Irishman Nick Murphy of Monaseed established contact between the capital, where he lived on New Street, and the insurgents encamped on Croghan Mountain in Wicklow. The rebels at Croghan numbered a Wexford corps commanded by Murphy's stepbrother Miles Byrne. They learned that the Dublin leaders were once again pursuing aggressive policies. Murphy became an ally of Emmet's in 1803 and may well have first dealt with him during the Rebellion of 1798.[109] Fresh contact was also established on 25 August 1798 between the Great Britain Street baronial and United Irishmen in Monaghan and Meath who requested 'a full and true account of what French force landed'.[110]

The news from Dublin encouraged rivals Holt and McMahon to combine forces and to embark on a recruitment drive in Carlow, Kildare and Wexford. It was generally assumed that government interests to the south of the capital would be threatened by them while the bulk of the armed forces were deployed in the west against the French. William Putnam McCabe also endeavoured to counteract the strategy of passivity he had been required to promote from mid-July to early August. Significantly, McCabe's mission to Kildare in September was underwritten by Philip Long of 4 Crow Street, a wealthy merchant and Donnybrook Hurler whose financial resources, personal contacts and leadership were indispensable to post-Rebellion United Irish plans. Long had served as a captain in the Neapolitan military and was deeply engaged in United Irish activities between 1794 and 1803. He was friendly with William Cole and probably others who had worked with Lord Edward Fitzgerald yet slipped through the Castle's intelligence net.[111] McCabe's brazen volte-face proved beyond doubt that the most committed elements of the United Irish movement outside prison, as well as the militants behind bars, viewed the Kilmainham pact as an expedient means to an end. Robert Emmet evidently supported this policy and, if not already a fully fledged member of the city leadership which advised this course of action, retained their confidence.[112] When obliged to make an incriminating statement in August 1803, Long admitted that he 'knew'

Emmet 'by living near him in 1798' without mentioning his secret dealings with Wright in the company of Emmet's brother-in-law John Patten.[113]

A new factor favouring United Irish intentions in August/September was the influx of thousands of rebel veterans returning to the capital, 1,064 of whom with city addresses admitted 'having participated in the late rebellion' when receiving certificates of pardon from Majors Sirr and Swan in Exchange Alley after late July. They evidently included hundreds who had fought with McMahon, Rourke, McClune and the other Dublin officers who had accepted terms in Kildare. Details emerged in the Commons on 13 September 1798 that a mere 124 weapons of all descriptions had been handed in by their followers. The vast majority of the rebels were from the city and county of Dublin and their combat experience was factored into Emmet's plans a few years later. Most hailed from the Green and Workhouse Divisions, the only areas of Dublin where serious skirmishing occurred in July 1803. South city spinners, weavers, servants and brewery workers enjoyed easier access to the fighting zones than their Rotunda and Barrack comrades and also happened to reside in the one part of the metropolis where the United Irish leadership functioned throughout the Rebellion. Their numbers were supplemented by the many hundreds of pardoned and unregistered United Irishmen who migrated to the capital in late 1798 on finding the threat of loyalist revenge attacks too great to remain at home. Others came from further afield, not least Longford's colonel Michael Farrell, who hid in Dublin after the defeat of Humbert before taking ship for Liverpool.[114] Privy Councillor Robert Ross claimed on 29 August 1798 that the 'Croppies of Dublin are as alert as possible, and we are threatened with an insurrection if great care is not taken'.[115]

Loyalist pessimism concurred with that of Felix Rourke, then imprisoned in Naas, Kildare. In a coded letter to his sister Mary, Rourke confirmed that the Dublin rebels would dishonour their surrender terms at the 'first opportunity, as many have done, and take to the mountains'.[116] It quickly became apparent that the Castle's dismissive accounts of the size of Humbert's force were correct and that this realisation had discouraged the turn-out of large-scale United Irish forces in the west. As had occurred in May 1798, several United Irish commanders instructed their men to stand back from the campaign in order to better serve the major landings they anticipated. Their ability to impose control was aided by the absence of large-scale dragooning in that sector in 1797–98 and the related lack of

Orange Order-linked ultra-loyalism which had incited the insurgents in southern Leinster. Matters may have taken a different course had Humbert been rapidly reinforced by troops massing at Brest. Even so, the prospect of a Franco-Irish breakthrough animated the city networks of which Emmet had become a part. They must have been encouraged by news that eight yeomen per city corps had been sent to augment the defences of Naas in support of two troops of the Fifth 'Royal Irish' Dragoons detached from Lehaunstown.[117]

Claims that Dunne of Thomas Court had discussed strategy with Kildare delegates and reports of seditious meetings in Meath served to remind Dublin Castle that the Rebellion was not over. Putnam McCabe met Neil of Plunket Street at this time to consider the unfolding events. Neil had been a member of the Liberty Rangers and had fought in Wicklow with Hugh O'Hanlon and Holt. Also present was the Barrack Division's Colonel Thomas Seagrave, a resident of Greek Street and former member of the Catholic Committee who was hanged shortly afterwards. Seagrave had been sponsored into the United Irishmen in November 1792 by Richard Dillon, a close associate of Bond's, whose name was mentioned as a Directory member in 1799. Dillon's brother in Donnybrook had supplied the McMahon faction. The citymen were unconvinced that a new uprising should be mounted in Leinster and vacillated as the strength of the Crown forces began to tell against Humbert. Repeated accounts of rebel activity, nonetheless, prompted Lieutenant General Craig to order a massive show of force in the city on 4 September. Yeomanry units paraded throughout Dublin and the guards on canal crossings were doubled as a precaution against rumours that a revolt would take place on the 5th.[118] None materialised, although the Wicklow rebels upped the ante by raiding and occupying Blessington that day and were notably aggressive at Greenan, Glenmalure and Keadeen. This followed minor clashes on 29–30 August at Clone Hill, Mucklagh Hill and Coolgreany in which several yeomen were killed by Holt's men. General Holt, one of the most determined and successful Irish guerrilla commanders, maintained close links with the Dublin leadership that had clearly called for an escalation of combat to take advantage of the transfer of troops to the west. It may have been reasoned that the best assistance they could offer the French was to oblige Cornwallis to retain a greater number of soldiers in Leinster than would have been the case had the province been quiescent. City rebels made their presence felt in more modest fashion on the 17th when they assassinated a suspected informer on Francis Street.[119]

Consultations between urban committees and rural factions continued even after Humbert's defeat at Ballinamuck on 8 September and the exceptionally destructive campaign of reconquest in the west, which culminated at Killala in the last week of the month. No quarter was shown in several skirmishes and the routine execution of United Irish officers created a deficit of experienced commanders which caused problems for the conspirators of 1803. Government ruthlessness, however, created new grievances and fresh enemies, who struck back in 1799. Buckingham noted the altered circumstances on 15 September 1798 when commenting: 'Ireland will be peaceable while it is governed (as at present) by the 150,000 men now armed in it.' The South Lincoln, West Suffolk and Herefordshire regiments arrived that day to further reinforce the Irish garrison. Buckingham echoed Broderick in stating that 'no arrangement will be formed to secure the country against the repetition of the same evils arising out of the same causes'.[120]

French officers were accommodated in the Mail Coach Hotel, Dawson Street, on the night of the 15th where 'persons of every description' thronged to catch sight of them. Their non-commissioned officers and men were taken by canal the following day to Ringsend where eight transports waited to carry them to Liverpool. They did not act like a defeated corps and sang marching songs and the national anthem in the packed barges to the delight of their local allies. Humbert's officers, amused by disparaging reports of their conduct and character in the Castle press, travelled in coaches to the Pigeon House knowing that they would be soon be exchanged for Britons held in France and free to campaign again.[121] The implications of Humbert's failure weighed heavily on the senior Dublin United Irishmen: the pragmatic McMahon dispersed his followers in Wicklow on 25 September having agreed 'to meet no more till the French make a landing in force'. The propriety of armed resistance may have been in doubt as the winter months approached but United Irishmen debated this and their other diminished options and prepared the ground for future ventures. Ballinamuck raised the highly contentious issue of the scale of French assistance required.[122]

In this respect the welcome extended by Donegal inhabitants to the arrival of Napper Tandy's small French party on 17 September was reassuring in that it suggested that the country people might well rise again given suitable military backing and leadership. Tandy landed on Rathlin Island with William Corbett, Emmet's Trinity colleague, and Anthony McCann, whom Emmet encountered in 1800–1802. Tandy's group, in view of the uncertainty engendered by Humbert's surrender, re-embarked on the *Anacreon* on the 18th and, after a gruelling ordeal, reached Bergen, Norway, before going to Hamburg in two parties. They were arrested in the German city on 24 November 1798 at the behest of the British representative, Colonel Sir James Crauford, and eventually extradited to Ireland for trial. Two other Dublin United Irishmen, George Grey and Lyndon Bolton (aka Gordon), remained safely ensconced in Hamburg and later had dealings with Emmet there and in Paris. Bolton, a close friend of Emmet's, had taken part in the Rebellion in Ireland and escaped to Hamburg by August 1798. He formerly ran a woollen drapery at 19 Francis Street, Dublin.[123]

Ballinamuck accelerated the transformation of the United Irishmen from its pre-Rebellion structure into the type of organisation of which Emmet assumed military command. New tactical and strategic possibilities were suggested by the campaign in consequence of the proven strengths and weaknesses of the rebels in battle. In the short term, the resurgence of widespread violence had caused Emmet to recede into obscurity once more, where his movements and actions cannot be accurately traced. It is unlikely that he was aware that two of his closest associates in Trinity, Michael Farrell and Peter McLoughlin, fought as rebel officers during the invasion crisis. Farrell was active in Longford and Westmeath, as was Emmet's future associate Denis Lambert Redmond, who had agitated with local leaders Hans and Alexander Denniston. McLoughlin had joined Humbert's Franco-Irish column in his native Mayo. United Irish officers in the French army included a third Trinity comrade, Corbett, as well as William Hamilton of Enniskillen, who later played a major role in the rising of 1803.[124]

Several further indications of French commitment to the United Irishmen were received during the autumn, albeit with simultaneous and highly discouraging demonstrations of British naval superiority. A small fleet under Admiral Bompard arrived off Donegal on 12 October and fought a running battle with the Royal Navy towards Tory Island until most of the outgunned ten-ship expedition was trapped and captured. Wolfe Tone, seized on board the *Hoche* flagship after a fierce and bloody struggle, was landed at Buncrana, Donegal, and conveyed as a prisoner to Dublin.[125] Against this run of bad luck, Commodore Savary, who had deposited Humbert's corps in Mayo, revisited Killala Bay on 27 October and withdraw in safety on learning of the fate of the earlier expeditions. As Elliott has shown, the inconsistent attitude of the French towards the United Irishmen was greater than they and the general public realised. French interest was affected by their limited resources, which were not as plentiful as they had been in 1796–97. Nelson's destruction of Napoleon's Egyptian army transports in Aboukir Bay on 1 August 1798 further strained French capacity to aid Ireland, as did attrition in the Caribbean and Indian Ocean. Official dispatches of Nelson's victory were released in the first week of October, just in time to steady the nerves of Lord Bridport's squadron when confronting Bompard off Donegal and Derry. What mattered for the United Irishmen was popular belief in Ireland that the landing of a substantial French force would eventually occur. This factor, irrespective of real conditions on the ground, was sufficient to encourage Robert Emmet and his comrades to work towards ultimate victory.[126]

The Dublin United Irish committees – which had decided against a city uprising during the French campaign in August and September – met in its aftermath to consider their next move. Such consultations did not always pass off without incident and on 7 October 1798 a thirty-strong meeting of 'journeymen, slaters, plasterers, shoemakers and ribbon weavers' was seized at Dwyer's in South Earl Street. Many of the participants had evidently migrated to the city from south Leinster and were drawn from the social tier which responded with the greatest vigour to Emmet's plans in 1803. The men were reputedly placed on a prison tender to await transportation or conscription. Major Swan compiled a list of over 200 untried men on the 'croppy ships' in the first week in October who were permitted to be 'turned loose to any regiment who will take them'.[127] Release from the tenders often entailed a one-way trip to the West Indies, although United Irishmen in uniform were stationed in Newfoundland, Guernsey and the Cape by 1800 and several who fought against the French in North Africa prior to 1802 participated in the Rising of 1803. Their conscription was resented by those who evaded detection.[128] The survivors in Dublin persevered, as evidenced by the discovery of arms and ammunition in a cart of provisions on Macartney Bridge.[129] Sproule reported to the Castle on the 7th that Francis McMahon, although returned from the mountains, was meeting O'Hara almost every night in Thomas Street and it seems that the most capable and militant Dublin United Irishmen had not given up hope.[130]

Another committee of 'active citizens' was raided on 14 October in Kevin Street as they prepared intelligence for the use of insurgents in Wicklow. They were possibly the adherents of Baird, Wright and

Emmet. An ailing Holt, the most likely candidate for such information, visited Dublin on the 16th and spent the night in a Francis Street cellar, despite having a bounty of £300 on his head. Fear of discovery forced him to lodge briefly on Plunket Street with Neil, who shortly afterwards defected to Sirr's staff in the Castle.[131] In his absence Michael Dwyer's men burned several houses owned by Rathdrum cavalrymen in reprisal for the acquittal in Dublin of their yeoman colleague who had been arrested for the summary execution of a pardoned rebel in Killincarraig. Holt was probably drawn to Dublin by an important gathering of city leaders at Wright's house in Great Ship Street on the 15th when McMahon, Shaw and Burke met to debate strategy. Account was taken of the latest news from France and the fresh demonstrations of British naval strength off the north coast of Ulster. Subordinate leaders awaited their deliberations with great interest. A spy reported that the delegates contemplated mounting 'one desperate attempt' in Dublin during the winter when security had lapsed, but little, if anything, was done to bring this about.[132] Instead, it was resolved that 'all sh[oul]d be over & not to act without the French or till the English troops are recalled'.[133] Wright also attended a meeting at Mahon's of Merchants Quay which drew a separate coterie together that reached similar conclusions. William Myler, a prime source for Higgins vis-à-vis low-level committees, spoke of the 'lamentable consternation they have been thrown into by the defeat of the French'.[134]

While Holt continued to wage a low-intensity struggle in Wicklow for several more weeks, the Dubliners who had often fought along-side him since the first days of the Rebellion were no longer available. A final decision seems to have been taken on 4 November 1798, 'the great night of deliberation'. On that occasion 'Holt's party' came together off Thomas Street, McMahon's officers met at O'Hara's home, 32 West New Row, Thomas Street, while Zachariah Shaw's group assembled at the Elephant Inn on Eustace Street. Sproule's agent informed him that 'they now conduct things with such secrecy as none but 2 men of themselves know of the meeting till they are brought to the spot'. The oft-wounded Holt was unwilling to continue fighting under the circumstances. Having dismissed the bulk of his followers at Ballylow, Holt accepted terms of surrender from Lord Powerscourt on 10 November. He was transported to New South Wales as a freeman on the *Minerva* in August 1799 where he was later reunited with several comrades who fought with Robert Emmet. Holt's demise brought an end to large-scale coordinated resistance in the Rebellion of 1798 and obliged the United Irish leadership to consider alternative strategies of advancing their cause.[135]

The sense that a new juncture had been reached for Irish republicans was grimly underlined by the death of Wolfe Tone in the Provost Marshalsea on 19 November 1798. Tried for high treason in the Royal Barracks on the 10th, and gravely injured by a self-inflicted wound to the neck the following day, the passing of Tone removed a key United Irishman from the revolutionary equation. Another popular and respected leader, Oliver Bond, had died in mysterious but apparently natural circumstances in Newgate on 6 September. While hardly creating a vacuum, the sudden demise of the single most important link with France and the linchpin of pre-Rebellion Dublin radicalism were far greater blows than the spate of state executions in July that claimed the lives of mid-ranking leaders. Both losses personally affected Addis Emmet. He had also come to realise that the state prisoners would not be permitted to emigrate to 'Germany' as previously intimated owing to government distrust of their long-term intentions. The opposition of US President John Adams to receiving Irish subversives virtually assured their confinement until the cessation of the Anglo-French war.[136] Indeed, on 10 October several Frenchmen deported on the instructions of Adams arrived in Bordeaux.[137]

While Robert Emmet's whereabouts at this time are unknown it is very likely that he was one of those consulted on the way forward. Reports of his activities in early 1799 indicate a level of authority which could not have developed in a short period and probably stretched back to August 1798. The future of the United Irishmen after the Rebellion rested on two major factors: the capacity of the organisation to regenerate its command structure and the ability of its agents to convince the French that an Irish campaign should be mounted. Arising from his Rebellion experiences Robert Emmet had become integral to the advancement of both strategies.

CHAPTER FOUR

Revival and Crisis, 1799

The new year of 1799 brought increased opportunities and challenges for the Emmets. Uppermost on the minds of most politically aware families in January 1799 was the prospect of legislative union being enacted between Britain and Ireland. Madden, drawing on John Patten's insight, claimed that Robert Emmet secretly attended debates at College Green on the Act of Union, discussions which drew to an acrimonious close in June 1800. The Emmets were by no means sympathetic towards the bastions of Protestant Ascendancy and state repression yet were prepared to brave the dangers pertaining to the adoption of an anti-government position on the issue. They were stirred by the mooted abolition of Ireland's only national political forum which, although flawed and undemocratic, was the same institution that the Patriots had influenced in the 1780s. In time of peace and under a progressive Viceroy, it could be argued that College Green might deliver on parts of the stalled liberal agenda that the Rebellion had proved was urgently needed. This was certainly the hope of several prominent pro-reformers who sympathised with the cause of the United Irishmen whilst deploring their methods.[1]

Denys Scully, stalwart of the Catholic Committee from 1804, was on close terms with the Emmets during their period of turmoil in 1798–99. Sharing their Tipperary and Limerick family background, Scully progressed from Trinity College, Cambridge, to the Irish Bar in late 1798. He lived in the capital on Suffolk Street and was the source of information on the Emmet family for a circle of socially privileged families of their acquaintance. These included the closely related Moiras and Mount Cashells and Lord and Lady Granard. All were displeased by the imminent prospect of legislative union and in early 1799 exchanged information, pamphlets and opinions on the matter with the extended Emmet family at Casino, Milltown. The loose network based around Milltown included Robert Emmet's sister, Mary Anne, and her secret fiancé, Robert Holmes, with whom Scully had served in the Lawyer's yeomanry and encountered at the Bar.

Jane and John Patten were also part of the group.[2] The families had
to be very careful in their political intrigue as, notwithstanding the
appointment of progressive viceroys Cornwallis and Hardwicke in
succession to the reactionary Camden, accusations of sedition risked
severe penalties after the Rebellion. Holmes, briefly imprisoned by
Lord Kilwarden in 1798, had been shot at by an over zealous guard.
Scully's conservative enemies, furthermore, were quick to accuse him
of having incited and led agrarian insurgents in the 1780s when his
pro-Catholic and anti-Union pamphlets were circulated in 1803.[3]

In late January 1799 Revd John Murphy forwarded Scully a confidential document addressed to Mary Anne Emmet by Margaret King,
who was known as Lady Mount Cashell after marriage to Lord
Stephen Moore, 2nd Earl Mount Cashell. The two women were
jointly interested in the life and legacy of Mary Wollstonecraft, whose
strident republicanism was clearly evident in her far-sighted and
provocative 1792 publication *A Vindication of the Rights of Woman*.
Wollstonecraft had been employed as King's Governess in 1787–88
and inculcated her charge with many of her radical opinions. The
accord which grew between student and pupil just prior to the French
Revolution laid the basis for long-term cordial relations. This
friendship terminated in tragic circumstances in September 1797
when Wollstonecraft died within ten days of giving birth to a daughter,
who, as the adult Mary Shelley, introduced the story of Frankenstein to
the English-speaking world.[4] By 1800 Wollstonecraft's equally progressive and more famous widower, the proto-anarchist philosopher
William Godwin, was also friendly with Mary Anne Emmet. He shared
an independent link with her through their mutual associate William
Drennan and, when visiting Ireland, sought his company. Robert
Emmet's familiarity with Godwin's writings as a student may have been
inspired in part by previous contact between the author and his family.
Revd Murphy regarded Mary Anne Emmet in early 1799 as an 'interesting and invaluable friend' and she was evidently a respected member
of a discreet circle of disaffected liberal intellectuals.[5]

THE ACT OF UNION

The timing of the Mount Cashell communication, probably written
at Moore Park, Kilworth, Cork, indicates that its contents referred to
the impending Union vote at College Green. Earl Mount Cashell was
one of twelve peers to vote against the motion on 22–23 January 1799
in the House of Lords. This contributed to the narrow defeat of the

various pro-Union motions and amendments in both Houses. The realisation that the sensitive enclosure had been compromised, despite apparently elaborate security precautions, alarmed Revd Murphy, who had a large measure of self-interest in this matter. The clergyman's perceived indiscretion in travelling to England with Lady Pamela Fitzgerald in 1798 had resulted in his ignominious removal from the chaplaincy of Dublin's Magdalene Church. She had been a guest in Moira House, Usher's Island, in May 1798 when her notorious husband was the most wanted man in Ireland. He had also known Lady Mount Cashell and, very probably, both Mary Anne and Jane Emmet née Patten. Mount Cashell House, the city residence of the earl's family, was conveniently located close to that of the Emmets on Stephen's Green.

The women were also near neighbours of the Fitzgeralds in 1798 and members of the extended Emmet family with whom Lord Edward had social and political associations in the advent of the Rebellion. Fitzgerald, of course, had operated at the highest levels of United Irish subversion with Thomas Addis Emmet until the spring of 1798, when Robert Emmet was engaged in a more modest capacity. From mid 1798, however, the younger man numbered Fitzgerald's former assistants, Palmer, Lawless, Long and Farrell, if not also Walter Cox, amongst his colleagues. By the winter of 1798–99, when Mary Anne Emmet's social and political links to the Fitzgeralds evidently remained strong, her younger brother was a leading member of the United Irish revivalist clique.

Murphy wrote to Scully on the day of the first Union clash to voice his concern for the welfare of Jane Emmet, who remained under voluntary confinement in Kilmainham with her husband. It was widely held that the Union controversy would ignite public discontent that might elicit reprisals from the city garrison. Indiscriminate slaughter of those out of favour with the government could not be ruled out given the atrocious behaviour of the army in south Leinster and north Connacht between May and September 1798. The clergyman's fears, nonetheless, were largely misplaced. Popular disinterest in the fate of the Ascendancy parliament, heavy winter rain and an oppressive security presence combined to ensure that no harm befell imprisoned United Irishmen and their dependents. On 21 January 1799, however, Sir William Worthington, commanding officer of the Liberty Rangers, reviewed his corps when they substituted the regimental colours for a standard inscribed 'For our King and Constitution of Ireland'. Within days of this peaceful protest several men were reputedly shot by the garrison after a public anti-Union demonstration was joined by aggravated United Irishmen who began breaking windows. The political complexion of the Rangers was overwhelmingly loyalist by 1803 when they clashed with Emmet's followers in the Coombe.[6]

Ultra-conservative opponents of union with whom the Emmets shared no other strand of political ideology were similarly unsettled by the perceived likelihood of violence. They expected yeomen, Orangemen and other plebeian anti-Unionists to ferment disorder. Ironically, when armed conflict finally encroached on the streets of Dublin in July 1803, it was primarily attributed to the one Emmet whose name and circumstances were kept out of the Scully corre-spondence: Robert Emmet. By then the Mount Cashell family had made or renewed contact with him when visiting the Continent in 1802 and Scully's allegiances had passed into the camp of their opponents.[7]

A more immediate source of hazard for the Milltown group was the furore which greeted the January 1799 publication of *A demonstration of the necessity of a legislative union of Great Britain and Ireland involving a refutation of every argument that has been or can be urged against the measure*. Ostensibly the pro-Union musings of 'Philosopher', as Robert Holmes was credited, the pamphlet was quickly identified as subversive in character owing to such content as the exhortation: 'LET NO COUNTRY SUBMIT TO BE A PROVINCE WHICH HAS STRENGTH TO BE A NATION'. Although reputedly suppressed by the Castle, the inclination and ability of the government to do so is unproven and the pamphlet enjoyed at least limited circulation. Lady Granard professed her difficulty in laying her hands on a copy, or, more probably, being seen to do so, and requested that Scully obtain one for her 'at Milltown'. It would appear that Casino was then regarded, along with Moira House, Dublin, as a centre of anti-unionist sentiment. Such attention undoubtedly encouraged Robert Emmet to carefully maintain his various bolt-holes and tunnels.[8]

Thomas Addis Emmet may also have been placed in jeopardy by unfounded assumptions that he was 'Philosopher'. From mid-January he had been denied correspondence, exercise and visitation privileges in Kilmainham. A copy of the pamphlet had been found during a search of his cell and to suspicions that he was its author were added allegations that he had assisted Arthur O'Connor in writing a letter that Castlereagh deemed offensive. Elizabeth Emmet sought an inter-view with Marsden on 27 February to refute both stories, which she presumed accounted for the sudden privations he encountered in jail. She explained to her acquaintance Thomas Ellis, whom she wished to intervene with Marsden, that 'O'Connor . . . has never at any time, consulted any man upon his publications' and that the pamphlet was sent to him by a friend. The strictness of the new regime, however, also owed much to the secrecy surrounding government plans to intern the state prisoners in Scotland.[9] Ellis, a Dublin barrister, was probably an acquaintance of Holmes. While Mrs Emmet evidently understood he could access the Castle administration, she was almost certainly unaware of his secret service function, which, in 1803, extended to dealing with Walter Cox as a means of spying on her son's United Irish associates.[10]

Madden ascertained that Mary Anne Emmet authored the noted pamphlet published in early 1799 as *An Address to the People of Ireland, showing them why they ought to submit to an Union*. The work condemned John Claudius Beresford, John Foster and other leading conservative politicians for their invocation of patriotic motives in justifying their opposition to union. The convoluted logic and strong tone of the pamphlet marked it as one of the most eccentric contributions to the Union debate in print. It may have been pertinent that Beresford and Foster belonged to the political elite that had overseen coercion in the 1790s, sponsored the Union, imprisoned one of her brothers and made the other a fugitive. If actually written by Mary Anne Emmet, the influence of Holmes, whom she secretly married in September 1799, and that of Robert Emmet, may be suspected. By the same token, the possible impact of her well-informed opinions on the two men must also be considered.[11] Robert Emmet certainly held very strong views on the Union and its possible effect on discouraging the French from invading Ireland on behalf of the United Irishmen. In September 1800 he signed his name to a memorial submitted to the French government which insisted that 'the English union has in no way eased the discontent of Ireland . . . the silence of that part of the Nation, in the mind of which the oppression of six hundred years has excited an unfailing hatred against the name of England, has been but the silence of politics, under a state of persecution, or the silence of the greatest nonchalance for an event which it deems to be in no way connected to that which it regards as ardently as ever – revolution'.[12]

Mary Anne Emmet was keenly aware that her surname alone invited Castle interest. As Drennan learned, the September 1799 match was concealed from the public owing to fears that 'such a connection' with the Emmets would exacerbate the trouble Holmes had brought upon himself for resigning from and criticising the Lawyer's yeomanry. In March 1800 Mary Anne alternated her nights between her husband's cell in Newgate, where he was held for six months, and her father's home at Casino. This was not the type of company the upwardly mobile Scully wished to keep and the dearth of references to the Emmets in his subsequent correspondence indicates that he withdrew from their circle. The Granards and Moiras remained well informed of Emmet family affairs and in October 1800 raised the fate of Addis Emmet and other prisoners held at Fort George in their letters.[13]

The backdrop to the Union was a deteriorating security situation in which anti-state violence reached a geographic extent it failed to attain during the Rebellion. Many protagonists, moreover, believed that the worst had yet to come. In January 1799 Denis O'Neil, a rebel officer who had fought to the bitter end with Holt in south Leinster before escaping abroad, informed the French Directory that the United Irishmen were 'ready on the first opportunity to support the banners of liberty'. While this optimism may have been well founded, there was no republican body capable of coordinating a national rising. This was particularly serious in Dublin city where prospective revolutionaries would have to act with great speed and purpose to have any chance of overcoming the garrison. It was to address this fundamental failing that efforts were made in the first month of 1799 to re-establish an authoritative United Irish Executive Directory in Dublin. Its members were drawn from the slew of city committees and trusted individuals who had proved their dedication in 1798, particularly former associates of Lord Edward Fitzgerald.[14]

THE EXECUTIVE DIRECTORY

The state prisoners anticipating exile on the Continent encouraged the project, with Arthur O'Connor and Thomas Russell proving particularly enthusiastic. Their seeming compliance with government parliamentary investigations in July/August 1798 had never been more than a stalling tactic and they had nothing to lose by further agitation. Robert Emmet's candidacy for co-option to high command was strong in early 1799 and was presumably supported by his influential brother, Addis Emmet. The younger Emmet's record of reliability prior to and during 1798 would have boosted his standing and he was one of the few members of the reformed Executive on close personal terms with the majority of the original incumbents. Another able, if less known activist, Henry Baird of Kevin Street, had served as secretary to the Leinster Provincial Directory in succession to John McCann after the March 1798 arrests. Baird's grouping had first attempted to replace the imprisoned high command in late August of that year when Humbert's expeditionary corps was on Irish soil. In all likelihood, it was Baird who convened the Kevin Street meeting that sought to recruit Robert Emmet at that time.[15] Emmet, in a rare security lapse, was the unwitting source of information obtained by the Castle on the more successful United Irish revival of January 1799. On 2 February James McGucken of Belfast, legal advisor to the Ulster Directory and a double agent since August 1798, reported that he had

> conversed with [Thomas Addis] Emmett[']s [sic] brother [Robert] who told him means were taking [sic] to form a new Committee & Executive in Dublin, that the plan was the appointment of colonels in each county who were to form their regiments secretly but no committees to be appointed. Emmet mentioned Wright the surgeon & [Con] McLoughlin [sic] of Usher's Island as two of the present leaders in Dublin.[16]

Many other names were subsequently added to the profile of the two-tier city leadership and their contacts in the provinces. Other than warning that the process was not only underway but advanced, the most important details gleaned by McGucken were the names of Wright and McLaughlin as members of the 'inactive' transitional Executive. This provided the Castle with the first inkling that survivors of the military committee which operated under Fitzgerald from February to May 1798 were assuming control of the entire republican movement. Emmet confirmed that the new committee, with the coop-eration of both the interim and imprisoned leadership, was putting the venture on a firmer footing. McGucken met Robert Emmet – along with O'Hanlon – once again on 6 February 1799. He learned from them that the new Executive would select three or four 'military men' per county as adjutant-generals, who would personally recruit their subordinate officers. More alarming for the Castle was the claim that three Dublin divisions were 'completely officered', albeit poorly equipped, and that the Rotunda was lagging behind. Their task was to prepare the ground for a revolution in a city with over 180,000 residents, or at very least, the officer cadre who would command republican elements during a French invasion crisis.[17]

The recreated Executive was evidently completed on 11 February 1799 when it allegedly consisted of 'old members' Wright and McLaughlin plus '[Robert] Emmet jun[io]r, [Hugh] O'Hanlon & George Teeling'. O'Hanlon, a veteran of the Spanish army's Irish Brigade and the previous summer's fighting in Wicklow, advanced to national-level leadership in early 1799. He worked out of lodgings with his brother-in-law, Michael Byrne, at 10 Eustace Street. George or John Palmer, an associate of Lord Edward Fitzgerald, was also promoted, as were two other Fitzgerald aides, James Farrell and the redoubtable William Putnam McCabe. They brought a wealth of experience in clandestine affairs to the new leadership. Like Emmet, Farrell and McCabe had assisted the state prisoners during the July 1798 pact negotiations and consequently trusted each other's capabilities. McLaughlin, furthermore, had arranged for the publication of the controversial August 1798 letter in which Addis Emmet et al. had contradicted the government's account of its dealings with the prisoners. News that Palmer and McCabe had gone secretly to London ahead of their illegal crossing to Paris, was relayed to Thomas Russell in Newgate in January 1799. Russell was the natural sponsor of the re-organisation and evidently followed its progress with great interest until 1803.[18]

The new Executive comprised, for all intents and purposes, secondary leaders promoted to positions of influence in a manner reminiscent of that in which the original had come into being in 1796. All were men of action: Farrell, seized by Sirr on 18 December 1798 in possession of weaponry and seditious documents, had only been released from Newgate in February 1799.[19] His colleague, Patrick Gallagher, was another ex-Fitzgerald assistant and freemason. After various adventures during the Rebellion, Gallagher had emancipated himself from a prison tender in Ringsend in December 1798 when awaiting transportation to New South Wales. His wife had called to see him in a row boat and passed him the end of a rope used to pull him to shore after her departure.[20] Gallagher was well regarded in the United Irish stronghold of 'James St & Tho[ma]s St' and reputedly never slept two nights in one place until he went to the Continent. He made a fleeting visit to Dublin in the autumn of 1801 and undoubtedly reported his impressions of the United Irish community to his close friend Robert Emmet upon returning to Paris. George Wilkinson of 32 Queen Street and Quinn, who had been 'in the American service', were more obscure and junior associates in 1799. Quinn had fought with Francis McMahon during the early months of the Rebellion and, like Colonel John Doyle of Plunket Street, managed to slip back into his former peaceful pursuits without arousing serious interest from the Castle.[21] Wilkinson, an 'old offender', was an associate of McCabe who travelled through London to Paris in early 1799.[22]

George Teeling could have entertained no illusions as to the seriousness of his commitment in view of the execution at Arbour Hill of his brother, Bartholomew, on 24 September 1798. Captured at Ballinamuck in the uniform of a French army officer, the elder Teeling's commission had been disregarded by the military tribunal, which also prevented him from delivering a prepared speech. Emmet's contact with Teeling may have inspired him to write 'Arbour Hill', which was published in March 1799. The poem commenced with the line 'No rising column marks the spot' which was equally applicable to the grave in which its author was laid in 1803. When Emmet was confronted with similar hostility at his own trial he doggedly persevered with a speech which included instructions as to how he was to be memorialised.[23] George Teeling hailed from his family's Antrim heartland of Lisburn but lived in Dublin's Lurgan Street, near the Linen Hall, during the Rebellion period. He had facilitated contact between Arthur O'Connor and northern United Irishmen prior to 1798 and was evidently called on to resurrect inter-provincial communications. Dr Christopher Teeling of 35 Great Ship Street, uncle of the younger Teelings in Dublin, was also deemed to be disaffected.[24]

After the Rebellion another Teeling brother, Charles, operated a linen bleaching operation at the Naul on the Meath/Dublin borderlands, which employed James Hope of Templepatrick from 1799 until 1802. Hope, a spinner and weaver by trade, had fought at the Battle of Antrim in June 1798 and, aided by the Palmers of Cutpurse Row, had eluded Sirr's men when a fugitive in Dublin. The Palmers, in turn, were close friends of Gallagher, a leader in their city neighbourhood, and hid him in their family home prior to his escape to France. The Teelings had been to the fore in promoting Defender–United Irish links in the mid 1790s and, as such, it is not surprising that Charles and George Teeling and Hope, a committed proto-socialist, were jointly engaged in the 1803 plot along with Gallagher and the Palmers. The Teelings also connected Bernard Coile and William Todd Jones, influential Armagh-born radicals, to the Emmet circle in 1802. Pre-eminent amongst their associates in exile were Alexander Lowry and Richard McCormick, men whose endorsement in the political clubs of Hamburg and Paris would have carried much weight. Bonds flowing from United Irish membership, strengthened immeasurably by the experience of the Rebellion, contributed much to the formation of the leadership networks that enabled the Rising of 1803 to attain potentially formidable proportions.[25]

The near-simultaneous rise to prominence of so many Dublin-based United Irishmen confused Dublin Castle's intelligence operators. On 5 February 1799 a well-placed source reported, '[Richard] D[illon], arrested at Oliver Bond's, but now at large, is a member of the new Executive Committee lately chosen in Dublin'. This added the name of a known conspirator and a bailed state prisoner, whose interests had escaped McGucken's notice, to those of McLaughlin and Wright. Dillon's politics resulted in his expulsion from the Guild of Merchants but he still operated a major wholesale linen drapery at 16 Lower Bridge Street. There was also a reference to 'McCabe, P of Dublin' which, if meant for Patrick McCabe of Francis Street rather than Putnam McCabe of Belfast would be highly significant given his leading role in the Rising of 1803. The same spy was on more certain ground when naming '[Charles] O'H[ara], of Antrim, now a merchant in Dublin' as a 'great patron of United Irishmen'. O'Hara and Wright had collaborated from 1791 and their engagement represented a logical extension of machinations during the 1798 Rebellion. Their involvement conferred the new grouping with the legitimacy of continuity, something the imprisoned higher leadership could not do in person. This was further enhanced by the emergence of members of the Emmet, Teeling, Palmer and Lawless families, whose older brothers and near relatives were already men of high standing in the United Irishmen.[26]

Consultation between the new leadership and the state prisoners was carried out through Baird, the reputed 'instrument' of the imprisoned commanders. Baird worked as a clerk at Halpin and Hannan's Distillery and moved from Kevin Street to Paradise Row, close to the lodgings of emissary James Farrell. His employers were known to Ned Byrne of Ballymanus and regularly donated a portion of their profits to the United Irishmen. Baird was evidently a significant figure in the city United Irishmen who had known Fitzgerald and attended a meeting of United Irish colonels in the city just prior to the outbreak of rebellion in May 1798.[27] Baird remained in contact in 1799 with an alleged member of the 'old Directory', Counsellor Edward Lawson, whose interest in 'military studies' and seniority in the movement had largely escaped Castle scrutiny, barring his brief imprisonment in 1798. Lawson, Emmet, Baird and O'Hanlon, moreover, were known to have conferred in College Green in February 1799, although it is unclear how committed Lawson subsequently remained given his relative anonymity in extant Castle intelligence up to 1803.[28] Lawson fought a non-fatal duel with Wright in late 1801 over allegations of 'disloyalty to the cause' and may have withdrawn from the inner circle at that time.[29] Although a qualified barrister from 1793, Lawson's political allegiances apparently incurred professional sanctions which hastened his descent from the 'Directory' to 'poverty'.[30] Wright retained the confidence of many city United Irishmen and associated with William Myler and the sub-grouping of radical professionals which met at Mahon's of Merchants Quay.[31]

Baird passed directions from the state prisoners to a Michael or Thomas Doyle, a printer based in England, who arrived in Dublin in early 1799 bringing cards commemorating the June 1798 execution of Fr Coigley in Kent. Coigley had joined the select ranks of republican martyrs whose sacrifices had hitherto proved inspirational. That his death had occurred in England interested United Irishmen living in that country and provided them with a role in post-Rebellion propaganda designed as much for agitation as commemoration. Doyle stayed with his brother in Chancery Lane when in Dublin and frequently travelled between Ireland and England, where a number of important United Irishmen had settled by 1799. They included Valentine Lawless, John Binns and Major James Plunkett and, more briefly, senior veteran officers of the Leinster rebellion: William Aylmer of Kildare, Garret Byrne of Wicklow and Edward Fitzgerald of Wexford. Given their involuntary status as distrusted transients, contact with the more junior but largely hidden United Irish communities of London and Manchester was more important. The London grouping numbered John Russell, brother of Thomas, as well as Pat Finney and John MacNamara, whom Addis Emmet had represented in January 1798.[32]

Doyle's association with Binns and their joint participation with the United Britons hastened moves to suppress republican activities in Britain in March 1799. He remained an occasional courier of men and material across the Irish Sea until late 1803 and was consequently one of several human links between the 1799 resurgence and the Emmet conspiracy four years later. Valentine Lawless was another. He employed Emmet's close friend Richard Curran in London in February 1799, who reputedly declined an invitation to participate in United Irish plans. More importantly, Lawless was in contact with William Dowdall in April 1799. He had been the last proprietor of the *Press* and played a leading role in both the Despard plot of 1802 and the Dublin Rising of 1803. Philip Lawless, brother of the self-exiled Surgeon William Lawless, was also a United Irishman of note.[33]

John Allen was one of the few compromised United Irishmen who dared to travel from England to Ireland in the uncertain times of

1799. He had been acquitted of treason at the Maidstone trial that sent Fr Coigley to a Kent gallows and was working as a woollen draper at 36 College Green, Dublin, in the spring of 1799. No charges were brought against him pertaining to his alleged involvement in the killing of a loyalist in Kevin Street in January 1798. Allen very probably hosted the College Green meeting in February 1799 attended by Baird, Emmet, O'Hanlon and several others. He was, at the very least, on the fringes of the post-Rebellion leadership and central to the events of 1803. This mirrored the profile of his fellow merchant and United Irish comrade Philip Long, who was coyly described as being 'near the Ex[ecutive]' in 1799. The seemingly unqualified support afterwards offered to Emmet by Allen and Long transpired to be critical to his resumption of authority in Dublin in October 1802 upon returning from a lengthy absence on the Continent. This was predicated on the earlier discretion practised by Long and Allen that enabled them to withstand the crackdown which largely contained the 1799 revival.[34]

Allen, Long and Dowdall represented the third distinct strand of the post-Rebellion republican leadership: membership of the pre-1798 Donnybrook Hurlers Club. This quasi-masonic society-within-a-society numbered a disproportionate number of wealthy and influential United Irishmen, many of whom were gradually revealed as such when the more exposed upper leadership tier was swept away by the coercion of 1798. All three possessed money, the ability to travel and reputations for reliability. This accounted to a large degree for their status amongst the Dublin city United Irishmen of 1799–1803 and their intermittent contact with the United Britons. The pre-April 1798 'collegians' of Trinity were a similarly elite cell, although Robert Emmet was the only prominent member to remain active in the capital after the Visitation and the Rebellion. In 1799 positions of leadership had to be earned by merit and retained by good conduct as they could no longer be obtained through democratic advancement in the Society. By the same token, it was difficult for rising men to prove themselves. More than ever, the United Irish leadership comprised the amalgamation of intimate circles of veteran activists. When it is considered that ex-Hurlers James Alleyburn, David Fitzgerald, John Madden and Michael Meighan also surfaced as conspirators in 1803, it is evident that the Donnybrook network, allied to the remnants of the pre-Rebellion committees and the Fitzgerald group, merged to comprise a secure backbone of leadership in the capital.[35]

McGucken ascertained when visiting his United Irish friends in Kilmainham in early February 1799 that the prospective leaders in the counties included James Reilly in Westmeath, Francis O'Flaherty in Connacht and one Watson in Down. Bagenal Harvey's third in command during the Rebellion was evidently destined to take a leading part in Wexford. James Hope, furthermore, was identified as a northern delegate.[36] Hope allegedly renewed his links with Robert Henry, Robert Robinson, John Henderson and other friends in Antrim and Down. Armagh United Irishmen, Jackson of the county town and Wilson of Keady, were reportedly present in Dublin in early February 1799 when selected to command in their strategically critical county. They were joined by the highly respected Donaldson 'of the Fews' (south Armagh), a probable former member of the Ulster Directory. McGucken, expected to assist in communicating with such Ulstermen, discovered that 'Henry, a Presbyterian clergyman, a young man, will act for Monaghan'.[37] His information also implicated Tyrone Quaker John Shaw and Revd Wilson of Creeve, Monaghan, whose input testified to the failure of sectarian propaganda during the Rebellion to deter all non-Catholic northern United Irishmen. The Presbyterians of Keady subsequently astounded their synod and the government in late 1802 by inviting the notorious Revd William Steel Dickson to minister their congregation. In 1799 Revd Stawell (aka Stowell) was deputed by the Dublin leaders to bring the new system to Cork, where the fresh stirrings of suspected United Irish leaders gave superficial weight to rumours of an uprising in the city in April of that year.[38]

The post-Rebellion United Irish leaders differed from the state prisoners in that they were unelected, financially unsupported and unaccountable to their subordinates. Indeed, they had no subordinates as the co-option of the rank and file was only envisaged during or just before a French invasion. Formerly routine duties of electing officers, paying dues and obtaining weapons were discarded as being neither prudent nor necessary. The new strategy was to build a streamlined, more secretive movement around a hard core of long-term initiates who kept in intermittent contact with each other by meeting at social occasions. Written communications were minimised and overt signs of organisation generally eschewed. The intention of the United Irishmen in 1799 was to remain ready but inert in key zones until a substantial French force had landed. The French were required to make good in full the armament deficiencies of their primed auxiliaries. In essence, this was a stripped-down reversion to the strategy promoted by the leadership between 1796 and March 1798 and was heavily reliant on hardened operators.[39] Security was obtained at the price of insolvency and the appearance of 'yielding to the Defender system'.[40]

The magnitude of the task faced by the new Executive in early 1799 was daunting but not insurmountable. The United Irishmen had suffered up to 30,000 fatalities in 1798 and lost thousands more to deportation, imprisonment and flight abroad, but this was a small proportion of the minimum 280,000 sworn members it possessed in the spring of 1798 and the 600,000 adherents enumerated by the government. Moreover, whole sectors of the country had been almost untouched by the Rebellion and casualties in the range of multiple thousands were confined to Wexford, Wicklow, Kildare, Carlow and Mayo and probably also to Antrim, Down, Sligo and Meath. Hundreds of rebels from Westmeath, Monaghan, Longford, Leitrim, Tipperary, King's County (Offaly), Kilkenny and County Dublin were killed and lesser numbers in Cork, Queen's County (Laois), Louth and Armagh. On paper, if not in actuality, the majority of county networks were largely intact when the major outbreaks ceased in September 1798. The influence of such an assessment on Emmet became evident in July 1803 when he issued a proclamation in the name of the Provisional Government of Ireland which asserted that nineteen counties would rise.[41]

This latent potential of the United Irishmen reflected the 1798 strategy of non-mobilisation observed by mid-ranking leaders in the midlands, Munster, Ulster and parts of Connacht. They sought to preserve their numbers and war material once it was clear that the Dublin-centred Neilson/Fitzgerald plan had failed. Indeed, the contingency of unilateral rising may never have enjoyed the support it required to become viable in the provinces; John Sheares had berated Neilson in May 1798 for entertaining 'so pernicious an enterprise'. The Ulster Directory under Robert and William Simms prohibited armed actions on 6 June 1798 in the absence of the French, even though much of Leinster was then in revolt. Henry Joy McCracken's clique disregarded the consensus and initiated a revolt in Antrim, which made good progress in the county at first and was boosted two days later by the victory of Down rebels at Saintfield. Down insurgents under Henry Munro joined those headed by McCracken, who, denied the full assistance of the Ulster Directory, were obliged to concentrate their numbers at Ballynahinch before undertaking ambitious offensive actions. The chance to attack never came, as they were decisively defeated on 12–13 June.[42]

Hervey Montmorency Morres, adjutant-general-elect for North Munster, also held back his subordinates in May 1798 to husband resources that were locally irreplaceable. He evidently favoured a prior rising in the capital and accepted command of those intended to attack military installations in Phoenix Park. This too was counter-manded. Rebels in Westmeath and Longford were only roused by the fugitive Morres in early September when Humbert's force unexpectedly turned away from Ulster towards Dublin due to the clash at Collooney. This opportunity to strike was seized, with mixed results. Major James Plunkett, another United Irishman with professional military experience, restrained the Roscommon United Irishmen under his control on the ground that the weakness of the French in the West did not warrant a full-scale turn out. He was never forgiven for this by James Hope. In effect, Simms, Morres and Plunkett preserved the cohesion of tens of thousands of United Irishmen in Munster, Ulster and Connacht who might easily have been squandered in what they believed to be a doomed war of attrition. Humbert's corps was clearly not the 'respectable French force' required by the Addis Emmet/ MacNeven faction prior to their arrest in March 1798. Public realisation that the French vanguard would not be quickly reinforced created a powerful disincentive to rise en masse.[43]

Robert Emmet, regardless of his opinion of such commanders in 1798, would have appreciated that the incidence of rebellion was unrelated to numerical strength. Leadership, timing, martial law and geography had proven critical in transforming low-level violence into popular open warfare. Pre-Rebellion coercion, in turn, was affected by such inter-related matters as the strategic importance of individual counties, the determination of their magistracy and yeomanry and the depth of politicisation. The lessons of 1798 were not lost on Emmet, who faced the challenge with other recently advanced leaders, of ensuring that the dormant and damaged United Irish networks retained sufficient cohesion and political purpose to offer meaningful assistance to the French. In the meantime, supporting the activities of politically minded rebel bands offered a means of encouraging the French to return in force.[44] The survival into 1799 of rebel groups in Wicklow, Wexford, Kildare and Carlow provided their representatives on the Continent with proof of the continued receptiveness of Ireland to invasion. Factions led by Michael Dwyer and James Corcoran were deemed 'dangerous in case of invasion' as they had the capacity to mushroom into much larger rebel concentrations close to the capital.[45] United Irish activities in 1799 were described in hindsight by Castlereagh as 'partial insurrections in different parts of the country'.[46]

THE REPUBLICAN UNDERWORLD

The list of 1,064 persons who received conditional pardons from Sirr and Swan between July and September 1798 revealed something of the extent of the republican militancy in the capital. It was, necessarily, a considerable underestimate of United Irish strength given that several hundreds in custody were ineligible to apply and hundreds more were still in the mountains. Moreover, the exercise largely concerned those who believed themselves to have been compromised to the point that their involvement in the fighting in Leinster might yet incur legal penalties. Many of those who applied were too well known to evade detection, not least William Horish, who gave his address as Pye Corner. Richard Turner, the Earl Street silk weaver, had a lower public profile but was equally notorious in the Castle. He had been jailed for seditious activities in the mid-1790s and in 1796–97 assisted James Hope and William Putnam McCabe in forging links with Wicklow republicans. Turner was re-imprisoned in Dublin in July 1798 just after bringing fifty city United Irishmen to the mountain camps of Rourke, Rattigan, McClune and Holt. Horish and Turner had no option but to avail of the best terms on offer when permitted to do so. Others, however, exposed themselves to retaliatory measures by giving their names in Exchange Alley and those who could make and service weapons were afterwards closely monitored.[47]

Blacksmiths Henry Anderson of 17 Kevin Street, Luke Crone of 35 Thomas Street, Patrick Flannery of 34 Stonybatter, James Foley of 48 High Street, James Hussey of 4 The Poddle, James Langan of Hanbury Lane, Patrick Moore of 16 Kevin Street and James Wilson of 22 Little Mary Street all confessed to being active in the Rebellion. Gunsmiths William Beggs of 48 Temple Bar, John Clinch of 29 The Coombe, John Clotworthy of 22 Mary Street and Edward Coffey of 42 Plunkett Street also received conditional pardons in 1798. Given that not one of these men practised their original trades in 1803 it is evident that the authorities moved to ruin their businesses, just as Walter Cox later alleged and spymaster Francis Higgins had urged. This was easily effected by harassment by state officials and the strict enforcement of revenue and licensing regulations. That this occurred systematically and on a comprehensive scale is further suggested by the fact that just one of nineteen publicans pardoned in September

1798 was trading in that line in 1803. Republican committeemen and armourers, therefore, paid a heavy, yet unstipulated, price for their certificates. Not all were financially destroyed: ex-publicans Thomas Dunne, Patrick Ennis, and Nicholas Stafford operated bakeries at 53 South Great George's Street, 38 Exchequer Street, and Thomas Street respectively in 1803. Stafford was then one of the most senior conspirators of the Rising that year, along with fellow bankrupt publican Patrick McCabe. Both were then jailed, as was Coffey, who was committed to the Provost on 28 July 1803. Thomas Maguaran and other innkeepers who either escaped detection or avoided Castle spies conducted business as usual.[48]

Prominent Wicklow rebels Walter Byrne of Kiloughter, John Healy of Annamoe, James Kavanagh of Roundwood and Edward Short of Keelogue (Newcastle) were living in Dublin by September 1798. Kavanagh inducted Joseph Holt into the United Irishmen in 1797 and temporarily shared a Rathdrum cell with Daniel Muley, a gunsmith involved with Robert Emmet and Thomas Russell in 1803. Samuel Judd of Cronebane, an organiser in the mines of the Avoca district in 1797–98, obscured his seditious past by giving his address as 56 New Row. None of these men were entitled to conditional pardons owing to their high status in the organisation and it must be presumed that volume of paperwork led to Healy being given a protection. He had been implicated in several killings in May/June 1798 and later rejoined the rebel faction headed by Michael Dwyer, possibly in anticipation of being found out. Healy killed state's witness James Redmond in Clara on 4 December 1799 and was sentenced to death by a Special Commission on 11 April 1800. There were at least fifteen active United Irishmen from Rathfarnham in the capital by September 1798 exclusive of their comrades from Mount Venus, Kilternan, Ballyboden, Grange and other parts of the south county. Assessing the paramilitary potential of the republicans of Dublin was clearly no easy task and was complicated by unexpected external factors.[49]

Dublin's United Irish communities were bolstered in the early months of 1799 by released prisoners, amnestied migrants and fugitive rebels who established colonies in the south city. Over 400 had been released from the Dublin Bay tenders in October 1798 and hundreds more were disgorged in the spring of the following year. Thomas, Francis and Kevin Streets were inundated with Wexford and Wicklow men who found it impossible to live in their home counties owing to the unofficial loyalist 'white terror'. South Leinster yeomanry corps, especially those which embraced the Orange Order in 1799, frequently exploited their legal indemnity to persecute amnestied United Irishmen and to attack Catholic infrastructure and clergymen. In Wicklow the Rathdrum, Newtownmountkennedy, Arklow and Donard units were responsible for murdering two priests and burning approximately eighteen Catholic chapels between September 1798 and June 1801. Wexford loyalists of the Gorey, Ballaghkeen and Wingfield corps (aka 'The Black Mob') ensured that house-burning was more prevalent and that over twenty six chapels were razed by 1802.[50] Higgins, Cooke's main informant and a frequent visitor to Bray, admitted in December 1799 that the Wicklow yeomanry 'have much to answer for. Regardless of protections granted [to] these misguided people who were concerned in the late rebellion but who have endeavoured to make some atonement by a peaceable demeanour, many of them are dreadfully harassed, taken from their homes at the dead hour of night, tied on horses and sent before a court martial who on the solitary oath of an approver (interested to save his own life) are condemned or either hanged or sent for Botany Bay.'[51]

Pluralist United Irishmen had no interest in retaliating in kind but their attacks on offending loyalists undoubtedly perpetuated the cycle of violence. Both elements carried out killings to avenge incidents that had occurred during the Rebellion. Meath, much less affected by the Rebellion and the subsequent sectarianism of Orange yeomen, did not reseed the pockets of its native Defenders and United Irishmen that had taken work and residence in the north city in the mid 1790s. The migrants of 1798–99 tended to live near each other, often engaging in the same type of labouring work and typically socialised in pubs owned by fellow countymen. James Barrett's inn on Kevin Street primarily served Wicklowmen, many of whom probably belonged to the United Irish group which met on the premises in March 1799. His Kevin Street competitor, John Lacey of Wicklow Town, was a former member of the county committee and conspired at a senior level with Emmet in 1803.[52] Francis Street publican John Butterfield hailed from Redgap, Wicklow, and was known to be 'a deep man and was a capt[ai]n in 98 in the field'. Michael Daly, in the same line on Great George's Street South, also fell under suspicion in 1799 and lost his business in consequence.[53]

Patrick McCabe of Francis Street 'gained a reputation for patriotism and bravery' in 1798 and kept an inn 'much frequented by many who had escaped to Dublin' until forced out of the trade. McCabe may have been on the Directory and his apparent intimacy with John Allen, Charles O'Hara and other leading city rebels from the pre-Rebellion period is indicative of his own high standing in the organisation. Dublin rebels also drank in Francis Street's Sun Inn, where the most senior south Leinster United Irishmen had convened in November/December 1797 to regulate the composition of the Provincial Directory. McCabe emerged as one of the leaders of the south city United Irishmen during the Rising of 1803.[54] Plunket Street publican John Doyle almost certainly also served men who had fought with Green Division companies during the Rebellion. Kildare rebel veterans tended to cluster on and around Thomas Street to take advantage of the easy access to their home county via the Canal Harbour and the roads which radiated from the west side of the city towards Palmerstown and Naas. They frequented the Thomas Street pubs run by the Dillon, Connor and Ryan families as well as Madden's of 47 Lower Bridge Street. All were owned by survivors of the fighting in Kildare and their immediate relatives. The Rourke brothers of Rathcoole, County Dublin, operated the Yellow Bottle on Thomas Street, another premises on Marlborough Street and perhaps a third on High Street.[55]

Pre-existing bonds of common politics, county loyalties and inter-marriage were reinforced by the unfamiliar phenomenon of refugee status, a novel experience for most south Leinstermen. Escaping persecution in their native counties, however, did not entail freedom from threat in the metropolis. The considerable level of Dublin support for the Rising of 1803 proved that the social and economic realities of rural life were by no means required to dispose Irishmen to revolution. Assistant Town Major Swan, who had documented the particulars of over 1,000 amnestied rebels in September 1798, persecuted the proprietors of their favourite haunts in his capacity as Inspector General of Excise and License. Swan had brought the Revenue corps yeomanry to Cusack's pub at Ely Place in April 1798, a United Irish haunt, and in March 1801 prosecuted Bryan Rourke of High Street for selling stolen wine in his Marlborough Street pub.[56] Many city rebels would have also recalled Sirr's raid on an alleged 'Dagger-Club' meeting at Dwyer's of South Earl Street in October 1798 after which thirty men were 'put on board a vessel, to be sent from this kingdom'.[57] This type of arbitrary repression merged civil and political despotism in a manner that was anathema to United Irishmen. Little had changed in 1799. Rebel migrants and the publicans who preserved the hegemony of the displaced communities were an exceptionally useful resource for the new city leadership. Emmet readily factored them into his plans in 1802–3 to the extent that one informant alleged that the Francis Street insurgents who rose in 1803 were 'principally from Wexford and Wicklow'.[58]

Prominent amongst the incoming United Irishmen in late 1798 and 1799 were rebel commanders Edward 'Ned' Byrne, William 'Billy' Byrne and John Lacey from Wicklow, Wexfordians Miles Byrne, Morgan Kavanagh and Nicholas Gray and Kildare's John Doorley and Michael Reynolds. Gray, an attorney and Secretary to the 'Council for directing the affairs of the People of the County of Wexford', acted as Bagenal Harvey's aide at the Battle of New Ross.[59] Their presence facilitated the restoration of high-level communications between the city and provinces and supplemented personal contacts developed during the Rebellion by Dubliners Rourke, McMahon, McClune and Rattigan.[60] McClune was temporarily removed from the scene in mid April when he and fifteen United Irishmen were arrested whilst meeting in Abbey Street.[61] Many of the newcomers had taken part in the second battle of Hacketstown on 25 June 1798 in which Dublin city and county forces had fought side by side with Wexford, Wicklow and Kildare rebels. They included insurgent commanders Reynolds, Dwyer and John Mathews of Tallaght, as well as Garret Byrne.[62]

Ned Byrne of Ballymanus worked as a clerk in a city distillery and retained the confidence of outstanding Wicklow rebel groups he supplied with money and gunpowder. His popular brother, William 'Billy' Byrne, was arrested on 14 May 1799 in the home of Nicholas Passmore, 6 Francis Street. Passmore, then in prison, was one of the Thomas Street committee that had sent emissaries and intelligence to Wicklow rebels under the command of William Byrne and Holt in June 1798.[63] News of Byrne's court martial and execution in Wicklow in September 1799 reached his former comrades in New South Wales. Such men would not have been pleased to learn that the drummers of the Fermanagh militia had executed thirty-one rebel prisoners in Wicklow Town in 1799. Murphy, the Hanover Lane gunsmith, Master Sweep Horish and Donnelly of Baggot Street, a building contractor who employed many ex-rebels, also assisted the Wicklowmen who fought on in the mountains and raised cash for them by soliciting donations and holding benefit auctions. 24 Patrick Street publican Thomas Maguaran harboured Dwyer during his visits to the city and participated with him in the 1803 conspiracy. Maguaran's politics, like Rourke's and Doyle's, probably rendered him vulnerable to the harassment he received from Majors Sirr and Sandys. Sympathisers and support networks were aided by the rescinding of martial law procedures in December 1798, which allowed freedom of association last enjoyed in May of that year. Dublin's yeomanry were stood down from permanent duty and guards and barriers were removed from the Liffey and canal crossings that had divided the city and hindered travel.[64]

Miles Byrne, the teenaged rebel captain from Monaseed, dared not solicit amnesty documentation which might expose him to the risk of being court-martialled. He was obliged to rely heavily on the network of contacts maintained by his step-brother Ned Kennedy. Byrne arrived in the city from Bray in mid November 1798 and stayed in Kennedy's New Street home. William Byrne had dined with Kennedy on the night of his arrest and Miles Byrne had formed part of their company the previous night. Socialising in the home of non-fugitive United Irishmen was usually safe and it seems the seizure of the Wicklow leader marked a departure, largely due to the fact that his certificate of protection was retrospectively invalidated. Miles Byrne availed of the United Irish underground by going to Lucan to stay with the recently released Fr John Barrett, who had ministered the state prisoners in Kilmainham in July 1798. Fr Barrett may have then encountered Robert Emmet. On venturing back to the city, Byrne was fortunate to avoid the notorious killer and 'active' magistrate Hunter Gowan of Mount Nebo, who was trawling Kevin Street with several 'Black Mob' yeomen looking for wanted insurgents. Byrne spent a week hiding in Maynooth while the 'Wexford and Wicklow Orangemen . . . were generally seen parading the streets' of Dublin. When this died down Byrne reappeared and assembled a gang of workers in similar circumstances to carry out contracts for his brother.[65]

Two Wicklow insurgents, Henry Downes and Patrick Barry, used knives to fend off Sirr's men when confronted in early 1799 at the carman's stage in Francis Street. Barry stabbed one of the Castle employees and escaped whereas Downes was captured and court-martialled on 2 April 1799. He was prosecuted by Sirr's employee John Neil, a former comrade in arms, and executed. His life and death were immediately commemorated in a popular rebel song bearing his name. Barry joined the 54th Regiment under an assumed identity and was killed fighting the French in Egypt.[66] François Joseph, a French soldier who landed in Mayo with Humbert and afterwards fought as an officer with Holt in Wicklow, was arrested by Sirr in Ormond Market on 27 April 1799. Joseph had found on arriving in the city that his former associates in the mountains were 'very glad' to see him but could not offer effective protection.[67] Another noted

Wicklow rebel, Hugh 'Vesty' Byrne of Kirikee (Glenmalure), was seized at his father-in-law's house in Charles Street in late June or early July 1799. Byrne was Dwyer's first cousin and, although sentenced to death on 14 November 1799, lived to conspire with Emmet four years later by escaping from Wicklow Gaol in February 1800.[68] Incredibly, Barney Colligan, the King's County militia defector who commanded a section of Holt's substantial mainforce in the autumn of 1798, managed to avoid being recognised and shot after settling in Dublin. There were probably many such stories to keep the fugitive city migrants in a perpetual state of tension.[69]

The gradually improving political atmosphere in the capital in mid-to-late 1799 enabled Fr Barrett to return to his Francis Street chapel, where he resumed his position as a trusted intimate of the rebel fugitives. Byrne became acquainted with Ned Byrne of Ballymanus, who introduced him to Daniel Maguire of 34 Francis Street, an extensive merchant and ship owner, who had visited Garret Byrne and other United Irishmen living in Hamburg. Maguire had been Castledermot's delegate to the Catholic Convention in 1792 and in mid-1801 was accused of holding a meeting of United Irishmen at his Bloomfield country house. Miles Byrne and Ned Kennedy functioned as the the hub of a transplanted Monaseed/Ballyellis insurgent group that lived and worked in and around Kevin Street. This clique was positioned not only within the south city United Irish stratum but had access to allies in adjacent counties. Owing to the cooperation of Maguire and others it was even possible to send messages to the international Irish republican community. Contact with their home county was maintained by using the carmen and carters who worked the Wexford route, as well as by frequenting rebel pubs where visiting friends could obtain directions to ex-comrades in the city. These ready-made cells of veterans slotted neatly into the street- and district-oriented Dublin organisation and proved more difficult to penetrate than pre-Rebellion societies. In many respects the internal dynamics and methodology of these elements more closely resembled Defender lodges and the independent radical societies of 1795–96 than the formally regulated United Irish societies of 1797–98.[70]

Maguire was a link between the street committees and the more socially privileged United Irishmen; his circle included prominent men such as James Dixon, Ambrose Moore and Nicholas Gray. Moore, in turn, was 'intimate' with John Russell of 11 Russell Place (Mountjoy Square), a large and prosperous contractor who had been implicated in 1798.[71] Ned Byrne, Maguire's Wicklow associate, was one of the

key city-based 'collectors . . . for the support of the United Irishmen'
and allegedly coordinated the donations from distillers Halpin and
Hannan, David Hinchey, Laurence Nihills and John and George
Edwards. It is likely that Philip Lawless, a brewer at 6 Warren's Mount,
Mill Street, also contributed given that he was a United Irishman and
brother of the Paris-based Surgeon Lawless. The pooling of resources
provided limited funds for the dependents of prisoners, select fighting
groups and United Irish projects. Most importantly, the periodic
availability of cash grants from the elite members eliminated the
innumerable difficulties attending the collection, protection and
disbursement of the pre-Rebellion subscription levies. The post-
Rebellion Dublin city United Irishmen, therefore, had lateral and
hierarchical command structures, comparative internal security,
reasonable finances and an extensive communications capacity.[72]

RESISTANCE

The chronic state of much of south Leinster offered reassurance to the
United Irish leadership and to the French that the republican cause
retained appeal. Wicklow factions headed by Dwyer, James Hughes,
Michael Dalton, William Pluck, James Ryder and John Mernagh
remained potent into late 1799. Dwyer's men, closely allied to
Mernagh's group in Glenmalure, were the best known of several rebel
groups whose resistance to authority spanned the period intervening
1798 and the conspiracy of 1803. A similar network in Kildare was
led by brothers John and Michael Doorley, rebel officers in the
Rebellion, who provided continuous leadership to Lullymore-area
insurgents until early 1804. As with Dwyer and the Corcoran/Cody
faction in Wicklow, Wexford and Carlow, United Irish membership
was a prerequisite of membership of the group and personal political
objectives were, or at least seemed, significant.[73]

Michael Doorley, as late as the winter of 1802–3, liaised with
Mathew Donnellan, leader of a low-profile faction in the Clane area,
and with associates in King's County and Carlow. Other Clane-area
rebel veterans remained undetected and largely unsuspected in their
homes, waiting for the chance to rise. Dwyer often visited United
Irishmen in Carlow town, north Wexford and Dublin for weeks at a
time. Maintaining communications with those with whom cooperation
would be required in the event of an invasion was high on the agenda.
Mere survival against the odds was also important in the broader
United Irish underground, which had come to cherish a culture of

resistance. Munster rebel leader Daniel Cullinane of Cashel, aka 'General Marcus Cleark', sent a letter to Dwyer in June 1801 crediting his 'good name and republican virtues' with having 'given much hopes to your suffering countrymen'. Cullinane, reputedly a graduate of the Irish College in Paris, had agitated in Tipperary, Waterford, Kilkenny, Limerick, Cork, Donegal and Down. He clearly appreciated the necessity of supporting a United Irish presence outside the capital.[74]

United Irish bands were distinguishable in the post-Rebellion period from those composed of criminal opportunists, ex-rebel brigands and military deserters in that they tended to act defensively in their home localities and avoided personal enrichment. Reported instances of rebels refraining from robbing loyalist prisoners and their killing of criminals were viewed as sinister aberrations in the Castle press. Confusingly, Clare militia deserter Michael Bryan, leader of a gang who terrorised adjacent parts of Cork and Waterford, also looked 'forward with confident hope to the arrival of a French force'. Groups such as Bryan's robbed the mails on no less than sixty-six occasions between 1798 and February 1803, a point of astonishment in England.[75] Sergeant Beatty and thirty-two members of the Meath militia became brigands in 1799, some of whom were still at large in 1801. Kilkenny and Tipperary, regarded in January 1799 as places where invasion had been expected 'for some time', were also disturbed by robberies and shootings.[76] Judge Robert Johnson claimed on the basis of such disruption that the United Irishmen were 'more general and systematic than ever'.[77]

Mounting instability in the winter of 1798–99 was indicated by fresh politically motivated disturbances in Antrim, Down, Armagh, Louth, Mayo, Cork, Limerick and Tipperary. A full-blown rebellion broke out in Clare on 4 January 1799 when 2–4,000 United Irishmen overran Ennis, Corofin, Milltown Malbay and Ennistymon. Clare had been comparatively quiet during the summer of 1798 but a group of fifty men reputedly made their way to the fighting in Wexford in June. Rebel strength in Clare had swollen after the Franco-Irish campaign, undeterred by the harrowing executions in Longford, Leitrim, Mayo and Sligo. The Clare uprising was led by Francis Lysaght and Hugh Kildea and had been triggered by their misplaced confidence in further large-scale landings from France and reports that military reinforcements were approaching. The declarations issued by the Claremen indicate that Lysaght, a minor landowner, and Kildea, a schoolteacher, had channelled popular agrarian discontent into pro-French paramilitary activity. Clare rebels went to Seafield on

14 January 1799 declaring that they would 'get arms and ammunition from a vessel they expected from France, and if they had any arms they need not fear the king's troops'. The only arms to arrive were borne by the New Romney fencibles and other British forces which rushed from Limerick with Brigadier General Meyrick to re-occupy Ennis. Nonetheless, the Clare incident confounded those who had hoped that the harshness of 1798 and numerous courts martial had terrified the people into passivity. Lysaght was delivered to the *Friendship* transport in Cobh the following summer in his own carriage and died from natural causes in Table Bay en route to New South Wales. His experience posed the question of what might have occurred had a French corps really disembarked on the Clare coast.[78]

Dublin conservative W. A. Crosbie, a Commissioner of the Barrack Office until 1798, claimed in December of that year that the 'public mind' had been 'very much inflamed' by rebel activity. Loyalists were allegedly 'in a dreadful state, and only less dreadful than a few months ago, as much as private assassination and general plunder and robbery can be called less dreadful than open rebellion'.[79] Castlereagh was warned that opposition to union had 'given the almost annihilated body of United Irishmen new spirits, and the Society is again rising like a phoenix from its ashes'.[80] While the Union was not a major bone of contention for the rank-and-file United Irishmen, the general import of the letter was correct. Republicans associated with Robert Emmet queried in February 1799 whether the yeomen would 'rise in consequence of the Union'. Government distrust of ultra-loyalist elements led to the imposition of sanctions on the recalcitrant Lord Downshire and the troublesome William Saurin.[81]

A massive upsurge in cattle mutilation in Mayo and Galway in the early months of 1799 reputedly threatened the 'total destruction' of livestock. Walsh, a Galway farmer, had 250 cattle houghed on refusing his brother-in-law's invitation to swear the United Irish oath. The raiders left a threatening note instructing Walsh to distribute the flesh of the slaughtered animals to the poor. While the severe winter and poor potato crop obviously increased the social and regional dimension of rebel activities, the demarcation of enemies on political as well as class fault lines was significant. Cattle owned by the Ennis Cavalry yeomanry captain and landlord Thomas Crowe had previously been singled out by the rebels during the Clare uprising. Conversely, farmers who supported the United Irishmen or were themselves republicans were ignored. The overwhelmingly Catholic demography of the district offered little scope for allegations of sectarianism by ultra-loyalists and the lack of severe coercion in 1798–99 reduced the level of grievances, which had resulted in revenge killings elsewhere. It was reported in London that 2,500 cattle and 25,000 sheep had been killed in Galway alone and that the economy was facing dire consequences.[82]

Cornwallis placed Galway under the Insurrection Act and issued orders on 20 February 1799 for the military to execute 'martial law with vigour'. This had unmistakable connotations of proactive severity given the notoriously indiscriminate nature of the crackdown which had accompanied the army's reconquest of the Connacht Republic in September 1798. The Viceroy was unequivocal in divining political pretexts 'connected with the system of United Irishmen . . . intended to prevent the supply of the navy with provisions'.[83] Judge Robert Day concurred in the view that the attacks were politically inspired, an impression which deepened on his arrival in Tralee on St Patrick's Day, 1799. He found seditious notices 'reprobating tithes, taxes & even rents, some reprobating Union – all under different forms & pretences . . . to agitate & excite the "Men of Kerry"'.[84] Houghing, according to Cornwallis, was linked to the concurrent resurfacing in Cork of the usual 'resistance' to tithes. As before, the root cause of the disturbances was held to be the chronic disaffection cultivated and exploited by the United Irishmen. Violent opposition to Government was consequently equated with 'Rebellion'.[85] The United Irish perspective on tithes, as set down by Addis Emmet, was that they were the 'frequent subject of partial insurrection, and were always the fertile source of general discontent; so that the French reformers, by abolishing them, exceedingly encreased [sic] the numbers, and awoke the energy of their Irish admirers'.[86]

Robert Emmet's relative, the Marquis of Buckingham, believed that

> the mischief done to private property by the new system (as ordered by the [United Irish] Directory here) is out of all calculation; none of the roads to Dublin are passable at any hour of the day save to large parties or military escorts; and this system is openly talked of as being more certain, and more destructive, than that of open force till their friends arrive, who are most impatiently looked for in the counties of Antrim, Galway, and Cork.[87]

This probably gave the reformed Directory too much credit for the state of unrest which, in places, testified to their lack of control over forces. An assessment of their capabilities by William Wickham on 28 February 1799 was only slightly less alarmist. He reported that there were 'many concurrent circumstances independent of the present state of the country in Ireland which must naturally tempt the enemy to an Invasion [sic]'. Wickham ascertained that the new Directory had informed its contacts that the French fleet fitting out in Brest was bound for Ireland, as one of Robert Emmet's letters revealed in late March. Wickham also knew that the state prisoners had sanctioned the formation of a replacement Directory that had determined on a 'general rising . . . as soon as the French shall appear on the Coast'.[88] The Clare incident was proof that this was entirely possible. MacNally warned that 15,000 French troops would land in Ireland in late May 1799 who, according to an intercepted letter from a United Irish officer in Hamburg, would be met by rebels 'better organised, and more eager in the glorious cause of freedom than they ever have been'.[89]

The signal from Cornwallis to utilise strong methods against the rebels in the provinces led to measures that would have been viewed as remarkably severe had they not closely followed the massive bloodshed of the Great Rebellion. The Inspector General of Prisons, Revd Foster Archer, discovered 120 men crammed into the county jail of Galway in 1799, which was 'not large enough for forty . . . twenty-two were executed by Martial Law, and fifty-two sentenced to Transportation'. The jailers of Galway city had executed a further eighteen of their twenty-six court-martialled prisoners.[90] One hundred and thirty Galwaymen were tried by the military between February and June 1799 on charges arising from the attacks on live-stock; most of them were described as United Irishmen, their ranks – if known – supplied in the trial listings.[91] On 16 March a crackdown on Cork was proclaimed in the midst of numerous attacks, sometimes fatal, on tithe proctors and magistrates. Forty-one were arrested arising from the killing of Timothy MacCarthy and dozens more were implicated in the shooting of Robert Hutchinson of Codrum (Macroom) on 19 April. The heads of five United Irishmen accused of seeking 'to "free" their country by desolating it and murdering every one of prop-erty and loyalty' were spiked on Macroom's bridewell on 14 May.[92]

Meanwhile, British-based agent handlers discovered plans to support a French invasion of Ireland with diversionary activity in London, Manchester and Bristol, where Irish republican migrants and fugitives had settled. Versions of this conspiracy were mooted over the following three years. Roscommon's major James Plunkett was said in March 1799 to have conspired in Bath and Bristol with United Irish exiles Byrne of Ballymanus, Fitzgerald of Newpark and Aylmer of Painstown. Aylmer's presence in London had also been resented by

Irish loyalists and he and other leading republicans were obliged to depart for the Continent. John Binns, the comrade of Emmet's associate James Farrell, was also implicated in contacts with the United Britons at this time and had been well known to Addis Emmet from the Society's early days. Binns and Doyle, the messenger from Dublin, escaped when London's Royal Oak pub was raided on 10 March 1799; Valentine Lawless, was not in attendance as expected. Their survival lessened the impact of the crackdown and alerted the United Irish community in Britain to the fact that their security had been compromised. Lawless was subsequently arrested and detained in the Tower of London along with Robert Emmet's Trinity friend Richard Curran, who acted as his secretary. Sufficient documentary evidence of sedition was recovered at the Royal Oak to cause serious disruption to United Irish plans in the London region. This success lulled the British authorities into a state of over-confidence and insufficient resources were deployed to monitor the traffic of emissaries between Dublin, London and Paris between 1799 and 1803.[93]

Britain was of secondary importance to the United Irishmen in comparison with advancing their national reorganisation and improving relations with the French government. The scope for United Irish resurgence was, to a degree, dependent on the ability and political will of the Executive to combat the process. The military drive in the west of Ireland was not sustained once the houghing threat subsided in late 1799 and was untypical of the post-Rebellion climate. Edward Cooke was preoccupied with promoting the Act of Union in early 1799 and increasingly depended on the imperfect, self-serving insights offered by McGucken, Pollock, Turner and others. Cooke never recovered his enthusiasm for the covert side of his duties and moved back to England in mid 1801, leaving the intelligence-gathering and assessment capacity of the Castle in disarray. Major Sirr, confirmed in his post in November 1798 owing to sterling service during the Rebellion, was under-resourced in Dublin Castle and primarily engaged in rooting rebel fugitives out of their newly formed south city ghettos.[94]

Little comfort could be taken in Dublin Castle in March/April 1799 from the glimpses of United Irish activity provided by MacNally, Turner, McGucken and Timothy Conway, 'one of the Directory at Cork'.[95] Robert Emmet's assumption of responsibility for shoring up contacts with the Connacht United Irish networks was noted at this time. Death, imprisonment and exile had thrown Ulster communications into disarray, notwithstanding the best efforts of James Hope and Putnam McCabe to salvage what they could with

George Teeling's assistance. East Ulster was highly agitated in early 1799 when it was alleged that arms had been landed from Holland at Ards and at other locations on the Antrim coast.[96] More immediate unrest stemmed from the almost nightly actions of Antrim rebel leaders Thomas Archer and general James 'Holt' Dickson (aka Dickey and Dixon). Both were veterans of the rebellion in Ulster who had remained active in 1799 at the head of small but well-armed and determined bands of followers. Attuning such men to the strategy of the new leadership and building up command structures that could be activated during an invasion were a priority in Dublin.[97]

EMMET UNMASKED

When attending the Carrickfergus assizes in late March, James McGucken received an unsigned letter from Robert Emmet containing a message written in invisible ink. This seemed to be a favoured mode of writing for Emmet whose familiarity with and access to chemicals proved useful. McGucken was asked to direct 'any persons that have occasion to come' to Dublin to the temporary lodgings of James Farrell in 33 Paradise Row. McGucken was clearly expected to use his knowledge of northern United Irish figures to encourage their cooperation with the new national leadership. Emmet enhanced McGucken's prospects of bringing such men forward by disclosing: 'there is every expectation of the French coming immediately to the amount of 17,000. Gov[ernmen]t are dreadfully alarmed. Be exceedingly cautious. Everything should be kept as quiet as possible. Fix upon one or two persons to send down communications to in case of anything happening and write this name up.'[98]

Using the postal service was a calculated risk on Emmet's part and one taken with reasonable precautions: the document was unsigned and contained an agreed code word to alert its recipient to the presence of invisible ink. Only McGucken could have easily detected the hidden message; his treachery was not suspected. He had, nonetheless, been waiting for such a moment and on 11 February passed on intelligence that 'Emmet resides with his father at Milltown' to facilitate his planned arrest. The letter provided the authorities with physical evidence of Emmet's treasonous activities and further grounds to launch a crackdown in Dublin. Warrants were issued for Emmet's detention on 3 April 1799 along with Hugh O'Hanlon, James Farrell and Thomas Wright. McCabe and Palmer were also sought without success, having apparently departed for the Continent via England in December 1798. O'Hanlon was the first man detained but, remarkably, broke out of Dublin Castle in time to alert his comrades and fled to France.[99]

Emmet immediately went into hiding and may, as the English poet Robert Southey claimed four years later, have lain concealed for six weeks in a secret chamber built under his father's study. This was probably a room in the secluded Casino, a rurally located house at Milltown, rather than in the more obvious family home on Stephen's Green. A tunnel led from a plank-lined basement room at Casino to a summer house within its grounds fifty yards away. Emmet reputedly made use of this excellent escape route in 1798 and on at least one occasion in December 1802. O'Hanlon was sighted in Dublin on 21 April 1799 where he apparently lingered, in part, owing to 'the entreaties of Emmet' who had his total confidence and with whom he dined during his last days in Ireland.[100] Baird also managed to elude those in pursuit of him and followed O'Hanlon abroad, although Edward Lawson was detained for questioning. Wright was arrested on 28 April 1799 and, fearing execution, assisted his captors, and suspicions that he may have done so probably accounts for his distancing from United Irish affairs between 1799 and 1803.[101]

Extant statements made by Wright when in the Castle on 1 May 1799 left much unsaid but pinpointed Robert Emmet, 'a young man with military talent', as the driving force behind the plebeian city United Irishmen. Emmet and the other 'young men' were allegedly 'fired with military ideas'. This was accepted at face value by Castlereagh, who expressed no surprise that Emmet's political commitment had garnered him authority. Emmet must have derived some benefit in this regard from the reflected glory of his elder brother, a noted populist and public United Irish leader, but the great faith he invested in the 'lower orders' in 1802–3 indicates that he had forged an independent and cogent connection with the city radicals. John Pollock, the government lawyer with whom Addis Emmet had locked horns the previous year, was sufficiently impressed by Wright's disclosures and those of McGucken to order the searching of the various Emmet family homes and those of their friends prior to 6 May 1799.[102] Information that 'Emmet is concealed' was received by the Castle three days before Pollock's failed attempt to seize the young fugitive. It was then ascertained that he intended to go abroad as soon as possible.[103]

Emmet's security precautions when on the run were such that his whereabouts between April 1799 and the spring of 1801 are uncertain. He may, as John Patten alleged, have continued to attend the Union debates at College Green, which drew to a sudden and anti-climactic close in June 1800. More certain is that Emmet had undertaken a writing project in early 1799 that required far more discretion than those of Mary Anne Emmet and Robert Holmes. He assisted Malachy Delaney and others in revising a military handbook produced by Surgeon Wright as a primer for United Irish cadres. It had been intended to circulate the book amongst the organisation in the countryside in order to improve their field craft and grasp of tactics. William Dowdall and Philip Long both committed to paper their advanced theories on such matters by 1803. Emmet was probably greatly interested in this work given his penchant for studying and writing military treatises. Delaney, a former officer in the Austrian army, had commanded the Kildare rebels who captured Ballitore in the first week of the Rebellion of 1798 and in 1799 was a fugitive from an old murder charge in Narraghmore. Wright's disclosures on Emmet and Delaney went undetected by his peers yet failed to provide the Castle with incriminating information of the type required to plan treason trials for men who could not be found. It is likely that Wright refused to testify in court, a problem encountered by the authorities with frustrating frequency in 1797–98.[104]

The low-key nature of the crackdown of March/April 1799 probably reflected the extreme delicacy of the political climate in which the Union Bill was enacted. Another factor was the diversion of the scarce human and financial resources of Dublin Castle to securing the bill's slow passage through parliament. Even so, it is surprising that Emmet not only managed to avoid arrest in the Dublin environs for over a year but moved closer towards the centre of the conspiracy. In late September 1800 McGucken confirmed that Wright, O'Hara, Lawless or Lawson and 'young Emmet [were] . . . at the head' of the new organisation. If correct, Wright had reintegrated himself with the survivors of the arrests after his own release from custody. William Metcalfe, one of McGucken's unwitting informants in 1800, had assisted McCabe and Hope in spreading the United Irish system to south Leinster in May 1797 and was selected by Emmet to improve contacts with the Ulster network in 1802–3. Metcalfe was the most active northern emissary in Ireland in 1799–1800 owing to the migration of McCabe to France and Hope's temporary retirement. Hope, who had not obtained a certificate of protection (amnesty), was working with Blue Bells linen bleacher Edward Finn and deemed it prudent to relocate to the Naul in June 1799. McGucken, crucially,

had felt obliged to distance himself from the Dublin-based conspirators in mid-1799 believing that O'Hanlon had uncovered his
treachery. The lawyer was consequently out of touch with the main
United Irish players by the time Emmet returned from overseas
in 1802.[105]

EXILES

A more proactive approach was taken by the government to the state
prisoners whose confessions and token compliance had dispelled any
doubts as to their capabilities. Humbert's campaign and the perceived
effrontery of Addis Emmet, O'Connor, Neilson and MacNeven in
writing to the press in August 1798 had thrown into relief the problems posed by keeping the prisoners in Ireland. The main concern of
the Castle was preventing the return of the voluntary exiles, an
impolitic proposition with serious consequences for state security.
This issue was addressed by the Banishment and Fugitive Acts of
October 1798, which made it a capital felony for named United
Irishmen to return to Ireland unauthorised or to enter British
Dominions. The prisoners were also prohibited from migrating to
countries hostile to Britain and the Banishment Act classified travel to
France, Spain and the United Provinces (Netherlands) as treason.
Given the disregard shown for the French army commissions of
Mathew and Wolfe Tone and Bartholomew Teeling there was every
reason to believe that the authorities would act upon this threat if the
opportunity presented itself.[106]

The political fallout of the near-farcical Tandy affair in Hamburg
prevented the government from publicly sending United Irish exiles
to that city as had been intended. The United States of America, the
country originally envisaged for the reception of the state prisoners,
had been ruled out for the purpose as early as September 1798 by
President Adams' representative in London, Rufus King. On learning
of the Irish government's plans to send the prisoners to America, King
had made known the hostility of the president to the immigration of
Irish 'traitors'.[107] The impossibility, however, of policing the movements
of the prisoners once they were ejected from the islands of Britain and
Ireland led to the detention of the twenty most 'dangerous' men at Fort
George, in the highlands of Scotland, for the duration of the French
war. They were said to have been 'transported to Scotland'.[108]

Although the object of press speculation, the identities of those
earmarked for internment in Scotland were not made public. On 12

February 1799 Dr Robert Emmet complained that he had been prevented from visiting his son in Kilmainham for over a month, an embargo primarily intended to limit state prisoner influence on the leadership that had replaced them in Dublin.[109] It was not until 18 March 1799 that the men were informed that they would be departing for an overseas location the following day. No destination was specified, although Fort George had been mooted for several months. Addis Emmet complained: 'I am just informed by an order from the Castle that I must prepare to embark at six o'clock tomorrow morning without knowing for what place or what purpose.' As with several other prisoners, he had no money and had not been permitted to contact relatives and friends owing to the 'close confinement' of the previous months.[110] Word of the move reached Mary Anne Emmet on the 18th who requested an audience with Cornwallis that evening to press him on the government's intentions. Cornwallis, a conciliatory man, offered assurances that Addis Emmet would be fairly treated and revealed that the decision to detain the prisoners had been influenced by fears that Ireland might be invaded.[111]

The selected inmates of Kilmainham and Newgate were not actually embarked in Dublin until 26 March 1799. They were then taken on board the *Ashton Smith* and sailed up the east coast to Belfast, where they were joined by four northern comrades. The Ulstermen had also been kept in the dark as to their fate until the last moment. On 30 March the prisoners made the rough passage to Scotland and were eventually disembarked at Gooroch near Greenoch.[112] Arthur O'Connor occupied himself during the crossing to Scotland by composing a short poem. A long road trip from Glasgow to Fort George followed, which was finally reached on 9 April. The remaining state prisoners in custody were quietly deported to Hamburg, one of the few Continental ports open to British shipping due to the French military and diplomatic blockade. Thereafter, the predictable spread of the exiles to France and Holland occurred, as well as to Switzerland, Denmark, Norway, Austria, Spain and Portugal, where small and ephemeral United Irish colonies were created.[113]

The revived notoriety of Thomas Addis Emmet and fresh stigmatic representation of Robert Emmet in early May 1799 obliged the ever-cautious William Drennan to resume a defensive posture regarding his relationship with the family. In reply to his sister's reproaches for not sending news of the Emmets, Drennan admitted: 'I have not visited the Emmet family lately and I have my reasons which I will not trouble you with at present.' Drennan chose his words carefully, having grounds to believe that his mail was monitored by the Post Office, a virtual adjunct of the Castle intelligence system. His dismissive allusion to a once-common topic of correspondence established that Drennan was aware of Robert Emmet's latest difficulties and unwilling to commit his thoughts on the matter to paper.[114] Drennan acknowledged on 24 June 1799 that Dr Emmet had visited him from Casino, where he spent more and more time, but no details of their conversation were recorded. This was a studied omission and Drennan hinted that sensitive matters were in play by stating: 'the weather has been too warm for me to walk out to the country. I have not many visitors because I don't give dinners.'[115] When made aware of the background details, Martha McTier professed her sense of 'hurt' that her brother had abandoned 'the intimacy of such old and respectable friends as Dr Emmet's family . . . in a season of distress to them'.[116]

The spring of 1799 was also a season of distress for Irish loyalists. Numerous reports reached the Castle of intended French-assisted risings and seditious dealings of the state prisoners with their successors. An elaborate plot to seize Cork on Easter Sunday was thoroughly investigated by Major-Generals William Myers and Charles Ross. Depositions referring to different locations and time frames confused the authorities and, as before, United Irish 'agitators' were known to be 'exceedingly active and busy throughout the whole kingdom'. Trends in the Continental balance of power also began to favour the United Irishmen as uneasy Franco-Austrian relations deteriorated in early March. French admirals Bruix and Story made their fleets at Brest and Texel ready to sail.[117]

Bruix's twenty-five ship fleet took advantage of favourable winds and a cloak of fog to leave Brest on 26 April 1799 without interference from the Royal Navy screen on station off the coast. By various ruses the authorities in London and Dublin were convinced that its destination was Ireland rather than the Mediterranean. Indeed, Lord Bridport's squadron were apprised that the French had gone to Texel while he was personally convinced they were bound for Cape Clear. The only positive aspect to the scare was intelligence that Bruix had sailed without troop transports and, lacking reinforcements, was unlikely to present a major invasion threat to Ireland or England. The French received United Irish support in obscuring their real objective of collecting the Spanish fleet at Cadiz and sailing for Genoa, presumably by giving assurances that Ireland would feature in their plans at a later stage. When ordered from Bantry Bay against the phantom French fleet on 30 May, Bridport was confronted by a mutiny on *L'Impetueux* off Berehaven. Not for the first or last time, Irish Royal Navy mutineers, many of whom had been transported to the fleet for seditious practices, acted as if in concert with the French. Their gambit coincided with reports of renewed infiltration of militia regiments in Munster.[118]

Against Castle expectations, there was no discernible reaction to news of the Brest fleet's sailing in Ulster where Major-General Nugent claimed that republican agents had assured supporters that there was an 'intention of a landing'. This may well have been a ruse suggested by the rump leadership in Dublin at the behest of their French allies.[119] Matters were far from quiescent in the north, however, and the followers of Dickson and Archer still terrorised loyalist families with arms raids, whippings and their ability to evade the authorities. Also worrying were the revelations of Samuel Hume of Moneyduff who detailed Defender/United Irish interaction in Antrim, Down, Derry and Tyrone. His information suggested that a systematic revival was underway notwithstanding the increased efforts of the yeomanry and Orange Order. Hume claimed that Patrick Mitchel of Tyrone and other emissaries had 'for some time . . . been travelling this county for the purpose of encouraging Defenderism'.[120]

The French threat had been cited in Randalstown, Ballymena and other parts of Antrim during an upsurge in arms raiding in early 1799 but this had levelled off by the time of the Brest incident. Revd Edward Hudson suspected that the United Irish Directory had disseminated spurious invasion dates to 'keep up' the 'spirits' of their followers until Ireland actually became the destination of the French. There was a limit to the number of times this could be done without demoralising the grass roots, and travelling the militarised lowlands of Ulster for propaganda purposes could not continue indefinitely.[121] The arrest of Dickson near Toome on 8 May 1799, just prior to the major invasion threat, and Archer's capture ten months later all but wiped out Rebellion-era factions in the north. Thereafter, intermittent disturbances of a quasi-political nature in north-eastern Ulster were attributable to isolated opportunists. This changed in the early summer of 1803 when Emmet's agents began to organise political agitation. In late June 1799, though, Castlereagh's sources informed him that the dispatch of the French to the Mediterranean was regarded 'by the disaffected as . . . an abdication of their cause'. The dashing of such high hopes in 1799 may well have informed the scepticism which greeted the once-revered Thomas Russell when he attempted to prepare Antrim and Down for the Rising of 1803.[122]

The Rebellion Act of March 1799, parliament's main response to the violent outbreaks, initiated a host of courts martial of suspects while also acting as the spur for the release of compromised United Irishmen from the Dublin Bay hulks and prisons. Those whose crimes were no longer deemed serious in the light of the liberal terms of the Amnesty Act or whose alleged offences were not easily proved were generally freed in 1799–1800. Hundreds of rebels were excused their sentences, bailed or simply sent home if they enjoyed gentry and military patronage. A minority of less fortunate men were conscripted into army regiments bound for the West Indies or the Prussian military or were dispatched to the penal colonies of New South Wales.[123]

This dispersal exported Irish sedition across the globe in 1799–1800. The consequences of this became apparent when United Irishmen conscripted to fight anti-British forces in Jamaica defected to the enemy. Impressed Irish recruits also planned a September 1799 'conspiracy' in the Prince of Wales Regiment on Guernsey and the almost 400 rebels shipped to Emden for induction into the Prussian military that month were refractory from the outset. United Irishmen in the Royal Newfoundland Regiment revolted in April 1800 and several temporarily avoided the repercussions by seizing the vessel taking them for trial in Nova Scotia. Given the migrant links between Newfoundland and the southern maritime counties of Ireland, it is quite possible that some of the fishery's United Irishmen had opposed the island's military governor, John Skerret, when he commanded the Durham Regiment at the Battle of Arklow (9 June 1798). Rebel convicts bound for New South Wales on the *Minerva* and *Friendship*, furthermore, mutinied unsuccessfully on leaving Cobh in August 1799. Upon arrival, they fostered the interconnected 'Irish plots' of February, September, October and December 1800 in Sydney, Parramatta and Norfolk Island. Eighteen died in an attempt to take the *Hercules* on 29 December 1801 and those who survived the subsequent punishments fomented great unrest when landed. Irish republicans were also held responsible, probably incorrectly, for a riot which broke out in Philadelphia in 1799 and were closely watched that year in the midlands and south of England. These disparate episodes signalled that United Irishmen who had fought before would do so again, even if the odds were very much against success. This remained the case in Ireland where their critical mass, revolutionary ideology and latent strength posed the gravest threat to the authorities.[124]

Attacks on cattle in Connacht had all but ceased by early June 1799, possibly due to a sense of futility engendered by the non-arrival of the Brest fleet. Severe losses had also been sustained by the United Irishmen and in March 1799 Major-General Trench wrote to the Castle from Castlebar with news that a rebel officer named Faherty had been mortally wounded in an arms raid. If this was the O'Flaherty identified in February as the rebel Directory's Connacht liaison, the devastation of livestock may indeed have been imbued with the direction discerned in the Castle. His death was followed up by the arrest of 'seven rebel chiefs . . . [who were] taken in the mountains'.[125]

Despite these successes, small numbers of insurgents who had been active since the Rebellion remained at large. Trench claimed that the appearance of Bridport's squadron off the Mayo coast on 3 June 1799 had drawn rebels into the nearby mountains in the forlorn hope of catching sight of their French allies. The influence of Westport's James Joseph MacDonnell was said to have motivated United Irishmen in the north of the province, specifically a 'regularly organised and well armed' group on the Mayo/Galway border. The personal involvement of MacDonnell is highly doubtful given his flight to France after the Battle of Ballinamuck. He met Robert Emmet in Paris in 1802 and allegedly corresponded with political allies in Mayo the following year, as he may have also done in 1799.[126] In Dublin, Patrick Dillon of Donnybrook, who had supported rebel factions during the Rebellion, financed McMahon's passage to New York in early 1799. McMahon had evidently tired of awaiting the French and believed they would not come before the authorities brought him to the scaffold. This fate had befallen his fellow city colonels Thomas Seagrave and Thomas Bacon, as well as Wicklow's William Byrne. Southwell McClune was also arrested in April and faced an uncertain fate. Michael Reynolds, a Kildare rebel colonel who had been highly active in the early days of the Rebellion, followed McMahon abroad. Although so grievously wounded at Hacketstown that a £300 bounty was paid to his supposed yeoman killer, Reynolds recuperated with the Powers in the Cherry Tree Inn on Thomas Street until well enough to go to London and disappear into obscurity. Edward Rattigan also left the country and died at the Battle of Marengo in 1800 when serving in the French army. The indirect fallout of the Brest scare, therefore, deprived the Dublin city leadership of five experienced rebel colonels.[127]

Ultra-loyalist violence surged in Wexford, Wicklow, Kildare, King's County and parts of Antrim in spite of the efforts of the Privy Council and brigade majors of the yeomanry to curtail illegal excesses. As before, the backlash was characterised by chapel- and house-burning, assassination attempts on Catholic clergy and the harassment, sometimes fatal, of suspected United Irishmen. Many loyalists were frustrated by the workings of the Amnesty Act, which had freed men known to have committed seditious acts from prison and allowed them to return to their pre-Rebellion residences and employment. Four hundred and sixty Wicklow claimants applied to the Committee for the Relief of Suffering Loyalists seeking compensation for houses destroyed or badly damaged by rebel activity in 1798. Many, presumably, remained in the Orange Order-influenced yeomanry units that mounted numerous revenge attacks into 1801. Amnestied rebels forced back into the mountains by threats and harassment included Michael Dwyer and William Genoud of Baltinglass; others simply retained their arms and kept fighting. Loyalist depredations in Ulster, while not as dramatic, sustained or as deadly as in Leinster, forced the Caldwell brothers, Trinity College friends of Emmet, into exile in New York.[128]

UNREST IN THE PROVINCES

The dispiriting absence of the French and the recall of the yeomanry to permanent duty in May 1799 apparently inhibited fresh outbreaks of violence during the summer months. Wicklow, Wexford, Carlow, Kildare and Limerick remained volatile and a major upsurge took place in September/October 1799 arising from inter-provincial agitation by Tipperary-based militants with links to Kerry, Limerick, Clare and Waterford. Something of the contagious and near-spontaneous dynamism of the Rightboys and earlier Whiteboys was in play, although the outbreaks were sufficiently systematic as to raise questions in the Castle. Undersecretary Alexander Marsden sent dispatches to London concerning these 'new attempts at rebellion', surmising that 'as the hopes of the disaffected are kept up partly by what the agitation of the question of Union may produce, and partly by promise of succour from France, it is of the utmost importance that our military force should not be too much reduced'. Livestock were once again targeted and General Lake reported on 29 October that 'cattle have been houghed or piked near Castle Otway'.[129] Kerry-born United Irish captain Phil Cunningham, who in 1798 had fought in the Clonmel area of Tipperary where he kept an inn and worked as a mason, came to regional prominence in mid 1799. He had no agrarian agenda but with Roger Guiry had visited Dungarvan on 1 August 1799 and 'other places in the county Waterford with intent to foment rebellion and excite divers[e] subjects . . . to raise & take up arms against his Majesty'. Cunningham had previously pursued this objective at Carrick-on-Suir and Kilmacthomas and was part of a network stretching from the Listowel district of Kerry to the south coast. A technicality spared his life when court-martialled in October 1799. Undeterred by his experiences, Cunningham was executed with Samuel Hume at Castle Hill, New South Wales, for leading the last uprising of the United Irishmen in March 1804.[130]

The arrest of Cunningham was exacerbated by the transportation of several of his associates within a short period, including Thomas Langan of Glin, Bill Leonard of Ahanagran and Manus Sheehy of Duagh. Notwithstanding these setbacks, Limerick and Kerry retained the services of higher-ranking United Irishmen who managed to evade prosecution into the early 1800s. A loose circle of influential republicans remained, of whom the most important was Gerald Fitzgerald, brother of the Knight of Glin, who employed the Langans as stewards. One of the family, schoolteacher Mícheál Óg Ó Longáin, lived in Kerry and Limerick in 1802. He had been a United Irish emissary in Cork in 1797–98 and wrote resistance poetry in Irish. Also prominent in north Munster from the days of the pre-Rebellion organisation were Nicholas Sandes of Listowel and the astronomer James Baggott of Ballingarry. Baggott had met Lord Edward Fitzgerald in 1798, and in early 1803 re-emerged along with Sandes and Gerald Fitzgerald as a supporter of Emmet and Russell. Self-sustaining networks of this kind had been developed prior to 1798 and were evidently maintained independently of Dublin until contact was re-established with the new Directory in 1799–1803. Limerick was one of the few places where the conspirators of 1803 hoped to launch attacks at the same time as the revolt in Dublin.[131]

The north Munster arrests of 1799 coincided with an insurgent scare in Tipperary in September. Clonmel, Carrick and Fethard yeomen and magistrates were repeatedly attacked by men deemed to be United Irishmen, leading John Bagwell to become convinced of 'an immediate intended rising of the rebels'. The revolt expected on 6 September did not occur but the spate of serious incidents led to the declaration of martial law in Tipperary and Waterford the following week.[132] An informer confirmed that 'Ireland was all new organized' and suggested that the Union would trigger a 'rising all over the kingdom', a comment which revealed more about the correspondent's anti-Union attitude than it did about United Irish policy. The Castle noted the gathering strength of the United Irishmen in King's County, Carlow and Kildare during the autumn and feared that organisers like Cunningham or Putnam McCabe would harness a wide range of economic grievances towards a revolutionary struggle. There were even rumours of a coup d'état in Dublin in mid October and 'General Clarke' was expected by some to deluge his home town of Cashel with 8,000 followers. In the event, it was Robert Emmet and his associates who reignited the United Irish cause in 1803 and it was to further this plan that he travelled to Britain and the Continent in 1800.[133]

CHAPTER FIVE

Emmet Abroad, 1800–1802

The early months of 1800 witnessed ongoing efforts to rejuvenate the United Irishmen. There were also numerous examples of chronic anti-state sentiment. It was reported in the first week of January that a sergeant in the Angushire fencibles had been shot dead in Dunboyne, Meath, and that the jailer of Athy prison was waylaid and killed when transferring prisoners to Naas in Kildare. Before the month was out another soldier was sniped in Dublin, where 'placards of the most inflammatory and treasonable nature' had been posted up.[1] The authorities learned in January that William Putnam McCabe had visited Belfast to inform the United Irishmen that an invasion would be mounted from Brest. McCabe had been implicated in virtually every phase and aspect of the United Irish conspiracy from the late 1790s. His Belfast message, if genuine, may have been widely disseminated in republican circles and there was certainly an appreciable upsurge in rebel and agrarian activity in the spring of 1800. A point of corroboration was that the Metcalfe who attended insurgent meetings in Antrim and Down in March was a former associate of McCabe's and later assisted Emmet.[2]

The killing of two Tipperary loyalists near Cahir in early March 1800 was, naturally, viewed with concern in the Castle, as was the flogging of several others near Newcastle. The fusion of quasi-political and agrarian violence in Clare and Limerick led to the dispatch of military reinforcements to Connagh, Emly, Bruff and Cappagh in the hope that this would inhibit the agitators from becoming 'more daring'.[3] These towns – and Bruff in particular – had been notably violent during the Defender outrages of the early 1790s. No doubt the more recent troubling precedent of what had occurred in Clare and Galway in 1799 encouraged the decisive response in 1800. Killings also occurred in Carlow and Wicklow, as they had since late 1797, while 'a formidable Banditti' of Defenders apparently took 'deep root' in Antrim and Down, despite Brigadier General Drummond's execution of several ringleaders and numerous followers. Those behind the Antrim raids were considered the 'better kind of Farmers', whom Emmet and the United Irishmen wished to recruit as officers and delegates.[4] Rebels hanged in Ballymena, of whom there were many, reputedly marched to the gallows in their burial shrouds as much for the psychological effect as the convenient disposal of their remains. No shroud was required by the 'wretched [Thomas] Archer', whose corpse festered on a Ballymena gibbet on 22 March 1800.[5] United Irishmen wanted for 1798 offences which were not covered by the Amnesty Act were also tried in considerable numbers.[6]

EMMET DEPARTS

The Castle gained its first insight into what appeared to be a centrally controlled attempt to enhance United Irish cooperation in Leinster in March 1800. Contact was then established between the resilient Dwyer group and three emissaries from Kildare who had been 'long expected' in Imaal. They called to the Eadestown home of Dwyer's father and, once their bona fides were accepted, spent several days in west Wicklow with local rebel leaders. The delegates then moved on to Carlow where one was arrested on 4 April, possibly intending to seek out the highly dangerous Corcoran faction. When apprehended the man claimed to have administered a new oath in Wexford to 'assist the French whenever they effect a landing' and presumably had done so in Wicklow.[7] This simple formula of fidelity was used by Emmet's agents in 1802–3 and its utilisation in early 1800 may reflect his input in the Directory. Of more immediate concern to Emmet, as he prepared to go overseas, was the demonstrable fact that Ireland was beset with seemingly endemic instability that favoured revolutionaries and anti-British foreign powers willing to assist the United Irishmen to overthrow the government.[8]

Emmet's family was also in turmoil. Dr Emmet vacated Stephen's Green shortly after the marriage of Mary Anne Emmet to Robert Holmes and moved with them to Casino House where he had been spending more of his time since 1797. Their presence would have made it difficult, if not impossible, for Robert Emmet to use Milltown as a hideout without incurring adverse consequences for all those in residence. Transportation was the penalty for harbouring in areas where martial law was in force and Emmet's departure from Ireland undoubtedly relieved his close relatives of their most immediate source of anxiety.[9] William Drennan found that Mary Anne Emmet, with whom a coolness was long manifest, 'appeared cheerful and

even happy' at Casino in March 1800. On renewing contact with Dr
Emmet, Drennan concluded that the Emmets were 'at present the
suffering family of the time'. Mary Anne was treated by Drennan
when she fell ill again in early July 1800 and, while detained at
Milltown, missed a call from William Godwin, the English radical
philosopher and widower of Mary Wollstonecraft. Robert Emmet
had been influenced by Godwin's writings when a student in Trinity
and would probably have attempted to meet the author had he
remained in Ireland. Emmet's allusions to America, France and
Poland when on trial reveal that he regarded himself as belonging to
an international movement of patriotic revolutionaries inspired by
thinkers such as Godwin.[10]

Robert Emmet slipped out of Ireland sometime after April 1800
and arrived in Hamburg from England by August at the latest. While
the precise timing and itinerary of the trip were concealed by Emmet
and cannot be established with certainty, the probability is that he left
Ireland in early August in company with John Patten. If they
remained in Dublin into August it is very likely that Emmet met
Monaghan United Irishman Edward Carolan of Carrickmacross who
arrived from Hamburg that month on a mission from the Paris
leadership. Carolan's movements on the Continent were tracked by
Hamburg-based spy Samuel Turner but he evaded close observation
upon arrival in Ireland and conferred with the Dublin Directory
before returning to France in February 1801. His discussions were
attended with secrecy which defied the efforts of MacNally to ascertain
their precise nature but the outcome may well have convinced the city
United Irishmen that the time had come to send Emmet and Malachy
Delaney to Paris.[11] Also significant was the assertion of Francis
Higgins in September 1800 that the Military Committee formed by
Lord Edward Fitzgerald 'has been revived again by the United
Irishmen'. This assumed particular importance in the context of
Carolan's clandestine interaction with Major McDermott, James
Dixon, Ambrose Moore and other suspected militants. They included
Walter Cox, Philip Long and William Cole who were not named by
Higgins' sources but were certainly engaged with Fitzgerald in 1798
and Emmet in 1803.[12] Higgins further ascertained that 'the medical
men' attached to Thomas Wright 'act as part of a Directory' and from
the winter of 1800/1801 attempted to liaise with United Irish groups
which met 'in the Liberty' and 'every public house in Thomas St and
Francis St' under the guise of 'Funeral Societies'. One of those implicated in May 1801, 'Mr Gray, late of Wexford but now of William

St', was evidently Robert Emmet's 1803 associate Nicholas Gray. The mission of Emmet and Delaney, therefore, coincided with tentative efforts to rebuild a Dublin-based leadership with a Military Committee and lines of communication to those prepared to fight.[13] They clearly regarded themselves as having a strictly defined role and in the memorial presented to the French authorities after arrival in Hamburg specified that they had been 'ordered' by an 'Irish Executive' with 'executive power'.[14]

En route to Hamburg, Emmet and Patten travelled to Fort George, near Inverness, Scotland, where Thomas Addis Emmet and the other state prisoners had arrived on 9 April 1799. The Highlands prison was a much stricter environment than he had generally experienced in Kilmainham and Newgate. Major J. H. Ballie, the guard commander, ordered his staff to avoid conversation with the prisoners to discourage fraternisation and to prevent illicit messages circumventing official channels. Addis Emmet was singled out for repressive treatment and held in isolation from the other prisoners for around a year. He endured this discrimination in the jurisdiction of Hope, Lord Advocate of Scotland, whom he had befriended as an undergraduate in Edinburgh University. Addis Emmet wrote to Hope in December 1801 to inform him that the Fort George inmates would not permit the authorities to decide the destination of their foreign exile lest it 'be construed . . . [that] government could send us to Botany Bay'.[15]

The security of Fort George was tested in April 1800 when St John Mason, a United Irishman and Addis Emmet's first cousin, travelled to the prison from London. He had recently met up with McCabe and Palmer in London, who then preceded him to Fort George, where they obtained a letter of introduction to the French government from Arthur O'Connor. In contrast, St John Mason found on arrival shortly afterwards that Addis Emmet was closely confined and that the Governor, Lieutenant Colonel Stuart, brother of the Earl of Murray, would only permit exchanges of letters. Some inkling of O'Connor's activities and the identity of his Irish visitors may have led to a clampdown. This tightly controlled and transparent communication spanned the several days St John Mason spent at Fort George, but as no such impediment was met with by Robert Emmet when in Scotland shortly afterwards it appears that the conditions of confinement were relaxed in the interim. This probably occurred shortly before 14 July 1800 when Mrs Elizabeth Emmet, mother of Robert and Thomas, wrote to Fort George referring to the absence of both sons as the 'present vacancies in our family'. It is unclear whether the date of writing, the eleventh anniversary of the French Revolution, was an intentional irony. The suggestion that Robert Emmet was no longer in the family home may also have been an intentional signal that he was preparing to travel.[16]

Any explicit mention of Robert Emmet is absent from the otherwise comprehensive letters sent to Addis Emmet by his parents between April 1800 and October 1801. They probably feared that discussing his affairs would contravene the draconian correspondence regulations at Fort George. On 3 June 1800 Drennan and his wife Mary walked from their city home at 33 Marlborough Street to Casino, where they were kindly received. They found the family once more in difficulty, with Holmes attending his ailing wife, Mary Anne, and Jane Emmet preparing to bring her children to Fort George via Donaghadee, County Down. Although refused permission to reside with her husband in the Scottish prison, Jane Emmet went to London with her three eldest children, Robert, Margaret and Elizabeth, to raise the matter with the Duke of Portland. On being rebuffed by unsympathetic officials of the Home Office, she remained in London until her powerful Temple relatives made representations on her behalf. This enabled her to go to Fort George within weeks and it seems that patronage, rather than compassion, alleviated the harshness of Addis Emmet's open-ended detention. Thomas Russell admired her determination and wrote a poem to commemorate the visit of 'Mrs Emmet'.[17] William Steel Dickson shared Russell's interest in her fortunes and noted on 19 July that she had received permission to reside in the complex with the children.[18]

Robert Emmet also travelled to Scotland, probably in company with John Patten, in early August 1800. Addis Emmet had written to Patten, his brother-in-law, requesting that he bring over a set of duelling pistols for him to settle a dispute with O'Connor. Long-standing difficulties of personality and politics between the two had broken out once they had been permitted to associate freely. Patten dutifully brought the pistols to Fort George but, no doubt, was pleased to have his efforts nullified when Robert Emmet made a successful intercession between the rivals. While his reputed skill as a negotiator and persuader may very well have helped secure this outcome, it is also likely that the new accord was facilitated by the positive news he had brought from Ireland. At the very least, Emmet could claim that the revival of United Irish structures had reached the point that a coordinated response to the French was again within reach. He may well have sought their imprimatur for the specific secret proposals he intended laying before Napoleon Bonaparte in Paris on behalf of the new Executive Directory. Carolan may have indicated in Dublin that a new approach might meet with approval. Addis Emmet, O'Connor and the other Irish rebels incarcerated at Fort George clearly assented given the ease with which the diplomatic contacts that had been painstakingly developed by the original leadership were put at Robert Emmet's disposal in 1801–2.[19]

Emmet family tradition asserted that Robert Emmet spent two months in the vicinity of Fort George and returned to Dublin before setting out for the Continent. This is very unlikely in view of the unnecessary risks entailed and the supreme importance of the unfulfilled mission in France. Madden's sources informed him that Emmet went 'immediately' from Fort George to the European mainland, a brusque departure confirming that his presence in Scotland had not been occasioned by fraternal concern alone. Emmet reappeared in Hamburg before the end of August 1800 in company with co-conspirator Malachy Delaney, with whom he presumably rendezvoused in England before making the crossing from Yarmouth. Delaney used the name 'Bowens' when travelling which, in addition to his fluency in German, helped conceal his identity from casual investigation. Emmet had evaded at least one arrest warrant in Ireland and may also have used a pseudonym, regardless of whether William Wickham believed that his detention was not planned in mid-1800.[20] Pollock was incorrect in surmising that Emmet's travels coincided with the lapse in the Habeas Corpus Suspension Act on 31 December 1800 and its re-enactment in March 1801. It was claimed that Emmet and Delaney 'lived a good deal' with Garret Byrne and Edward Fitzgerald in the Hamburg suburb of Altona, the two most experienced United Irish combat leaders on the mainland.[21]

MacNally learned on 19 September 1800 that Emmet and Delaney had departed 'on business to France'. His news was several weeks out of date and indicative of his increasing distance from the post-Rebellion Directory. They rarely called upon the services of barristers presumed to be sympathetic as had been the practice prior to the summer of 1798. Newry's Samuel Turner (aka Roberts and Richardson), the organisation's main contact in Hamburg, reported the arrival of the delegates to the British authorities in the city. It was believed that they had come from Dublin to replace the inactive and out-of-touch United Irish Paris intermediary, Edward Lewins. This was not strictly accurate even though Emmet acted as secretary to Delaney to bolster the impression that he was the real ambassador of the United Irish

Directory in Dublin. Delaney was then forty-two and Emmet twenty-two, an age difference reflected by their assumed roles in Hamburg. While Lewins was embroiled in myriad difficulties it does not seem that supplanting him was an option in the late summer of 1800. Lewins was estranged from the spirit and personalities of the new commanders in Ireland yet remained a respected member of the circle created by Wolfe Tone.[22] Nonetheless, Emmet reputedly 'wrote several memoirs which were delivered to the French Government', communications that effectively sidelined Lewins. If, as seems likely, the plans had been verbally ratified in Fort George, they could be expected to carry a degree of authority and purpose that had been lacking since the Rebellion. McCabe and Palmer had been previously dispatched on a similar mission but due to the vagaries of travel in wartime Europe reached Paris after Emmet and Delaney.[23]

HOLLAND AND FRANCE

Crossing into Holland from Hamburg, a territory under French military jurisdiction, required the permission of General P. F. C. Augereau, with whom Delaney was acquainted from his days in the Austrian service. This probably accounted for the warm reception they encountered from the general, which contrasted with difficulties faced by many United Irishmen seeking access to France. Augereau allowed the delegates to enter Holland and was impressed by the pragmatic Franco-Irish relationship they outlined to him in a memorial written in French and endorsed by him on 15 September 1800. Emmet and Delaney revealed that 25–30,000 French troops, rather than 10,000, were sought by the Dublin leadership. This was a decisive force when backed by the 75,000 stand of arms they required to equip the United Irish auxiliaries. Victory was virtually assured if such an expedition could be mounted. A prescient consideration was the promise of reimbursing the French for their investment when the new Irish Republic found its feet, a point of dispute between the American revolutionaries and France in the 1780s.[24]

Emmet and Delaney informed the French that while 500,000 men had been 'included in the organisation of the Irish Union [United Irishmen] . . . threefold that number would cooperate, when the invasion would actually take place'. Of these, 200,000 were promised 'to fight alongside the French army and extort the peace of the World from the heart of England'. The document also sought to assure the French of confidentiality and revealed their instructions to avoid unnecessary contact with the Irish exiles in Hamburg other than an unnamed former member of the United Irish Directory for whom they also requested a passport. This was almost certainly Richard McCormick, whose engagement with the visitors from Ireland on this occasion escaped the notice of Turner. The final part of the memorial requested that Augereau communicate the contents to 'the brave [Napoleon] Buonaparte' who, they hoped, would issue three passports in false names for the delegation to enter France. When transmitted to Paris, the plan met with the approbation of Bonaparte, who personally signed the memorial in January 1801 and instructed Tallyrand to interview the delegates. Bonaparte also recommended that Tallyrand receive the opinion of General Jean Bernadotte. Travel expenses were then authorised for the United Irishmen to come to the French capital indicating a wish to expedite whatever arrangement might be agreed.[25]

Tallyrand, the great survivor of French politics and the country's foreign minister, received Emmet and Delaney in Paris in January 1801. They were not accompanied by McCormick or any other Hamburg-based United Irishman whose sudden disappearance or travel to Paris might have raised questions. Tallyrand was distrusted by MacNeven who allegedly told Walter Cox in 1798, when both were imprisoned in Kilmainham, that the Frenchman had 'sold' Ireland.[26] Whatever their reservations, the United Irishmen sent to Paris were obliged to discuss the invasion project in detail with Tallyrand who had no hesitation in commending it to the First Consul as worthy of development. Bernadotte must also have concurred. Emmet continued to draft memorials outlining the United Irish position which were examined by the various military departments concerned. While the logistics of a possible expedition were being explored, the French moved to make immediate political capital from their strengthened alliance with the United Irishmen. Hoping to pressurise London into negotiating suitable peace terms, Delaney and other United Irish agents presumed to be under surveillance by the British agreed to go to Brest to intimate that Ireland was the destination of its fleet in the spring of 1801. This threat was wearing thin for men who looked forward to such an event and complicated the task of those responsible for convincing them to act in July 1803. St John Mason, McCabe, O'Hanlon and other associates of Emmet who had been forced into exile were on hand to assist the 1801 subterfuge. That many United Irishmen complied with the ruse suggests that Bonaparte was expected to initiate the strategy he had backed in principle in January.

This proved illusory, although, as Elliott contends, it is not certain that the United Irishmen had been deceived. The signing of a preliminary Anglo-French peace agreement at Leoben in August 1801, partly due to United Irish machinations, arose from matters beyond their control.[27]

Robert Emmet's Dublin associates awaited his return to Ireland in mid-March 1801 but the Brest ruse and political developments in France evidently changed his plans. Francis Higgins wrote to Cooke from Stephen's Green on 4 March claiming: 'I have been well informed that the younger Emmett [sic] is expected to arrive at Belfast from Cruxhaven [sic] in the course of the next week. It is mentioned that papers of consequence and some [French army] commissions are also expected.' This entailed a return to Hamburg and probable travel through England to Liverpool. Higgins did not specify the source of his information but it may be pertinent that his agents were relaying information to him in early 1801 from persons in contact with John Keogh, James Dixon and Hugh Fitzsimmons, all of whom were implicated to some extent in the Rising of 1803. Keogh was one of the first persons contacted by Emmet on his return from France in late 1802.[28]

Emmet reacted to the disastrous news of impending peace in Europe by seeking another audience with Tallyrand. That this was granted under the changed circumstances testified to French perceptions of him as an accredited plenipotentiary. He intended pressing Tallyrand to demand provisions for Irish Catholics and the remaining United Irish prisoners in any definitive peace treaty concluded with Britain. On detecting the statesman's 'evasive' demeanour Emmet left the meeting holding out little hope for progress. A major point of difficulty was that Bonaparte's administration contemplated suppressing Irish republican activity in France if the British reciprocated by clamping down on royalist émigrés in Britain. Consolidating the ascendancy won by French arms after almost a decade of war on many fronts was far more important to the First Consul than honouring tentative commitments to expendable United Irishmen. This realisation was obviously not only unwelcome but humiliating to men who had worked for years to bind Irish interests to those of France. The decision to invite overwhelming foreign assistance, however, permitted the United Irish leadership no alternative but to await a breakdown in Anglo-French relations.[29]

One consolation for the Emmets was the proposed release of the high-ranking United Irish prisoners held at Fort George in peacetime. They were prime candidates for government positions in the Irish Republic, whenever it could be established. The theme of family disunion and its relationship to the French war surfaced in an outwardly innocuous letter sent to Fort George by Dr Emmet on 1 January 1801. New Year's Day in a new century was evidently an occasion on which family absences seemed more poignant. It was also the first day on which the Act of Union made Ireland part of the United Kingdom. Overt mention of Irish political concerns was assiduously avoided, although inferences may have been drawn from Dr Emmet's comments on the continuation of the conflict. The discharge of Addis Emmet was contingent on peace being effected by the victory of either protagonist or the conclusion of an armistice; Robert Emmet's input into both scenarios was taken for granted by his parents. They could not have known that their youngest son had raised the issue of prisoners with Tallyrand and was embittered by his negative attitude. Emmet quickly divined what was contemplated by Bonaparte and informed Addis Emmet of certain 'expressions . . . from high authority, respecting the willingness of [the French] Government to deliver up the United Irishmen, tied neck and heels, to England'.[30]

The gradual onset of peace removed all urgency attending Emmet's stay on the Continent and he spent the summer of 1801 in Switzerland. He no doubt reflected on what bearing the altered international situation might have on the United Irish agenda. Emmet had returned to Paris by early October 1801 and wrote in French to a family friend from an address of 9 Rue D'Amboise. The contents of the letter indicated that they had previously been in close contact. On 6 October 1801 Emmet professed his ignorance to the Marquise de Fontenay of 'the time of my departure' from Paris but linked this to news that his father had put Casino House on the market. The proposed sale of the Milltown property raised the possibility of reuniting the Emmet family outside Ireland. Wales and the United States were both suggested as suitable locations.[31]

If shelving or abandoning radical politics seemed an option for Robert Emmet this was not reflected by his reading matter. When in Paris Emmet purchased and closely studied Colin Lindsay's edition of *Extracts from Colonel Templehoff's History of the Seven Years' War* published in London in 1793. Volume two of Lindsay's work came into the possession of Madden who marvelled at the detailed marginal notes made by Emmet. This was a compulsive habit formed by Emmet as a child and continued through his student years in Trinity. The first volume was found in a secret munitions depot on Thomas Street operated by Emmet's followers in 1803. News of the Dublin networks was very probably relayed to Emmet in October

1801 when Patrick Gallagher returned to Paris from a highly dangerous visit to the Irish capital on 'political business'. Gallagher, the man who had escaped from a Dublin prison tender in December 1798, left for Ireland from Bordeaux using the name Wilson when word of Leoben reached the United Irish community in or around August 1801. His short detention in Bordeaux on the return journey, ostensibly owing to passport irregularities, served as a reminder that the United Irish mission to Paris was entirely dependent on French tolerance.[32]

In mid December 1801 Emmet anticipated the release of the state prisoners from Fort George and was apprised by a London contact that the French threat to Ireland had encouraged British participation in the peace talks at Amiens. The presence of Cornwallis at Amiens, who as Viceroy of Ireland three years before had introduced the Amnesty Act, may have lent credence to rumours that a 'general amnesty' would be granted by the British that would exonerate Emmet and his associates. More importantly, a 'system of conciliation in Ireland' was also, incorrectly, said to have been on the table. The dashing of this optimistic forecast by March 1802 may account for Emmet's rededication to advancing the revolutionary option in Ireland. The state prisoners also became restive and, in November 1801, Robert Hunter wrote from Fort George claiming that his colleagues had discovered from a message passed to Jane Emmet that he had been providing information to the government. Addis Emmet and Neilson were reputedly then plotting to suborn the Scottish militia.[33] Addis Emmet certainly succeeded in smuggling letters out of Fort George to his associates in Dublin, several of which were read out at a United Irish gathering in mid-November.[34] By the close of 1802 a street ballad published in Dundalk contained a reference to 'E[mme]t' being in Brest, although, pointedly, not in a sense which reflected the presence of a leading United Irishman in an invasion port.[35]

PARIS

When not engaged in overt political intrigue or studying military texts, Emmet immersed himself in the vibrant Parisian social scene. He was financially supported by 'the liberality' of his father, who had raised extra funds by the oft delayed sale of Addis Emmet's unwanted share of the state physicianship. The sum of £67 was sent to Robert Emmet on 1 September 1801 and again on 10 February 1802. Between April and August 1802 a further grant of £202 was remitted in three instalments. Emmet's social life in Paris was hardly frivolous and several advantageous connections were formed. He befriended the American ambassador and Joel Barlow, one of the new republic's most radical citizens abroad. A poem by Barlow on the American War of Independence was printed in Ireland by Watty Cox seven years later.[36] Barlow introduced Emmet to the gifted Pennsylvanian engineer Robert Fulton, then thirty-seven, who shared the Dubliner's fascination with science and had acquired the wealth to conduct expensive experiments. Fulton, an associate of Benjamin Franklin, built the *Nautilus* submersible in France in 1800 and was researching other sophisticated forms of naval weaponry such as torpedoes and underwater mines when he met Emmet. It is very likely that Fulton convinced Emmet of the utility of advanced armaments given that the Dubliner was the first to introduce mines and multiple rockets to the armoury of Irish revolutionaries. Emmet, for his part, may have informed the American of Lord Edward Fitzgerald's far-sighted interest in the role of rocketry in urban zones. While Fulton may have provided his new friend with prototype plans for explosive devices, it is clear that further research and development was carried out under Emmet's auspices in Ireland in 1803. Their respect was evidently mutual and in August 1803 Fulton offered his rockets to the French government if they campaigned in Ireland. He became disaffected with Bonaparte when this and other opportunities to strike at the Royal Navy were passed over.[37]

Emmet also became acquainted in Paris with the noted Normandy chemist Louis-Nicolas Vauquelin, discoverer of quinic and camphoric acid, whose reputation was almost certainly known to him before arriving in France. Comtesse d'Hausonville recalled the Dubliner's visits to the salon of Madame de Staël (Anne Louise Germaine), her grandmother, and described him as having a 'pleasing' countenance with 'energy, delicacy and tenderness . . . expressed in his melancholy features'. Emmet re-encountered the Parisian family of the Marquise de Fontenay, who had last seen him as a young boy when they lived in Dublin. In the early 1790s the de Fontenays were refugees from the turmoil of French politics and had been befriended by Dr and Mrs Emmet at Stephen's Green.[38]

Robert Emmet's eyesight had always been less than perfect and in February 1802 he contracted an infection which took over two months to heal. Such problems ran in the family; Thomas Addis Emmet was said to have been 'remarkably short sighted', as was Christopher Temple Emmet.[39] The younger Emmet raised the subject of his troublesome eyes in a letter of April 1802 in which he lamented the absence of his friend, Surgeon, later General, William Lawless. He had lived on Eustace and French Streets in the mid-1790s and was a member of the Court of Assistants at the Royal College of Surgeons in Ireland. Lawless was the elder brother of Emmet's Trinity friend John Lawless and had been away from Paris 'for some time'. Another relative, Valentine Lawless, was an occasional resident of the French capital and known to the Emmet brothers for many years. William Lawless's brother and nephew were implicated in the Rising of 1803.[40]

Malachy Delaney, Hugh Ware, James Joseph MacDonnell and Patrick Gallagher, all popular veteran fighting rebel commanders of 1798, were foremost amongst Emmet's United Irish companions in Paris. Apart from other important considerations, Ware was the cousin of Joseph Perrot, one of Emmet's main assistants in organising Kildare for rebellion in 1803. Delaney could have vouched for Emmet's character and status had such guarantees been required by the Kildare group. Ware linked Emmet to Tyroneman Bernard Duggan, a fellow participant in the Rebellion in Kildare, who became the Dubliner's aide on his return to Ireland. An equally if not more significant connection was established with Michael Quigley of Rathcoffey who left France in the spring of 1803 to function as a key figure in Dublin-area plans. Wickham described him as 'by far the cleverest man' of Emmet's followers.[41] It was in Paris, therefore, that Emmet received introductions to several experienced and dynamic United Irishmen who were instrumental in preparing the ground for the Rising of 1803. This could not have been done at that time in any other city in the world. A more casual acquaintanceship was probably made by Emmet with Matilda Tone, widow of Wolfe Tone, who moved in the same compact Anglophone circuit. Emmet had probably met her in Ireland given the close friendship between Wolfe Tone and Addis Emmet.[42] His Longford and Trinity friend Michael Farrell, furthermore, participated in 'meetings at Lawless's [and] Mrs Wolfe Tone's' when in France.[43]

Emmet's Paris circle extended to fellow Dubliner Lyndon Bolton, in whose house he re-encountered a former Trinity student who later provided the authorities with the type of information which Fitzgibbon and Duigenan had striven to obtain in April 1798. Bolton, formerly a woollen draper in Francis Street and a member of the Liberty Rangers, had taken part in the Rebellion and reputedly shared a 'particular intimacy with Emmet'. His family connections in the Irish capital intersected with the social and political associations of

Delaney and he was clearly a United Irishman of note before fleeing to Hamburg.[44] As early as August 1798 Bolton's name had been raised by Castlereagh in relation to 'Captain Williams, Despard, Tremlett, a naval officer, Palmer of Barnard's Inn' and other suspected subversives in Britain and, by 1802, he was also known to the Manchester radicals.[45]

Bolton initially struggled to make ends meet in Hamburg where he had assumed the name 'Gordon' and impersonated John Gray's brother. When living in better circumstances in Paris a few years later he hosted gatherings attended by Emmet, Delaney, Gallagher, McCormick and William Lawless, whose presence signified their trust of his politics. While Bolton's status within the United Irishmen on the Continent is unclear, his many levels of contact with republicans in Hamburg and Paris suggest seniority. A potentially important association with Colonel Despard from 1798 and their joint subsequent links with William Dowdall and Manchester's revolutionary cells, indicates prominence. Emmet's close association with Bolton is, therefore, significant. Also of interest are the series of detailed disclosures made by Bolton's lodger that ultimately attuned Dublin Castle to the depth of Emmet's involvement with the United Irishmen in 1796–1802. While Bolton was not above suspicion in this regard, the most likely candidate for providing this information was John Egan, whose public cooperation with the Trinity investigation was supplemented by secret betrayals.[46]

Egan was in France at the same time as Emmet acting as tutor to the three eldest boys of the Mount Cashell touring party. They stayed in Paris from 5 December 1801 until April 1802 and for brief subsequent periods. In addition to the Trinity, Dublin and United Irish links shared with Egan, Emmet was connected to the group by Lady Mount Cashell's association with his sister, Mary Anne Emmet. Catherine Wilmot's letters record the party's social engagements in Paris with such luminaries as the Polish patriot leader General Kosciusko, Tallyrand, the American Ambassador, the painter David and English radicals Tom Paine and Sir Francis Burdett. They also met General Louis-Alexandre Berthier, veteran of the American War and colleague of Bonaparte in the Italian and Egyptian campaigns. Berthier assumed responsibility for Franco-Irish military cooperation in 1803 and, as such, was probably a more active listener and observer than his dinner party guests could have realised.[47]

The circumstance of Emmet's being 'amongst the politically distinguish[e]d in Dublin College' intrigued Catherine Wilmot when they met in Paris. On 13 March 1802 she wrote to her brother Robert from the Hotel de Rome, Faubourg St Germain, bringing to an end a month of silence. She explained:

> we have lately become acquainted with Robert Emmett [sic], who, I dare say you have heard of . . . His face is uncommonly expressive of everything youthful and everything enthusiastic, and his colour comes and goes rapidly, accompanied by a such a nervousness of agitated sensibility, that in his society I feel in a perpetual apprehension lest any passing idle word shou[l]d wound the delicacy of his feelings. For tho[ugh] his reserve prevents one's hearing many of his opinions, yet one would swear to their style of exaltation, from their flitting shadows blushing across his countenance in everlasting succession. His understanding they tell me is very bright. But I am not likely to know much about it. For his extreme prejudice against French society will prevent our meeting him anywhere except at the House of an English gentleman, who is soon returning to London. At this house we have seen [Matilda Tone] the widow of the unfortunate [Wolfe] Tone, who is interesting to the greatest degree.[48]

The 'reserve' detected by the perceptive Wilmot indicates that Emmet was guarded when mixing outside the company of fellow United Irishmen. This accounts for the fact that 'Jones' or Egan could only furnish Dublin Castle with obsolete, low-grade information when detailing Emmet's associations in 1803 and evidently knew nothing of his negotiations with the French executive. It was clearly not apparent to the Mount Cashells or to the spy at Bolton's that Malachy Delaney had returned to Ireland in March 1802 and that Emmet had moved in with Patrick Gallagher. Emmet must have taken Egan's public conduct during the Trinity Visitation into account when in the company of the Mount Cashell group. This may explain why Wilmot was seemingly unaware of Emmet's dealings with the predominately Francophone de Staël salon. If Emmet's discernible exasperation with elements of Parisian society was genuine, as Wilmot's innocent comments suggest, it is clear that their political context was not understood by her. Frustration, ennui and personality clashes were more likely than anti-French sentiment to have muted Emmet's characteristic exuberance.[49] Another commentator noted that 'Emmet lived very privately at Paris'.[50]

During a short return visit to the French capital in August 1802 the Mount Cashells and their friends met a diverse range of Irish tourists. They included the well-known United Irishman Valentine Lawless, two sons of the conservative Wicklow politician Sir John Parnell, and James and Louisa Penrose of Woodhill, Cork. Lawless was then in frequent contact with the Emmet brothers while the Penroses, friends of John Philpot Curran, were destined to act as guardians to Robert Emmet's secret fiancée, Sarah Curran. Even though these associations were merely social and partly, if not entirely, coincidental, they reveal the ease with which prominent Irish liberal families encountered high-ranking United Irishmen. It is very likely that the Mount Cashells sent news of their meetings with Emmet to the Moiras, Granards, Edgeworths and other landed families who knew his father and sisters.[51]

In April 1802 Emmet lived at 298 Rue de la Loi and was uncertain whether to remain in Paris. He then claimed to be torn between the prospect of emigrating to North America with his brother's family or 'making a sacrifice by returning to Ireland' where his parents had resolved to stay. The 'sacrifice' alluded to was that of professional prospects, rather than his life. He was not listed on the Banishment Act and could rely on the eventual restoration of habeas corpus to shield him from Castle harassment. A crucial factor was apparently 'the intention of the British Government' and the continuation of the peace treaty signed at Amiens on 27 March 1802. He may have learned something of the mood in Amiens from the Mount Cashells who, as visitors to the French town, had narrowly missed running into Britain's chief negotiator, Lord Cornwallis. The United Irish partnership with France appeared less hopeful in 1802 than at any time since 1794 and the rationale for Emmet's ongoing presence in Paris was consequently in doubt.[52]

Returning to Ireland was conditional on his arriving 'without contracting any engagement that might compromise my honour'. Even at this nadir Emmet would neither renounce his United Irish oath nor repudiate the organisation's objectives. Emmet knew he had been sought for questioning along with several close political colleagues in April 1798 and April 1799, and this suggested prudence if travel to Ireland was contemplated. Whereas William Wickham believed Emmet had left his home country without fear of arrest hanging over his head, the subject of his enquiries felt otherwise in 1802.[53] His caution was vindicated in August 1803 when Cork United Irishman John James Finn was arrested on the basis of 'a Secretary of State's Warrant against him in 1798 at which time he fled' to France. In the final analysis, the threat Emmet perceived to his liberty was more important than the actual legal technicalities pertaining to his case.[54]

THE FORT GEORGE LEADERS

The release of Thomas Addis Emmet from Fort George on 26 June 1802 provided a terrific boost for the family. This was possibly an error. Alone of the Irish inmates, Addis Emmet's name was missing from the warrant sent to the prison from London ordering the discharge of the internees. The Governor interpreted this omission as a clerical oversight and took the principled step of releasing Addis Emmet regardless, an action for which he was allegedly reprimanded. If the government wished to retain Addis Emmet in custody it is far from certain that a legal pretext could have been invoked. Had specific offence been taken at the publication in London in 1802 of *Memoire, or detailed statement of the origin and progress of the Irish Union* it is likely that Addis Emmet's co-authors, O'Connor and MacNeven, would also have been detained. Given that this was not the case the Governor's initial assessment may have been correct.[55]

Barred from returning to Ireland by the Banishment Act, Addis Emmet was deported to Hamburg on 4 July with Mathew Dowling, John Sweetman, Thomas Russell and several less prominent men on board Captain P. Campbell's HMS *Ariadne*. Addis Emmet lost no time going to the Dutch port city of Amsterdam with his wife and four of their seven children. Most of the Hamburg party also went. A reunion with their other children was planned in Brussels where Addis Emmet wished to generate income by taking students. He also planned to complete a work of Irish history with MacNeven which they had drafted in Kilmainham in 1798 only to have the manuscript confiscated by their jailors. This project was complicated by MacNeven's shifting his residence from Hamburg to Munich and then from Prague to Paris within a period of months in 1802. Their friend Dowling went to live in Rotterdam while Sweetman made his home in Lyon. The dispersion of the emancipated United Irish leaders to locations where few, if any, of their comrades were living, suggests that no major seditious enterprise was then contemplated.[56]

Robert Emmet was probably in Spain when news reached him of his brother's release. He had journeyed to Cadiz with John Allen, an important United Irishman, who had been acquitted of treason at Maidstone and afterwards resumed his work in the cloth business in Dublin. Allen's legal entitlement to travel within British territories and his possession of sufficient personal wealth to embark on frequent trips overseas rendered him a valuable asset to the United Irishmen.

He almost certainly briefed Emmet on the 1801 dinner he shared in Liverpool with Thomas Cloney and William Todd Jones, both of whom emerged as prominent figures in the 1803 conspiracy. Allen's use of the name 'Captain Brown' when in Spain implies that the purpose of their presence may have been to make representations to the Spanish authorities on behalf of the United Irishmen. The Spanish government had long since directed the operations of its Irish Brigade towards its colonies in the Americas and Caribbean, but direct military assistance was not out of the question. The prospect of this was greatly boosted by Spain's tentative alliances with France in the early 1800s, which, if nothing else, increased the burden of the Royal Navy in the Mediterranean and Atlantic.[57]

Cadiz had a small United Irish community that, in 1803, temporarily sheltered William Dowdall, James Farrell and Thomas Brannigan when matters went awry in Dublin. Long-term Irish residents were very probably visited by Emmet and Allen in the summer of 1802, as were other expatriates living in the Iberian Peninsula. Health considerations and the wine trade brought many to the warmer climate including individuals whose assistance would have been useful to Emmet. Philip Long, one of Emmet's political mentors, had spent many years in Spain prior to the revolutionary period and could have provided written or personal introductions for United Irishmen in the region.[58] William Sampson, the friend of Surgeon Lawless and Addis Emmet, had nominated the Portuguese city of Oporto as his destination of choice when obliged to leave Ireland. Michael Farrell of Longford, however, simply required a convenient Continental port of entry in order to remain an active United Irishman. Farrell first escaped to Liverpool after fighting with the Franco-Irish forces in August/September 1798 and proceeded to London, from where, after a period hiding in Soho, he crossed to Portugal. Having availed of this insecure but legal trade route, Farrell contravened passport restrictions on British and Irish subjects by going to Bordeaux to meet Putnam McCabe and Palmer. He was in Paris by the end of 1800 where he was reunited with his Trinity comrade, Robert Emmet. Cork United Irishman John O'Finn went in the opposite direction and arrived in his native city from Lisbon on 5 August 1803.[59]

Michael Farrell was suspected by British intelligence of being a United Irish courier in England and was, like Emmet, close to both Lawless and Palmer. His return to England by late July 1803, from either Hamburg or France, raised fears in Whitehall that the United Irishmen still hoped to coordinate republican activity in both islands of the newly formed United Kingdom. A spy made the significant allegation that Farrell's 'first coming from France [to England] in May or June [1803] was at the request of Emmett [sic] who placed great reliance on him'.[60] Allen was also rightly suspected of such intrigue yet was free to travel between Britain and Ireland owing to his refusal to sign the Kilmainham agreement in 1798. William Dowdall and Roger O'Connor had also successfully gambled on obtaining this rare privilege. Emmet may have personally conspired in Britain but his intimacy with Allen, Dowdall, Farrell, Long, John Binns and James Farrell ensured that his views were well represented when he was engaged elsewhere. Their plans to seed revolution in Britain and Ireland were effectively provisional until the backing of Addis Emmet's clique was obtained in conjunction with a signal from the French.[61]

Robert Emmet wrote to John Patten from Amsterdam on 7 August 1802 mentioning that he had left Paris 'too suddenly' to obtain letters of introduction from Vauquelin for 'one of the first chemists of Europe'. This was possibly Vauquelin's mentor Foureroy, the follower of the great Lavoiser, but Emmet's abiding interest in chemistry took second place to political affairs. He returned to Paris from Spain for a brief stay before setting out to meet Addis Emmet. That he left most of his belongings in Lawless' house indicates that he did not intend a prolonged absence; his hurried departure from the French capital may also suggest that he had not positively ascertained his brother's exact address in Holland. Supporting this statement is that the two allegedly met by chance in Amsterdam's main post office when enquiring after each other's missing correspondence. Not mentioned in Emmet's letter to Patten was that he travelled in company with Hugh Wilson, who had arrived in Hamburg with Addis Emmet. Wilson, former associate of Wolfe Tone and Oliver Bond, may have been deputed to bring Robert Emmet to Holland for an informal conference with the released state prisoners.[62]

Emmet briefed his elder brother on the state of the French alliance and his dealings with Tallyrand. Addis Emmet then informed MacNeven, whom he had last seen in Hamburg, that Robert Emmet had advised against publishing their history of Ireland claiming 'that it would be as safe in London as in France'. This disappointing news, while not entirely unexpected, affirmed Addis Emmet in his plan to emigrate to the United States. That this did not occur, however, reflected his belief, shared by most leading United Irishmen in Europe, that the Treaty of Amiens might not hold. If it collapsed there was every prospect of Bonaparte renewing his support for the Irish cause.

18 The Trinity College expulsions (Trinity College Dublin MS 1203)

By the Lord Lieutenant and Council of Ireland.

A PROCLAMATION.

CAMDEN.

WHEREAS by an act of Parliament passed in this kingdom in the 36th year of his Majesty's reign, entitled "an act more effectually to suppress insurrections, and to prevent the disturbance of the public peace," it is enacted, that it shall be lawful for the Justices of the Peace of any county, assembled at a special session, in manner by the said act directed, not being fewer than seven, or the major part of them, one of whom to be of the quorum, if they see fit, upon due consideration of the state of the country, to signify by memorial, by them signed, to the Lord Lieutenant, or other Chief Governor or Governors of this kingdom, that they consider the county, or any part thereof, to be in a state of disturbance, or in immediate danger of becoming so, and praying that the Lord Lieutenant and Council may proclaim such county or part thereof to be in a state of disturbance, or in immediate danger of becoming so; and thereupon it shall be lawful for the Lord Lieutenant or other Chief Governor or Governors of this kingdom, by and with the advice of his Majesty's Privy Council, by proclamation to declare such county, or any part of such county, to be in a state of disturbance, or in immediate danger of becoming so; and also such parts of any adjoining county or counties as such Chief Governor or Governors shall think fit, in order to prevent the continuance or extension of such disturbance.

And whereas twenty-two Magistrates of the county of the city of Dublin, being the Major part of the Magistrates, duly assembled, pursuant to the said act, of a special session of the peace, holden at the Session house, in and for the county of the said city of Dublin, on Friday the 18th day of May instant, have, by memorial by them signed, signified to his Excellency the Lord Lieutenant that they consider the county of the city of Dublin to be in immediate danger of becoming in a state of disturbance, and have thereby prayed that the Lord Lieutenant and Council may proclaim the said county of the city of Dublin to be in immediate danger of becoming in a state of disturbance.

Now we the Lord Lieutenant do, by and with the advice of his Majesty's Privy Council, in pursuance of and by the authority to us given by the said act of Parliament, by this our proclamation, declare the said county of the city of Dublin to be in immediate danger of becoming in a state of disturbance, of which all Magistrates of the said county of the city of Dublin, and all others whom it may concern, are to take notice.

Given at the Council Chamber in Dublin, the 19th day of May, 1798.

Clare, C.	Portarlington.	Rossmore.
Char. Cashel.	Ely.	John Foster.
W. Tuam.	Dillon.	J. Beresford.
Waterford.	Pery.	J. Blaquiere.
Drogheda.	O'Neill.	D. Latouche.
Westmeath.	Castlereagh.	Robt. Ross.
Shannon.	H. Meath.	Isaac Corry.
Altamont.	G. D. Kildare.	Lodge Morres.
	Glentworth.	

19 Dublin Castle Proclamation, *Saunder's Newsletter*, 27 August 1798

Rebell. Captains found Entered in Commisary Brennan's Book as having been supplyed with Provisions out of his Stores — (Ross Army & Corbett Hill)

Genl. Ryan — County Wexford
Genl. Roach — Do
Col. McClune — Dublin
Col. Holt — Wicklow
Col. Byrne — Ballymanus Do
Col. Fitzgerald — Co. Wexford
Captain Dixon — Town Wexford
Captain Perry — Do
Captn. Rourke — Dublin
Captn. Dixon Jun. Wexford
Captn. Rossiter — town Do
Captn. Murphy — Do
Captn. Doyle — Do
Captn. Greene — Town Do
Captn. Clomay, B. Barge Do
Captn. O'Brien, Fookes Mills, Co. Wexford
Captn. Wm. Furlong, Ambrosetown Do
Captn. Breen — Taughmoe
Captn. Butler — Do
Captn. Bryan — Do

Captn. Richd. Howlin — Do
Captn. Tool — Ross
Captn. Sharkey — Burrows
Captn. Ryan — Glinn
Captn. Codd — B. Fort
Captn. Devrs — Adamstown
Captn. Treuman — Wexford
Captn. O'Farrell — Waterford
Captn. Barry — Wexford
Captn. Shannon — Ross
Captn. Prendergast Wexford town
Captn. Maguire, Island, Co. Wexford
Captn. Quirke — Dublin
Captn. Jno. Murphy — Wexford
Captn. J. Barry — Do
Captn. Cullen, Tintown Co. Wexford
Captn. Charley — old Ross Co. Wexford

(turn

20 Dublin rebels in Wexford (National Archives of Ireland, Rebellion Papers, 620/51/223)

21 Joseph Holt

22 Henry Charles Sirr by T. Martyn

23 James Hope by William Charles Nixon

24 Edward Cooke

Lodge (John and Co.) Merchants, 16, *Abbey-street.*
Lodge (Mary) Haberdasher, 35, *College-green.*
Logan (James) Shoemaker, 22, *Clarendon-street.*
Logan (Mary) Linen-draper, 10, *Aungier-street.*
Logan (Thomas) Paper-stainer, 23, *Temple-bar.*
Logan (William and Co.) Merchants, 60, *Marlborough-street.*
Long (Abraham) Shoemaker, *Nassau-street.*
Long (Ann) Tallow-chandler, 119, *James's-street.*
Long (George) Grocer, 6, *Luke-street.*
Long (John) Carpenter, 17, *gt. Ship-street.*
Long (Mark) Grocer, 11, *Anglesea-street.*
Long (Philip) Merchant, 4, *Crow-street.*
Long (William) Coach-maker, 12, *Mary-street.*
Longford & Cahill, Chip and Straw-hat-manuf. 61, *S. gt. George's-street.*
Lord (Mary) Hatter and Hosier, 19, *Capel-street.*
Loughlin (James) Apothecary, 13, *King-street.*
Louch (Richard Lucius) Architect and Measurer, 27, *Poolbeg-street.*
Love (William) Woollen-draper, 25, *Francis-street.*
Lovely (Robert) Slate-merchant, 26, *Poolbeg-street.*
Lowe (Mary) Metal Sash-maker, 12, *Marlborough-street.*
Lowe (Robert) Carpenter, 18, *Montgomery-street.*
†Lowry (James) Merchant, 54, *Pill-lane.*
Lowry (Michael) Brewer and Merchant, 11, *Meath-street.*
Lowth (Edmond) Brush-maker, 2, *S. gt. George's-street.*
Lowther and Co. Straw-hat & Fancy Feather-merchants, 11, *Dame-co.*
Lube (Patrick) Wholesale Woollen-draper, 41, *Bridge-street.*

25 Listing for Philip Long from *Wilson's Dublin Directory*, 1803

26 Michael Dwyer by
George Petrie

27 Insurgents

28 Fort George, Scotland

29 William Corbett

30 Arthur O'Connor

31 Samuel Neilson

32 Napper Tandy

33 Philip Yorke,
Earl Hardwicke
(courtesy of the
National
Library of
Ireland)

Accordingly, Robert and Addis Emmet went to Brussels where, within a short period, the future of Irish republicanism appeared far less bleak than it had during the summer.[63] In mid-September an impatient Thomas Russell wrote from Paris to his brother John in London 'wishing and expecting' to see him 'in *free* Ireland'.[64]

After months of travelling to Franco-Swiss battle sites MacNeven arrived in Paris from Switzerland in October 1802. He had lived in Prague as a boy with his uncle, physician to Habsburg Empress Maria Theresa, and obtained his MD at Vienna in 1783. An account of MacNeven's 1802 sojourn was published the following year in Dublin by John Stockdale.[65] MacNeven found on returning to Paris that William Lawless and other United Irish figures were once again keen to act if war was resumed. Robert Emmet went to see MacNeven in Paris and evidently stayed on this occasion with Lawless given that he left a quantity of books and papers with him on departing for Ireland. Thomas Russell, who had serious reservations as to Bonaparte's interest in Ireland, was also in the capital when Emmet returned from Brussels. He had struck up a strong relationship with General Humbert, leader of the French expedition to Ireland in August/September 1798. The general remained a staunch supporter of the United Irishmen, despite the uneven performance of the rebels with whom he had fought in 1798. He and other French advocates of an Irish campaign required and received guarantees that an invasion would be met with a substantial response by the United Irishmen.[66] Arthur O'Connor, by no means an impartial commentator, informed the historian Madden many years later that Russell's enthusiastic dealings with Robert Emmet had convinced the Dubliner to act in 1803.[67]

NAPOLEON BONAPARTE

It was around this time that Robert Emmet was invited to discuss United Irish affairs with Bonaparte. The First Consul, as Emmet later informed Miles Byrne, apparently feared that the Act of Union had changed the attitude of the Irish towards liberty, a concern previously addressed in the memorial presented by Emmet and Delaney to General Augereau in September 1800. This crucial misconception was quickly dealt with by Emmet when face to face with Bonaparte as the two sounded each other out, although the resurfacing of the issue in 1802 may have had important bearing on the events of July 1803. Emmet confided in John Patten that he had gained an 'unfavourable impression' of Bonaparte but agreed to meet once

more with Tallyrand. Emmet credited Tallyrand with backing the
creation of an independent Irish republic and providing sufficient
French assistance for the purpose. This was the type of military aid
which the Addis Emmet coterie in Fort George had wished to obtain:
ideally, financial, logistical and military support on a par with that
extended to the American insurgents twenty years before. Bonaparte
was suspected by Robert Emmet and others of seeking to 'aggrandize
France' if his army established a major presence in Ireland, a risk
which Arthur O'Connor's much smaller faction was more than
willing to take. The most important realisation arising from Emmet's
negotiations was that the French anticipated the resumption of war
with Britain. This placed the United Irish cause back on the international agenda, albeit not on centre stage.[68]

Emmet dined with Valentine Lawless on the night before he
commenced the ensuing journey from France to Ireland. In his often
unreliable autobiography, Lawless recalled that his guest 'spoke of his
plans with extreme enthusiasm; his features glowed with excitement,
the perspiration burst though the pores and ran down his forehead'.
According to Lawless:

> both [Emmet] brothers dined with me in Paris the day before Robert
> returned to Ireland for the last time previous to his fatal outbreak; and
> although that catastrophe was not then thought of, I remember the
> most urgent entreaties being vainly used by his friends, to dissuade him
> from a visit, which all felt to be full of danger to him, and the sad
> consummation of which so fully justified those gloomy forebodings.[69]

This perspective is undermined by the improbability that Lawless
really disapproved of Emmet's intentions. Madden's sources informed
him that Valentine Lawless was actually supportive in 1802, as were
William Lawless, Thomas Russell, William MacNeven, William and
Thomas Corbett, John Sweeney, Hugh Wilson, Hugh Ware, William
Hamilton and Colonel Lumm. Emmet's old friend William Corbett,
a former associate of Napper Tandy and Anthony McCann from his
days in Hamburg, was lecturing in the new French military college of
Saint-Cyr in 1803. Corbett had used a rope ladder to escape from
Kilmainham prison, where he had been held after being extradited
from Hamburg with Napper Tandy. Tandy's son James was in Brest,
Bordeaux and Paris for much of September/October 1802 and met
with Russell, Lawless and Hampden Evans. His movements were
primarily dictated by the wine trade in which he engaged, although
his socialising placed him in an ideal position to report on the affairs

of the Dublin United Irishmen.[70] The younger Tandy's information was frequently passed to Leonard MacNally, a perceived confidant who communicated what he saw fit to the Castle. Little of note reached the Irish authorities on this occasion with the result that the significance of Emmet's return to Dublin and its wider context was not realised.[71]

It is generally believed that Emmet left Holland for England in early October 1802 and reached Ireland before the end of the month. He probably saw Addis Emmet in Brussels in the first week of October while going to or from Hamburg, where he had last visited with Delaney in August 1800. Emmet's typically overlooked return to Hamburg in late 1802 suggests that he may have considered making the familiar crossing to Yarmouth. More certain is that he held a series of meetings with fellow United Irishmen which assumed retrospective importance in the aftermath of the Rising of 1803. The waning Irish community in Hamburg and its Altona suburb had been replenished in the months preceding Emmet's 1802 arrival by that of many Fort George deportees. The city was once again a centre of intrigue and a key interface for United Irishmen based in the south of England and those on the Continent. Emmet dined with the noted Richard McCormick at the country house of Robert or John Gray in company with Thomas Johnson, an Irish merchant with London connections. Gray, an intimate of Emmet's friend Lyndon Bolton, lodged with a man named Schon and met 'young Emmett [sic]' at the Schlaffen-hoff garden.[72]

McCormick was a former member of the United Irish Executive and had adhered in the early-to-mid 1790s to the grouping headed by Addis Emmet, MacNeven and Keogh. They had factored the Catholic masses into revolutionary plans over the reservations expressed by William Drennan.[73] In early 1798, moreover, Addis Emmet, MacNeven and McCormick had counselled caution in negotiations with the French when Arthur O'Connor, Lord Edward Fitzgerald and Samuel Neilson clamoured for action. While too much has been read into the nuances of these apparent command divisions, Robert Emmet's disproportionate dealings with his brother's faction indicates that a degree of acrimony remained. When in Fort George, O'Connor had reputedly denounced his former friend Lord Edward Fitzgerald as a man who 'had neither nerves nor spirit'. He went on, according to Lady Moira's sources, to castigate Addis Emmet as 'a sensualist and voluptuary' and MacNeven as 'a paltry mixture of duplicity and meanness'.[74] Emmet and Michael Quigley apparently had 'a very serious quarrel' with O'Connor 'on the subject of French assistance' shortly before the Dubliner left for Ireland. Quigley claimed in October 1803 that O'Connor remained resolutely opposed in late 1802 to any United Irish project of which the French were not a major and decisive element. McCormick declined to participate in the 1803 plan outlined by Robert Emmet.[75]

On the positive side, Robert Emmet had been accepted in Dublin by January 1799 as the virtual heir to the position of chief military strategist, which had been vacated by the death of Fitzgerald. The succession evidently passed from Fitzgerald to Neilson and from Charles O'Hara to Robert Emmet, an appointment which was evidently recognised, if not ratified, by the leading members of the United Irishmen in exile.[76] Shifting contexts in the Anglo-French war between 1797–98 and 1802–3 also rendered the old tactical disputes far less compelling. It is significant that the Addis Emmet–O'Connor falling out, although exacerbated by their joint internment in Fort George, flared to its greatest extent after the failure of the Rising of 1803. Indeed, O'Connor's belligerence required the defeat of the conspiracy to claim vindication on the basis that he had been marginalised during its planning stages and was consequently blameless. The contingencies developed by General Berthier for an Irish campaign suggest that O'Connor's reputedly good relationship with Bonaparte was not essential to French commitment. In late 1802 and early 1803, therefore, the endorsement of figureheads like Neilson, Russell, Keogh and MacNeven was more important to Emmet than appeasing O'Connor. It is not surprising that they were canvassed by him in Paris, Hamburg and Dublin before concrete preparations to rise again were initiated.

The extraordinary breadth of Emmet's consultations defied the capacity of pro-British agents in Whitehall and Dublin Castle to track and account for them. It consequently remains unclear whether he took ship in Hamburg, retraced his steps to Holland or even returned briefly to Paris before setting out for Ireland via England. One version of the trip claimed that Emmet delayed crossing the Channel for up to two weeks by staying in the Normandy village of Andemar, between Honfleur and Caen. Emmet told Miles Byrne that he met a Scottish republican named Campbell in a coastal town in Normandy who gave him an insight into the 'patriots' who still resided in their own country and those who had settled in Ireland.[77] The Andemar story avers that Emmet roomed with an English tanner named Lawrence and disguised himself as a working man. Emmet, supposedly, rarely ventured far from the house until he embarked for England at Honfleur. Secrecy was obviously a consideration for Emmet given that his return to Ireland pre-dated the November 1802 lapse of the Habeas Corpus Suspension Act. This, as far as he knew, could have been renewed by Westminster notwithstanding the opposition this would have incurred from the Whigs in parliament. Emmet, therefore, had good reason to conceal his intentions and only narrowly escaped seizure in Dublin the following December.[78]

RETURN TO IRELAND

In November 1802 Addis Emmet asked MacNeven to have William Lawless send Robert Emmet's documents to Brussels so that they could be forwarded to Dublin. That this was unfulfilled prior to his departure indicates that the younger Emmet had not ruled out the possibility of a rapid return if things went badly in Ireland. Addis Emmet spent the winter in Brussels and finally moved to Paris in February 1803 to link up with his comrades. He was partly motivated by the arrival in Brussels of William Hamilton, the husband of Russell's niece, who had received encouraging news from Dublin. MacNeven and Russell had been in contact with Tallyrand in late 1802 and remained keen to meet Bonaparte. They probably wished to confirm Robert Emmet's somewhat negative account of his discussions with the French leader. Hamilton's report of progress in Dublin threw up new possibilities which were later outlined to the French government by the Paris representatives of the United Irishmen. Addis Emmet expressed the hope to MacNeven in early 1803 that they 'may, perhaps, give us some insight; as, if they look to war, they will scarcely treat us with neglect'. This new found optimism was informed by his working knowledge, if not familiarity, with a series of important developments with bearing on his brother's departure for Ireland.[79]

John Russell, brother of Thomas, had left his London home in September/October 1802 and crossed to France from Dover. He fell ill during the trip and was treated by MacNeven, as mentioned in a cryptic message sent to James Farrell in London from Dover on or around 4 November. The letter contained guarded comments on 'Hamilton and Coningham [sic]' whom Russell believed Farrell was likely to encounter in London. This referred to William Hamilton and Edward Carolan (alias Cunningham) who secretly visited the English capital in late 1802.[80] Russell had previously sent an unsigned and undated letter addressed to Farrell from Paris which discussed Malachy Delaney, 'C[arolan/Cunningham] & H[amilton]'.[81] A further partially encoded communication to Farrell cited 'Tom [Russell]'s' opinion that William Putnam McCabe's 'manufacture [in Rouen] is in such a state as to warrant his hopes of making a great fortune'. McCabe's dealings in France with Philip Long and Kildare exile James Smith were noted in brief without explicit comment. The subtext evidently concerned the continuing military preparations of the United Irishmen in France which had previously been masked by the 'Louisiana' cover story.[82]

The Russell/Farrell correspondence pertained to a concerted effort by the United Irishmen to establish much tighter control of their activities across the Irish Sea, as well as across the English Channel. William Dowdall was highly active in this respect and already committed to several linked endeavours which formed the genesis of the Rising of 1803. Dowdall's whereabouts were raised by Addis Emmet in October 1802, who may not have realised that his former comrade had left the Continent to advance the republican plot masterminded by Colonel Edward Marcus Despard in England. The trigger for this was a letter dated 19 September 1802 which was forwarded by William St John in London to Dowdall in Paris. It stated: 'never on my part shall cooperation be wanting where there appears the smallest prospect of benefiting the most injured of Countries'. The letter was endorsed 'D' with '[Malachy] Delany [sic]' added in a different hand.[83] St John urged Dowdall to respond and he obviously did so given that he was soon in Ireland with Delaney and Robert Emmet.[84] It seems that Dowdall had met their mutual associate Philip Long and quite possibly St John in London as recently as 4 September when important political developments were anticipated. Long furnished Dowdall at that time with a letter of introduction to a Liverpool associate whose 'attention' was required 'on his way to Dublin'.[85]

Despard was another midlands United Irishman from Coolrain, Queen's County, and a close friend of naval hero Horatio Nelson. He learned that Dowdall had spoken without reserve of the London-centred plot when at an autumn dinner in Dublin. They had apparently first met in the Irish capital in February 1802 to discuss the viability of striking simultaneous blows against Westminster in both islands. If the Peace of Amiens dampened their initial enthusiasm further consultations, nonetheless, had taken place in London in late July to which Long was privy. Long then apprised Dowdall of his 'pretty sure prospect of . . . entering into the undertaking', a comment indicative of his commitment of United Irish resources in Dublin.[86] Dowdall was strongly rebuked for his ill-disciplined volubility in late 1802 by James Hope, the most experienced United Irish agitator in Ireland. Hope had only recently moved into the populous Coombe district of Dublin's south city to evade arrest in the Naul. He was not then actively engaged in sedition and formed a poor impression of Dowdall and, by association, the 1802 conspirators. The detention of Despard in England on 16 November 1802, however, put paid to twin risings in Dublin and London and undermined whatever had been agreed in September/October when John Russell sailed to France and Robert Emmet to Ireland.[87]

Despard's arrest prompted Dowdall to flee once more to France yet he had returned to Ireland by December at latest to assist Long, Delaney, Emmet and others who had been involved in the 1802 discussions without being seriously compromised. Their combined efforts were then focussed on a Dublin-centred revolution which was attempted in July 1803. There was an ironic symmetry to these complex and dangerous manoeuvres if Hope was correct in his claim that Emmet's return from the Continent was determined by the need to counteract Dowdall's indiscretion in Dublin. Dowdall was clearly important, not least in that he had participated in the London talks attended by McCabe, Long, Despard and Sir Francis Burdett in the summer of 1802 when an all-island revolt was still contemplated. Emmet almost certainly learned of what transpired arising from Long's subsequent visit to Paris, even if absent in Belgium when his former comrade arrived. Emmet was also in close contact with Valentine Lawless, Bolton and others who had dealt with Despard when living in England and counted Delaney, the subject of the September 1802 exchanges between Dowdall and St John, as a close friend. While shoring up Hiberno-English sedition attributed to Despard's leadership may well have affected the timing of Emmet's departure for Ireland there were clearly other important considerations.[88]

Hope informed Madden that he had met the notorious Samuel Neilson in Ireland in late 1802 who had reappeared in his native country 'at the risk of his life' under the proscription of the Banishment Act. Details of Neilson preceding Emmet to Ireland were re-evaluated by the authorities in the context of the Dubliner's subsequent actions.[89] A Hamburg-based informer known to Emmet learned that Thomas Ridgeway had transported Neilson and

Anthony McCann from Hamburg in the *Providence* to a place 'four miles from Dublin, and that they went to Emmett's [sic] country house' in Milltown. McCann was part-owner of the *Providence* and frequently made the vessel available for clandestine trips from the German and Dutch coast to Britain and Ireland. McCann had actually collected Neilson from Holland in early August 1802 and crossed to Drogheda before going on to Dublin. Emmet had not then returned from the Continent although the three may well have met at Casino in October, when they all reappeared in Dublin. The clear inference drawn by the informer after a conversation with McCann was that the visitors were received by Emmet in his father's house.[90] Moreover, when safely back in Bordeaux, McCann expressed his gratitude to 'that extraordinary man Mr Long' whom he met in Ireland with Dowdall and who evidently played a large role in their affairs. Ridgeway paid for his when imprisoned in Kilmainham in the aftermath of the Rising. It would appear from this intense trafficking of prominent figures that the United Irishmen on the Continent were anxious to re-establish communications with persons capable of furthering their cause in Ireland and England. Emmet, Long, Dowdall and others were jointly engaged in this ambitious resurgence by October 1802 when the Despard plot, referred to in rueful terms in McCann's January 1803 letter, was still in prospect.[91]

Neilson's first week in Dublin in the late summer of 1802 was spent in the home of Bernard Coile at 13 Lurgan Street. Coile hailed from Lurgan, Armagh, and in the early 1800s operated a cambric and muslin workshop at 14 Linen Hall Street.[92] He had close ties with Neilson in the early-to-mid 1790s along with the Teelings, Coigleys, O'Hanlons, McCrackens and other radical northern families. 'Linen factor' George Teeling, Emmet's associate in 1799, was a near neighbour of Coile's in Dublin and a man with influence in the Defenders of south Ulster and north Leinster.[93] Coile, for his part, had acted as a Defender delegate to Dublin city in the late 1790s, along with the martyred Fr James Coigley, and had been imprisoned in 1798. He was famous for duelling in Dublin with Wexford privy counsellor George Ogle, a powerful champion of 'Protestant Ascendancy'. Ogle fought, according to Barrington, 'because [Coile] . . . was a papist', and exchanged eight shots with his adversary without result. Coile and the Teelings were undoubtedly capable of garnering support for another rebellion amongst the manufacturing workers of Dublin and their willingness to assist the United Irish grouping represented by Emmet was probably a matter of discussion.[94]

McCann returned to Hamburg, but not before meeting Protestant radical William Todd Jones at Coile's house. Todd Jones, also from Lurgan, was a former collaborator of Richard McCormick and John Keogh and an old friend of Lord Moira's. His early days in the moderate Northern Whig Club were followed by years of vehement advocacy of Catholic rights and propaganda work for the United Irishmen. Todd Jones was afterwards suspected of acting as the leader of the 1803 conspiracy in south Munster and his liaison with men who formed the bridge between Ulster activists and those in the capital is therefore significant. Also noteworthy were their dealings with elements of McCann's Hamburg network, of which Robert Emmet had also availed himself. That Teeling and Hope, if not also Coile, featured in the plans devised by Emmet's circle strongly suggests that political matters were high on the agenda of McCann and Neilson's risk-laden venture.[95]

James Hope, Neilson's assistant in the 1790s, was invited to Lurgan Street in early September 1802 to meet Coile's distinguished visitor. He was greeted with the warning: 'Do not mistake; this is not a party of pleasure; if we are discovered, the event will be banishment to you and death to me.' The serious tone may have served to mollify Hope's anger at Dowdall's inappropriate nonchalance.[96] After a few days of discreet discussions in Coile's, Neilson and Hope set off on horseback for Belfast. They stopped in the Naul for the first night to rest and to visit Charles Teeling. This endangered Hope, who had been forced to quit his employment with Teeling a few months before when a hostile Ulsterman and co-worker, John McCarroll, passed word of his presence to the Castle. The night was clearly not entirely social: Hope stayed awake outside the house and at dawn crossed the fateful River Boyne with Neilson. After three days lying low in Belfast, where Neilson made arrangements with his family, he rejoined Hope outside the town and called with him to John Jackson's house at Creeve.[97]

The main purpose of this diversion may have been personal given that Jackson was taking care of one of Neilson's daughters, but their common United Irish background was by no means incidental. Jackson's brother Henry, exiled as a state prisoner in 1802, was formerly one of the highest-ranking United Irishmen in Dublin. The Jacksons of Church Street and Pill Lane were iron founders known to the Emmets in 1803 and, together with Bond and the executed John McCann, had been staunch promoters of city republicanism when the Society was proscribed. Another brother, Hugh Jackson of Cremone,

Monaghan, was a trusted activist prior to the Rebellion and his eponymous nephew and United Irishman, Hugh, son of Henry, ran the family business in Dublin in 1802–3.[98] Neilson returned to the capital after just one day at Creeve and reputedly met in private with Robert Emmet. The northerner certainly relied upon two men steeped in metropolitan intrigue who were already well known to the Dubliner: Charles O'Hara and 'old [John] Palmer' of Cutpurse Row. Neilson was concealed by O'Hara in Irishtown until his passage to New York was arranged, and he was seen to the boat at Ringsend by Palmer when it was ready to sail.[99] A city-based informer named Kennedy lodged an obsolete report in May 1803 stating that 'Lawless, Neilson and Mat Dowling have been here, the latter very lately as an accredited agent to the Irish Executive, which has always existed'. Kennedy, who had known Dowdall in England, did not understand the context of such endeavours and found that it was 'next to impossible' to identify the new United Irish leadership.[100]

The sickly Neilson envisaged no personal engagement in the nascent conspiracy and departed for New York City in December 1802. He died aged forty-four in Poughkeepsie, New York State, on 29 August 1803. Neilson's tacit support was very likely given his legendary militancy, and a diplomatic role in the eastern States may also have been considered. He envisaged starting a newspaper 'devoted to Irish interests' but was driven from his preferred domicile of New York City by an outbreak of yellow fever. The moral backing of Neilson, together with that of Addis Emmet, Russell and MacNeven, would have conferred the authority of four of the five most influential United Irishmen on Robert Emmet's endeavours. The fifth, O'Connor, could hardly have opposed any French-supported initiative, notwithstanding his embittered relations with Addis Emmet. Quigley's account of October 1803 suggests that O'Connor was indeed aware of and interested in the French-backed rising under consideration. The assent of Richard McCormick, a shadowy figure on the Continent whose former status evidently brought Robert Emmet to Hamburg, was desirable but not required. Indeed, the release of the Fort George internees lessened the cachet of securing the input of a pre-Rebellion Executive Directory member. Far from being an impetuous, romantic and self-absorbed maverick, Emmet consulted widely with key republicans in the advent of July 1803 and was a key player in what remained a broad movement. To a far greater extent than previously acknowledged, the Rising of 1803 was envisaged by the United Irishmen as the natural sequel to the

Rebellion of 1798. It was also, in some respects, a by-product of the abortive Despard conspiracy in London.[101]

DUBLIN

Emmet returned to Ireland in late October 1802 convinced that he would be followed in the near future by a French army. The accompanying United Irish insurrection anticipated by virtually all commentators under such circumstances would, he hoped, overthrow the colonial government, sever the constitutional link with England and reassert Irish sovereignty. When living in America many years later, William MacNeven claimed that Emmet had left France with no precise knowledge of a planned rebellion in Ireland. This must have been the case as the Peace of Amiens negated the possibility of specific undertakings from the French. A general expectation of another contest in Ireland if war resumed was a different matter. On arrival in Dublin, MacNeven ascertained that 'communications were soon made to him [Emmet] . . . supported by returns and details, which gave him assurance that the population of seventeen counties would be brought to act, if only one successful effort were made in the metropolis'. This explains the confidence of Emmet's assertion, when dining at Mount Jerome with the Keogh family and John Philpot Curran shortly afterwards, that nineteen Irish counties would rise if called upon. Keogh, Curran and Grattan, as well as Addis Emmet, MacNeven and Russell, were amongst those likely to form part of an Irish government in the event of success.[102]

The emphasis on the role of the city in a future rising reflected the uncomfortable legacy of the collapse of the rebel effort in Dublin in May 1798. Too great a burden had been devolved onto rural cadres in Leinster, which had been previously ravaged by martial law. This issue was raised time and time again by Emmet's provincial adherents in 1803 and was not only a major grievance but a stark precedent of tactical incompetence. Within a few months of his return to Ireland, Emmet had improved on the blueprint for urban warfare conceived by Lord Edward Fitzgerald's military committee in early 1798. Drawing, as it appeared, on his familiarity with Fitzgerald's work and his own extensive warfare studies, Emmet devoted an exceptional level of attention to the theory and practice of city fighting. By July 1803 he and Long had perfected detailed plans for a coup d'état with the aid of a small staff of trusted assistants known as the 'Council of War'. Emmet was a highly competent strategist whose handiwork was later privately admired by those who found it necessary to deride him in their public pronouncements.[103]

MacNeven's comments on Emmet omit the crucial fact that the assessment of United Irish strength presented to him emanated from the same republican circle that sent him to Paris with Delaney in August 1800. This accounts for his acceptance of their less than ideal forecast and their willingness to furnish him with incriminating written estimates which government spies failed to procure. The association of veteran United Irishmen who comprised the post-Rebellion Directory had continued to function during Emmet's absence, even though Wright and O'Hara had stepped back from the forefront. Illness may have stricken O'Hara, who died in November 1803, although the spy McGucken ascertained that he was still engaged in sedition with 'old friends' Emmet, Lawson and Teeling in June of that year.[104] His dealings with Neilson in late 1802 suggest that this was the case and Castle surveillance of Henry O'Hara was a sign that the family remained committed. Wright was probably suspected of making inappropriate compromises after his arrest in April 1799, although there is evidence that he met Thomas Russell in August 1803. More than ever, Robert Emmet was the primary link between the new militants based in Dublin and the old ideologues in exile overseas. McGucken detected superficial signs of his resumed influence on 8 July 1803 when informing Marsden that the conspiracy 'goes entirely on the old system of 1799, formed by young Emmet etc'.[105]

During Emmet's absence United Irish agitators in various parts of the country had attempted to maintain contact with rebel leaders who had survived 1798. This was casual, ad hoc and regional with centrally located republicans acting independently of the United Irishmen in the capital. It was speculated in July 1801 that the Dublin Directory had 'dissolved' having appointed 'consuls' to await 'a rising in England . . . and then a rising . . . here aided by four or five French squadrons in different parts of the Kingdom'. Unfounded rumours that the French were in Killala created alarm in Galway that month but no modes of popular response indicated systematic preparations. William Putnam McCabe, the personification of conspiracy, was sighted in various parts of Ireland in 1801–2 but never apprehended. Messengers were sent to and from United Irish leaders living in Dublin, addresses were updated and news was exchanged within the republican community. Consequently, when it was decided to lay concrete plans for a rising, the assistance of Felix Rourke, Miles

Byrne, Thomas Cloney, Michael Dwyer, Bernard Duggan and Nicholas Gray was easily obtained.[106] Soundings were taken of rank-and-file attitudes towards revolt after Emmet's return. Walter Cox ascertained that he could 'bring forward 500' city men in 1803, approximately 50 per cent of those he had influence over in 1798.[107] Kildare leader Michael Doorley reorganised and retrained the Lullymore district insurgents after November 1802 in consequence of news there was 'to be a turn out again'. Several hundred conducted manoeuvres in the Wood of Allen, along with contingents from other parts of Kildare, Carlow and King's County. The Irish authorities underestimated the willingness of such men to fight again and were ultimately obliged to review and overhaul intelligence files which had been neglected after the Union.[108]

A report of Thomas Bernard, MP of Ballyboy, ex-High Sheriff of King's County and a banker at Birr, was typical of those reaching the Castle in the autumn of 1801. In response to a circular concerning the disposition of the 'lower orders' Bernard wrote:

> I am perfectly satisfied that their inclinations and intentions are to assist the French on their landing. I have received some private information that there are persons going through the country endeavouring to organize them, and I have every reason to believe that much evil is likely to arise from Hurlings, Dances and constant meetings which they hold . . . They are to all appearance perfectly quiet, but I cannot doubt their inclinations to be otherwise should opportunity offer.[109]

Judge Day concurred in August 1802 when noting the 'immense assemblages of people who habitually meet under innocent pretences' outside Cork city. Day believed 'no rational mind will be persuaded that a mere hurlying [sic] match or any other object of mere amusement & recreation can collect 10,000 of your lower orders repeatedly every week'.[110] Gatherings were more easily effected in Dublin where large workforces, trade combinations and pub life offered opportunities for United Irishmen to keep in contact. From time to time events occurred that permitted apparently spontaneous mass displays of disaffection. Jemmy O'Brien's capital conviction for murder on 19 July 1800 was one such occasion when 'bonfires were [lit] thro[ugh] the Liberty'. O'Brien was Sirr's most hated assistant and the Town Major was outraged that the republicans who set the fires ablaze had shouted 'Bloody Sirr's Blood next'.[111]

News of the Peace of Amiens devastated the morale of the domestic United Irish organisation but the Dublin-based leaders attempted to persevere. Miles Byrne was 'unnerved and disappointed' as it seemed much less likely that 'something good would be done for poor Ireland'.[112] An immediate response was made to a warning that the Dwyer faction in Wicklow, the most disciplined and effective in Ireland, was on the point of disbanding. They had never contemplated life in the mountains as a mere opportunity to engage in brigandage or to settle scores arising from the repression of 1797–98. Rathdrum magistrate Thomas King reported: 'soon after the Peace, Dwyer and his party having no hope of succour proposed to separate and each man to shift for himself – as soon as it was known in Dublin a written paper was sent down signed by many names amongst whose was Napper Tandy's assuring Dwyer of immediate support and desiring the Party by all means to continue out'. The Dublin leaders valued the positive propaganda generated by special groups such as Dwyer's and played a decisive role in prolonging political unrest in Wicklow until December 1803. Emmet fully supported this strategy.[113] It was probably not a coincidence that the fourth edition of *Paddy's Resource*, a collection of United Irish and pro-French ballads, appeared in 1803 for the first time since 1798. This timely effort to raise the spirits of republicans was, if nothing else, proof that the movement still possessed the means to edit, print and distribute propaganda.[114]

EMMET AND LONG

Shortly after arriving back in Ireland Emmet dined with Philip Long at 4 Crow Street. Long, a wealthy merchant and veteran United Irishman, had been a prime mover in the mid-1802 negotiations between the republicans of Dublin, London and Paris. He agreed to underwrite future revolutionary operations to the tune of £1,400 and may have furnished greater amounts and was certainly applied to by Emmet for supplementary funds. This fact, when considered alongside Long's authorship of an address to the 'Citizens of Dublin', recovered in the Thomas Street arms depot on 24 July 1803, suggests that his patronage of the Emmet conspiracy was considerable.[115] A government document compiled after 1807 noted that Long had been 'a very deep conspirator, nephew to John Roach the Merchant, frequently met at Surgeon Wright's Ship Street, John Patten etc on the subject of Rebellion'.[116] Long was probably the most significant single financial supporter of the Rising of 1803 and his early provision of cash marked him as one of the plot's originators. Kildare's

Michael Quigley went so far as to claim that the state prisoners held in Kilmainham in 1805 'all consider Long to have been the principal instrument in creating the late Insurrection'.[117] He traded Spanish wines and was acquainted, if not friendly, with James Tandy, whose travels on similar business in France in the autumn of 1802 and independent connections with William Dowdall were subsequently deemed suspicious by Wickham and another wine dealer, Major Sirr. The younger Tandy also knew Charles O'Hara and the ubiquitous John Allen.[118] Dowdall, for whom Long had a 'particular regard', was his guest when they met McCann in Ireland in the late autumn of 1802. He returned to Crow Street from France prior to January 1803.[119]

James 'Duke of Marlborough' Ryan of 77 Marlborough Street, a future follower of Daniel O'Connell and reputed financier of insurrection in 1803, was introduced to Emmet by John Keogh shortly after the Mount Jerome dinner.[120] Keogh was one of the few United Irishmen capable of opening such doors at will. He was identified by Wright in May 1799 as a member of the reformed Directory, along with his friend Con McLaughlin, and went in person to Casino to arrange Emmet's meeting with Ryan. Keogh greatly admired the French form of republicanism and probably disengaged from the United Irishmen when it became apparent that they were prepared to rise without Bonaparte's assistance. He had not survived over ten years of radicalism only to risk his personal fortune and quite possibly his life in a doomed enterprise. In the winter of 1802–3, however, the implications of Emmet's return warranted careful consideration by Keogh's circle of prosperous Catholic merchants.[121]

That Emmet was the recipient of substantial cash overtures even before a specific plan of action had been agreed indicates that his status, considerable in 1798–99, had been boosted by the time of his return. This is not altogether surprising as his credentials as a dedicated United Irishman were virtually unimpeachable. Emmet had exchanged the safety of Paris for the life of a fugitive obliged to hide in his parent's house in Casino. Moreover, Emmet, as Long and Dowdall could confirm, had fulfilled his Continental mission of fostering new channels of communication with the French government during a period of international crisis. His fresh and reliable insights into the thinking of the most important state prisoners released from Fort George must have been valued by their former comrades in Dublin who had evaded the authorities. If vital information was to come from France it must have been obvious that Emmet was one of the most suitable conduits.

Notwithstanding the fragments of intelligence supplied to the Castle by MacNally, Turner, McGucken, Kennedy and others, Emmet's position in the United Irishmen was only understood in hindsight. Extant documentation is consequently skewed towards lesser figures whose movements were more easily documented by state agents. In late 1802 the Castle had yet to receive comprehensive proof of Emmet's sedition in Trinity in 1797–98 and doubt surrounded reports naming him as a high-ranking conspirator in 1799–1800. His prolonged absence in Europe until late 1802 lessened the urgency in resolving the often conflicting profiles of the United Irish leadership to the point that the tireless Major Sirr had no physical description of Emmet until June of the following year. The notion that Emmet was somehow inveigled by enemies to return to Ireland is belied by his relative anonymity in official documentation prior to the summer of 1803 and the inability of the authorities to lay their hands on him when he wished to avoid their attention.[122]

Emmet, a secretive and capable leader with an established reputation amongst metropolitan radicals, was an ideal coordinator of the pro-French uprising in the offing. It was a role he assumed with alacrity. When his prominence became apparent to all in the summer of 1803, Emmet had overseen the maturation of a sophisticated conspiracy. He arrived home at a time when reports were circulating in Whitehall of extensive United Irish interest in a French fleet bound for Louisiana. The linking of General Humbert's name to those of the deported Napper Tandy, James Joseph MacDonnell, Hugh Ware, William Hamilton and Thomas Russell suggested that Ireland was its real destination. William Putnam McCabe, with Long's backing, was known to have obtained weapons in Rouen for the use of an Irish contingent while Russell, John Sweeney and Surgeon Lawless stockpiled muskets in Le Havre. A Louisiana destination was ruled out in October 1802 when France agreed to cede the vast Mississippi valley territory to America for 60 million livres and it was not immediately apparent how the small fleet might then be tasked. It was probably significant that money sent to France by Robert Emmet was used by McCabe and Russell to underwrite emissary traffic to and from Dublin.[123]

Confusion also stemmed from the arrest in England on 16 November 1802 of Colonel Edward Marcus Despard, leader of the British-based revolutionaries. Almost thirty of his followers were also detained, many of whom were United Irishmen. *Faulkner's Dublin Journal* deemed it extraordinary that 'a plot of such an extent' existed 'at such a time' and hinted at the uncertainty this created in Dublin by stating 'the French Revolution, surely, has few partisans in this country'.[124] Irish republican leaders in 1802 and 1803 recognised the value of creating simultaneous ferment in Britain and Ireland to overstretch the military and encourage greater levels of mobilisation to facilitate the French. United Irishmen in Paris and Dublin certainly explored the possibility of conjoining an Irish revolt to the one sparked in England by Despard. Counter-insurgency and poor communications led to the chronic setback of his seizure but hopes were afterwards entertained that English and Scottish republicans would act as they had undertaken to in 1798. Addis Emmet attempted to develop such contacts when held at Fort George; the extent of his success is open to question.[125]

Robert Emmet, as the generally authoritative James Hope contended, may have come to Ireland to bolster the Irish dimension of Despard's conspiracy, an ambitious plan which had already begun to unravel at its London core. What is known of Emmet's actions points to his immediate reintegration into the Dublin United Irish leadership and in a manner that brought fresh impetus, if not a new direction, which required the raising of finance. He soon engaged Dowdall, John Binns, Benjamin Pemberton Binns, Michael Farrell, James Farrell, John Russell and other United Irishmen who plotted in Britain. Michael Farrell evidently left France at Emmet's request and went to London while Pemberton Binns soon turned up in Corke Abbey (Bray), County Wicklow. Similarly, Thomas Cloney lived in exile in Liverpool from September 1801 until February 1803 when he too slipped back to Dublin to renew his contacts with the United Irishmen. Dubliner Patrick Finney returned from four years of residence in London around the same time. Several of his associates had been arrested for complicity in the Despard conspiracy. He had worked as a tobacco importer under an assumed name and was deeply engaged in the activities of the United Irishmen in England.[126]

The seemingly unqualified support of these leaders for Emmet's conspiracy indicates a rededication of the movement's resources towards a French-backed Irish insurrection along with possible secondary actions in Scotland and England. Alternatively, if Britain was invaded, as many in London believed was possible in 1803, Irish rebels could strike without fear of significant army reinforcements being redeployed from England and Wales. This was an important consideration in Ireland where the Dublin regime's reconquest of Wexford in June/July 1798 and its difficult campaign in the west of

Ireland the following autumn had depended on the emergency transfer of over 10,000 soldiers from England, Scotland, Wales and the Channel Islands.[127]

In November 1802 Emmet went through the motions of entering the tanning business in Dublin with John Patten, an interest possibly whetted by the weeks spent above a Normandy workshop. More probable is that he sought a plausible explanation for his return to Ireland should it be required by the Castle. Patten apparently provided the full investment for a Dolphin's Barn operation managed by Limerick-born United Irishman William Norris. A former teacher who studied for the priesthood in Cork prior to the Rebellion, Norris had been an insurgent officer in 1798 and apparently remained a fugitive five years later. He met Robert Holmes in Dublin in 1799 who introduced him to Patten and other members of the extended Emmet family.[128] This seditious background explains why the North Cork Street tannery which Edward Condon claimed was operated by Norris was not listed under his name in the directory of merchants. Alternatively, its owners may have hoped to evade the excise regulations introduced in 1798, which had severe economic consequences for practitioners. Regardless of the status of the operation, Emmet's dealings with Norris were not primarily centred on business given that the Limerickman was dispatched to his native province to organise United Irish support. His subversive activities in Munster came to the notice of Major-General William Payne in Limerick and, when sought for questioning, Norris turned up in Dublin on the day of the Rising of 1803.[129] He was described in retrospect as 'one of the provisional Government with Emmet'.[130]

Suspicions were aroused in April 1803 that William Todd Jones, the most likely overall commander of Munster United Irishmen, had gone 'several times' to the western coast. Greater attention would have been paid to these trips by the authorities had it been realised that he had previously met the Hamburg visitor Anthony McCann in Dublin in company with Armagh republican Bernard Coile. It was also not widely known that Todd Jones had two years before met with the notorious Thomas Cloney and other members of the United Irish community in Liverpool.[131] Cloney ascertained, possibly before returning to Ireland, that 'young Emmett [sic] . . . was organising the country, to be ready to rise when a French army should land'. Todd Jones, Coile and Cloney were arrested in the weeks following the 1803 Rising.[132]

While Emmet's presence in Dublin was reported to the Castle within weeks of arriving from France, it was not until early December

1802 that an attempt was made to bring him in for questioning. He was not regarded as a major threat and the expiration in November of the Habeas Corpus Suspension Act meant that police agents had little hope of prosecuting him arising from his evasion of earlier, possibly lapsed, warrants. Even so, Major Sirr routinely monitored United Irish movements and Emmet's name was sufficiently well known to arouse his interest. Confirmation that Emmet was once again in residence at Casino led to a raid on the house by Sirr's deputy in the first week of December 1802. William Bellingham Swan, who had been assaulted during an anti-Orange riot in the city on 12 July, got no closer to his quarry than finding a warm bed. Its occupant presumably vacated the ground floor room in a hurry to avoid an interview with state officials. Emmet disappeared into one of the building's purpose-built bolt-holes, realising that it would be necessary to redouble his personal security.[133]

This dispiriting event presaged another: the death of Dr Emmet in Casino on 9 December aged seventy-three. He was buried three days later in St Peter's Church, Aungier Street after a very small funeral for such a socially prominent man. Wary friends, not least William Drennan, chose not to attend Revd J. J. MacSorley's service. Robert Emmet's return unsettled the family circle who could have entertained no illusions as to the implications of Swan's raid. Lady Anne Fitzgerald, one of those who offered condolences to the Emmets on the 11th, owed Dr Emmet her life and shared his widow's Kerry origins. Fitzgerald arrived at Casino that day to find Robert Emmet in attendance, who undoubtedly observed and vetted those calling to the house. The death forced Drennan to break his latest self-imposed silence on the subject of his former colleague's errant son. He belatedly informed his sister that Emmet had been in Ireland for 'about two months . . . but will not I suppose reside in this country'. For all intents and purposes, Emmet was already a fugitive.[134]

Elizabeth Emmet no longer wished to live at Casino after the death of her husband and moved to Bloomfield House off Morehampton Road, Donnybrook, a property formerly owned by William Saurin. The Emmets shared Saurin's abhorrence of the Act of Union but whereas their concerns centred on the threat it presented to Irish national aspirations, Saurin, Orangeman and officer in the Lawyer's corps yeomanry, feared the weakening of Protestant Ascendancy. Bloomfield had been only recently purchased by Dr Emmet for £900 and was probably intended for the use in adulthood of his 15-year-old ward, Catherine, orphaned daughter of Christopher Temple

Emmet. The discovery that Dr Emmet's will directed this settlement was regarded as one of many 'errors' made by the addled doctor as death neared. The problematic codicils were drawn up by attorney Joseph Rawlins, who had caught sight of Robert Emmet in Casino and identified him at his September 1803 trial. Michael Leonard, the family gardener, confirmed to Madden in 1836 that Emmet continued to use the vacated estate house, which had proved its worth for his clandestine purposes on more than one occasion.[135]

Emmet spent much of the early winter of 1802–3 investigating the attitude of the Dublin United Irishmen towards a future revolt and their capacity to perform as required by the leadership. This was not simply prudent but absolutely necessary owing to the standing down of the stratified, democratic organisation of May 1798 with its elected officers and chain of command. The various societies, fronts and cliques which constituted the post-Rebellion United Irishmen were all but autonomous and of uncertain revolutionary potential. While no definite plans could be made until war seemed imminent, Emmet was anxious to lay as much groundwork as possible. Norris and Long provided him a route back into the warrens of the south city, where many of those Wright claimed admired Emmet in 1798 and 1799 still resided. Coile, Miles Duigenan, James Dixon and other more obscure figures in the Dublin area may have assisted in this tentative phase while Emmet's access to the friends of Patrick Gallagher and Lyndon Bolton would have boosted his standing in Thomas, James's and Francis Streets. John Allen may have provided an introduction to Patrick McCabe of Francis Street, who knew of Emmet's secret travels to England in 1800 and may have been part of the revived Directory. Emmet needed the aid of men like McCabe to establish contact with the Dwyer group in Wicklow and other active outstanding factions whose longevity, militancy and popularity rendered them important. In keeping with the practice of the post-Rebellion leadership, only those who had distinguished themselves in 1798 were deemed suitable adherents. Emmet later admitted that 'all' his followers 'had fought before'.[136] Walter Cox became aware of the conspiracy at an early stage and believed that 'young Emmet' had come under the 'influence' of 'a few men of desperate fortunes'.[137]

The big push to open communications did not commence until the spring of 1803, although unusually frequent emissary activity took place over the winter. Rathdrum magistrate Thomas King believed that the Wicklow United Irishmen in December 1802 were 'ready to rise at a moments notice' and, while new passwords and recognition signs had been created, only 'select men' received the oath. This was Emmet's policy in 1799–1803 and that of the leadership which had quietly agitated during his absence. Dwyer's group were visited on a number of occasions by a Wexfordman of 'gentlemanlike appearance' in late 1802.[138] In January 1803 suspicion also fell on William Holt, brother of the transported rebel general Joseph Holt who, in 1798, had close contacts with Dublin leaders Wright, O'Hara, O'Hanlon and McMahon. William Holt lived in the city after the Rebellion yet was sighted in the Avoca district for the first time in five years 'swearing the rebellious to a new oath'. The seriousness of this overture was underlined by the fact that he dared not live in his home county, where he had very nearly been lynched by the Rathdrum yeomanry in August 1798. Such episodes reflected preliminary overtures by Emmet's men in strategic areas where support for a rising could be taken for granted. As matters stood, the danger to loyalist interests in Wicklow and Kildare in 1802–3 was such that both counties hosted Special Commissions that dispensed summary justice from ostensibly civil forums.[139]

Limerick was also highly disturbed in the winter of 1802–3 with large illegal assemblies taking place by night around the city area. Magistrates and yeomen clamoured for bodyguards and the reinforcement of garrisons yet, while the number of reported incidents was high, few were actually harmed or robbed of arms. The main concern of Lord Lieutenant Hardwicke was that the French government would attach the 'greatest weight' to reports of internal unrest in Ireland. Hardwicke acted when Major-General Edward Morrison panicked on 8 January 1803 and withdrew outlying detachments to Limerick city to repulse a non-existent insurgent threat. General Payne, brother of Rear Admiral John Payne, assumed command and the astute Wickham commenced an investigation which ascribed the unrest to agrarian protesters and gentry rivalry.[140] General Payne concurred with Wickham at first but in March 1803 revised his initial assessment after a spate of seditious incidents, the most daring of which involved 100 armed raiders carrying off twenty guns from a single parish. Attempts were made to suborn and disarm soldiers and illegal oaths were administered in Limerick and Kerry. By June Payne predicted a 'serious public calamity' if the new 'system of terror' was not vigorously counteracted. Emmet observed the growing unrest in Munster with keen interest and made reference to it in a revolutionary manifesto issued on 23 July 1803. He may have helped stimulate disturbances by sending agents into the province, as he did in the Dublin region.[141]

Emmet was wary of appearing in public at this time and rarely sighted prior to March 1803 when his understanding of events on the Continent excited frenetic activity. The first indication of an improved situation came in January 1803 when William Hamilton of Enniskillen arrived from France with a message from the Paris circle. Perhaps in response to positive reports of the United Irish revival and rural agitation sent by Emmet, a reduced figure of 10,000 French troops was being sought by MacNeven and Russell. It may not be a coincidence that Hamilton's departure followed closely on the arrival in Paris of Robert Carty of Birchgrove, a Wexford rebel leader in 1798, who was introduced to Humbert. Hamilton had fought in French uniform in 1798 and participated in the 'Louisiana fleet' preparations. He travelled to Ireland in 1803 in company with Edward Carolan of Monaghan, whom Emmet had met in Hamburg and probably earlier in Dublin.[142] Hamilton, Carolan, John Russell and John Byrne of Dundalk, a friend of James Tandy and Anthony McCann, also conferred in London in December 1802 despite the risk of meeting in the aftermath of the Despard arrests. When safely in Ireland, Hamilton pressed Emmet to estimate the likely level of support for a French-assisted uprising, possibly to confirm what Carty had claimed. He also urged Emmet to secure as much finance as possible without recourse to levying membership dues. Emmet had already done much to meet these requests and immediately furnished the Fermanaghman with £80 drawn from Long's resources. The proving of Dr Emmet's will on 10 January 1803 paved the way for Robert Emmet's inheritance of £1,500, some of which was sent to Paris with Hamilton. A greater amount was due when the tangled affairs of his father's many properties and neglected debts were sorted out. Other sums were provided by Dowdall's associate James Barrett, a lace merchant at 15 Cutpurse Row.[143]

Hamilton carried Emmet's encouraging preliminary assessment back to Paris in February and called to Addis Emmet and MacNeven in Brussels. It was evidently in response to what Addis Emmet heard that he overcame his instinctive disdain of the First Consul and some of his O'Connerite admirers. Addis Emmet's plans to migrate with his family to Baltimore, America, were consequently shelved in late March. He moved instead to the French capital to add his authority to the unfolding conspiracy and, in so doing, renewed the intriguing with Arthur O'Connor. This new dynamism led to a flurry of secondary activity as Russell began to disburse monies raised by Robert Emmet to pay for the return to Ireland of several men listed on the Banishment Act. Russell also obtained cash from his Belfast friend and fellow United Irishman Robert Simms. Such assistance may have served to inflate Russell's notions of the receptiveness of Ulster to another contest. Sending banished men to Ireland was attended with fatal risks in the event of capture and it is evident that the exiled United Irishmen accepted Emmet's reading of the situation and believed, as he did, that a French invasion would be attempted in or around August 1803. It was imperative that the United Irishmen attained the organisational strength necessary to break the connection with England without becoming an Atlantic province of a French empire.[144]

Notes

PREFACE

1 For evidence of Robert Emmet's United Irish membership from late 1796 see 30 Nov. 1803, NA (National Archives), Rebellion Papers, 620/11/130/59.

2 Robert Emmet, 'Account of the late plan of Insurrection in Dublin and cause of its failure', BL (British Library), Hardwicke Papers, MS 35740/199–200. See Appendix One.

3 Hardwicke to Dudley, 1st Earl of Harrowby, 27 Feb. 1804 in A. P. W. Malcomson (ed.), *Eighteenth-century Irish official papers in Great Britain, private collections* (Belfast, 1990), II, p. 69. See also [Lieutenant General Henry Edward Fox], 13 Dec. 1803, 'Memoranda relation [sic] to 23[r]d July [1803]', NLI (National Library of Ireland), MS 57 (1).

4 T. A. Emmet, *Memoir of Thomas Addis Emmet and Robert Emmet, with their ancestors and immediate family*, 2 vols (New York, 1915), I, p. 372. There is no mention of Robert Emmet in Addis Emmet's 'Part of an essay towards the history of Ireland' in W. J. MacNeven et al., *Pieces of Irish history* (New York, 1807), pp. 1–144.

5 Henry Grattan, *Memoirs of the life and times of the Rt. Hon. Henry Grattan, by his son, Henry Grattan, esq. M.P.*, 3 vols (London, 1839–41); Thomas Moore, *Memoirs, Journal and Correspondence of Thomas Moore, edited . . . by the Right Hon. Lord John Russell* (London, 1860); Thomas Moore, *The Life and death of Lord Edward Fitzgerald* (Glasgow, 1875) 1st edn, 2 vols (London, 1831); Valentine Lawless, *Personal Recollections of the life and times, with extracts from the correspondence, of Valentine Lord Cloncurry* (Dublin, 1849); John Newsinger (ed.), *United Irishman, The autobiography of James Hope* (London, 2001). Moore's 'Oh breathe not his name' and 'When he who adores thee', concerning but not naming Emmet, first appeared as early as 1807 in *Irish Melodies*. Later editions of *Melodies* added the subtitle 'Emmet in Ireland' to the second song. See Mathew Campbell, 'Thomas Moore's wild song: The 1821 Irish Melodies' in *Bullan, An Irish Studies Journal*, 4, 2 (1999–2000), p. 87.

CHAPTER ONE

1 Emmet, *Memoir*, I, p. 149 and 'The Emmett family', *Clonmel Historical and Archaeological Society*, I, 2 (1953–54), pp. 43–4. A tradition of Kent origins of the family stems from the discovery of a will made there by Robert Emmott in 1650. *Burke's Irish Family Records* (London, 1976), p. 387.

2 *Annual Register*, 1803, p. 433. See also Emmet, *Memoir*, I, p. 165; A. M. E. McCabe, 'The medical connections of Robert Emmet', *Irish Journal of Medical Science*, 6th series, 448 (April 1963), pp. 171–2; J. J. Reynolds, *Footprints of Emmet* (Dublin, 1903), p. 12; Emmet family pedigree, NLI, MS 10,752.

3 Emmet, *Memoir*, I, p. 184.

4   John T. Collins, 'The Emmet family connections with Munster', *Cork Historical and Archaeological Journal*, LVIII, 187 (1953), pp. 77–80.

5   See William Drennan to Martha McTier, 15 Jan. 1805 in Jean Agnew (ed.), *The Drennan-McTier Letters*, 3 vols (Dublin, 1999), III, p. 306.

6   R. R. Madden, *The United Irishmen, their lives and times*, 2nd edn, 4 vols (Dublin, 1857–60), III, pp. 4–5, 10–11; *Wilson's Dublin Directory for the year 1794* (Dublin, 1794), p. 138.

7   See F. Elrington Ball, *A history of the County Dublin: The people, parishes and antiquities*, reprinted (Dublin, 1979).

8   *Wilson's Dublin Directory . . . 1794*, pp. 115, 139; Reynolds, *Footprints*, p. 13; Emmet, *Memoir*, I, pp. 175–6; McCabe, 'medical connections', p. 172; David Dickson and Richard English, 'The La Touche dynasty' in David Dickson (ed.), *The gorgeous mask, Dublin 1700–1850* (Dublin, 1987), p. 25; *Irish Times*, 5 Mar. 2001.

9   Madden, *United*, III, p. 344. Robert Emmet's grandmother was buried at St Anne's, Dawson Street, when the family lived around the corner on Molesworth Street. This was the probable basis of rumours that he too may have been interred in the plot. See Michael Barry, *The mystery of Robert Emmet's grave, a fascinating story of deception, intrigue and misunderstanding* (Cork, 1991), p. 13. The original St Peter's church had fallen into disrepair in the early 1700s and was replaced by the building on the present site. This church was enlarged in 1773 and reconstructed in 1867. Further alterations were made in the late 1800s. See Brian Mac Giolla Phádraig, 'Speed's Plan of Dublin, part 1', *Dublin Historical Record*, X, 3 (1948), pp. 89–96.

10 Raymond Postgate, *Robert Emmet* (London, 1931), p. 13. See also William Drennan to Martha McTier, 16 June 1802 in Agnew, *Drennan-McTier Letters*, III, p. 51. For the Emmet family Bible see RIA (Royal Irish Academy), MS 12.G.14.

11 Emmet, *Memoir*, II, p. 4. See also Joseph W. Hammond, 'Town Major Henry Charles Sirr', *Dublin Historical Record*, IV, 1 (1941), p. 15.

12 Emmet, *Memoir*, II, p. 3 and J. T. Gilbert, *A history of the city of Dublin*, 3 vols (Dublin, 1861), I, p. 200.

13 Robert Welch (ed.), *The Oxford Companion to Irish literature* (Oxford, 1996), pp. 520, 597.

14 Cited in Emmet, *Memoir*, II, p. 4.

15 Emmet, *Memoir*, I, p. 176 and Madden, *United*, III, p. 34.

16 Madden, *United*, III, p. 5 and Anne Fitzgerald to La Touche, 31 July 1803 in Michael MacDonagh (ed.), *Viceroy's post bag, correspondence hitherto unpublished of the Earl of Hardwicke, first Lord Lieutenant of Ireland after the Union* (London, 1904), pp. 333–4.

17 Quoted in Postgate, *Emmet*, pp. 15–16. See also Emmet, *Memoir*, I, p. 194.

18 *Walker's Hibernian Magazine*, June 1783, p. 390; Gerard O'Brien, *Anglo-Irish politics in the age of Grattan and Pitt* (Dublin, 1987), pp. 28–45; Thomas P. Power, *Land, politics and society in eighteenth-century Tipperary* (Oxford, 1993), p. 219.

19 *Transactions of the General Committee of the Roman Catholics of Ireland during the year 1791* (Dublin, 1791), p. 19.

20 *Annual Register*, 1803, p. 433. See also *Walker's Hibernian Magazine*, June 1783, p. 333; W. J. Fitzpatrick, *The Sham Squire, Rebellion in Ireland and the informers of 1798*, 6th edn (Dublin, 1872), pp. 32–3; Postgate, *Emmet*, pp. 11, 15; Madden, *United*, III, p. 4; *The Gentleman's and Citizen's Almanack . . . 1800* (Dublin, 1800), p. 50.

21 *Annual Register*, 1803, p. 433.

22 *Walker's Hibernian Magazine*, Oct. 1784, p. 556. See also Reynolds, *Footprints*, p. 13.

23 Jonah Barrington, *Personal sketches and recollections of his own time*, reprinted (Dublin, 1997), p. 80. See also Eugene Coyne, 'Sir Edward Newenham, the 18th Century Dublin Radical', *Dublin Historical Record*, XLVI, pp. 15–30.

24 *Alumni Dublinenses, a register of the students, graduates, professors and provosts of Trinity College in the University of Dublin (1593–1860) ed[ited] by George Burtchaell and Thomas Sadlier, new edn.* (Dublin, 1935), p. 180; Madden, *United*, I, p. 584; Emmet, *Memoir*, I, p. 177. Catherine's birth was announced as 'At Stephen's green, the Lady of Temple Emmett [sic], Esq: of a daughter' in *Walker's Hibernian Magazine*, April 1785, p. 223.

25 Thomas Davis (ed.), *The speeches of the Right Honorable John Philpot Curran*, 6th edn (Dublin, n.d.), p. xvii; McCabe, 'medical connections', p. 174; David Quaid, 'Robert Emmet' in *United Irishman*, 21 June 1902. An account in *Hibernian Magazine*, erroneous in several respects, noted that Temple Emmet died in February 1788. See Emmet, *Memoir*, I, pp. 191–2.

26 Drennan to Martha McTier, 15 January 1805 in Agnew (ed.), *Drennan-McTier Letters*, III, p. 306.

27 *Alumni Dublinenses*, p. 180; Madden, *United*, III, pp. 5, 11; *Dictionary of National Biography*, VI, p. 781; Emmet, *Memoir*, I, pp. 202–4; *United Irishman*, 21 June 1902. Knox was MP for Dublin University and captain of 2nd company, Lawyers' yeoman infantry in 1803 when Robert Emmet was tried and executed.

28 Postgate, *Emmet*, pp. 35–6; Madden, *United*, III, pp. 76–7; William Ridgeway, *A report of the trial of Robert Emmet upon an indictment for high treason* (Dublin, 1803), pp. 79–92; Anthony Cronin, *An Irish eye, viewpoints by Anthony Cronin* (Kerry, 1985), pp. 9–13. Murphy of Smithfield was implicated in the Rising of 1803 but vehemently denied to Madden that he was involved. Madden, *United*, I, p. 530.

29 Theobald Wolfe Tone, 'Memoirs' in Thomas Bartlett (ed.), *Life of Theobald Wolfe Tone, memoirs, journals and political writings compiled and arranged by William T. W. Tone, 1826* (Dublin, 1998), p. 37.

30 Thomas Addis Emmet to William James MacNeven, 3 Dec. 1798, NA, Rebellion Papers, 620/15/2/16.

31 Henry Grattan, *Memoirs of the life and times of the Rt. Hon. Henry Grattan, by his son, Henry Grattan, esq. MP*, 3 vols (London, 1839–41), III, pp. 460–1; James Kelly, *Henry Grattan* (Dublin, 1993), pp. 24–5 and *Irish Magazine*, Jan. 1811, p. 17.

32 Drennan to Sam McTier, 3 May 1790 in Agnew (ed.), *Drennan-McTier Letters*, I, p. 349.

33 Emmet, *Memoir*, I, pp. xv, 165. See also ibid., II, p. 11; Nancy Curtin, *The United Irishmen: popular politics in Ulster and Dublin, 1791–1798* (Oxford, 1994); pp. 40–42, Helen Landreth, *The pursuit of Robert Emmet* (Dublin, 1949), p. 13; and *Wilson's Dublin Directory . . . 1794*, p. 138.

34 Jim Smyth, *The men of no property, Irish radicals and popular politics in the late eighteenth century* (Dublin, 1992), pp. 53–69, 91–9; *Faulkner's Dublin Journal*, 11 April 1793.

35 *Burke's Irish Family Records*, p. 387; Madden, *United*, III, pp. 29, 340; Landreth, *Pursuit*, p. 17, Drennan to McTier, 3 July 1794; Agnew (ed.), *Drennan-McTier Letters*, II, p. 79; ibid., III, p. 299; Hammond, 'Sirr', p. 17; 'Emmett family', p. 44.

36   Richard Sadlier to Addis Emmet, 25 Dec. 1790, NA, Rebellion Papers, 620/15/2/1. Addis Emmet corresponded with Sadlier in late 1790 on the will of his aunt in Tipperary who left Dr Emmet and his male heirs a half-share of 72 acres at Raheen, 150 acres at Crossail and 5 lots plus a garden at Boheracrow. This generated £110 a year rental income. An English friend commented: 'I need not, I find, wish you may be successful at the Bar, as I learn from Nolan that you have experienced even more than you could have expected.' J. Calvert Clarke to Addis Emmet, 9 June 1791, NA, Rebellion Papers, 620/15/2/2.

37   David Dickson, 'Paine and Ireland' in David Dickson, Dáire Keogh and Kevin Whelan (eds), *The United Irishmen, Republicanism, Radicalism and Rebellion* (Dublin, 1993), pp. 135–50; Marianne Elliott, *Wolfe Tone, prophet of Irish Independence* (London, 1989); Landreth, *Pursuit*, pp. 16–17; 'Essays for the political club formed in Dublin, 1790' in Bartlett (ed.), *Tone*, p. 433.

38   Brendan Clifford (ed.) *Scipture Politics, selections from the writings of William Steel Dickson, the most influential United Irishman of the North* (Belfast, 1991), p. 52. Revd Dickson's sermon to the Echlinville Volunteers on 28 March 1779 foreshadowed the pro-Catholic agenda of the United Irishmen which he joined in December 1791. His writings were distributed by Samuel Neilson in February 1793. Neilson and Dickson had both backed the young Robert Stewart as a reform candidate for Down in 1790.

39   *Walker's Hibernian Magazine*, July 1791. See also Sir Richard Musgrave, *Memoirs of the different Rebellions in Ireland*, 2nd edn (Dublin, 1801), p. 94.

40   Quoted in Elliott, *Tone*, pp. 139–40.

41   Elliott, *Tone*, pp. 139–40; Frank MacDermot, *Tone and his times*, rev. edn, (Dublin, 1980), chapters four and five.

42   Tone, 'Memoirs' in Bartlett (ed.), *Tone*, p. 37.

43   R. B. McDowell (ed.) *Proceedings of the Dublin Society of United Irishmen* (Dublin, 1998), pp. 7–8. Perry of Inch, Co. Wexford, a Co. Down-born resident of Longford Street (Dublin) in 1791, and 'Major' Bacon of Ship Street, both lost their lives in the 1798 Rebellion. The David Fitzgerald of Suffolk Street inducted in January 1792 was evidently Philip Long's nephew and a man destined to play a role in the Rising of 1803. Ibid., p. 9. 'Mr [Thomas] Wright and Mr [Edward] Maguire' were also implicated in the post-1798 United Irishmen, as were James Tandy, Richard Dillon of Francis Street and Edward Keane of Chancery Lane. All three were named as activists by Thomas Collins in late January 1792. Patrick Byrne of Grafton Street, co-sponsor of G. J. Browne with Leonard MacNally, was obliged to emigrate in consequence of his seditious interaction with Henry and John Sheares in early 1798. Ibid., p. 10. By February 1792, United Irishmen 'Captain' Daniel Muley of Abbey Street, 'Major' James Plunkett of Roscommon, Robert Fyans of Thomas Street, John Byrne of Mullinachack and John Stockdale had all embarked on the path that would result in their cooperation with Robert Emmet in 1802–3. Ibid., pp. 4–15.

44   Lord Redesdale to Anon., 14 Dec. 1803 in Malcomson (ed.), *Irish official papers*, II, p. 435. See also Emmet, *Memoirs*, II, p. 11.

45   Madden, *United*, III, p. 29. MacNeven, a neighbour of the Emmets, was another chemist and United Irishman in a position to assist Robert Emmet's experiments. See William J. Davis, 'William James MacNeven: chemist and United Irishman' in Patrick N. Wyse Jackson (ed.), *Science and engineering in Ireland in 1798: a time of revolution* (Dublin, 2000), pp. 7–24.

46   *Transactions of the General Committee*, pp 9–10, 16, 19–23.

47   Addis Emmet, 'Part of an essay', p. 114. See also *Hibernian Journal*, 13 Dec. 1792; Dáire Keogh, 'Archbishop Troy, the Catholic Church and Irish Radicalism' in Dickson, Keogh and Whelan (eds), *United Irishmen*, p. 126;

R. B. McDowell, 'The personnel of the Dublin society of United Irishmen, 1791–4', *Irish Historical Studies*, II, 1940–41, pp. 12–53.

48 Tone, 'Journals' in Bartlett (ed.), *Tone*, p. 163. See also ibid., p. 165; Curtin, *United Irishmen*, pp. 48–9.

49 Tone, 'Journals' in Bartlett (ed.), *Tone*, p. 167.

50 Drennan to Sam McTier, 27 Jan. 1794 in Agnew (ed.), *Drennan-McTier Letters*, II, p. 8. See also McDowell (ed.), *Proceedings*, pp. 54–6.

51 Addis Emmet, 'Part of an essay'; p. 57, Curtin, *United Irishmen*, p. 52; Emmet, *Memoir*, I, pp. 207–8. Tandy had been sent to Newgate on 18 April 1792. He escaped to Delaware, America, in March 1793 and soon made his way to France. *Irish Magazine*, September 1808, pp. 415–17; ibid., Oct. 1808, pp. 463–7. Dublin United Irish leaders Dowling, Tandy and 'Major' Thomas Bacon had commanded the Dublin Independent Volunteers which held manoeuvres at Roebuck, County Dublin, in the summer of 1783. It may not be a coincidence that Roebuck was the country home of Henry Jackson, another leading city radical in the 1790s. Bacon, a tailor by trade, reputedly made 200 uniforms for the National Guard in 1792, a Volunteer-style front for the United Irishmen. The Dublin Independent Volunteers evidently prefigured a republican city leadership in the way in which rural units, such as Rathdrum-based Wicklow Foresters maintained their loyalist politics when progressing under the leadership of Thomas King from the Volunteers to the masonic 'Friendly Brothers', Rathdrum yeoman cavalry and Rathdrum Orange Lodge between 1794 and 1800. See Musgrave, *Rebellions*, p. 43 and O'Donnell, *Rebellion in Wicklow*, pp. 34–5. See also Thomas Bartlett (ed.), *Revolutionary Dublin: The Letters of Francis Higgins to Dublin Castle, 1795–1801* (Dublin, 2003), p. 425. William Steel Dickson believed Dowling was COI. Clifford (ed.) *Dickson*, p. 100.

52 Quoted in Madden, *United*, III, p. 37.

53 Ibid., p. 41; McDowell (ed.), *Proceedings*, p. 45; *Hibernian Journal*, 2 May 1793.

54 McDowell (ed.) *Proceedings*, p. 46. See also ibid., pp. 8, 19–20; Power, *Eighteenth-century Tipperary*, p. 304.

55 See Edward Moore to Addis Emmet, 29 July 1797, NA, Rebellion Papers, 620/15/4 and Power, *Eighteenth-century Tipperary*, p. 285.

56 McDowell (ed.), *Proceedings*, p. 53.

57 McDowell (ed.), *Proceedings*, p. 57. See also ibid., p. 58; Addis Emmet, 'Part of an essay', p. 81.

58 *Freeman's Journal*, 3 Jan. 1793. For Corbally's trial and transportation see Barbara Hall, *A desperate set of villains, the convicts of the Marquis Cornwallis, Ireland to Botany Bay, 1796* (Sydney, 2000), pp. 79–81.

59 McDowell (ed.), *Proceedings*, p. 63. See also Addis Emmet, 'Part of an essay', pp. 42–3.

60 Thomas Bartlett, *The fall and rise of the Irish nation, the Catholic question, 1690–1830* (Dublin, 1992), pp. 168–72.

61 McDowell (ed.), *Proceedings*, pp. 62–6.

62 Brian Inglis, *The freedom of the press in Ireland, 1784–1841* (London, 1954), p. 77. See also McDowell (ed.), *Proceedings*, p. 92; *Dublin Evening Post*, 1 May 1794; Madden, *United*, III, p. 41. Judge Robert Day commented that 'Driscool [sic] Journ[alis]t circulates all the sedit[io]n of [the] Un[ited] Irishmen of Dublin papers & his own'. Journal of Judge Robert Day, 17 Mar. 1794, RIA, MSS 12. W. 14., p. 7. For Driscoll's later career see Inglis, *Press*, p. 89; John Paul Waters (ed.), *The African Traveler: a radical's tale of Ireland in the year of the Great Irish Rebellion by Denis Driscol*, unpublished MS; David A. Wilson, *United*

Irishmen, United States, immigrants, radicals in the early Republic (Dublin, 1998), pp. 46, 61–2.

63 Marianne Elliott, 'The Defenders in Ulster' in Dickson, Keogh and Whelan (eds), *United Irishmen*, pp. 226–7; Smyth, *Men of no property*, p. 67.

64 Bartlett, *Fall and Rise*, chapter eight; Wilson, *United Irishmen, United States*, pp. 23, 34.

65 *Hibernian Journal*, 25 July 1793, *Faulkner's Dublin Journal*, 15 Mar. 1794; Thomas Bartlett, 'An end to the moral economy: the Irish militia disturbances of 1793', *Past and Present*, 99 (1983), pp. 41–64.

66 Drennan to Sam McTier, 17 Jan. 1794 in Agnew (ed.), *Drennan-McTier Letters*, II, pp. 2, 4. See also Drennan to Sam McTier, 3 Feb. 1794 in ibid., p. 14; Davis (ed.), *Curran*, pp. 153–4, 363; McDowell (ed.), *Proceedings*, pp. 105–6.

67 *Alumni Dublinenses*, p. 180; R. R. Madden, *The life and times of Robert Emmet* (Glasgow, n.d.), pp. 4–5; Emmet, *Memoir*, II, p. 294; *The Gentleman's and Citizen's Almanack, compiled by Samuel Watson, for the year of our Lord, 1794* (Dublin, 1794), p. 85. Fry was the godson of ultra-loyalist Earl Kingston. Having abandoned his studies to assist his brother in fighting the Boyle Defenders, he obtained a lieutenancy in the Royal Regiment of Artillery in October 1794. Fry had joined Masonic Lodge 338 in 1792, the Athlone Friendly Brothers 'Knot' and the Orange Order in which the King family exerted influence in the west of Ireland. Major Oliver Fry, 'Narrative', privately published book, Roscommon County Library, pp. 23, 26.

68 Tone, 'Memoirs' in Bartlett (ed.), *Tone*, pp. 100–1; *Faulkner's Dublin Journal*, 24 May 1794; *Hibernian Journal*, 10 Nov. 1794.

69 Drennan to Sam McTier, 3 May 1794 in Agnew (ed.), *Drennan-McTier Letters*, II, p. 48.

70 Quoted in Landreth, *Pursuit*, pp. 39–40.

71 2 Oct. 1805 [sic, 1803], NA, Rebellion Papers, 620/11/130/43. See also *Alumni Dublinenses*, p. 312. Alternatively, Dubliner Abraham Fuller, several years older than James, progressed from Trinity to the Irish Bar in 1773 and thus shared possible legal connections with both brothers. Ibid. Landreth believed that 'F' was Thomas Collins. She noted that Drennan had received a similar warning from John Pollock in April 1793, whom he had known in Newry. Landreth, *Pursuit*, pp. 31–2, 41.

72 Information of Thomas Collins, n.d. [c. May/June 1794], NA, Rebellion Papers, 620/54/18.

73 *Saunder's Newsletter* and *Faulkner's Dublin Journal*, 20 May 1794.

74 Drennan to Ann Drennan, 26 June 1794 in Agnew (ed.), *Drennan-McTier Letters*, II, p. 69. See also John Francis Larkin (ed.), *The trial of William Drennan, on a trial for sedition, in the year 1794 and his intended defence* (Dublin, 1991), pp. 92–6.

75 Information of Thomas Collins, n.d. [c. May/June 1794], NA, Rebellion Papers, 620/54/18. See also Drennan to Sam McTier, 29 Sept. 1792 in Agnew (ed.), *Drennan-McTier Letters*, I, p. 416; Drennan to Sam McTier, 20 Aug. 1794 in ibid., II, p. 91; Drennan to Martha McTier, n.d. [Oct. 1794] in ibid., II, p. 101; Drennan to Martha McTier, 20 July 1796 in ibid., II, p. 252.

76 William Rowan to Addis Emmet, 31 Nov. 1794, NA, Rebellion Papers, 620/15/2/8.

77 Deirdre Lindsay, 'The Fitzwilliam episode revisited' in Dickson, Keogh and Whelan (eds), *United Irishmen*, p. 199.

78 *New Cork Evening Post*, 3 Sept. 1795. In August 1804 an anonymous and moralistic Englishman arrived in Hollyhead from Chester on a tour which took him into Dublin's republican communities. He recalled: 'After service I walked

again through the St. Giles's of Dublin, the Poddle in Meath-street and Thomas-street, to the Foundling-hospital. In these streets there seemed to be nothing which indicated Sunday; not even that difference of apparel with which, in other great towns, even the most depraved distinguish it. For the drunkenness, noise, beating of drums and fifes at the doors of alehouses, and low gambling in the streets, the police is reprehensible; and how is the full growth of rebellion to be wondered at, when it is thus fostered in its infancy?' Seamus Grimes (ed.), *Ireland in 1804, with an introduction by Seamus Grimes* (Ireland, 1980), p. 28.

79 *Belfast Newsletter*, 19 May 1797. An intelligence digest prepared for the Duke of Portland in July 1795 claimed: 'Some of the heads of the United Irishmen are Mr. Hamilton Rowan, Counsellor the Hon. Simon Butler, Emmett [sic], MacNally, the two Sheares, Sampson and Tone.' Quoted in Bartlett (ed.), *Higgins*, p. 597.

80 MacNeven et al., *Pieces of Irish history*, p. 277. See also Moore, *Lord Edward Fitzgerald*, p. 228; David W. Miller, *Peep O'Day Boys and Defenders, selected documents on the county Armagh disturbances, 1784–96* (Belfast, 1990).

81 Addis Emmet, 'Part of an essay', p. 143. See also Madden, *United*, III, p. 41.

82 In mid-March 1796 a group of forty Defenders were arrested when meeting in Church Street; on the same day it was reported that nine had been sentenced to death in Mullingar and fifteen in Trim. In August 1796 Thomas Kennedy and almost forty other Dublin Defenders sentenced by the show trials were put on board a vessel at the North Wall to be shipped to Cobh. They were transported to New South Wales on the *Britannia* and arrived, after a fatal mutiny attempt, in May 1797. Their comrade, Joseph Corbally, had preceded them on the *Marquis Cornwallis* in 1796. *Walker's Hibernian Magazine*, Aug. 1796, p. 192; *Faulkner's Dublin Journal*, 15 Mar. 1796; *Hibernian Journal*, 30 Mar. 1796.

83 Tone, 'Memoir' in Bartlett (ed.), *Tone*, pp. 106–7. See also Denis Carroll, *The Man from God Knows Where, Thomas Russell, 1767–1803* (Dublin, 1995), pp. 104–5.

84 Cited in Smyth, *Men of no property*, p. 118.

85 Thomas Addis Emmet to Tone, n.d. [June 1795], quoted in Emmet, *Memoir*, I, p. 214. See also Addis Emmet, 'Part of an essay', p. 130.

CHAPTER TWO

1 *Faulkner's Dublin Journal*, 30 June 1795 and Moore, *Memoirs*, pp. 20–1.

2 Moore, *Lord Edward Fitzgerald*, p. 142. Moore, born in 12 Aungier St., entered Trinity College on 2 June 1794. *Alumni Dublinenses*, p. 595.

3 Emmet, *Memoir*, I, pp. 194–5.

4 Jane Maxwell, 'Sources in Trinity College Library Dublin for researching the 1798 Rebellion', *Irish Archives, Journal of the Irish Society for Archives*, 5, 1 (Summer 1998), p. 144; Madden, *United*, III, pp. 14–19.

5 *Belfast Newsletter*, 24 Mar. and 7 April 1797.

6 See Hugh Gough, 'Anatomy of a failure' in John A. Murphy (ed.), *The French are in the bay: the expedition to Bantry Bay 1796* (Cork, 1997), pp. 9–24.

7 Tone, 'Journals' in Bartlett (ed.), *Tone*, p. 531.

8 Quoted in León Ó Broin, *The Unfortunate Mr. Robert Emmet* (Dublin, 1958), p. 18.

9 For a discussion of the evolving upper command structure of the movement see Tommy Graham, 'United Irish leadership, 1796–1798' in Jim Smyth (ed.), *Revolution, counter-revolution and Union: Ireland in the 1790s* (Cambridge,

2000), pp. 55–66. For Bond's imprisonment in Newgate in May 1793 see NA, Official Papers, 30/4/17. For Dowling and Richard Dry see *Faulkner's Dublin Journal*, 2 April and 22 October 1793. It was alleged that Thomas Dry and William Coffey were Defender leaders when they convened a meeting in Drury Lane. *New Cork Evening Post*, 14 Mar. 1796.

10 Madden, *United*, III, p. 62. Emmet attended a meeting in the home of Henry and John Sheares along with republican lawyers Mathew Dowling, William Sampson, Beauchamp Bagenal Harvey, Edward Lewins and Edward Keane (aka Kane). H[iggins] to Sackville Hamilton, 24 June 1795 in Bartlett (ed.), *Higgins*, pp. 128–33.

11 W. J. MacNeven, 'An account of the treaty between the United Irishmen and the Anglo-Irish government in 1798' in MacNeven et al., *Pieces of Irish History*, p. 171. The camps were by no means rigid. MacNally claimed O'Connor's language, in late 1797 or early 1798, was 'as severe as that of Robespierre in Paris . . . [and] shock[e]d' the 'moderate minds . . . the friends who strictly adhere to O'Connor are Lord Edward Fitzgerald whom the moderate republicans describe as his dupe, and Dr. McNeven [sic], whom they represent as his subservient tool. His other associates are mostly new in the lower Orders of Society; a few priests and a number of merchants. The moderate party, who wish for the independency of Ireland, though of republican principles . . . consists of the men of Education and Wealth. Among those are Lawless, [Thomas Addis] Emmett [sic], the two Leesons, McCormick, [Thomas] Dillon of [7] Parliament Street, and [Richard] Dillon of Bride Street. The opinion of Bond and Jackson on this business I do not at present know.' [MacNally], n.d. 1797–98, NA, Rebellion Papers, 620/10/121/148.

12 Madden, *United*, III, pp. 47–8; Marianne Elliott, *Partners in Revolution, the United Irishmen and France* (London, 1988), pp. 189–213; Curtin, *United Irishmen*, pp. 86–8.

13 Dixon, Edward Lewins, James Moore and John Byrne were amongst the south city delegates to the Catholic Convention. Also active in the United Irishmen were Charles O'Hara, Ambrose Moore, Thomas Bacon, Thomas Wright, Robert Fyan, Philip Long, Miles Duigenan and many others who remained committed in 1802–3. [Collins], n.d., NA, Rebellion Papers, 620/54/20. Dixon was imprisoned on several occasions during the Rebellion years and was known to have harboured Fr. James Coigley in his Kilmainham home. Higgins claimed that Dixon had care of Coigley's papers in 1801. [Higgins] to [Cooke], 27 Feb. 1801 in Bartlett (ed.), *Higgins*, p. 530.

14 Bird to Sirr, n.d., 1798 in Madden, *United*, I, pp. 498–9. Bird's information mainly concerns early-to-mid-1797 when he was active in Wicklow, Dublin and Meath, but must have been written after March 1798 as it refers to the 'committee . . . taken at Bond's house [on 12 Mar. 1798]'. Ibid., p. 500. For the original version of the document see Sirr Papers, TCD (Trinity College Dublin), MS 869/84–5. On 18 February 1798 *Faulkner's Dublin Journal* refuted United Irish claims that Bird, a former employee, had been assassinated. See also *Wilson's Dublin Directory . . . 1803*, p. 42.

15 Duigenan, also referred to as Dignam, Dignan and Duignan, was an active United Irishman from 1794, at which time he would have formed links with Bond, Wright, Jackson, Charles O'Hara, Hampden Evans and others later revealed as the sponsors of the armed republicans of Dublin. See McDowell (ed.), *Proceedings*, p. 118. For Dublin's political societies see Kevin Whelan, *The Tree of Liberty, Radicalism, Catholicism and the construction of Irish identity, 1760–1830* (Cork, 1996), pp. 78–80. Duigenan was reputed to have owned a share in the *Morgan* or *Morgan Rattler*, a Rush-based smuggler and privateer

used in gun running. Another shareholder, Thomas Richard of Abbey Street was related to Arthur O'Connor. [Higgins] to [Cooke], 15 July 1796, NA, Rebellion Papers, 620/18/14. In the aftermath of the Rebellion years Duigenan was regarded as 'a desperate man [who] forwarded assassination'. 'Suspect list', n.d., NA, Rebellion Papers, 620/12/217.

16 *Report from the Committee of Secrecy appointed to take into consideration the treasonable papers presented to the House of Commons of Ireland on the 17th day of July last* . . . (Dublin, 1798), p. 117.

17 See Musgrave, *Rebellions*, p. 157; Smyth, *Men of no property*, pp. 150–6; *Faulkner's Dublin Journal*, 18 April 1797.

18 Quoted in Emmet, *Memoir*, II, p. 9.

19 Madden, *Emmet*, p. 7. See also Landreth, *Pursuit*, pp. 65–6 and Moore, *Lord Edward Fitzgerald*, pp. 122, 126. Moore was incorrect in stating that Addis Emmet was not in the United Irishmen in early 1796. Ibid., p. 122.

20 30 Nov. 1803, NA, 620/11/130/60.

21 Donal Kerr (ed.), *Emmet's Casino and the Marists at Milltown* (Dublin, n.d.), p. 6.

22 For a basic outline of Egan's career see *A catalogue of graduates . . . University of Dublin* (Dublin, 1869), p. 177 and Thomas U. Sadlier (ed.), *An Irish Peer on the Continent (1801–1803) being a narrative of the tour of Stephen, 2nd Earl Mount Cashell, through France, Italy, etc., as related by Catherine Wilmot* (London, 1920), p. 70. Landreth believed that 'Jones' left Trinity in 1797 and travelled to France with George Orr. This implicates Orr's associate John Murphy of Tandragee, Armagh, who knew Fr James Coigley. Orr and Murphy took part in Napper Tandy's *Anacreon* expedition to Donegal in September 1798 and 'Jones', apparently following arrest in England in 1799, cooperated from time to time with the British authorities. While Orr betrayed details of the March 1799 revival of the United Irishmen in Britain there is no evidence that either he or Murphy encountered Robert Emmet abroad. See Landreth, *Pursuit*, p. 66 and Elliott, *Partners*, pp. 176–7, 232–3, 252–4.

23 30 Nov. 1803, NA, Rebellion Papers, 620/11/130/60.

24 3 Nov. 1803, Public Record Office (PRO) London, Home Office Papers, 100/114/149. See also Blacker, 'Extracts' in Constantia Maxwell, *A History of Trinity College Dublin, 1591–1892* (Dublin, 1946), p. 269; John Edward Walsh, *Sketches of Ireland sixty years ago* (Dublin, 1847), pp. 168–9; *Alumni Dublinenses*, p. 274. Walsh's insights were informed by his having published political items which aroused the interest of the College authorities. Emmet, *Memoirs*, II, p. 5.

25 Lawless, *Life and Times*, pp. 163–4. Lawless was sent by his father to study law in London in late 1797 in the hope that he would evade prosecution as a United Irishman. Ibid., p. 48. See also *Alumni Dublinenses*, p. 485.

26 Emmet, 'Part of an essay'. See also Whelan, *Tree of Liberty*, pp. 62–4, 74, 190 and M. Butler, *Burke, Paine, Godwin, and the Revolution controversy* (Cambridge, 1984). Postgate referred to Emmet's annotated copy of Locke's *An Essay Concerning Human Understanding*. Postgate, *Emmet*, p. 180.

27 Francis Plowden, *An historical review of the state of Ireland from the invasion of that country under Henry II to its union with Great Britain on the 1st of January 1801*, 2 vols (London, 1803), I, pp. 559, 617, 625.

28 *Belfast Newsletter*, 20–24 Mar. 1797 and 5 May 1797.

29 *Belfast Newsletter*, 17–24 Mar. 1797.

30 John Giffard to Cooke, 5 June 1797, NA, Rebellion Papers, 620/31/36 and Anon. to Wilkinson, 14 July 1797, NA, State of the Country Papers, 3097. See also Madden, *United*, I, p. 298.

31 *Belfast Newsletter*, 15 May 1797.

32 *Faulkner's Dublin Journal*, 25 April 1797. See also ibid., 8 June 1797.

33 Thomas Pelham to Sheffield, 29 May 1797 in Anthony Malcomson (ed.), *An Anglo-Irish Dialogue: a calendar of the correspondence between John Foster and Lord Sheffield, 1774–1821* (Belfast, 1975), p. 69. See also *Belfast Newsletter*, 14–17 April and 15 May 1797.

34 *Report from the Committee of Secrecy*, pp. 120–21. See also Smyth, *Men of no property*, p. 153 and Curtin, *United Irishmen*, p. 109. For Dry and the Defenders see Ruán O'Donnell, '"Desperate and Diabolical": Defenders and United Irishmen in Early New South Wales' in Richard Davis et al. (eds), *Irish–Australian Studies* (Sydney, 1996), pp. 360–72. United Irish committees connected to Jackson's network met in the Black Bull on High Street in early 1796. Information of John Dawson, 1799, NA, Rebellion Papers, 620/8/72/1. Francis Higgins reported in May 1797 that 'pikes have been made in numbers at Clonskeagh and Milltown Mills and continue making there'. This referred to Jackson's operations which Higgins wrongly credited to one Waters. [Higgins] to [Cooke], 18 May 1797, NA, Rebellion Papers, 620/18/14.

35 27 Aug. 1797, NLI (National Library of Ireland), Frazer Papers, MS/1/17.

36 R. R. Madden, *The autobiography of James (Jemmy) Hope* (Belfast, 1998), pp. 15–16; *The Annual Register, or a view of the history politics and literature for the year 1798* (London, 1800), Chronicle, pp. 38, 50; R. R. Madden, *Down and Antrim in '98* (Dublin, n.d.), pp. 115, 170–3. In late October 1797 delegates from Wicklow met in McVeagh's of Dorset Street where Patrick Byrne of Great Britain Street, treasurer of the Rotunda Division, received their subscriptions to the projected Leinster Provincial Directory. See Ruán O'Donnell, *The Rebellion in Wicklow 1798* (Dublin, 1998), pp. 82–3.

37 [Higgins] to [Cooke], 24 Nov. 1797, NA, Rebellion Papers, 620/18/14.

38 Thomas Addis Emmet, *Montanus' Letters, being a selection from the writings of T. A. E, contributed to the "The Press" (The journal of the United Irishmen, 1797–8). Edited with notes and a memoir* (Dublin, n.d. [1898]). See also Emmet, *Memoir*, I, pp. 234–5. The 'Literary men' believed that Arthur O'Connor 'directs' the *Union Star* and he was certainly on good terms with Cox prior to 1799. MacNally reported: '[Addis] Emmett [sic] in particular is exerting himself to suppress this execrable publication and probably it will be suppressed.' [MacNally], n.d. [1797–98], NA, Rebellion Papers, 620/10/121/148. Valentine Lawless was the first 'principal proprietor of the *Press*' in late 1797, as MacNally discovered when offered a share by him for £50. [MacNally], 8 Nov. [1797], NA, Rebellion Papers, 620/10/121/147. The 'Private Committee' with input into the paper met in Chamber's house on Abbey Street. The fact that MacNeven and 'Cox the printer' attended illustrates the complex inter-relationship of United Irish propagandists. Ibid. A post-Rebellion Castle entry for Cox as '*engraver, gunsmith* and was bred a *Priest*, author of the Union Star and a Deep Conspirator' is indicative of his near fanatical commitment and the administration's distrust of his motives. 'Suspect list', n.d., NA, Rebellion Papers, 620/12/217. He occasionally passed information to the Castle during the Rebellion years but was by no means a double agent. See 10 Mar. 1798, PRO London, Home Office Papers, 100/75/189.

39 Cox did not warn of the 1803 conspiracy. Cooke briefed Wickham: 'Cox, a gun smith who was author of the Union Star & who finding himself on the point of detection obtained the promise of a pardon on condition that he was to discover the author of that shocking publication. He then disclosed himself to be sole publisher & author of the *Union Star*. Another condition of his pardon was that

he should give me every possible information as to the United Irishmen.' Cox disclosed details of the Binns brothers and one Bonham, agent of the London Corresponding Society. He learned of their travel plans in John Stockdale's office on Abbey Street with whom he was 'very intimate'. Cooke to Wickham, 10 Mar. 1798, PRO, Home Office, 100/75/189.

40 Miles Byrne, *Memoirs of Miles Byrne*, 2 vols (Paris, 1863), II, p. 180; Inglis, *Press*, pp. 99–103; Curtin, *United Irishmen*, pp. 213–5; Moore, *Memoirs*, p. 24.

41 Madden, *United*, III, p. 578. See also ibid., p. 6. For Kirwan and St Peter's see Fintan Cullen, 'The cloak of charity: The Politics of Representation in late eighteenth-century Ireland', *The Irish Review*, 21 (Autumn/Winter 1997), p. 68. In July 1797 Addis Emmet corresponded with Edward Moore of Mooresfort, Tipperary, a family friend, who considered running for Parliament. Moore's address 'To the Free and Independent Electors of the COUNTY OF TIPPERARY' acknowledged support 'From enlightened Protestants, who think all Sects of Religion equally entitled to Privileges with themselves, and who do not taint their Love of the Constitution with an Adoration of those Impurities which have no natural Connection with it'. Edward Moore to Addis Emmet, 29 July 1797, NA, Rebellion Papers, 620/15/2/4.

42 The disaffected Sweetmans of Francis Street had a porter brewery at 83 St Stephen's Green in the mid-1790s. See *Wilson's Dublin Directory . . . 1794*, p. 98. John Sweetman was described as an 'eminent porter brewer'. Dickson, *Narrative*, p. 110.

43 John Burke (aka Burk), a Cork relation of Edmund Burke, was expelled from Trinity in early 1794 for seditious activities and atheism. He belonged to a group of senior United Irishmen known as 'the Strugglers' which included Oliver Bond, John and Henry Sheares and Beauchamp Bagenal Harvey. Their host, Luke Dignan/ Duigenan, owned the pub which gave the group its name at 42–43 Cook Street. He participated in the Rising of 1803. Dignan knew John Farrell of Clara, a senior King's County/Westmeath United Irishman. See Thomas Barnard to Marsden, 16 Aug. 1803, NA, Rebellion Papers, 620/64/198; Wilson, *United Irishmen, United States*, p. 23.

44 Emmet, *Memoirs*, I, p. 176 and II, p. 22. See also Reynolds, *Footprints*, p. 21; Postgate, *Emmet*, p. 33; Kerr (ed.), *Emmet's Casino*, p. 6. Christopher Temple Emmet was also interested in 'mighty Neptune' and mermaids, both of which featured in one of his published allegorical poems. See *The Decree, written during the administration of, and inscribed to, his Excellency, John, Earl of Buckinghamshire, by Christopher Temple Emmet, Esq.* (Dublin, n.d.). This indicates that the Milltown sculptures, if executed by Robert Emmet, were created as a form of memorial or tribute to Temple Emmet.

45 For McCabe and Palmer in 1797–98 see 30 Aug. 1801, NA, Rebellion Papers, 620/49/125.

46 McDowell (ed.), *Proceedings*, pp. 128, 135 and Maxwell, *Trinity*, pp. 144–6. For Stokes see TCD, MS 3363. Moore had spoken in favour of Grattan and Fitzwilliam in April 1795 when Trinity students presented an address to the MP and rallied in Francis Street chapel. The informer Francis Higgins claimed that Moore was 'secretary' of the group, a role which accounts for his subsequent United Irish membership and vulnerability to punishment in 1798. See H[iggins] to Hamilton, 10 April 1795 in Bartlett (ed.), *Higgins*, p. 111.

47 Lawless, *Life and Times*, pp. 63, 86. See also Davis (ed.), *Curran*, p. xxviii. For Richard Curran and Valentine Lawless see [MacNally], n.d. [1798?], NA, Rebellion Papers, 620/10/121/150.

48 Leslie Hale, *John Philpot Curran, his life and times* (London, 1958); p. 176, Madden, *United*, III, p. 285; *Alumni Dublinenses*, pp. 203, 463. For Hudson,

who lived at 28 Grafton Street, see Gilbert, *City of Dublin*, III, p. 217 and *The trial of William Michael Byrne for High Treason* (Dublin, 1798), p. 6. For Bunting and Moore see Mary Helen Thuente, 'The Literary Significance of the United Irishmen' in Michael Kenneally (ed.), *Irish Literature and Culture* (London, 1992), p. 52.

49   TCD, MSS 1203, quoted in Maxwell, 'Sources in Trinity College', p. 14. Egan admitted paying his 6d subscription to Flinn, the secretary of his simple society. Ibid.

50   Maxwell, *Trinity*, pp. 146–7; Landreth, *Pursuit*, pp. 71, 78; *Report from the Committee of Secrecy*, pp. 169–72.

51   Robert White, a former apprentice of Chambers, printed United Irish handbills as well as 'political song books . . . watch papers, with a monument to [William] Orr'. Bird to Sirr, n.d., 1798 in Madden, *United*, I, p. 501. In 1803 White owned a bookshop at 80 Great Britain Street. *Wilson's Dublin Directory . . . 1803*, p. 106. The *Press* was published in 62 (renumbered 67) Middle Abbey Street. NLI, MS Ir 92 E 43, II.

52   30 Nov. 1803, NA, Rebellion Papers, 620/11/130/60. Years later William Wickham ascertained that Farrell 'was very intimate with young Emmet while they were at College'. Wickham to John King, 3 Nov. 1803, PRO London, Home Office Papers, 100/114/149.

53   Information of Thomas Reynolds, n.d. [Mar. 1798], PRO London, Home Office Papers, 100/75/105.

54   Landreth, *Pursuit*, p. 66; *Wilson's Dublin Directory . . . 1794*, pp. 147–8; Graham, 'United Irish leadership', p. 60; Michael Durey, 'Marquess Cornwallis and the fate of Irish rebel prisoners in the aftermath of the 1798 rebellion' in Smyth (ed.), *Revolution*, p. 132.

55   30 Nov. 1803, NA, Rebellion Papers, 620/11/130/60.

56   See McDowell (ed.), *Proceedings*, p. 135.

57   Byrne, *Memoirs*, III, pp. 37–8.

58   Moore, *Lord Edward Fitzgerald*, p. 142. Dr Robert Emmet and Arthur Chichester McCartney (aka Macartney) senior were joint assignees under a Commission of Bankruptcy in 1795 for a house on Dawson Street. Item 740, *Whyte's Ephemera: Irish Interest*, (June, 1998). They were neighbours in Stephen's Green into the 1800s. Thomas Langlois Lefroy entered TCD in 1790 and graduated five years later. He was called to the Bar in 1797 and was King's Council in 1806. W. G. Strickland, *A descriptive catalogue of the pictures, busts and statues in Trinity College Dublin and in the Provost's house* (Dublin, 1916), p. 61.

59   Madden, *Robert Emmet*, pp. 4–5.

60   Revd Thomas Elrington to Major Sirr, 7 June 1803 in Madden, *United*, III, pp. 336–7.

61   Davis (ed.), *Curran*, p. 276 and Gilbert, *City of Dublin*, III, pp. 320–1. Moore acknowledged that his first published essay appeared in the *Press* and that 'among those extracts from its columns which are appended in the Report of the Secret Committee, for the purpose of showing the excited state of public feeling at that period, there are some of which the blame or the merit must rest with an author who had then but just turned his seventeenth year'. Moore, *Lord Edward Fitzgerald*, p. 147. See also Moore, *Memoirs*, pp. 24–5.

62   *Press*, 4 Nov. 1797.

63   The five were 'Arbour Hill', 'Genius of Erin', 'The Exile', 'The London Pride and Shamrock' and 'Help from Heaven'. He had earlier written 'Erin's Call'. Madden, *United*, III, pp. 495–502; Ó Broin, *Unfortunate*, 31; *Press*, 21 Oct. 1797. Madden stated in relation to Emmet poems in his possession that 'for

these interesting documents in the original I am indebted to Miss Mary McCracken'. Mary Anne Emmet may have placed the manuscripts in McCracken's care through their joint connections with the Drennan and Russell families. Madden, *United*, III, p. 495. A long but incomplete poem was found in the 'Thomas Street' arms depot on 23–4 July 1803 which was almost certainly written by Emmet. See NA, Rebellion Papers, 620/12/158/8.

64   *Report from the Committee of Secrecy*, p. 195. While Moore may not have realised that his article had been accepted for publication by Neilson, its submission establishes a greater input into such circles than he was ever prepared to acknowledge in print. Moore could not have known, unless informed by Castle agents, that Higgins had passed detailed reports of his radical 1795 activities to the authorities. For the literary dimension to Moore's engagement with the United Irishmen see Thuente, 'Literary Significance' in Kenneally (ed.), *Irish Literature*. pp. 52–4.

65   Blacker, 'Extracts' in Maxwell, *Trinity*, p. 271 and Charles Dickson, *Revolt in the North, Antrim and Down in 1798* (Dublin, 1960), pp. 177–8. Power published a 'patriotic' letter 'of excessive ardour' after his expulsion. He was 'implicated' in the 1798 Rebellion and pressurised by Judge Robert Day into giving evidence against the Cork Directory. Although detained for two years on Spike Island and in Cork City, Power refused to prosecute Timothy Conway. Ironically, Conway became an informer and double agent. Madden, *United*, I, p. 515. Power was, however, subjected to 'a little flogging' and reputedly divulged information of a plot to seize Cork in May/June 1798. He became a captain in an English militia regiment based in Devon after his release in 1800. Hartigan to Downshire, 20 June 1798, PRO Belfast, D. 607/F/258. See also TCD, MS 869/7.

66   Madden, *United*, III, pp. 270–4. A reconstructed account of the 'Visitation' of April 1798 is provided by Maxwell in 'Sources in Trinity College', pp. 3–22. Newry historian W. H. Maxwell claimed that the anti-loyalist demonstrators of February 1798 had taunted their enemies with calls of 'Orange rascals' and that a plot by one Ward to admit city rebels to the College precincts was then averted. W. H. Maxwell, *History of the Irish Rebellion in 1798: with Memoirs of the Union, and Emmett's* [sic] *Insurrection in 1803* (London, 1845), p. 54.

67   Madden, *United*, III, p. 43.

68   R. B. McDowell, *Ireland in the Age of Imperialism and Revolution, 1760–1801* (Oxford, 1979), p. 573.

69   Madden, *United*, III, p. 43. See also Plowden, *Historical Review*, II, pp. 638–9 and *Press*, 25 Nov. 1797.

70   John Pollock to Addis Emmet, 5 Dec. 1797, NA, Rebellion Papers, 620/15/2/6.

71   D to Addis Emmet, 21 Jan. [1798?], NA, Rebellion Papers, 620/15/2/7. 'D' may have been William Dowdall whose background in the Whig Club, republicanism and brief proprietorship of the *Press* brought him into contact with Addis Emmet and other members of the United Irish constitutional subcommittee. Dowdall certainly had input into the 1803 proclamation of the Provisional Government which set an upper limit of 300 MPs. See Appendix Two. For Pollock's interrogation techniques and agent running see William Steel Dickson, *A narrative of the confinement and exile of William Steel Dickson . . .* (Belfast, 1812), pp. 65, 70–2. Dickson had been a friend of Alexander Stewart and incurred debts to help bring the future Lord Castlereagh, Stewart's son, into parliament in 1790. Ibid., pp. 6, 239.

72   *Union Star*, n.d., 1797.

73   *Belfast Newsletter*, 22 Jan. 1798. See also *Freeman's Journal*, 11 Jan. 1798; *Saunder's Newsletter*, 17 Jan. 1798; Davis (ed.), *Curran*, p. 314; *Irish*

Magazine, May 1809, pp. 205–23. O'Brien was suspected of murdering one Adare of Dunboyne, Co. Meath, during a robbery in 1795. He worked as a gardener for David La Touche of Marley (Rathfarnham) and, when accused of the Adare killing, turned state's witness. He was encountered in Dublin in 1797 by Miles Duigenan and the spy John Bird, to whom he offered to supply 160 muskets and 5,000 cartridges obtained from the army camp at Loughlinstown 'at prime cost'. O'Brien's dealings with Sirr may have led to Duigenan's arrest in May 1797. See Madden, *United*, I, pp. 498–501. Mathew Dowling's clerk, Hugh Crook, claimed that George Howell 'swore very hard against O'Brien and was the   chief means of saving *Finn*[e]*y* from being hanged'. Ibid., p. 503. See also ibid, pp. 467–8.

74   [Higgins] to [Cooke], 16 Jan. 1798, NA, Rebellion Papers, 620/18/14.
75   Luke Brien to [Marsden?], 23 Aug. 1803, NA, Rebellion Papers, 620/11/130/3 and *Saunder's Newsletter*, 19 Jan. 1798. Finney used the name Hyland when in England, that of a January 1798 co-defendant. *Freeman's Journal*, 21 Jan. 1798. He was considered an activist in 1798 and 1803. 'Suspect list', n.d., NA, Rebellion Papers, 620/12/217.
76   *Report from the Committee of Secrecy*, pp. 190–1; Madden, *Literary Remains of the United Irishmen of 1798 and selections from other Popular Lyrics of their Times . . .* (Dublin, 1887), p. 205; Gilbert, *City of Dublin*, III, p. 328.
77   *Freeman's Journal*, 11 Jan. 1798. See also *Belfast Newsletter*, 22 Jan. 1798; *Saunder's Newsletter*, 18 Jan. 1798; Landreth, *Pursuit*, p. 85. One Murphy was killed at Astley's Circus on Eccles Street, off Dorset Street, in March 1798, probably the incident associated with Allen and Kelly. Cooke to Wickham, 23 Mar. 1798, Public Record Office, Home Office Papers, 100/80/136. Allen was evidently an earthy character. According to government sources he was: '5 feet 10 inches, dark crop[pe]d hair, much pock mark[e]d, hollow blue eyes, rather a pug nose, dresses slovenly, generally in black, in kneed, seems when walking to drag his legs after him, has completely the slang accent peculiar to the lower order, vulgar & uncouth in manner, addicted to swearing, stoops, always wears Pantaloons & Boots'. 'Suspect list', n.d., NA, Rebellion Papers, 620/12/217.
78   Information of Patrick McCabe, n.d., 1803 in Madden, *United*, I, p. 493.
79   [Higgins] to [Cooke], 16 Jan. 1798, NA, Rebellion Papers, 620/18/14.
80   *Belfast Newsletter*, 9 Feb. 1798.
81   See Thomas Cloney, A *Personal Narrative of those transactions in the County of Wexford in which the author was engaged at the awful period of 1799* (Dublin, 1832), p. 229.
82   *Press*, pp. 478–9 and Senior to [Cooke], 24 Jan. 1798, NA, Rebellion Papers, 620/18/13.
83   Lawless, *Life and times*, pp. 66–7 and *Faulkner's Dublin Journal*, 8 Mar. 1798. Binns was mentioned as a United Irishman in Castle correspondence as early as July 1792. McDowell (ed.), *Proceedings*, p. 27.
84   'GH' to Thomas Ellis, 25 July 1803, NA, Rebellion Papers, 620/65/74. Cox knew Thomas Boyle who may have learned of O'Connor's movements from him in the summer of 1798. Boyle, 9 June 1798, NA, Rebellion Papers, 620/18/3.
85   Reynolds claimed to have been inducted by Bond in February 1797. See Bartlett (ed.), *Higgins*.
86   Quoted in Gilbert, *City of Dublin*, III, p. 286. See also PRO London, Home Office Papers, 100/75/203–9.
87   See Musgrave, *Rebellions*, Appendix Twenty-Two, 12, pp. 845–7 and ibid., p. 680. Fitzgerald failed to take account of the possible effects of government forces being supported by cannon, as had occurred in Bruff, Limerick, during a contest against the Defenders in 1793. The use of cannon against massed

pikemen inflicted thousands of rebel fatalities in Carlow, New Ross and Arklow between 25 May and 9 June 1798 and generally proved decisive in keeping the rebels out of military lines. The critical point was that the military were not surprised and had time to prepare positions in small urban centres to ward off external attack. Fitzgerald's preoccupation with a surprise internal city revolt seconded by external reinforcements establishes the primacy of Dublin to United Irish strategy in Leinster.

88 'GH' to Ellis, 25 July 1803, NA, Rebellion Papers, 620/65/74. Carhampton was the landlord of the Cox family. His 'interference' led to Walter Cox being released from custody on two occasions. Ibid. The recipient, Ellis of 6 Trinity Street, was evidently the man of that name called to the Bar in 1796. *Wilson's Dublin Directory . . . 1803*, p. 115. In 1812 Dr John Brennan, publisher of the *Milesian Magazine*, claimed that Cox had written the document attributed to Fitzgerald. Madden noted that Brennan confused the Leinster House raid with Fitzgerald's arrest, although Cox may well have acted the part of scribe. Madden interviewed Isabella Powell in 1840, who had attended Cox in his later years, and ascertained that his father had been a master-blacksmith on Carhampton's Westmeath estate. Cox senior was apparently jailed for sedition but 'liberated after some weeks'. This may account for Cox's erratic behaviour towards Government. Madden, *United*, II, pp. 270–71.

89 'Citizens of Dublin', NA, Rebellion Papers, 620/12/155/5. See also Appendix Three.

90 Sirr was a former army officer and wine merchant of English, including Anglo-Catholic, parentage. He was Lord Heathfield's nephew and reputedly born in Dublin Castle where his father was Town Major from 1761–68. An enthusiastic freemason, Sirr formed a lodge in the 68th Foot in 1790 and retired from the army with the rank of captain in 1791. In late 1796 Sirr became adjutant of the Stephen's Green Light Infantry yeomanry corps (aka 5th Company, Royal Dublin Volunteers) and on 4 January 1797 founded the loyalist French Street Association, where he lived in number 35, with his brother-in-law Humphrey Minchin of Merrion Square. Sirr's zeal is implied by the fact that his Association was unique in Dublin. Sirr was apparently appointed acting Town Major in November 1796 and in late September of the following year detained seventeen men in Temple Bar suspected of being members of a United Irish baronial committee. He shortly afterwards arrested Peter Finnerty of the *Press* staff. Sirr lived at 77 Dame Street in 1798 when a powerfully built 34-year-old. Minchin moved to Grafton Street after the Rebellion. See Hammond, 'Sirr, part one', pp. 14–20 and *Faulkner's Dublin Journal*, 1 Oct. 1797. Sirr was appointed sheriff on 10 November 1798. See NA, Official Papers, 46/5.

91 John Beresford to Lord Auckland (William Eden), 15 Mar. 1798 in Malcomson (ed.), *Irish official papers*, II, p. 291. See also *Report from the Committee of Secrecy*, pp. 133–8.

92 *Report from the Committee of Secrecy*, pp. 131–2. See also Musgrave, *Rebellions*, Appendix Nine, pp. 627–8 and Smyth, *Men of no property*, p. 176. Traynor was described as 'one of the worst that was taken up'. In early April he 'made his escape [from Dublin Castle] through the shore [i.e. sewer] to the river'. Earl Shannon to Viscount Boyle, 6 April [1798] in Esther Hewitt (ed.), *Lord Shannon's Letters to his son. A calendar of the letters written by the 2nd Earl of Shannon to his son, Viscount Boyle, 1790–1802* (Belfast, 1982), p. 77. See also Shannon to Boyle, 17 April [1798], ibid., p. 85. Traynor (aka Trenor) was proclaimed a fugitive in May 1798 and eventually recaptured. He was one of several men 'bailed and transported' on 3 April 1799 when Carlow's delegate at Bond's, Peter Ivers, was sent to Cork for transportation to New South Wales.

3 April 1799, NA, Register of Kilmainham Gaol, 1798–1814. Higgins claimed that Traynor had reappeared in Poolbeg Street in April 1801 and used an American passport to participate in a United Irish club known as 'The States'. Higgins to Marsden, 16 April 1801 in Bartlett (ed.), *Higgins*, p. 539. McCann's handwriting was identified in July 1798 by Dublin brewer Arthur Guinness who had employed the United Irishman as a 'clerk for some years in my office'. *Trial of William Michael Byrne*, p. 7. Guinness was closely aligned with many leading ultra-loyalists in Dublin. He had been sub-sheriff in the city in 1793 when William James was mayor and John Giffard high sheriff. Giffard Papers, NLI, MS 35,961/1.

93 Camden to Portland, 12 Mar. 1798, PRO London, Home Office Papers, 100/75/213–5 and *Faulkner's Dublin Journal*, 20 Mar. 1798. Reynolds named the Executive of March 1798 as Jackson, McCormick, McCann, Teeling and Lord Edward Fitzgerald. McCormick, MacNeven and John Sweetman were also identified as the subcommittee that drafted the 1 February 1798 'Address of the County Committee of Dublin City to their constituents'. PRO London, Home Office Papers, 100/75/203–5.

94 Richard Annesley to Downshire, 15 Mar. 1798, PRO Belfast, D. 607/F/96.

95 'Papers got at Coun[sello]r Emmetts [sic], Steph[e]ns Green, 12 Mar[ch] between 12 & 3 o'clock by William Alexander.' NA, Rebellion Papers, 620/15/2.

96 Camden to Portland, 12 Mar. 1798, PRO London, Home Office Papers, 100/75/215; 'State Prisoners in custody, received and discharged in Kilmainham Gaol, commencing 17th Sept[ember] 1796', NA, Rebellion Papers, 620/7/79/31; Curtin, *United Irishmen*, p. 240. Addis Emmet had stayed away from the pillorying of Finnerty in late December 1797 when his associates Fitzgerald, Bond, O'Connor, Sampson, Jackson, Sheares and MacNally attended. [Higgins] to [Cooke], 3 Jan. 1798, NA, Rebellion Papers, 620/18/14.

97 Madden, *United*, III, pp. 50–1 and Camden to Portland, 13 Mar. 1798, PRO London, Home Office Papers, 100/75/218.

98 Madden, *United*, III, pp. 52–3. Lady Louisa Connelly noted Jane Emmet's feat a few weeks later: 'Poor Lady Edward [Pamela Fitzgerald] is to go [to England], when I brought her the passport this morning it threw her into sad distress . . . if Mrs [Jane] Emmet saw her husband it was by stealth, and contrary to the most positive order.' Lady Louisa Connolly to Lady Sarah Napier, 22 May 1798, NLI, MS 35,003/2.

99 Dr Robert Emmet to Mrs Macoubry, 27 Mar. 1798 quoted in Emmet, *Memoirs*, I, p. 248.

100 8 Mar. 1798, 'To the United Irishmen', NA, Rebellion Papers, 620/15/2/9.

101 *Freeman's Journal*, 17 Mar. 1798. Kelly, Rooney and O'Donnell were hanged for the killing on 31 October 1798, for which they indicated political motivation. Ibid., 1 Nov. 1798.

102 Ibid. See also Landreth, *Pursuit*, p. 75 and *Belfast Newsletter*, 2 Mar. 1798.

103 Moore, *Memoirs*, p. 27. See also ibid., p. 22 and Moore, *Lord Edward Fitzgerald*, p. 147. Fr. Peter Moran of Adam and Eve Chapel, Francis Street, passed 'most interesting intelligence' to the Castle via Higgins in 1798 and may have earlier implicated Moore. [Higgins] to [Cooke], 18 Mar. 1801 in Bartlett (ed.), *Higgins*, p. 536.

104 Report of the National Committee of United Irishmen, 26 February 1798, PRO London, Home Office Papers, 100/75/132. Captured returns for April were as follows: Carlow, 11,300 members; Kildare, 11,910; Kilkenny, 6,700; Dublin county, 7,412; Dublin city, 8,597; Meath, 8,596; Wicklow, 14,000; King's County, 6,500 and Westmeath, 5,250. 19 April 1798, PRO London, Home Office Papers, 100/76/132.

105 *Freeman's Journal*, 31 Mar. and *Saunder's Newsletter*, 2 April 1798, and Camden to Portland, 30 Mar. 1798, PRO London, Home Office Papers, 100/80/161 and Castlereagh to Abercromby, 30 Mar. 1798, PRO, Home Office Papers, 100/75/351.

106 Castlereagh to Abercromby, 30 Mar. 1798, PRO, Home Office Papers, 100/75/351 and Camden to Portland, 30 Mar. 1798, PRO, Home Office Papers, 100/80/161. See also O'Donnell, *Rebellion in Wicklow*, pp. 88–163.

107 *Freeman's Journal*, 5 April 1798.

108 *Freeman's Journal*, 31 Mar. and 3 April 1798. Alderman Carleton returned with yeomen cavalry from the Phoenix Park on 1 April in time to prevent a mob pulling down the Elbow Lane home of one Metcalf who was 'charged with being an informer'. Eleven men were committed to Newgate. *Saunder's Newsletter*, 4 April 1798.

109 *Saunder's Newsletter*, 6 April 1798. See also *Freeman's Journal*, 31 Mar. and 10 April 1798 and Robert Ross to Downshire, 22 Jan. 1798, PRO Belfast, D. 607/F/24.

110 Shannon to Boyle, 11 [April 1798] in Hewitt (ed.), *Letters*, p. 81. See also Shannon to Boyle, 12 April 1798 in ibid., p. 82. Lieutenant Winslow absconded to avoid trial and upon surrendering in late April 1798 was reprimanded for being drunk on duty. 12 and 24 April 1798, PRO London, War Office Papers, 68/422/257–8.

111 *Freeman's Journal*, 7 April 1798. Weapons were seized on the 6th by Captain White's Upper Cross Fusiliers in Harry Street off Grafton Street. Ibid.

112 Patrick N. Wyse Jackson, 'Tumultuous Times: Geology in Ireland and the Debate on the Nature of Basalt and other Rocks of north-east Ireland between 1740 and 1816' in Jackson (ed.), *Science*, p. 39.

113 Shannon to Boyle, 19 April [1798] in Hewitt (ed.), *Letters*, p. 88.

114 *Saunder's Newsletter*, 16 Mar. 1798. See also Walsh, *Ireland sixty years ago*, pp. 159–72.

115 Ann C. Kavanaugh, *John Fitzgibbon, Earl of Clare* (Dublin, 1997), pp. 340–1; Reynolds, *Footprints*, p. 23; Deirdre Lindsay, 'The sick and indigent room keepers' society' in Dickson (ed.), *Gorgeous Mask*, pp. 135–6.

116 Blacker, 'Extracts' in Maxwell, *Trinity*, p. 269. See also ibid., p. 264. Lady Moira also deemed Egan 'vulgar & absurd' with 'conceited airs'. Moira to Scully, 15 Feb. 1803 in Brian MacDermot (ed.), *The Catholic Question in Ireland and England, The Papers of Denys Scully* (Dublin, 1988), p. 63. See also ibid., pp. 64–5.

117 Walsh, *Ireland sixty years ago*, pp. 158, 172.

118 30 Nov. 1803, NA, 620/11/130/60. The informer 'M', probably Egan, specified that Farrell 'had [taken] the precaution before this to take his name off the College books to prevent being expelled'. Ibid.

119 TCD, MS 1203 quoted in Maxwell, 'Sources in Trinity College', p. 16.

120 Shannon to Boyle, 19 April [1798] in Hewitt (ed.), *Letters*, p. 88.

121 Anon., n.d., [c. 23 April 1798], NA, 620/36/96. The Castle source claimed: 'It is thought the expulsions that have taken place in College must produce the happiest effects to the [United Irish] cause, as well in gaining proselytes as binding more firmly to the party those already engaged, they talk with the greatest confidence of the number of their friends in the University.' Ibid. Thomas Reynolds had informed the Castle that there were forty-seven United Irishmen in Trinity. n.d. [Mar. 1798], PRO London, Home Office Papers, 100/75/203.

122 Caldwell's brother John was a member of the Down county committee of United Irishmen in January 1798. See Durey, 'Irish rebel prisoners' in Smyth

(ed.), *Revolution*, pp. 132–3; PRO Belfast, T/3541/5/3; 'Suspect list', n.d., NA, Rebellion Papers, 620/12/217.

123 TCD, MS 1203 quoted in Maxwell, 'Sources in Trinity College', p. 17.

124 Madden, *United*, III, pp. 277, 280, 285; Moore, *Memoirs*, pp. 27–9; Musgrave, *Rebellions*, p. 517; John Patrickson to [Downshire], 21 April [1798], PRO Belfast, D.607/F/149. The students were Thomas Robinson, Dacre Hamilton, George Keogh, Robert Emmet and James Thomas Flinn (aka Flynn) of Dublin; Thomas Corbett, William Corbett, Edmund Barry, Thomas Bennett, Martin John Farrell (aka Ferrall) of Cork; David Shea and John Carroll of Limerick; Arthur Newport of Waterford; John Browne of Belfast, Peter McLaughlin of Mayo; Bernard Killian of Fermanagh; Michael Farrell of Longford, John Pennefather Lamphier of Tipperary and Patrick Fitzgerald of Kerry. See PRO Belfast. List reprinted in Kavanaugh, *Fitzgibbon*, p. 355 and Walsh, *Ireland sixty years ago*, pp. 152–72. According to Trinity historian Maxwell: 'Nine of the students were expelled for refusing to be sworn, eight for refusing to appear before the visitors, one because he admitted that he had been connected with these and one [i.e. Robinson] for lending his rooms for meetings of the United Irishmen.' Maxwell, *Trinity*, p. 147. Emmet and Michael Farrell were technically not students when expelled and others omitted from the Fitzgibbon/ Duigenan list, such as John Keogh junior and one Dogherty, informally withdrew from College at this time. Cooperative United Irishmen like Thomas Moore and John Egan were sufficiently contrite to escape serious censure.

125 Madden, *Robert Emmet*, p. 7.

126 *Annual Register*, 1803, p. 434. The same source understood that Emmet had been 'publically expelled'. Ibid.

127 Drennan to McTier, 23 April 1798, in Agnew (ed.), *Drennan-McTier Letters*, II, p. 391. See also Drennan to McTier, 17 Jan. 1795, ibid., p. 121. Blacker described Browne as 'a very gentlemanlike and talented young man from Belfast'. Blacker, 'Extracts' in Maxwell, *Trinity*, p. 269.

128 James McGucken to Anon., n.d. [April 1799] in Landreth, *Pursuit*, p. 110.

129 Drennan to McTier, n.d. [late April 1798] in Agnew (ed.), *Drennan-McTier Letters*, II, p. 395. The property was leased by Dr Emmet on 7 July 1796 from city resident Anne Elizabeth Moulds, whose family had owned the land since the 1760s. The transaction was witnessed by 'Rob[er]t Emmet, jun[io]r' and 'William Goodwin'. Registry of Deeds, 495/50/321029 cited in Kerr (ed.), *Emmet's Casino*, p. 6.

130 Information of Thomas Reynolds, n.d. [Mar. 1798], PRO, Home Office Papers, 100/75/205. Valentine Lawless was an elected colonel in the Kildare organisation. Ibid.

131 Ruán O'Donnell, 'The Bray area in the years of Rebellion', *Bray Historical Record*, I, 7 (2000), pp. 34–59; Kevin Murray, 'Loughlinstown Camp' in *Dublin Historical Record*, VII, 1, 1944; James Scannell, 'The Lehaunstown Camp 1795–1799', *Dun Laoghaire Borough Historical Society Journal*, 8 (1999), pp. 22–7; Madden, *United*, IV, p. 153.

132 *Freeman's Journal*, 8 May 1798.

133 *Report from the Committee of Secrecy*, pp. 169–70. The instructions comprised advice on tactics, insignia and equipment. Ibid.

134 Anon., [c. 23 April 1798], NA, 620/36/96. A baronial committee meeting composed of fourteen officers was held on the 23rd in Colbert's, No. 3, Schoolhouse Lane. 23 April 1798, NA, Rebellion Papers, 620/36/199.

135 Hammond, 'Sirr', p. 21.

136 *Report from the Committee of Secrecy*, p. 157. See also PRO, Home Office Papers, 100/75/132.

137 Anon. to Sirr, 21 April 1798, NA; Rebellion Papers, 620/36/191; 23 April 1798, NA, Rebellion Papers, 620/36/199. See also Curtin, *United Irishmen*, pp. 257–8.

138 Camden to Portland, 11 May 1798, PRO, Home Office Papers, 100/76/175. See also *Freeman's Journal*, 8, 10 and 12 May 1798. For Newell see Madden, *United*, I, p. 486.

139 *Freeman's Journal*, 12 May 1798.

140 *A list of the counties of Ireland and the respective yeomanry corps . . . 1 June 1798* (Dublin, 1798).

141 Fitzpatrick, *Sham Squire*, pp. 111–12, 181–2; Maxwell, *Irish Rebellion*, p. 39; Kathleen Flynn and Stan McCormack, *Westmeath 1798, a Kilbeggan Rebellion* (Kilbeggan, 1998), pp. 84–5. James Moore was a delegate to the Catholic Convention in Back Lane and a United Irishman. He also owned 119 Thomas Street, the Yellow Lion pub and had storehouses off Bridgefoot Street. Sirr and Jemmy O'Brien were observed searching fields beside Moore's warehouse by an armed rebel named Clayton who decided not to open fire. Fitzpatrick, *Sham Squire*, p. 185 and McDowell (ed.), *Proceedings*, pp. 128, 134. McCabe, according to James Hope, prevented Palmer from stabbing Sirr in the neck. Palmer was arrested two days later but escaped from Newgate when his sister, Biddy, pestered a guard into letting him go. John Newsinger (ed.), *James Hope*, p. 67. McCabe's 'great friend' Horan, a Stoneybatter publican and United Irishman, was Palmer's brother-in-law. Horan may, therefore, have been married to Biddy. 'Suspect list', n.d., NA, Rebellion Papers, 620/12/217. Gallagher had the Westmeath men send details of garrison strengths to 12 Thomas Street, a letter drop or occasional residence. He may have been the Patrick Gallagher who ran an earthenware shop at 42 Meath Street in the mid-1790s, a circumstance that would explain his high-level city contacts. See *Report of the Committee of Secrecy*, p. 238, Patrick C. Power, *The Courts Martial of 1798–99* (Kilkenny, 1997), p. 117 and *Wilson's Dublin Directory . . . 1794*, p. 46.

142 30 Aug. 1801, NA, Rebellion Papers, 620/49/125.

143 *Freeman's Journal*, 22 May 1798.

144 Walsh, *Ireland sixty years ago*, p. 60. See also Shannon to Boyle, 17 May 1798 in Hewitt (ed.), *Letters*, p. 96.

145 Fitzpatrick, *Sham Squire*, pp. 182–3. See also Madden, *United*, IV, p. 255. Fitzgerald was believed to have spent the first week of May in Portobello, near the newly constructed canal. If Dr Kennedy's role was suspected by the authorities it evidently went unpunished as he remained a practitioner of midwifery in the home in 1803. *Wilson's Dublin Directory . . . 1803*, p. 131. This is surprising, as Collins had named him as a United Irishman prior to 1798. See McDowell (ed.) *Proceedings*, p. 135.

146 Diary of Richard Farrell, 18 May 1798, NLI, MS 11,941. Farrell graduated BA in 1802 at which time he had been practising at the Bar for a year. *Catalogue of Graduates*, p. 187.

147 *Saunder's Newsletter*, 7 April 1798 and Madden, *United*, IV, pp. 56–7. The Murphy and Rattigan families ascertained that the door had been left unsecured by a servant and in 1832 testified that Neilson, far from being responsible, had warned the occupants of this lapse about an hour before the raid. Neilson had also called to the house at lunchtime and another person arrived during the afternoon to deliver a uniform to Fitzgerald. Joseph Hamilton, *An impartial enquiry respecting the betrayal of Lord Edward Fitzgerald, and Robert Emmett* (Dublin, 1832), p. 7. Fitzgerald, recovering from a heavy cold in bed, fired a shot at Swan, which missed its target, then stabbed him on the left side of his

body with a dagger. After Swan returned fire, 'Ryan threw himself upon Lord Edward and Swan; Lord Edward made a strong effort and rushing on Ryan, gave him three desperate wounds on the breast and the belly [from which he died on 30 May] . . . Lord Edward, when he saw Major Sirr, grinned, and made an effort to get at him. The Major immediately fired and lodged several lugs in his shoulder.' *Freeman's Journal*, 22 May 1798. It may be significant that Ryan was taken into Laurence Tighe's house on Thomas Street after being shot and that Tighe not only knew Walter Cox but gave information on the United Irishmen in 1802–3. Madden, *United*, II, p. 275. Ryan was believed to have written the Orange ballad 'Croppies lie down' in 1798. See Georges-Denis Zimmerman, *Songs of Irish Rebellion, political street ballads and rebel songs, 1780–1900* (Dublin, 1967), pp. 307–8. Martial law was technically authorized from 29 May when the Privy Council endorsed the petition of the magistrates. *Saunder's Newsletter*, 27 Aug. 1798. A letter written in Newgate at 6.00 a.m. on 4 June informed the Fitzgeralds of 'the melancholy intelligence of Lord Edw[ar]d Fitzgerald's death. He drew his last breath at two o'clock this morning after a struggle that began soon after his friends left him last night.' [Dr Armstrong] Garnett to Lady Louisa Connelly, 3 [sic, 4] June [1798], NLI, MS 35,003/1. Lady Sophia Fitzgerald claimed: '"It is heaven to me to see you" these were my beloved blessed Edward's own angelic words to aunt Louisa [Connelly] on her first & last visit to him in his prison where the adored angel died of his wounds . . . the names of Camden & Castlereagh I should ever hear with the utmost horror & detestation.' Notes, n.d., NLI, MS 35,004/21. Fitzgerald was guarded in Newgate by Captain Samuel Stone of the Derry militia who was requested to perform this special duty by Castlereagh. See PRONI, D.584 (4–5).

148 Farrell Diary, 19–20 May 1798, NLI, MS 11,941.
149 Fitzpatrick, *Sham Squire*, pp. 113–16, 13 July 1798, NA, Rebellion Papers, 620/3/16/9; Madden, *Hope*, pp. 17–18; *Freeman's Journal*, 22 May 1798; [Higgins] to [Cooke], 20 May 1798, NA, Rebellion Papers, 620/18/14; TCD, Sirr Papers, MS 869/8/155. Murphy, when a prisoner in Newgate in November 1798, sought the assistance of the Fitzgerald family to recover his home. This indicates an acquaintanceship between the Murphys and Fitzgeralds and gives lie to his understandable, yet disingenuous, claim to have tolerated the United Irish leader's presence on sufferance. He was actually a member of the baronial/district committee. The Murphy home was still 'occupied as a barrack' at the close of 1798 when much of his stock had been taken from his warehouses to other locations for private sale. He protested, incredibly, to have 'never interfered in politics or belonged to any political society'. NLI, MS 35,014/1. Murphy persevered in his quest for compensation into the 1830s. He then sought payment of 'five guineas each day for a sergeants guard living at free quarters for 15 days . . . 60 dozen port claret and sherry wine used destroy[e]d and sold by the soldiers . . . damages and loss of property by soldiers and females connected with them when in possession of the concerns [£]500'. The total reached £1,275 but unsatisfied with financial reparation, Murphy sought additional 'compensation . . . for 55 weeks confinement as a State Prisoner 386 days at 20[shillings?] a day'. Murphy Accounts, 20 Oct. 1831, ibid.
150 See Edward Farrell's entry on 'Suspect list', n.d., NA, Rebellion Papers, 620/12/217.
151 Higgins to Marsden, 15 Nov. 1801 in Bartlett (ed.), *Higgins*, p. 577. Magan convinced Higgins that the original plan of Fitzgerald and Sheares was to 'massacre . . . the Lord Lieutenant, nobility, judges, Members of Parliament etc,

assembled (on the trial of the Earl of Kingston for murder) in the House of Commons' on 18 May 1798. Ibid. This was allegedly cancelled 'on the ground that they could not be properly armed or assemble in the daylight without the certain loss of thousands of lives; but they have decided on an attack on the Castle'. [Higgins] to [Cooke], 18 May 1798 in ibid., p. 407.

152 John Beresford to Lord Auckland, 9 August 1798 in William Beresford (ed.), *The Correspondence of the Right Hon. John Beresford*, 2 vols (London, 1854), II, p. 171. Lumm was a colonel in the Kildare organisation and 'deeply involved' with Lord Edward Fitzgerald. John Patrickson to Downshire, 7 May 1798, PRO Belfast, D. 607/F/163. Hamilton, an associate of the Neilson family, confirmed that Lumm, Ogilvie and Plunkett were politically connected to Fitzgerald in May 1798. One of these men may have been Fitzgerald's relation William Ogilvie, former tutor to the family at Frascati, Blackrock (Dublin). Hamilton, *Impartial Enquiry*, p. 12. Plunkett was from Roscommon and was deemed to have served in Talbot's regiment in the French army. See McDowell (ed.) *Proceedings*, p. 140. Ex-officer Lumm was escorted to Dublin from Macclesfield, England, by a King's Messenger named Breton on 21 May. *Freeman's Journal*, 22 May 1798. Major Anthony James McDermott, formerly of the Austrian army, was another frequent visitor to Frascati and Military Committee member. Its composition was frequently altered by arrests but at various times included Neilson, Morres (ex-Austrian army), Arthur O'Connor, Henry Jackson, Miles Duigenan, Walter Cox, William Cole and probably also McDermott's friend Garret Byrne of Ballymanus (Wicklow), Ambrose Moore, Philip Long (ex-Neapolitan service), Malachy Delaney (ex-Austrian army), Patrick Dillon of Donnybrook (ex-Dillon's regiment, France) and James Dixon of Kilmainham. See [Higgins] to [Marsden], 29 Sept. 1800, NA, Rebellion Papers, 620/18/14. Moore, Mathew Dowling's stepbrother, hosted a meeting of the 'secret committee' in his 69 Dame Street home in September 1797. This may have been the inaugural session and was attended by Fitzgerald, O'Connor, Jackson, Plunkett and McDermott. [Higgins] to [Cooke], 15 Sept. 1797 in Bartlett (ed.), *Higgins*, pp. 304–8. A MacDermott of Ballymahon, Longford, formally joined the United Irishmen in May 1792, which, if same man as the Major, would account for the prominence of Michael Farrell of Ballymahon in Trinity. McDowell (ed.) *Proceedings*, p. 22. It may be significant that the meeting which ratified MacDermott's membership also accepted that of one Michael Farrell of 'Cock-hill'. Ibid.

153 Camden to Portland, 24 May 1798, PRO London, Home Office Papers, 100/76/258.

154 n.d. [1798], PRO London, Home Office Papers, 100/77/144. Lord Leitrim had informed Earl Shannon in April that 3,000 Westmeath rebels were 'ready to rise on the first signal, but they wait for its beginning at Dublin, which will be the signal to the kingdom'. Shannon to Boyle, 14 April [1798] in Hewitt (ed.), *Letters*, p. 83.

155 Shannon to Boyle, 21 May [1798] in Hewitt (ed.), *Letters*, p. 100. Byrne was sworn into the United Irishmen in November 1792 by John Stockdale, at the same time as 'Captain' John Sweetman and Charles O'Hara. McDowell (ed.) *Proceedings*, p. 40.

156 *Freeman's Journal*, 22 May 1798; *Annual Register* [England], Chronicle, p. 38; *Report from the Committee of Secrecy*, pp. 151–2. The proclamation was discovered by Alderman William Alexander. For the original see NLI, MS 8079 (1). This item has been occasionally misattributed to Robert Emmet. The Hayes listing for Emmet's speech, NLI, MS 8235, is also incorrect. Hayes, *Manuscript Sources*, Dates, p. 446.

157 See *Report from the Committee of Secrecy*, pp. 153–7.
158 Farrell Diary, 22 May 1798, NLI, MS 11,941. Farrell was unfamiliar with the Liberties which he regarded as a 'place that contains as much misery & as much wickedness as any street in Europe of the extent'. He was unaware that the military 'system' had been extended from the county to the city. Ibid.
159 [Higgins] to [Cooke], 27 Feb. 1801 in Bartlett (ed.), *Higgins*, p. 530.
160 Farrell Diary, 22 May 1798, NLI, MS 11,941.
161 Hammond, 'Sirr', pp. 21–3. The irresolute Cormick, named by Thomas Reynolds, fled overseas and was arrested in Guernsey on 10 July 1798. William Lawless escaped to France by disguising himself as a butcher and carrying meat onto a vessel which left Dublin. *Report from the Committee of Secrecy*, p. 123 and Madden, *United*, IV, p. 255.
162 Farrell Diary, 23 May 1798, NLI, MS 11,941.
163 [Higgins] to [Cooke], 18 Mar. 1801 in Bartlett (ed.), *Higgins*, p. 536.
164 *Irish Magazine*, July 1808, p. 323. See also Maxwell, *Irish Rebellion*, pp. 57–8; Musgrave, *Rebellions*, p. 193; *Faulkner's Dublin Journal*, 24 May 1798. McClune was a cabinet maker at 185 Abbey Street. *Wilson's Dublin Directory . . . 1794*, p. 71. The informer John Hughes, an unreliable source, claimed that Edward Rattigan told him that the United Irishmen would 'begin the insurrection in Dublin by liberating the prisoners in Kilmainham – Rattigan shewed [sic] him a plan of the intended attack on Kilmainham'. *Freeman's Journal*, 13 Sept. 1798. For the maltreatment of Neilson see Madden, *United*, IV, p. 58. Neilson had pretended to be 'dead drunk' in mid-April 1798 when he and Lord Edward Fitzgerald were briefly detained near Palmerstown by a patrol of artillerymen who did not know who they were. Sirr memo, n.d. in Madden, *United*, I, p. 504. Magan, Fitzgerald's betrayer, informed Higgins: 'Lord Edw[ard] [Fitzgerald] lurks about town and its vicinity. He with Ne[i]lson was a few days ago in the custody of a patrole [sic] or party in the neighbourhood of Lucan but not being known and assuming other names they were not detained for any length of time. Ne[i]lson is now the most active man.' Francis Magan to Higgins, 22 April 1798 in Bartlett (ed.), *Higgins*, p. 601. The insightful Hamilton claimed the Church Street meeting was that of 'the New Directory' and claimed that Neilson's detention was a critical reversal which meant that the 'inferior officers sat waiting for instructions until midnight'. Hamilton, *Impartial Enquiry*, p. 12. Newgate was described in the Rebellion period as being 'surrounded by streets distinguished for filth and infamy. The iron drop is a fixed balcony, having bars below, which when drawn in leave the criminal suspended'. Grimes (ed.), *Ireland in 1804*, p. 21.
165 Anon. to Swan, n.d. [late July 1803], NA, Rebellion Papers, 620/64/121.
166 Sproule to Anon., 23 May 1798, NA, Rebellion Papers, 620/51/18 and Walsh, *Ireland sixty years ago*, pp. 173–4. A loyalist connected to Dublin Castle claimed: 'there can be no doubt that, prior to the rebellion of 1798, in spight [sic] of all the bustling activity of that day, 100,000 pikes were, at very least, prepared in this city'. While this was an exaggeration intended to minimise the importance of the 1803 effort by comparison, weaponry was certainly not in short supply in May 1798. *The opinion of an Impartial Observer, concerning the late transactions in Ireland*, 3rd edn (Dublin, 1803), p. 26. A horde of pikes was found buried two and half feet deep under cabbages in a garden to the rear of Eccles Street. Others were recovered from a yard in Bridgefoot Street, along with a hammer and new nails for mounting the blades. Musgrave, *Rebellions*, p. 195. Thomas McKenny, future Lord Mayor of Dublin in 1818, reputedly guarded a horde of thirty pikes in late May 1798. [Higgins] to [Cooke], 26 May 1798, NA, Rebellion Papers, 620/18/14. John Beresford MP approved the use

of the triangles and noted on the afternoon of the Rebellion: 'I have seen none of the flogging, but it is terrible to hear the perseverance of these madmen. Some have received three hundred lashes before they would discover where the pikes were concealed. The extent of the conspiracy is amazing . . . all the gaols are full.' Beresford to Auckland, 23 May 1798, BL, MS 34454/272. See also Diary of Richard Farrell, 23 May 1798, NLI, MS 11,941.

167 n.d., Feb. 1799, NA, Rebellion Papers, 620/7/74/15.

168 Musgrave, *Rebellions*, pp. 194–5. Mountjoy Square was built on the site known as the 'Barley fields'. Madden, *United*, IV, p. 58.

169 Information of Thomas Halpin, 4 April 1801 in Charles Dickson, *The Life of Michael Dwyer with some account of his companions* (Dublin, 1944), p. 165. In 1800–1 Taker allowed the notorious Wicklow rebels associated with Michael Dwyer and Martin Burke to use his employer's home. Ibid., pp. 165–6. See also Musgrave, *Rebellions*, p. 193.

170 Walsh, *Ireland sixty years ago*, pp. 173–4. See also Landreth, *Pursuit*, p. 91.

171 Boyle senior to Cooke, n.d., [May 1798], NA, Rebellion Papers, 620/18/2. See also Mrs Maria H to Helen Clarke, 23 May 1798, NLI, MS 13,837; Robert Ross to Downshire, 24 May 1798, PRO Belfast, D. 607/F/183; [MacNally] to [Cooke?], n.d., May 1798, NA, Rebellion Papers, 620/10/121/157; Musgrave, *Rebellions*, p. 192. Rooney was evidently Walter Rooney, a brewer at 61 Newmarket and Chambre Street in 1803 and resident of 28 Watling Street. He owned a distillery at 47 Bridgefoot Street prior to the Rebellion of 1798, when his servant, Thomas Regan, was described as 'a big rebel'. Anon., n.d. [1798] in Madden, *United*, I, p. 509. See also *Wilson's Dublin Directory . . . 1794*, p. 90 and ibid., 1803, p. 91

172 Shannon to Boyle, 23 May [1798] in Hewitt (ed.), *Letters*, p. 102. John Patrickson also noted that 'some burnings and some whippings are doing well'. Patrickson to Downshire, 23 May [1798], PRO Belfast, D. 607/F/181.

173 Musgrave, *Rebellions*, p. 191. Camden sent Lieutenant O'Reilly and a troop of the Fifth Dragoons towards Rathfarnham to investigate reports of rebel activity. O'Reilly fell in with Lieutenant Colonel Richard Puleston of the Ancient Britons and Lord Roden and, on nearing the village, was redirected west in pursuit of the insurgents. As they approached Rathcoole the patrol met a local yeomanry force which had been driven back by the rebels. On dividing the cavalrymen into two groups, the element led by Roden made contact with the rebels close to the Rathcoole turnpike and drove them towards O'Reilly's body. Two rebels were killed and many wounded before the protagonists pulled back. Ibid., p. 201. The Rathfarnham area rebels on the first night of the Rebellion shot Philip Prosser at Tibbraden for resisting an arms raid, took Richard Davis' guns at Kilgobbin and carried away goods from the Grange home of Humphrey Minchin. The Grange raiding party included their employees Curran and McDonagh. Minchin, Sirr's brother-in-law, might well have been killed had he been at home. Joseph Sirr, however, father of the Major, was present and unharmed. The Major survived an assassination bid on 23 June 1798 when returning from visiting his father at Grange. Ibid., p. 202 and Hammond, 'Sirr', p. 22. Martin Byrne was charged with shooting Prosser. *Saunder's Newsletter*, 19 Sept 1798. Carroll of Baldwinstown, a cotton manufacturer, led a successful attack on Westphalstown House in which twenty Fermanagh militiamen were captured. Their officer, Ensign Cleland, was badly injured when ambushed in a separate incident but escaped to Swords to raise the alarm. Musgrave, *Rebellions*, pp. 204–5. David La Touche, owner of Marley, was a staunch supporter of Government, unlike his Fitzwilliamite brother, John La Touche of Bellvue (Delgany), Wicklow. David La Touche donated £1,000 to the Treasury

'towards the defence of the country, at this important crisis' in April 1798. *Freeman's Journal*, 1 May 1798. He became highly religious in the late 1790s having previously fallen 'into Deism' and 'lost' his 'religion'. By March 1799 La Touche was in no fit mental state to monitor the political allegiances of his employees. The Rebellion probably claimed the lives of some of the spouses of Marley widows Mary Flinn, Mary White, Sarah Maguire, Esther Doyle, Anne Long, Catherine McDaniel, Mary Byrne, Margaret Byrne, Mary Duffy, Mary Behan, Catherine Byrne, Elizabeth Hayden and Molly Byrne. 'Diary of John David La Touche of Marley', NLI, MS 3153.

174 *Freeman's Journal*, 24–5 May 1798; Robert Ross to Downshire, 25 May 1798, PRO Belfast, D. 607/F/185; [MacNally] to [Cooke?], [c. 24] May 1798, NA, Rebellion Papers, 620/10/121/157; Patrick Archer, 'Fingal in 1798', *Dublin Historical Record*, XL (1986–87), pp. 66–79, 108–16. For Dublin participants in the Rebellion who, for the most part, evaded detection see 'An account of the number of persons who have surrendered themselves in the city of Dublin, confessed themselves being engaged in the present rebellion, and the number of arms surrendered, from 29 June last to 9 September 1798' in *Journal of the House of Commons of the Kingdom of Ireland*, XVII, pp. dccccxlvi–dcccclix. See also Bartlett (ed.), *Higgins*, Appendix III.

CHAPTER THREE

1 8 Mar. 1798, NA, Rebellion Papers, 620/15/2/9.
2 30 Nov. 1803, NA, Rebellion Papers, 620/11/130/60. William Sampson used an address at 43 Abbey Street. See 4 Oct. 1798, NA, State Prisoners Petitions, 275. Cox, Chambers and McClune were all neighbours. Cox, moreover, had attended political meetings in Chambers' house in late 1797 with MacNeven and other leaders. [MacNally], 3 Nov. [1797], NA, Rebellion Papers, 620/10/121/147.
3 *Saunder's Newsletter*, 2 Sept. 1798.
4 Musgrave, *Rebellions,* pp. 191–2.
5 Information of Thomas Foy, 28 Mar. 1799, NA, Rebellion Papers, 620/17/30/18.
6 Anon., 23 April 1798, NA, Rebellion Papers, 620/36/199.
7 *Freeman's Journal*, 26 May 1798.
8 Cox to Marsden, 29 June 1803, NA, Rebellion Papers, 620/64/150. Cox had been compromised as a leading city United Irishman in December 1797 and had been 'dismissed' as armourer of the Commissioners of the Revenue 'on account of his bad character'. 'GH' to Ellis, 25 July 1803, NA, Rebellion Papers, 620/65/74.
9 See Musgrave, *Rebellions*, pp. 199–200.
10 Farrell Diary, 24 May 1798, NLI, MS 11941. Farrell, who evidently knew Braughall, claimed that the 'Attorney's yeomanry behaved in a most indecent man[ner] at this Gentleman's house which they seized on for a barracks, they broke open his cellar & drank his wines'. For a man abroad in the city 'it was chance if he returned home without having his eyes scared by the sight of a fellow creature suspended from a lamp post or his ears assailed by the cries of some unhappy wretch groaning beneath the lash and begging for immediate death as a boon, innocence was not secure, nor without its fears, for in the search for arms, if any were found on a man's premises, his house was burned or himself put to the halberds in order to extort confession'. Ibid. The case against Braughall was weak and he faced down pressure to sign the Banishment Act in October 1798. He was consequently freed in early November when one

Houston was bailed from Newgate. *Hibernian Journal*, 5 Nov. 1798. Braughall had been disgraced on 15 October when the Guild of Merchants disenfranchised him along with Napper Tandy, Archibald Hamilton Rowan, Henry Jackson, Richard Dillon and Henry Grattan. *Finn's Leinster Journal*, 17 Oct. 1798.

11 The trial, summoned by General Eustace, was attended by Farrell. He recalled: 'I gained admittance with great interest into a court martial which was sitting in one of the rooms of the house of Commons upon trial of two yeomen belonging to the Rathfarnham corps who fought on the side of the rebels the evening before. There was not a person beside myself in plain coloured clothes, it was to me a hard sight to see the lives of my fellow citizens disposed of in this summary manner . . . a fiery ordeal to pass through.' Farrell Diary, 25 May 1798, NLI MS 11941.

12 Thomas Keogh, 25 Aug. 1798, NA, State Prisoners Petitions, 189. One Macready, whose mother knew Lord Edward Fitzgerald, informed W. J. Fitzpatrick that 'the blood flowing from the block [on Bridgefoot Street] whereupon the poor rebels were quartered clogged up the sewers, and some dogs were licking it up. The Lady Lieutenant was driving past, and got such a fright from this horrible scene that she fainted in the carriage. Having arrived home, she wrote to her brother, who was high in the then Government, for God's sake to stop this wholesale massacre of the defenseless. Her humane appeal had the desired effect; an order came to stem all further executions.' Fitzpatrick, *Sham Squire*, p. 184. See also *Freeman's Journal*, 26 May 1798. Carroll, West, Manning and possibly other Fingal leaders had considered escaping to France. Sirr to Bird, n.d., 1798 in Madden, *United*, I, p. 502. A Down gentleman going to a party at Lord Blayney's house on Merrion Square on 23 May allegedly saw a lamplighter being flogged for putting water instead of oil in the lamps. See McDowell, *Ireland*, p. 614. P. Rourke, a publican, John Habbott and one Lewis were hanged on the New Bridge of Waterford on 2 July. *Finn's Leinster Journal*, 4 July 1798.

13 Sproule to Lees, 25 May 1798, NA, Rebellion Papers, 620/51/19; Francis Gerard, *Picturesque Dublin old and new* (London, 1898); *Freeman's Journal*, 5 June 1798. Dr Esmonde was the brother of Sir Thomas Esmonde. For details of the Raymond conspiracy and subsequent expulsion of Catholic yeomen from the corps see Maxwell, *Irish Rebellion*, p. 80. Raymond was implicated in 'the death of young Mr. Marturine'. *Freeman's Journal*, 2 June 1798. See also ibid., 5 June 1798. Bacon was believed to have concealed himself for several days in the home of James Tandy, 4 Marlborough Street. [Higgins] to [Cooke], 2 June 1798, NA, Rebellion Papers, 620/18/14. Much of Higgins' information duplicated that of Thomas Collins in the early 1790s. While cross-referencing was undoubtedly valuable, it gave the erroneous impression to Cooke et al. that men like John and Samuel Dudgeon of Pill Lane, Patrick Thunder of Ballaly and Edward Kelly of Church Street were significant anti-government conspirators. McDowell (ed.), *Proceedings*, pp. 28, 38–9.

14 Quoted in Stella Tillyard, *Citizen Lord, Edward Fitzgerald, 1763–1798* (London, 1997), p. 288. 'John Clinch, Esq. Rathcoole' was sworn into the United Irishmen in March 1792 in the same session which recruited Tighe and Moore of Thomas Street. Moore was proposed by Esmonde which indicates his possible role in Clinch's induction. McDowell (ed.), *Proceedings*, p. 19. Clinch was reputedly influenced in 1798 by Fr James Harold, parish priest of Rathcoole and Saggart, and was a close associate of Felix Rourke. Musgrave gives the date of Clinch's execution in Dublin as 2, not 4, June 1798. All three United Irish leaders were implicated in the killing of one Buckley, a loyalist farmer who was bayoneted to death on 13 March 1798. See Musgrave,

Rebellions, pp. 207–8. Richard Farrell knew one Ennis and other members of Lord Gormanstown's yeomanry corps which contained at least six United Irishmen. Farrell and Pat Smyth visited Gormanstown on 25 May and learned that 'nothing could equal the distracted state of mind these men displayed undetermined what side to take, wavering between inclination & prudence'. A loyalist member of the Attorney's Cavalry threatened Farrell on Kevin Street the following day. He was aghast to witness the yeomen 'with a scissors in his hand cropping the hair & ears of a decent man because he discovered him with a false tail [i.e. hair extension]'. On noticing Farrell's disgust the yeoman enquired 'if I was a crop & then made me pull off my hat'. This incident convinced Farrell to leave the country for Birmingham, England, after a fruitless search for bank notes and a difficult experience obtaining a passport in the Castle from Alderman James. Farrell Diary, 25–7 May 1798, NLI, MS 11941.

15 Maxwell, *Irish Rebellion*, p. 80.
16 n.d., May 1798, NA, Rebellion Papers, 620/10/121/159. A banker named Finney was shot outside Dublin in mid-August 1803, who, if the same man, was evidently unpopular with the United Irishmen. *Times*, 15 Aug. 1803. Sergeant Archibald McClaren of the Dunbartonshire fencibles was initially disturbed by the number of men being brought to his barracks by yeomen to be flogged. He became 'convinced' of the 'necessity' of such practices when 'many of them led to the very places where the rebels arms were concealed'. McClaren's unit afterwards took part in the massacre of wounded rebels near Newtownmount-kennedy, Wicklow, on 31 May 1798. Archibald McClaren, *A minute description of the battles of Gorey, Arklow and Vinegar Hill: together with the movements of the army through the Wicklow mountains* ([London?], 1798), p. 6. See also O'Donnell, *Rebellion in Wicklow*, p. 187. The Dublin authorities were obliged to discourage loyalists taking matters into their own hands by issuing a notice warning that only state agents were permitted to flog suspects. *Dublin Evening Post*, 9 June 1798.
17 *Freeman's Journal*, 31 May 1798. See also Musgrave, *Rebellions*, p. 191. The wrecking of Braughall's home was commemorated after his death in a poem published in 1803 by his friend Frederick William Conway. It read in part: 'Like the liquour of Circe, Braughall's wine, Transformed a corps of the Law into swine. No pikes in view, what feats do they perform? Taking an empty house at night by storm.' Quoted in *Dublin Historical Record*, XIV, no. 2, 1956, p. 49.
18 Beckwith to Major Sandys, 31 Dec. 1802, Kilmainham Papers, NLI, MS 1145, p. 99.
19 [MacNally], n.d., 'Tuesday' [May 1798], NA, Rebellion Papers, 620/10/121/155. MacNally claimed that the prospect of the insurgents breaking into Dublin and massacring the inhabitants worried several ex-United Irishmen. Ibid.
20 Beresford to Auckland, 9 Aug. 1798 in Beresford (ed.), *Correspondence*, II, p. 171.
21 *Finn's Leinster Journal*, 28 Nov. 1798.
22 *Dublin Evening Post*, 31 May 1798 and *Freeman's Journal*, 26 May and 2 June 1798. For McNally, (aka McAnally) see Bird to Sirr, n.d., 1798 in Madden, *United*, I, p. 502 and Cooke, 17 May 1798, NA, Rebellion Papers, 620/37/95. He may have been the James McNally who gave his home place as Rush and occupation as 'farmer' when seeking a conditional pardon in Dublin city after July 1798. 'Account of the persons'. Five companies of the Reays received orders on 22 May to march from their Lisburn camp at noon the following day. They had taken part in counter-insurgency operations with the Twenty-Second Light Dragoons and the Monaghan militia. Regimental orders issued at Kells, Meath, on the morning of 24 May required: 'all the men that is not sick is to be under

arms and in the ranks on the march'. Order Book of the Reay Highlanders, NLI, MS 5913. They lost seven (killed) at Dunshaughlin and suffered twenty-six casualties at Tara. John Jones, *An impartial narrative of each engagement which took place between his majesty's forces and the rebels during the Irish Rebellion of 1798*, 4th edn, part two (Dublin, 1800), pp. 159–62. Three constables and a revenue official named Creighton were killed in Dunboyne on 24 May by the group which later attacked the Reays. Dunboyne was evidently a flashpoint as it had been selected by Lord Edward Fitzgerald as a rallying point for Meath and Fingal United Irishmen. Captain Wynne of Clonsilla, aided by some local yeomen and eleven Angus Highlanders under Lieutenant George Armstrong of the Royal Artillery, rescued Captain Gorges MP, Lieutenant Corbally and several yeomen taken prisoner by the rebels at Ratoath. Musgrave alleged that the captives were 'on the point' of being hanged. Reinforced by eighteen Fifth Dragoons, the Ratoath rebels reputedly lost thirty-five men to Wynne's column. One insurgent group, however, rallied and pursued Armstrong's Highlanders to Clonee Bridge, where six soldiers were killed. Their determination may be attributed to the fact that Armstrong had earlier taken two rebel leaders prisoner near Eskar and had dispersed another group at Lucan. Elsewhere, a large rebel force under one Gilshanan had entered Dunshaughlin and killed a clerical magistrate, Revd Neilson, together with two other loyalists guarding an arsenal. On 25 May a large quantity of war material was captured at Blair's ironworks, Lucan, by rebels under command of George Cummins, a defector and Fitzgerald associate from the Clonsilla Cavalry. McNally may have been connected to this haul which was intended for the use of the Tara rebels. Musgrave, *Rebellions*, pp. 203–5. The battle at Tara was regarded as one of the most brutal of the Rebellion. Word reached the city that 'the rebels fought with the greatest bravery & yielded not an inch to the troops until some pieces of cannon were brought to bear with such effect that it is thought more than 450 of the rebels were slain'. Lieutenant Christopher Barnwell lost his nerve during the battle and was courtmartialled in Dublin for cowardice. Farrell Diary, 27 May 1798, NLI, MS 11941.

23 See Brian Cleary, *The Battle of Oulart Hill, context and strategy* (Kildare, 1999) and Ruán O'Donnell, 'King's County in 1798' in Timothy P. O'Neill and William Nolan (eds), *Offaly, history and society, interdisciplinary essays on the history of an Irish county* (Dublin, 1998), pp. 485–514. The actions of the troops at the Gibbet Rath were informed by their discovery of the body of the young Lieutenant William Giffard, piked by rebels who had stopped his coach. Duff's column included the Dublin City militia in which John Giffard of Dundrum Castle, the ultra-loyalist father of William, was a captain. He was driven into a psychotic state which evidently permeated the ranks. Giffard stated in a letter to his wife: 'If you pass through Kildare exult in the ruin that I have left behind me. Recollect five hundred slaughtered traitors and drop a tear on the grave of your heroic son.' Giffard to Giffard, n.d., Giffard Papers, NLI, MS 35,961/1.

24 O'Donnell, *Rebellion in Wicklow*, pp. 184–9.

25 B[oyle] senior to Anon., 29 May 1798, NA, Rebellion Papers, 620/18/7.

26 *Freeman's Journal*, 31 May and 5 June 1798 and Musgrave, *Rebellions*, p. 193.

27 Musgrave, *Rebellions*, p. 209. The Buckinghamshire militia, eager to fight the French, were 'cruelly used in being left [in Dublin] . . . to take care of Newgate gaol, Kilmainham gaol, Bridewell infirmary, Penitentiary House, Prevots [i.e. the Provost Prison], Marshalsea prison, Naval Hospital, Bank of Ireland, exclusive of the usual guards'. Buckingham to Lord Grenville, 26 Aug. 1798 in J. B. Fortescue, *Report of the Manuscripts of J.B. Fortescue, Esq., preserved at Dropmore* (Dublin, 1905), *Fortescue*, IV, p. 287.

28 Sproule to Cooke, 17 May 1798, NA, Rebellion Papers, 620/37/97; Sproule to Anon., 23 May 1798, NA, Rebellion Papers, 620/51/18; information of Joseph Thompson, 27 June 1798, NA, Rebellion Papers, 620/38/247. For discussion of the various 'key buildings' contingencies see Thomas Graham, 'An Union of Power? The United Irish Organisation' in Dickson, Keogh and Whelan (eds), *United Irishmen*, pp. 244–55.

29 'Suspect list', n.d., NA, Rebellion Papers, 620/12/217. Dillon owned a bleach green in Donnybrook and would have known Patrick Madden, the local publican, Donnybrook Hurler and United Irish leader in 1798–1803. Ibid. If this man was 'Captain Dillon late of *Dillon's Regiment*', who lived near his brother Robert Dillon of Francis Street in 1794, his connection to the city rebel colonels McMahon and Rattigan in 1798 is all the more explicable. It may also be significant that the information which noted Dillon's politics in February 1794 also concerned 'Captain [Philip] Long' and was imparted at a time when Thomas Wright was highly active. See McDowell (ed.) *Proceedings*, p. 113.

30 Information of Thomas Collins, [n.d., c. May/June 1794], NA, Rebellion Papers, 620/54/18. See also McDowell (ed.), *Proceedings*, pp. 74, 91; Sproule to [Lees], 26 May 1798, NA, Rebellion Papers, 620/51/26; Sproule to Lees, 25 May 1798, NA, Rebellion Papers, 620/51/20. Diana McMahon, a merchant of 31 Aungier Street in 1803, was probably one of the family, as was A. McMahon of 41 Aungier Street, a barrister from 1790. *Wilson's Dublin Directory . . . 1803*, pp. 73, 118. The McMahons were evidently Church of Ireland, as was fellow rebel colonel Thomas Bacon. Bond, their imprisoned mentor, was Presbyterian. John McMahon of Phibsborough was evidently a county Dublin colonel prior to his arrest in May 1798. He was apparently not related to Francis McMahon with whom he was frequently confused. Musgrave, *Rebellions*, p. 201.

31 Castlereagh to Wickham, 1 May 1799, PRO London, Home Office Papers, 100/86/299.

32 Information of Surgeon Thomas Wright, 1 May 1799, PRO London, Home Office Papers, 100/86/302. See also Drennan to Martha McTier, n.d. [Oct. 1794], in Agnew (ed.), *Drennan-McTier Letters*, II, p. 101; Drennan to Martha McTier, 20 July 1796 in ibid., II, p. 252; *Wilson's Dublin Directory . . . 1794*, pp. 140, 144.

33 See Long's entry in 'Suspect list', n.d., NA, Rebellion Papers, 620/12/217.

34 Information of Thomas Hawkins, n.d. [June/July 1798], NA, Rebellion Papers, 620/52/127; Anon., n.d., NA, Rebellion Papers, 620/17/77; Musgrave, *Rebellions*, pp. 192–4; n.d., NA, Rebellion Papers, 620/12/217; Sproule to Anon., n.d. [1798], NA, Rebellion Papers, 620/51/12; Castlereagh to Wickham, 11 Sept. 1798, PRO London, Home Office Papers, 100/82/66.

35 Anon., n.d., TCD, Sirr Papers, 69/8, fo. 153.

36 Castlereagh to Wickham, 11 Sept. 1798, PRO London, Home Office Papers, 100/82/66. There seems to have been a degree of confusion in Castle documents between Jonathan Gray and Nicholas Gray. Both Grays were regarded as members of the Liberty Rangers and were high in the councils of the city United Irishmen. Jonathan had been compromised prior to the Rebellion in which Nicholas fought with distinction in Wexford.

37 Anon., 25 May 1798, NA, Rebellion Papers, 620/51/15.

38 Felix Rourke to [Mary Finnerty], 24 Aug. 1798 in Madden, *United*, I, pp. 329–30. Rourke's father operated a coach and carriage inn outside Rathcoole and was well regarded in the community. Felix Rourke was described as 'a farmer' and in 1798 based himself in a city brewery when not in the mountains. Boyle senior to Cooke, May 1798, NA, Rebellion Papers, 620/18/3. See also Anon., n.d. [1798], TCD, Sirr Papers, 869/9, fo. 98 and Anon., n.d. [1798], TCD,

Sirr Papers, 869/8, fo. 160. The Golden Bottle was considered the premises of John Rourke of Rathcoole after the 1803 Rising, although all the Rourke brothers in Dublin were engaged in the drink trade. 'Suspect list', n.d., NA, Rebellion Papers, 620/12/217.

39 [John McGucken], 24 Sept. 1800, NA, Rebellion Papers, 620/49/54. See also 14 Nov. 1803, PRO London, Home Office Papers, 100/114/173 and McDowell (ed.), *Proceedings*, pp. 40, 47, 134–5, 142. Seagrave's high standing with the rank-and-file rebels is explained in part by his relations with Charles Teeling and his 'intimate' friendship with Mathew Dowling, both of whom were key figures in the Defender/United Irish merger. See Bird to Sirr, n.d., 1798 in Madden, *United*, p. 502. O'Hara was a grocer at 12 High Street and lived in New Row. *Wilson's Dublin Directory . . . 1794*, p. 82. He, or his son, was erroneously reported to have been transported, although one or both may have been briefly detained. *Freeman's Journal*, 19 April 1798. A Henry O'Hara of High Street was also deemed a United Irishman after 1803. 'Suspect list', n.d., NA, Rebellion Papers, 620/12/217. Francis Higgins maintained on 12 January 1798 that Dowling intervened to have Charles O'Hara and James Dixon appointed to the Petty Jury of Dublin County in order to influence verdicts in political cases. See Bartlett (ed.), *Higgins*, pp. 363–5. Higgins also named Moore as a member of 'a club in Thomas St' with influence over 'the lower order of United Irishmen'. Other leaders in 1801 included Philip Long's associate Robert Fyan of 21 Usher's Quay. [Higgins] to [Cooke], 18 Mar. 1801 in ibid., p. 535.

40 Information of Patrick McCabe, n.d., 1803, in Madden, *United*, I, p. 493.

41 See McDowell, *Imperialism and Revolution*, p. 574 and *Dublin Evening Post*, 25 November 1797.

42 *Wilson's Dublin Directory . . . 1794*, pp. 55, 82 and O'Donnell, *Rebellion in Wicklow*, pp. 23, 60, 66–7, 82. Wicklow's Rathdown barony captain and delegate, Thomas Miller of Powerscourt, was sworn in in Thomas Street by fellow rebel officer Charles Gallagher of Castletown. Both were close associates of William Michael Byrne of Parkhill, Wicklow's main delegate to the Provincial Directory and a man who agitated as far away as Cork in late 1797 and early 1798. O'Donnell, *Rebellion in Wicklow*, pp. 79–80 and William Ridgeway, *Trial of William Michael Byrne* (Dublin, 1798), p. 128.

43 Information of Thomas Wright, 1 May 1799, PRO London, Home Office Papers, 100/86/301–2. Their emissary, Fr Martin, claimed that they were the 'Committee of the District of Thomas Street'. He claimed that twenty-five men met in Nicholas Murphy's house on Thomas Street, including James Morn, John Passmore and John Parsons of Francis Street, Hugh McVeigh and one Hammond of Bolton Street, John White of Watling Street, Luke White, Charles Delahyde and others. McVeigh may have been the 'McVeagh' who had helped form the Wicklow County Committee in Dorset Street in the winter of 1797–98 where one Wall was considered the leading figure in June 1798. Information of Fr John Martin, 11 June 1798, NA, Rebellion Papers, 620/38/181.

44 O'Donnell, 'Rathdown Barony', p. 42; Alex Maguire, 'Who was Samuel Sproule?', *Dun Laoghaire Borough Historical Society Journal*, 8, 1999, pp. 28–38; Sproule to Lees, 2 June 1798, NA, Rebellion Papers, 620/38/22. Sproule had spoken against 'illegal and seditious practices' at a Dublin meeting as early as 19 Dec. 1790. *Faulkner's Dublin Journal*, 20 Dec. 1790. He was attacked and 'grossly abused' in his Rochestown home in late November 1794 by men described as burglars. Ibid., 1 Dec. 1794. Leech was a silk weaver at 85 New Street. He claimed and received a conditional pardon from Major Sirr between July and September 1798. 'Account of the number of persons'. The precise nature of his link to Sproule is unclear but it was insufficient to spare him from

being 'whipt at the Castle during the rebellion'. Sproule, remarkably, recommended that Leech be treated in this manner. Sproule to Lees, 2 June 1798, NA, Rebellion Papers, 620/38/22. Leech remained an active United Irishman five years later. Luke Brien to [Marsden], 5 April 1803, NA, Rebellion Papers, 620/64/112.

45 Brennan, n.d. [4–5 June 1798], NA, Rebellion Papers, 620/51/34. McClune's name was raised in connection with a United Irish clique which met in May/June 1798 at the Globe Coffee House, 51 Essex Street. [Higgins] to [Cooke], 5 June 1798, NA, Rebellion Papers, 620/18/14.

46 Shannon to Boyle, 5 June 1798 in Hewitt (ed.), *Letters*, p. 108.

47 Sproule to Lees, 5 June 1798, NA, Rebellion Papers, 620/38/57. See also William James to [Cooke], 6 June 1798, NA, Rebellion Papers, 620/38/67; John Kelly, 4 June 1798, NA, Rebellion Papers, 620/3/32/7; Higgins to [Cooke], 5 and 13 June 1798, NA, Rebellion Papers, 620/18/14. Rebel Captain Thomas Byrne, proprietor of 'Byrne's Arms', Cornelscourt, was arrested in late May and flogged in Lehaunstown camp for distributing fifty-three pikes under his control to his subordinates. *Freeman's Journal*, 31 May 1798. The Thomas Street combatants included Thomas Byrne (labourer, no. 120), Thomas Clare (carpenter, no. 113), John Colligan (shopkeeper, no. 15), James Cosgrove (paver, no. 124), Luke Crone (blacksmith, no. 25), Patrick Donigan (labourer, no. 9), Thomas Ellis (tape weaver, no. 65), Thomas Fegan (labourer), Denis Gaynor (labourer, no. 113); John and Thomas Gilligan (cobblers, no. 115); John Hews (labourer, no. 12); Morris Horan (rope maker, no. 87); Patrick Kelly (porter, no. 117); John Kenna (cobbler, no. 6); Joseph Lenihan (sawyer, no. 50); Patrick McLone (labourer, no. 113); Daniel Murphy (milliner, no. 111); Cormick O'Neil (clerk, no. 55); Stephen Shortall (carpenter, no. 104) and Sylvester Whelan (silk weaver, no. 149). 'An account of the number of persons who have surrendered themselves in the city of Dublin, confessed themselves being engaged in the present rebellion, and the number of arms surrendered, from 29 June last to 9 September 1798' in *Journal of the House of Commons of the Kingdom of Ireland*, XVII, pp. dccccxlvi–dcccclix and Bartlett (ed.), *Higgins*, Appendix III. Committee meetings were held in 1798 at the home of Sam Dixon of 6 Upper Ormond Quay and the Townsend Street rebels were sufficiently well organised to draw on the services of local apothecary Donovan. He was known to have 'sent drugs to the rebels in 98 and attended them'. 'Suspect list', n.d., NA, Rebellion Papers, 620/12/217.

48 Fr Michael Murphy to Thomas Houston, 6 June 1798 in Musgrave, *Rebellions*, p. 407. See also Maxwell, *Irish Rebellion*, p. 131. See also [Higgins] to [Cooke], 13 June 1798, NA, Rebellion Papers, 620/18/14.

49 Camden to Portland, 11 June 1798 in John T. Gilbert (ed.), *Documents relating to Ireland, 1795–1804* (Shannon, 1972), p. 132 and Cooke to Anon., 13 June 1798, PRO London, Home Office Papers, 100/81/80.

50 Boyle senior to Cooke, n.d., [1798], NA, Rebellion Papers, 620/18/1.

51 O'Donnell, *Rebellion in Wicklow*, pp. 228–36.

52 See Seamus Ó Loinsigh, 'The Rebellion of 1798 in Meath', *Riocht na Midhe*, V, 1, 1971, pp. 68–71; Liam Chambers, *Rebellion in Kildare, 1790–1803* (Dublin, 1998), pp. 92–3; Charles Dickson, *Revolt in the North*, pp. 148–55.

53 For Gallagher's arrest see Breandan Mac Suibhne, 'Up not out: Why did northwest Ulster not rise in 1798?' in Cathal Póirtéir (ed.), *The Great Irish Rebellion of 1798* (Cork, 1998), p. 94 and Flynn and McCormick, *Westmeath*, pp. 85, 101–2. For McManus see 'Suspect list', n.d., NA, Rebellion Papers, 620/12/217.

54 O'Donnell, *Rebellion in Wicklow*, pp. 225–6.

55 *Freeman's Journal*, 26 May 1798.

56 Petition of Michael Masterson, 18 Sept. 1798, NA, State Prisoners Petitions, 214. See also Captain William Griffin to Anon., 17 July 1798, NA, Rebellion Papers, 620/3/32/10; Ball, *County Dublin*; Hammond, 'Sirr, part one', p. 21. The same repentant United Irishman who told John Claudius Beresford that Horish 'was a sound good fellow, and much attached to the cause' named Masterson as a potential killer of informers. Anon., June 1798 in Musgrave, *Rebellions*, p. 674. Horish reputedly owned several houses in Dame Court and earned £400 per annum. Shannon to Boyle, 30 May 1798 in Hewitt (ed.), *Letters*, p. 105.

57 *Irish Magazine*, Aug. 1809, p. 383. Glindon never fully recovered and died aged 35 in 1809 after a 'lingering decline' which commenced during the 'reign of terror'. Ibid.

58 Order Book of the Reay Highlanders, 4 July 1798, NLI, MS 5913.

59 Petition of Luke Doyle, 19 Nov. 1798, NA, State Prisoners Petitions, 120. See also Petition of Peter Gaffney, 25 July 1798, NA, State Prisoners Petitions, 145.

60 Ruán O'Donnell, 'Marked for Botany Bay': The Wicklow United Irishmen and the development of political transportation from Ireland, 1791–1806', Ph.D. thesis, Australian National University, 1996, pp. 185–6 and 10 October 1798, NA, State Prisoner Petitions, 318.

61 *Freeman's Journal*, 14 June 1798.

62 O'Donnell, *Rebellion in Wicklow*, pp. 246–52; Madden, *United*, IV, pp. 554–5; Anon. to Sirr, 21 April 1798, NA, Rebellion Papers, 620/36/191. Fitzgerald may have been related to Benjamin Fitzgerald, a rebel captain who worked as a silversmith at Cole Alley and was held in the Provost prison. Madden, *United*, I, p. 492.

63 B[oyle] senior to Cooke, n.d. [1798], NA, Rebellion Papers, 620/18/1. Houses belonging to the Rourke, Russell and Doyle families of Lusk were identified as sanctuaries for 'wounded men that were in the engagements in the Co. Wexford'. Ibid. See also *Freeman's Journal*, 2 June 1798; [Higgins] to [Cooke], 30 June 1798, NA, Rebellion Papers, 620/18/14 and Freda Agnew (ed.), 'June 1798', *Dun Laoghaire Borough Historical Society Journal*, 8, 1999, p. 39.

64 Taylor to William Wickham, 25 June 1798, PRO London, Home Office Papers, 100/81/71–2; Foster to Sheffield, 7 July 1798 in Malcomson (ed.), *Anglo-Irish dialogue*, p. 26; *Faulkner's Dublin Journal*, 28 June 1798. Lady Sarah Napier informed her brother, the Duke of Richmond, of the outstanding rebel forces in Kildare in late June: 'I hear today from Cellbridge (where I fear our intelligence is too good) at Timahoe hill that forms a kind of peninsula in this end of the bog of Allen, we knew of many thousands [of rebels camped] between Timahoe and Cellbridge for this month past for Col [. . .] has by his personal attention kept them off from Cellbridge by odd means, too long to explain, but which being ruse de guerre – which they did not expect has answered the purpose . . . thank God that Brute [Camden] is treated with the contempt he deserves by his friend Pitt.' Napier to Richmond, 27 June 1798, NLI, MS 35,003/4.

65 John Mathews quoted in Fitzpatrick, *Sham Squire*, p. 355. The Westmeath men were led by Nugent and Mulligan in August 1798 and Reilly, who assumed command of the Longford rebels formerly headed by Farrell, was subsequently killed. 30 Nov. 1803, NA, Rebellion Papers, 620/11/130/60. John Byrne of Castletown, a member of the merchant Byrnes of Mullinahack, went to Hamburg with Anthony McCann and Bartholomew Teeling in 1797. See McDowell (ed.), *Proceedings*, p. 135 and Paul Weber, *On the road to Rebellion, The United Irishmen and Hamburg, 1796–1803* (Dublin, 1997), pp. 74–5. Warren may have been the associate of Richard McCormick, who opened communications with the Defenders in the early 1790s. See Smyth, *Men of no property*, p. 73.

66 O'Donnell, *Rebellion in Wicklow*, pp. 255–66.
67 Sproule to Lees, 12 July 1798, NA, Rebellion Papers, 620/39/60. See also Lord Enniskillen to Anon., 6 July 1798, NA, Rebellion Papers, 620/39/25.
68 Anon. to Cooke, 6 July 1798, NA, Rebellion Papers, 620/39/28; *Saunder's Newsletter*, 9 and 11 July 1798; Shannon to Boyle in Hewitt (ed.), *Letters*, p. 140. See also Taylor Diary, TCD, MS 10347.
69 *Saunder's Newsletter*, 11–14 July 1798 and J. B. Lyons, 'The Royal College of Surgeons in Ireland and its worthies', *Dublin Historical Record*, XLVIII, 1, 1995, pp. 40–54.
70 Sproule to Lees, 10 July 1798, NA, Rebellion Papers, 620/39/44.
71 [Higgins] to [Cooke], 12 July 1798, NA, Rebellion Papers, 620/18/14.
72 Information of Richard Turner, 9 July 1798, NA, Rebellion Papers, 620/39/38 and Foster to Sheffield, 23 July 1798 in Malcomson (ed.), *Anglo-Irish dialogue*, p. 26. It was claimed that 'The pass which the rebels go out to the Co. of Wicklow is through Dolphin's Barn by a gate and little lane and so on by a ditch [i.e. hedgerow] which conceals them untill [sic] they get to the mountain'. n.d. [1798], NA, Rebellion Papers, 620/51/212. Thompson may have been ex-Catholic Committee delegate in 1792 and apothecary, Anthony Thompson of 9 Stephen Street. He was a member of the United Irish circle which included John Keogh, Richard Dillon, John Sweetman and Richard McCormick. See *Wilson's Dublin Directory . . . 1803*, p. 100 and [Higgins] to [Cooke], 11 Oct. 1796, NA, Rebellion Papers, 620/18/14. There was also a 'Thompson of Pill Lane' who attended United Irish meetings in March 1798. Bartlett (ed.), *Higgins*, p. 394.
73 18 July 1798, NA, Rebellion Papers, 620/3/16/5.
74 Information of Bartholomew Connelly, 24 July 1798, NA, Rebellion Papers, 620/37/73. See also Bird to Sirr, n.d. 1798 in Madden, *United*, I, p. 498 and O'Donnell, *Rebellion in Wicklow*, pp. 276–8.
75 Bird to Sirr, n.d. 1798 in Madden, *United*, I, p. 502. See also Cornwallis to Portland, 6 July 1798, PRO London, Home Office Papers, 100/81/227 and Pole Carew to Downshire, 17 July 1798, PRO Northern Ireland, D. 607/F/326. Markey and his brother Nicholas, had been active at a high level in the pre-Rebellion United Irishmen. In early 1797 they had met with McCann, Turner, John Byrne, Bartholomew Teeling and other Dundalk/Newry area leaders. Fitzpatrick, *Sham Squire*, pp. 357–8.
76 Felix Rourke to Mary Finnerty, 27 July 1798 in Madden, *United*, IV, pp. 546–7. Rourke's letter exaggerated the success of the insurgents in the first phase of the action. Ibid. See also Bulletin, 19 June 1798, PRO London, Home Office Papers, 100/77/167. Richard Allen, a yeoman in Beresford's Loyal Dublin Cavalry, was mortally wounded at Clonard and died in Mullingar within two weeks. *Freeman's Journal*, 28 July 1798.
77 O'Donnell, *Rebellion in Wicklow*, pp. 276–86.
78 William James to Cooke, 16 July 1798, NA, Rebellion Papers, 620/39/90.
79 Foster to Sheffield, 23 July 1798 in Malcomson (ed.), *Anglo-Irish dialogue*, p. 26.
80 Sproule to Lees, 14 July 1798, NA, Rebellion Papers, 620/39/70.
81 Buckingham to Lord Grenville, 23 July 1798 in Fortescue, *Report of the Manuscripts of J.B. Fortescue, Esq.*, IV, p. 264.
82 28 July 1798, PRO London, Home Office Papers, 100/77/313.
83 Cornwallis to Portland, 29 Oct. 1798, PRO London, Home Office Papers, 100/82/218. See also Camden to Portland, 25 Feb. 1798, PRO London, Home Office Papers, 100/75/138 and 2 April 1798, PRO London, Home Office Papers, 100/76/7; Cornwallis to Portland, 26 July 1798, PRO London, Home

Office Papers, 100/77/301 and 12 Nov. 1798, PRO London, Home Office Papers, 100/79/100; Ross to Downshire, 26 July 1798, PRO Northern Ireland, D. 607/F/339.

84 Castlereagh to Wickham, 29 Oct 1798, PRO London, Home Office Papers, 100/79/66. See also Cooke to Wickham, 12 Nov. 1798, PRO London, Home Office Papers, 100/79/98 and Sproule to Lees, 10 July 1798, NA, Rebellion Papers, 620/39/44.

85 *Finn's Leinster Journal*, 4 July 1798.

86 Ross to Downshire, 30 July 1798, PRO Northern Ireland, D. 607/F/342. See also Castlereagh to Wickham, 30 July 1798 in Londonderry (ed.), *Memoirs and Correspondence of Viscount Castlereagh*, 4 vols (London, 1848), I, pp. 246–8; Maxwell, *Irish Rebellion*, p. 295; Charles Hamilton Teeling, *History of the Irish Rebellion of 1798, and sequel to the history of the Irish Rebellion of 1798* (Shannon, 1972), pp. 298–300.

87 Cornwallis to Portland, 7 Aug. 1798, PRO London, Home Office Papers, 100/78/19.

88 Thomas Addis Emmet to Rufus King, 9 April 1807 in Madden, *United*, III, pp. 85–6.

89 Londonderry (ed.), *Castlereagh Correspondence*, I, pp. 349–50. See also Dobbs to Castlereagh, 28 July 1798, NA, Rebellion Papers, 620/4/29/15 and Richard Annesley to Downshire, 22 Aug. 1798, PRO Northern Ireland, D. 607/F/358.

90 Charles Broderick, Bishop of Kilmore, understood the significance of Fitzgibbon's support. He wrote to a London friend: 'it will give you very great pleasure both on private and public grounds to hear that Lord Cornwallis's measures have the entire approbation of our Chancellor, and that every day brings something to light to prove the great wisdom of them'. Charles Broderick to Charles Townshend, 6 Aug. 1798, Ó Mathuna Collection.

91 Cooke to [Wickham?], 28 July 1798, PRO London, Home Office Papers, 100/77/311. John Foster believed the government was imprudent to publish 'the latter part of [Addis] Emmet's examination' which contained his justification of United Irish strategy. Foster to Sheffield, 11 Sept. 1798 in Malcomson (ed.), *Anglo-Irish dialogue*, p. 29.

92 Madden, *Robert Emmet*, p. 8. See also Castlereagh to Wickham, 2 April 1799 in Charles Ross (ed.), *Correspondence of Charles, First Marquis Cornwallis*, 3 vols, 2nd edn (London, 1859), III, p. 83.

93 MacNeven, 'Account of the treaty', pp. 181–4. In August or September Addis Emmet sent by 'the bearer' a letter to Russell enquiring 'whether (as we heard) a protest had been drawn up by the state prisoners in Newgate against the working & clauses of the Emigration Bill & whether that was communicated to Castlereagh with an intimation that it would be inserted in the Courier [newspaper]'. Addis Emmet to Russell, n.d. [Aug./Sept. 1798], NA, Rebellion Papers, 620/15/2/13. See also Madden, *United*, IV, p. 64.

94 O'Donnell, *Rebellion in Wicklow*, pp. 298–99 and Walsh, *Ireland sixty years ago*, pp. 180–81.

95 Broderick to Townshend, 6 Aug. 1798, Ó Mathúna Collection.

96 *Finn's Leinster Journal*, 21 July 1798. See also Examination of Henry Charles Sirr, 19 July 1798 in Hammond, 'Sirr', part one, p. 23. Tipped off by John Sandys, Sirr recovered weapons and documents from John Russell's home. Ibid. A rebel captain named Robinson was arrested in the city the following week. *Freeman's Journal*, 28 July 1798.

97 *Freeman's Journal*, 28 July 1798. The only two city traders of this name who were listed in 1794 but not in 1803 were Roger Hynes, a tailor, of 1 Price's Lane and James Hynes, a hatter, of 100 Grafton Street. *Wilson's Dublin Directory* . . .

1794, p. 57 and ibid, 1803, p. 60. Three men of this name received conditional pardons: Anthony Hynes (carpet maker, 25 Meath Street); John Hynes (silk weaver, 29 New Row) and Michael Hynes (paper maker, 6 Hammond Lane). 'Account of the number of persons'.

98 Felix Rourke to General Dundas, 9 Sept. 1798, NA, Rebellion Papers, 620/40/46.

99 Shannon to Boyle, 5 Aug. 1798 in Hewitt (ed.), *Letters*, p. 142. See also *Hibernian Journal*, 6 Aug. 1798 and Petition of Thomas Markey, 4 Dec. 1798, NA, State Prisoners Petitions, 213. It was reported that Rattigan 'one of the persons proclaimed . . . has come forward, and given himself into custody'. *Finn's Leinster Journal*, 4 Aug. 1798. Markey was sentenced to death in Dundalk, although this was commuted to transportation for life. He was held on a prison hulk off Howth before being transferred to Kilmainham on 12 March 1801. He was 'bailed before Alderman Rose and transported', i.e. deported, on 21 May. He went to France where he joined the Irish Legion and later rose to the position of Lieutenant Colonel and aide-de-camp to the Duke of Feltre, Minister for War. Kilmainham register quoted in Mary P. McConnon, 'The Kilmainham Gaol Registers 1798 to 1823: List of convicts from County Louth', *Journal of the County Louth Archaeological and Historical Society*, XXIII, 4, 1996, p. 415. See also Emmet, *Memoir*, I, p. 371.

100 *Freeman's Journal*, 4 Aug. 1798.

101 Castlereagh to Wickham, 4 Aug. 1798, PRO London, Home Office Papers, 100/78/13. See also MacNeven, 'Account of the treaty', p. 189.

102 Portland to the King, 11 Aug. 1798 in A. Aspinall (ed.), *The later correspondence of George III*, five vols (Cambridge, 1968), III, p. 104. See also *Report from the Committee of Secrecy*, Appendix XXXI, pp. 225–36.

103 See Buckingham to Grenville, 28 Aug. 1798 in Fortescue, *Fortescue*, IV, p. 290.

104 Emmet, *Memoir*, I, p. 323 and Samuel Neilson to Anon., 16 Sept. 1798 quoted in Teeling, *Sequel*, pp. 361–2.

105 Madden, *United*, III, p. 61.

106 See Harman Murtagh, 'General Humbert's campaign in the West' in Pórtéir (ed.), *Great Irish Rebellion*, pp. 115–24.

107 Information of Surgeon Thomas Wright, 1 May 1799, PRO London, Home Office Papers, 100/86/301. Charles O'Hara's name was also raised in connection with the new committees. See Castlereagh to Cornwallis, Aug. 1798 in Londonderry (ed.), *Castlereagh Correspondence*, I, p. 327.

108 James to Anon., 28 Aug. 1798, NA, Rebellion Papers, 620/39/223. Buckingham wrote from Dublin on the same day: 'In the midst of all this we have no Government, or any thing like one, in the capital, where people talk of a rising with the same coolness as they would of any other event. It is known that the rebel leaders (not in prison) all left Dublin yesterday, and the consternation in Dublin must invite all the mischief that can be done. I still am persuaded that there will be no rising in Dublin, but I am most sure that there will be risings in Meath and Kildare . . . The garrison of Dublin has been most wantonly thinned; we have barely 1,100 infantry in the town, and the whole neighbourhood calling out for troops.' Buckingham to Lord Grenville, 28 Aug. 1798, Fortescue, *Fortescue*, IV, p. 291.

109 Information of Surgeon Thomas Wright, 1 May 1799, PRO London, Home Office Papers, 100/86/301; McDowell (ed.), *Proceedings*, pp. 125–6; Byrne, *Memoirs*, I, p. 235.

110 [Higgins] to [Cooke], 26 Aug. 1798, NA, Rebellion Papers, 620/18/14. The source for this was one Myler, a frequent informant of Higgins and the Castle. Ibid.

111 'Captain Long' was a United Irishman in 1794 when he lived in Essex Street. McDowell (ed.), *Proceedings*, pp. 113, 139. When Long stayed in the Castle Hotel the spy Thomas Collins described him as 'Captain Long . . . French agent'. Ibid., p. 141. Collins, however, was uncertain of Long's Christian name, which he usually left blank in his reports. One letter mistakenly gave it as 'John' in February 1794, an error which may have confused the authorities. Ibid., p. 113. In an 1803 statement full of necessary evasions and half-truths, Long falsely claimed that he had been living in Spain from 1789 to 1795 and did not join the United Irishmen on his return. He certainly visited Ireland prior to 1795 and was listed in Castle files as a member by 1794. When forced to acknowledge that he knew several men included in the Banishment Act of 1798, Long, unaware of having been watched in the 1790s, downplayed such connections. He claimed, for instance, to have seen Samuel Neilson 'in 1798 in the street for a few minutes never since', although Collins had identified them as confederates years earlier. Philip Long, 18 Aug. 1803, NA, Rebellion Papers, 620/11/138/4.

112 O'Donnell, *Rebellion in Wicklow*, pp. 304–6. For McCabe and Long see Information of Michael Quigley, 30 June 1805, NA, Rebellion Papers, 620/14/187/11 and Chambers, *Rebellion in Kildare*, p. 102.

113 Long, 18 Aug. 1803, NA, Rebellion Papers, 620/11/138/4. Long claimed that one Darling introduced him to Emmet, possibly fellow merchant Richard Darling, who lived at 28 Townsend Street. Ibid and *Wilson's Dublin Directory . . . 1803*, p. 37. Luke and Patrick Darling were held in the Provost prison on 18 September 1803. 'Persons in confinement', *House of Commons*, VI, 1805, p. 449.

114 *Finn's Leinster Journal*, 15 Sept. 1798. See also *Freeman's Journal*, 15 Sept. 1798 and 30 Nov. 1803, NA, Rebellion Papers, 620/11/130/60. Another indication of the scale of Dublin-area commitment to the Rebellion is provided by the arms returns of General Craig. Although commander of the entire Eastern Division, his account of weaponry delivered to and recovered by his forces excludes Kildare and Wicklow war material claimed by General Sir Ralph Dundas and acting Brigadier General Joseph Hardy. From 18 May to 16 July 1798 Craig's officers collected 1,930 guns, 1,183 pistols, 70 blunderbusses and 13 pieces of ordnance. While some of this haul may have been obtained from non-yeoman loyalists, the 2,544 pikes were all United Irish owned. See 'Returns of arms seized and surrendered in several districts' in *Report from the Committee of Secrecy*, p. 245. The Commons returns pertained to the 'near 1,000 persons' who informed Sirr and Swan of their 'treasonable oaths' in late July. *Freeman's Journal*, 28 July 1798. See 'Account of the number of persons'.

115 Ross to Downshire, 29 Aug. 1798, PRO Northern Ireland, D. 607/F/377.

116 Felix Rourke to Mary Finnerty, 27 July 1798 in Madden, *United*, IV, p. 543.

117 *Finn's Leinster Journal*, 1 Sept. 1798.

118 Alderman James to Castlereagh, 29 Aug. 1798, NA, State of the Country Papers, 1017/26; John Brown to Anon., 29 Aug. 1798, NA, Rebellion Papers, 620/39/207; Hartigan to Downshire, 4 Sept. 1798, PRO Northern Ireland, D. 607/F/382; Anon. to Castlereagh, 3 Sept. 1798, NA, Rebellion Papers, 620/3/32/14–15; Anon., n.d., TCD, Sirr Papers, MS 869/8, fo. 92; Thomas Roche to Alexander Hamilton, 6 Sept. 1798, NA, Rebellion Papers, 620/40/25; *Saunder's Newsletter*, 7 Sept. 1798; *Dublin Evening Post*, 20 Sept. 1798; McDowell (ed.), *Proceedings*, p. 142. Neil (aka Fitzharris) 'served under O'Hanlon in the Co. Wicklow. He knows [James] Farrell too & can convict him'. Pollock to [Cooke?], 28 April 1799, NA, Rebellion Papers, 620/7/74/27. O'Hanlon was probably related to the Newry radical who, in early 1792, went

to France to deliver a donation of £300 to the National Assembly towards the war effort. Smyth, *Men of no property*, p. 92. The Thomas Seagrave of 1 Lower Kevin Street was evidently a close relative of the Greek Street colonel. A chandler and tobacconist, Seagrave of Kevin Street was considered 'a principal [United Irishman who] raised money for the outlaws in 98'. He was jailed in 1803. 'Suspect list', n.d., NA, Rebellion Papers, 620/12/217.

119 *Courier*, 10–12 Sept. 1798; 27 Mar. 1799, NA, Rebellion Papers, 620/17/30/43; Cullen, NLI, MSS 8339, pp. 190–91.

120 Buckingham to Grenville, 15 Sept. 1798 in Fortescue, *Fortescue*, IV, p. 315.

121 *Finn's Leinster Journal*, 15–19 Sept. 1798. Captain R. Hill of the *Van Tromp*, one of the transports used to carry the French to England, was awarded the Freedom of the City in October in recognition of his 'attention and hospitality to the citizens of Dublin'. *Hibernian Journal*, 19 Oct. 1798. The French officers left London for Dover and France where they were deemed to be on parole until formally exchanged. *Hibernian Journal*, 31 Oct. 1798.

122 Sproule to Lees, 25 Sept. 1798, NA, Rebellion Papers, 620/51/270. 25 September was notable in Dublin for the arrival in Kevin Street of twenty-five Dundrum yeomen who had been driven out of their village by 'a party of Holt's men'. Thirty-seven Fermanagh militiamen, including wounded, arrived in the city a few days later having lost their arms and equipment in another Holt ambush at Knockalt in the King's River Valley. *Courier*, 27 Sept. 1798. See also ibid., 29 Sept. 1798. The *Courier* also noted: 'a number of families have arrived at the inns in Kevin Street, from different quarters of that county [Wicklow]; having escaped with their lives, though most of them beggared [sic], their property having been destroyed . . . every hour brings some new account of assassination and carnage, which by their frequency seem to have already deadened every feeling of humanity . . . The most shocking enormities are daily committed by the rebels against the yeomanry, and the Protestant Orange families in Wicklow.' Ibid., 8 Oct. 1798.

123 Wickham to Castlereagh, 23 Nov. 1799 in Londonderry (ed.), *Castlereagh Correspondence*, II, p. 16. Grey and Bolton were described as 'very dangerous persons'. Another United Irishman using the name Murphy, 'lately expelled [from] Dublin College', was in the Hamburg suburb of Altona in late 1798 where he enlisted the support of the well-connected Kerry rebel agent William Duckett. Ibid. See also ibid., I, p. 326; 2 Nov. 1798, NA, Rebellion Papers, 620/41/2; *Wilson's Dublin Directory . . . 1794*, p. 19. Turner denounced Bolton as 'a most infamous blackguard . . . [who] ought not to be let back on any account'. [Turner] to Downshire, 27 Sept. 1798, PRO Northern Ireland, D. 607/F/432.

124 Wickham to John King, 3 Nov. 1803, PRO London, Home Office Papers, 100/114/149–50; Richard Hayes, *The last invasion of Ireland, when Connacht rose* (Dublin, 1979), p. 62; Walsh, *Ireland sixty years ago*, p. 173. The participation in separate French ventures of Hamilton and Corbett – also 'expelled [from] Dublin College' – had been predicted in August 1798. See 'Secret Information from Hamburg', 16 Aug. 1798 in Londonderry (ed.), *Castlereagh correspondence*, I, p. 306.

125 Elliott, *Partners*, pp. 233–4.

126 *Belfast Newsletter*, 26 Oct. 1798; *Hibernian Journal*, 29 and 31 Oct. 1798; Elliott, *Partners*, pp. 233–5.

127 Buckingham to Grenville, 26 Sept. 1798 in Fortescue, *Fortescue*, IV, p. 326.

128 *Finn's Leinster Journal*, 17 Oct. 1798.

129 *Freeman's Journal*, 2 Oct. 1798.

130 Sproule to [Lees], 7 Oct. 1798, NA, Rebellion Papers, 620/40/139. See also *Freeman's Journal*, 9 Oct. 1798 and *Saunder's Newsletter*, 10 Oct. 1798. Fifty

suspected rebels were placed on a tender on 31 July and a further fifty three weeks later. *Freeman's Journal*, 1 Aug. 1798 and *Finn's Leinster Journal*, 25 Aug. 1798.

131 *Saunder's Newsletter*, 17 Oct. 1798.

132 Sproule to Lees, 18 Oct. 1798, NA, Rebellion Papers, 620/40/170.

133 Sproule to Lees, 19 Oct. 1798, NA, Rebellion Papers, 620/40/172.

134 [Higgins] to [Cooke], 20 Oct. 1798, NA, Rebellion Papers, 620/18/14. Bartlett has identified the attendees in Merchants Quay as Surgeon Robert Hamilton, Lewis Alexander Lyons of Arran Quay, John Adrien of Meath Street, Dr Richard Kiernan of 16 Upper Ormond Quay and Malachy O'Connor. All those named by Higgins were professionals and several, like Wright, had medical careers. See Bartlett (ed.), *Higgins*, pp. 467–9 and McDowell (ed.) *Proceedings*, pp. 134–5. Lyons may have been the man of that name who harboured United Irish emissary Edward Carolan in late 1800. This is indicated by Carolan's contemporaneous visit to Mahon. Ibid., pp. 506–8. Myler was a merchant at 171 Abbey Street, an address which, along with his politics, explains his access to the McClune circle. *Wilson's Dublin Directory . . . 1803*, p. 80. Adrien, a member of the Royal College of Surgeons, was under observation into the early 1800s. 'Suspect list', NA, Rebellion Papers, 620/12/217. He lived on Fleet Street in 1803. *Wilson's Dublin Directory . . . 1803*, p. 142.

135 Sproule to Lees, 4 Nov. 1798, NA, Rebellion Papers, 620/41/12. A Castle document recorded that Henry O'Hara, a hardware merchant and United Irishman, lived at 30 West New Row. n.d., NA, Rebellion Papers, 620/12/148/18. His actual address in 1803 was 32 West New Row which suggests he inherited or otherwise obtained ownership of the business run by Charles O'Hara in 1798. He was probably the eldest brother of Charles O'Hara junior. *Wilson's Dublin Directory . . . 1803*, p. 83.

136 President Adams allegedly stated that 'no person who is unfit to live under the English government is fit to live under his'. Addis Emmet to Marsden, 11 Oct. 1798, NA, Rebellion Papers, 620/15/2/13. Tone bequeathed a ring containing a lock of Hoche's hair to Addis Emmet, who described him as 'a friend whose memory I shall never cease to esteem and love . . . Were it ever so dangerous, I should not hesitate to avow my attachment to Tone – he was dear to men in his misfortunes, his magnanimity has encreased [sic] & his death has perpetuated my affection.' Addis Emmet to Marsden, 3 Dec. 1798, NA, Rebellion Papers, 620/15/2/16. Castlereagh was also contacted by Addis Emmet. See Elliot to Castlereagh, 27 Nov. 1798 in Londonderry (ed.), *Castlereagh Correspondence*, II, p. 27.

137 *Hibernian Journal*, 24 Oct. 1798.

CHAPTER FOUR

1 For the background to the Union see Patrick Geoghegan, *The Irish Act of Union, A study in High Politics, 1798–1801* (Dublin, 1999) and Jim Smyth, 'The Act of Union and "public opinion"' in Jim Smyth (ed.), *Revolution, counter-revolution and union, Ireland in the 1790s* (Cambridge, 2000), pp. 146–60.

2 Revd John Murphy to Denys Scully, [20 Jan. 1799] in MacDermot (ed.), *Papers of Denys Scully*, p. 15. Moira House was the Dublin address of George Forbes, Earl Granard, during the Union controversy. This arose in consequence of Selina Frances Rawdon, Lady Granard, being the daughter of the 1st Earl of Moira by his third wife. Lord Mount Cashell was the Earl's grandson by his first wife. See ibid., pp. 146, 694 and *Gentleman's and Citizen's Almanack . . . 1803*, p. 39.

3   The anonymous loyalist editor of one of Scully's pamphlets claimed the lawyer had been 'General of a Crusade, in the County of Cork, in the year 1786, when after the example of the pious father Nicholas Sheehy, he incited the White Boys [sic, Rightboys] to commit various outrages'. Denys Scully, *An Irish Catholic's advice to his brethren, how to estimate their present situation, and repel French invasion, civil wars, and slavery*, new edn (London, 1803), p. 5. In 1803 the disturbing, if ludicrous, image of an anti-Protestant 'crusade' was used by Judge Robert Day when painting William Todd Jones as 'the holy Champion of the Catholic Religion' in Munster. Day to Marsden, 27 Sept. 1803, NA, Rebellion Papers, 620/64/160.

4   Revd Murphy to Scully, 23 Jan. 1799 in MacDermot (ed.), *Papers of Denys Scully*, p. 18 and William Godwin, *Memoirs of the author of the Vindication of the Rights of Woman* (London, 1798).

5   Murphy to Scully, 23 Jan. 1799 in MacDermot (ed.), *Papers of Denys Scully*, p. 18.

6   Thomas Grenville to Lord Grenville, 29 July 1803 in Fortescue, *Fortescue*, VII, p. 181 and Buckingham to Grenville, 17 Sept. 1803, ibid., p. 188. Buckingham noted: 'The very unquiet state of Dublin kept me on horseback till two o'clock last night: but the force in very numerous patrols, which I arranged in breach of Lord Cornwallis's order according to my own fancy, and the alertness of the troops in dispersing every assembly of people, prevented any serious mischief.' Buckingham to Grenville, 24 Jan. 1799, ibid., IV, p. 452.

7   Revd Murphy to Scully, 22 and 29 Jan. 1799 and 14 April 1799 in MacDermot (ed.), *Papers of Denys Scully*, pp. 16–17, 20–21, 29–30; Sadlier (ed.), *Irish Peer*, p. vii; Fitzpatrick, *Sham Squire*, pp. 144–5.

8   Lady Granard to Scully, 29 Jan. 1799 in MacDermot (ed.), *Papers of Denys Scully*, p. 22. See also Robert Holmes, *A demonstration of the necessity of a legislative Union of Great Britain and Ireland involving a refutation of every argument that has been or can be urged against the measure* (Dublin, 1799).

9   Elizabeth Emmet to Thomas Ellis, 27 Feb. 1799, NA, Rebellion Papers, 620/15/2/17.

10 See 'GH' to Thomas Ellis, 27 July 1803, NA, Rebellion Papers, 620/65/74.

11 For an in-depth survey of Union literature see W. J. McCormick, *The Pamphlet debate on the Union between Great Britain and Ireland, 1797–1800* (Dublin, 1996).

12 Memorial of Robert Emmet and Malachy Delaney, 28 fructidor 8 (15 September 1800), Archives des affaires étrangères: correspondance politique Angleterre: volume 593, folios 288–9, translated by Sylvie Kleinman.

13 Drennan to Martha McTier, 3 Mar. 1800 in Agnew (ed.), *Drennan-McTier letters*, II, p. 380. See also ibid., III, p. 716, Lady Moira to Lady Granard, 13 Oct. 1800, PRO Northern Ireland, T/3765/J/9/2/8; Madden, *United*, III, pp. 21–2; Postgate, *Emmet*, p. 37.

14 Memorial of Denis O'Neil, 30 Jan. 1799 in Londonderry (ed.), *Castlereagh correspondence*, II, p. 234.

15 Information of Surgeon Thomas Wright, 1 May 1799, PRO London, Home Office Papers, 100/86/301. O'Connor reputedly wrote to a fruit merchant named Morton who had been 'one of the leaders in the Rebellion in Wicklow'. 10 Feb. 1799, NA, Rebellion Papers, 620/7/74/10. This was very probably John Morron, 'fruiterer' at 24 Upper Ormond Quay. *Wilson's Dublin Directory . . . 1794*, p. 77.

16 [McGucken], 2 Feb. 1799, NA, Rebellion Papers, 620/7/74/6. McGucken would have been well known to United Irishmen for defending William Orr in Sept. 1797. See 'Information of James McGuckin' in Dickson, *Revolt in the North*,

p. 46 and A. T. Q. Stewart, *The Summer Soldiers, the 1798 Rebellion in Antrim and Down* (Belfast, 1995), p. 46.

17 McGucken, 7 Feb. 1799, NA, Rebellion Papers, 620/7/74/8.

18 McGucken, 11 Feb. 1799, NA, Rebellion Papers, 620/7/74/11. For John Palmer see 30 Aug. 1801, NA, Rebellion Papers, 620/49/125.

19 *Hibernian Journal*, 24 Dec. 1798. Farrell was arrested with a dagger of 'admirable workmanship' and 'libellous books professing to contain the creed and catechism of the United Irishmen'. Ibid.

20 Fitzpatrick, *Sham Squire*, p. 184 and 3 Jan. 1799, NA, Rebellion Papers, 620/7/74/2. Gallagher had requested permission to emigrate with his wife to America. Petition of Patrick Gallagher, 4 Oct. 1798, NA, State Prisoners Petitions, 146. Following his arrest in Derry on 17 June 1798 Gallagher was tried at the Royal Barracks on 7 July and charged with taking part in the attempt to rescue Fitzgerald on 19 May. He had actually stabbed Major Sirr in the leg the previous day. A Dublin story has it that Gallagher was being taken from the Provost for execution when the guard commander noticed his masonic apron and returned him to his cell on the grounds that he was incapable of hanging a fellow mason. See Fitzpatrick, *Sham Squire*, pp. 181–2.

21 n.d. Feb. 1799, NA, Rebellion Papers, 620/7/74/22. See also 31 Aug. 1803, NA, Rebellion Papers, 620/11/130/26.

22 Quoted in Elliott, *Partners*, p. 256. See also ibid., pp. 268, 278. A founding member of the United Irishmen, George Wilkinson of 8 Spital Fields was a silk and worsted manufacturer in 1792. McDowell (ed.), *Proceedings*, p. 56.

23 For 'Arbour Hill' see Emmet, *Memoir*, II, p. 15. The text of Teeling's undelivered trial speech is in Liam Kelly, *A flame now quenched, Rebels and Frenchmen in Leitrim, 1793–1798* (Dublin, 1998), p. 141. Bartholomew Teeling told Cooke that after Castlebar 'they resolved to attempt something daring, and to march for Dublin upon speculation of insurrection'. Cooke to Wickham, 11 Sept. 1798 in Ross (ed.), *Cornwallis Correspondence*, II, p. 404. The hanging of Teeling was witnessed by an English officer who noted: 'he was perfectly unconcerned at the gallows, and although they bungled about with ladders, and tyeing [sic] the cord round his neck, and throwing it over the gallows for nearly $\frac{3}{4}$ of an hour, he seemed totally indifferent, and sometimes smiled, he said just before he went off "well, it is better to die thus in one's youth (about 35 years old) than to be physicked [sic] to death in old age"'. Diary of Captain Thomas Law Hodges of the West Kent militia, 24 Sept. 1798, BL, MS 40166N. Another account claimed: 'Teeling just hanged, and [Mathew] Tone under trial; all the prisoners made at Ballinamuck brought up to Dublin, and all reprieved for transportation and put on board what is termed a croppy-ship.' Buckingham to Lord Grenville, 24 Sept. 1798 in Fortescue, *Fortescue*, IV, p. 321.

24 See Smyth, *Men of no property*, pp. 158–9.

25 Information of Surgeon Thomas Wright, 1 May 1799, PRO London, Home Office Papers, 100/86/301; Madden, *Hope*, p. 28; Byrne, *Memoirs*, II, p. 183; Walsh, *Ireland sixty years ago*, pp. 155, 180–81; *Finn's Leinster Journal*, 26 Sept. 1798.

26 Castlereagh to Wickham, 5 Feb. 1799 in Londonderry (ed.), *Castlereagh Correspondence*, II, p. 224. The same source named 'St J . . . one C . . . O'M of the county of Meath'. Ibid. William St John and St John Mason were both very close to Robert Emmet. See also Castlereagh to Cornwallis, ibid., I, p. 327; Information of Thomas Wright, 1 May 1799, PRO London, Home Office Papers, 100/86/301–2; Elliott, *Partners*, p. 247. For the bailing of Dillon see 5 Sept. 1799, NA, Rebellion Papers, 620/7/79/31 and *Saunder's Newsletter*, 15 March 1798. Dublin Castle believed that James Tandy, son of Napper Tandy,

occupied a similar position of authority in the United Irishmen. Wright, however, entertained 'very strong doubts' as to the 'sincerity' of the younger Tandy and evidently kept him at arm's length. James Tandy was probably too useful to arrest given his naïve willingness to discuss his father's political correspondence to the double agent Leonard MacNally. MacNally, 6 Feb. 1799, NA, Rebellion Papers, 620/7/74/7.

27 Wickham to Castlereagh, 26 March 1799, PRO London, Home Office Papers, 100/86/198. See also McGucken, 9 Feb. 1799, NA, Rebellion Papers, 620/7/74/9.

28 Information of Thomas Wright, 1 May 1799, PRO London, Home Office Papers, 100/86/301–2.

29 [McNally], 28 Sept. 1801, NA, Rebellion Papers, 620/10/121/133.

30 'Suspect list', n.d., NA, Rebellion Papers, 620/12/217. Lawson lived at 5 College Green, near Allen and Hickson. Ibid.

31 [Higgins] to [Marsden], 18 May 1801 in Bartlett (ed.), *Higgins*, pp. 544–1.

32 Castlereagh to Wickham, 30 March 1799, PRO London, Home Office Papers, 100/86/224–6; n.d. Feb. 1799, NA, Rebellion Papers, 620/7/74/15; Wickham to Castlereagh, 7 March 1799, PRO London, Home Office Papers, 100/86/124; Wickham to Castlereagh, 8 March 1799 in Londonderry (ed.), *Castlereagh Correspondence*, II, p. 200; *Wilson's Dublin Directory . . . 1803*, p. 117.

33 'Suspect list', n.d., NA, Rebellion Papers, 620/12/217.

34 n.d. Feb. 1799, NA, Rebellion Papers, 620/7/74/22. See also 21 April 1799, NA, Rebellion Papers, 620/7/74/24.

35 See Sirr memo, n.d. in Madden, *United*, I, p. 526.

36 [McGucken], 2 Feb. 1799, NA, Rebellion Papers, 620/7/74/6. Reilly, aka O'Reilly, had been investigated by the spy Bird in 1797–98 and was closely connected through the Fingal United Irishmen to William McDermott and north Dublin rebel leaders. Bird to Sirr, n.d. 1798 in Madden, *United*, I, p. 501.

37 McGucken, 7 Feb. 1799, NA, Rebellion Papers, 620/7/74/8. See also Information of Robert Henry, 23 July 1799, NA, Rebellion Papers, 620/47/100 and Elliott, *Partners*, p. 250. Donaldson may have been Alexander Donaldson of Keady, who attended the Ulster Provincial Directory meeting in Armagh on 29 May 1798. n.d. [1798], PRO London, Home Office Papers, 100/77/144.

38 McGucken, 9 Feb. 1799, NA, Rebellion Papers, 620/7/74/9. See also Dickson, *Narrative*, p. 281.

39 Wickham to Castlereagh, 1 May 1799, PRO London, Home Office Papers, 100/86/302 and J.W. [MacNally] to Downshire, 17 April 1799, PRO Northern Ireland, D. 607/G/159.

40 Wright, 1 May 1799, PRO London, Home Office Papers, 100/86/299.

41 *Report from the Committee of Secrecy*, p. 131; Cooke to Castlereagh, 20 Dec. 1798 in *Castlereagh Correspondence*, II, pp. 49–50 and Madden, *United*, III, Appendix One.

42 See J[ohn] S[heares] to Samuel Neilson, n.d. [c. 19 May 1798], in *Report of the Committee of Secrecy*, p. 237.

43 MacNeven, 'Account of the treaty', p. 171. See also Memorial of Citizen Hervey Montmorency Morres, n.d. [1798], in Londonderry (ed.), *Castlereagh Correspondence*, II, pp. 92–6; Madden, *Hope*, pp. 18–19; M. Gormley, 'Castleplunkett', *Tulsk Parish in Historic Maigh Ai, Aspects of its history and folklore* (Tulsk, 1989), pp. 82–3; Buckingham to Grenville, 5 Sept. 1798 in Fortescue, *Fortescue*, IV, p. 301; Hayes, *The last invasion of Ireland*, pp. 208, 276, 295–6. Morres' first cousin, Esmonde Kyan of Mount Howard and Mount Pleasant, was executed in Wexford after playing a leading role in the rebellion in south Leinster, as was another cousin, Dr John Esmonde of Naas. Morres was

related through Kyan to Leinster leaders Garrett Byrne of Ballymanus, Edward Fitzgerald of Newpark, William Michael Byrne of Parkhill and Edward Hay of Enniscorthy. Madden, *United*, IV, p. 549.

44 See Ruán O'Donnell, *Aftermath, Post-Rebellion insurgency in Wicklow 1799–1803* (Dublin, 2000); Chambers, *Rebellion in Kildare*; Daniel Gahan, "The Black Mob" and "The Babes in the Wood": Wexford in the wake of the rebellion, 1798–1806', *Journal of the Wexford Historical Society*, VI (1990), pp. 92–110; Dickson, *Dwyer*.

45 Henniker to Dundas, 23 Aug. 1801, PRO London, Home Office Papers, 100/104/71. See also O'Donnell, *Aftermath*, pp. 141, 147 and Madden, *United*, III, p. 349.

46 *Parliamentary Debates*, I, 1803–1804, p. 1627.

47 O'Donnell, *Rebellion in Wicklow*, pp. 55–6, 271–2.

48 'Account of the number of persons' and *Wilson's Dublin Directory . . . 1803*, pp. 42, 44. The publicans were: Thomas Boyle of Clanturk, Michael Browne of 46 New Row, John Burke of 41 Kevin Street, Peter Coughlan of 43 Golden Lane, William Curran of Carman's Hall, Patrick Downey of 84 Bride Street, John Dungan of 39 Bolton Street, Thomas Dunne of 15 Cook Street, Patrick Ennis of 49 Thomas Court, John Fitzpatrick of 39 Robert Street, Patrick McCabe of Francis Street, Mathew Manwarring of 31 Aston Quay, William McGuinness of 57 Manor Street, Mark Molloy of Capel Street, Patrick Murray of 4 New Row, James Quinn of 18 Kevin's Port, Patrick Rooney of Kevin Street, Nicholas Stafford of 131 James's Street and Philip Sweeny of 8 George's Street. Sweeny was the only man still in the drink trade in 1803 when he was listed as a 'vintner'. *Wilson's Dublin Directory . . . 1803*, p. 98. City schoolmasters Hughes Brennan of 131 New Street, Thomas Coyne of Great Ship Street, James Murphy of 20 Abbey Street and one attorney, Patrick Cullen of 91 Camden Street, fared no better. The use of licensing as a means of control and extortion was still prevalent in 1814 when ex-rebel general Joseph Holt returned from transportation. Having received a license from a reluctant Major Sirr, Holt opened the Plough Inn on the corner of Redmond's Hill and Kevin Street. He soon relinquished the successful business: 'One vagabond set would come in and call me "a bloody croppy". Them I used to kick properly. And if I showed them I had the protection of the law because I suffered under laws of my country for being so, whether guilty or not, another gang of ruffians would come in and call me "a bloody Orange man". And I am sure many of them was bribed for doing so, to rise a mutiny in my house by my ill hearted neighbours . . . I was so tormented with those rascals I thought better to get shut of trouble at once, so I gave up public business and came to the country, for it is impossible for a publican to live in Dublin when he pays forty-six pounds and ten pence for his licence, and ten shillings for police licence, and a guinea to the Lord Mayor's office. Then he has only paid one half his expenses. There is so many of those disturbers of the peace – if you don't bribe them every week you are sure to be fined selling one pint of porter or one glass of spirits.' *Joseph Holt, A rum story, the adventures of Joseph Holt, Thirteen years in New South Wales (1800–12)* edited by Peter O'Shaughnessy (Perth, 1988), p. 146. See also 'Persons in confinement', *House of Commons*, 1805, VI, p. 445.

49 The Rathfarnham United Irishmen were: Andrew Byrne, William Carr, Bryan Clark, Timothy Colligan, Arthur Doyle, Laurence Dunn, Robert Ennis, Michael Finn, James Hart, Michael Lynch, Thomas Owens, Christopher Peppard, George Phillips, John Reynolds, Thomas Thompson. 'Account of the number of persons' and O'Donnell, *Rebellion in Wicklow*, pp. 22, 36, 50–51, 75–6, 292 and *Aftermath*, pp. 47–8, 92.

50 See O'Donnell, *Aftermath*, pp. 26–8, 222 and Buckingham to Genville, 23 Oct. 1798 in Fortescue, *Fortescue*, IV, p. 351.

51 [Higgins] to [Cooke], 2 Dec. 1799 in Bartlett (ed.), *Higgins*, p. 476.

52 Thomas Archer to Marsden, 24 March 1799, NA, Rebellion Papers, 620/49/88 and 14 Nov. 1803, PRO London, Home Office Papers, 100/114/173, and O'Donnell, *Rebellion in Wicklow*, pp. 85–8.

53 'Suspect list', n.d., NA, Rebellion Papers, 620/12/217. Daly's obituary appeared alongside that of Alderman Fleming who died the same month after 'shooting himself through the head'. *Irish Magazine*, Aug. 1809, pp. 382–3.

54 Byrne, *Memoirs*, I, p. 366. See also Information of Patrick McCabe, n.d. 1803 in Madden, *United*, I, p. 493.

55 *Annual Register*, 1803, p. 303 and *Wilson's Dublin Directory . . . 1803*, pp. 73, 92.

56 *Freeman's Journal*, 10 April and 15 Sept. 1798 and 21 Feb. 1801, and *Gentleman's and Citizen's Almanack*, p. 85. Rourke was flogged from Newgate to College Green on 9 March 1801 for paying 16 shillings per dozen bottles of stolen wine. *Freeman's Journal*, 10 March 1801.

57 *Freeman's Journal*, 9 Oct. 1798.

58 Brien to Marsden, n.d. 1804, NA, State of the Country Papers, 1030/38.

59 For Gray see David Goodall, 'A divided family in 1798: The Grays of Whitefort and Jamestown' in *Journal of the Wexford Historical Society*, no. 15, 1994–5, pp. 52–66. Gray was discharged at the 1799 Lent assizes in Wexford due to a *nolle prosequi*. Ibid., p. 57. Doorley stayed with a relative who ran a 'huxter shop' in Meath Street and one Dunne of Thomas Court, a notorious United Irishman. Information of Boyle, n.d., quoted in Peadar Mac Suibhne, *Kildare in 1798* (Naas, 1978), p. 226.

60 Byrne, *Memoirs*; Thomas Archer to Marsden, 24 March 1799, NA, Rebellion Papers, 620/49/88; *Freeman's Journal*, 19 Oct. 1799.

61 Castlereagh to Wickham, 16 April 1799, PRO London, Home Office Papers, 100/86/375.

62 Madden, *United*, IV, p. 555. Perry, a native of Down, had been re-sworn as a United Irishman in Mathew Dowling's Dublin home in early 1797. Perry then availed of the services of William Putnam McCabe and Mathew Doyle of Polahoney (Arklow) to spread the military format in north Wexford. He was captured and executed by King's County loyalists on 21 July 1798 after the expedition to Kildare and Meath. O'Donnell, *Rebellion in Wicklow*, pp. 61–2, 283.

63 O'Donnell, *Aftermath*, pp. 41–4.

64 25 Sept. 1801, NA, Rebellion Papers, 620/49/133; n.d. [1799], TCD, Sirr Papers, MS 869/8, fo. 47; Sir Henry McAnally, *The Irish Militia, 1793–1816, a social and military study* (Dublin, 1949), p. 204; *Freeman's Journal*, 31 May 1798. Maguaran allegedly gave either Sirr or Major Sandys a house in Tallaght to secure his release from the Provost prison. See Madden, *United*, I, p. 472 and *Wilson's Dublin Directory . . . 1803*, p. 73.

65 Byrne, *Memoirs*, I, p. 326. See also ibid., pp. 322–8.

66 2 April 1799, NA, Rebellion Papers, 620/5/6/5 and Dickson, *Dwyer*, p. 326.

67 Petition of Francois Joseph, 29 June 1799 quoted in Dickson, *Dwyer*, p. 377.

68 O'Donnell, *Aftermath*, pp. 40, 50.

69 'Suspect list', n.d., NA, Rebellion Papers, 620/12/217.

70 Byrne, *Memoirs*, I, pp. 329–30; *Wilson's Dublin Directory . . . 1794*, p. 72; O'Donnell, *Aftermath*, pp. 39–40, 138; [Higgins] to [Marsden], 24 June 1801 in Bartlett (ed.), *Higgins*, pp. 564–5.

71 See 'Suspect list', n.d., NA, Rebellion Papers, 620/12/217.

72 Higgins to Marsden, 22 Oct. 1801 in Bartlett (ed.), *Higgins*, pp. 568–9. In 1803 Nihills distillery was at 20 Great Strand Street, Edwards' at 148 James's Street, Hinchey's at 37 Queen Street and Halpin and Hannan operated in Petticoat Lane. *Wilson's Dublin Directory . . . 1803*, pp. 43, 54, 81. For Lawless see ibid., p. 67 and 'Suspect list', n.d., NA, Rebellion Papers, 620/12/217.

73 O'Donnell, *Aftermath*, ch. 1 and Carysfort to Grenville, 23 Jan. 1799 in Fortescue, *Fortescue*, IV, p. 449.

74 See Marcus Cleark [Daniel Cullinane] to Dwyer, c. 15 June 1801 quoted in Dickson, *Dwyer*, pp. 355–6. See also Chambers, *Rebellion in Kildare*, p. 110 and O'Donnell, *Aftermath*, pp. 106–8.

75 William Kirby to Castlereagh, 12 Jan. 1799, PRO London, Home Office Papers, 100/85/95; *Freeman's Journal*, 2 June 1801; *Observer*, 6 Feb. 1803.

76 Cornwallis to Portland, 16 Jan. 1799, PRO London, Home Office Papers, 100/85/87. See also Thomas Judkin Fitzgerald to Castlereagh, 18 Jan. 1799, NA, State of the Country Papers, 1018/22.

77 Robert Johnson to Downshire, 14 Feb. 1799, PRO Northern Ireland, D. 607/G/67.

78 Information of James Taaffe quoted in Kieran Sheedy, *The United Irishmen of County Clare* (Ennis, 1998), p. 53. See also ibid., pp. 38–40; *Hibernian Journal*, 26 Dec. 1798; Revd Edward Hudson to Charlemont, 30 Nov. 1798 in Charlemont, *The manuscripts and correspondence of James, First Earl of Charlemont*, 2 vols (London, 1891–94), II, pp. 340–41; PRO London, Home Office Papers, 100/86/272; *Finn's Leinster Journal*, 19 Sept. 1798. For Clare rebels at Vinegar Hill (Wexford) see Ignatius Murphy, *The Diocese of Killaloe in the Eighteenth Century* (Dublin, 1991), pp. 238–9.

79 William Crosbie to Duke [of Montrose], 25 Dec. 1798 in Fortescue, *Fortescue*, IV, p. 424.

80 J. C. Beresford to Castlereagh, 19 Dec. 1798 in Londonderry (ed.), *Castlereagh Correspondence*, II, p. 51.

81 McGucken, 7 Feb. 1799, NA, Rebellion Papers, 620/7/74/8.

82 Adjutant General George Hewitt to Major-General John Moore, 20 Feb. 1799, PRO London, Home Office Papers, 100/85/261. See also Robert Johnson to Downshire, 14 Feb. 1799, PRO Northern Ireland, D. 607/G/67; Cornwallis to Portland, 9 Feb. 1799, PRO London, Home Office Papers, 100/85/237–8; Pelham to Sheffield, 10 Mar. 1799 in Malcomson (ed.), *Anglo-Irish dialogue*, p. 74. For Crowe's activities in 1797–98 see Murphy, *Diocese of Killaloe*, pp. 238–41.

83 Cornwallis to Portland, 23 Feb. 1799 in Ross (ed.), *Cornwallis Correspondence*, III, p. 66.

84 Diary of Judge Robert Day, 5 Mar. 1799, Royal Irish Academy (RIA), MS 12. W. 11, p. 65.

85 Cornwallis to Portland, 14 Feb. 1799, PRO London, Home Office Papers, 100/85/235.

86 Addis Emmet, 'Part of an essay', pp. 14–15.

87 Buckingham to Grenville, 11 Mar. 1798 in Fortescue, *Fortescue*, IV, p. 497. See also [Emmet] to McGucken, n.d. [March 1799] in Landreth, *Pursuit*, p. 108.

88 Wickham to Castlereagh, 28 Feb. 1799, PRO London, Home Office Papers, 100/85/281. General Gerard Lake toured the south of Ireland in April/May 1799 and reported that 'the disposition of the people is not good. They are ready to rise should the French land . . . they will not shew [sic] unless the enemy arrive and make a successful stand in arms in any part of the Kingdom.' Lake to Cornwallis, 3 June 1799, PRO London, Home Office Papers, 100/89/55.

89 Memorial of Dennis O'Neill, 30 Jan. 1799 in Londonderry (ed.), *Castlereagh Correspondence*, II, p. 234. See also [MacNally] to D[ownshire], 17 April 1799, PRO Northern Ireland, D. 607/G/159.

90 Quoted in James Mitchell, 'The prisons of Galway: Background to the Inspector General's reports, 1796–1818', *Journal of the Galway Archaeological and Historical Society*, 49, 1997, p. 8.

91 See Feb. to June 1799, NA, Rebellion Papers, 620/7/78/9.

92 Herbert Webb Gilman, 'Muskerry Yeomanry, Co. Cork, and their times, part one, 1796–1799', *Journal of the Cork Historical and Archaeological Society*, second series, II, 17, May 1896, p. 208. The crackdown netted 'Captain Thunderbolt' (John Duggan) and 'Captain Slasher'. Ibid, pp. 206–8.

93 Lieutenant General James Rooke to Anon., 23 Mar. 1799, PRO London, Home Office Papers, 100/66/421; Shannon to Boyle, 26 Mar. 1799 in Hewitt (ed.), *Letters*, p. 183; McDowell (ed.), *Proceedings*, p. 90; Elliott, *Partners*, pp. 254–5.

94 Wickham to Castlereagh, 7 and 23 Mar. 1799, PRO London, Home Office Papers, 100/86/124, 179.

95 Castlereagh to Wickham, 2 Apr. 1799, PRO London, Home Office Papers, 100/86/242.

96 McGucken, 2 Feb. 1799, NA, Rebellion Papers, 620/7/74/6.

97 Report of Major-General Nugent, 10 May 1799, PRO London, Home Office Papers, 100/88/340. See also J. G. Patterson, 'Continued Presbyterian Resistance in the Aftermath of the Rebellion of 1798 in Antrim and Down', *Eighteenth-century life*, XXII, (1998), pp. 45–61 and O'Donnell, *Aftermath*, pp. 51–2.

98 [Robert Emmet] to James McGucken, n.d. [Mar. 1799], quoted in Landreth, *Pursuit*, p. 108.

99 McGucken, 11 Feb. 1799, NA, Rebellion Papers, 620/7/74/11. The warrants were signed by Castlereagh and addressed to Major Sirr. Madden, *United*, I, p. 525 and Castlereagh to Sirr, 3 April 1799, TCD, Sirr MS, 869/6, fo. 10.

100 McGucken, 21 April 1799, NA, Rebellion Papers, 620/7/74/24.

101 Castlereagh to Wickham, 30 Mar. 1799, PRO London, Home Office Papers, 100/86/224–6; [MacNally] to Downshire, 2 May 1799, PRO Northern Ireland, D. 607/G/170A; Emmet, *Memoir*, II, p. 31; Ó Broin, *Unfortunate*, pp. 31, 39; Drennan to Ann Drennan, 1 May 1799 in Agnew (ed.), *Drennan-McTier Letters*, II, p. 495. MacNally was surprised at Lawson's arrest and clearly had no idea of his political activity. Castlereagh claimed that one of the Sheares brothers had named Lawson as a United Irish leader in or before July 1798. Castlereagh to Wickham, 6 May 1799, PRO London, Home Office Papers, 10/86/325. A Castle list headed 'Private Papers' may concern documents recovered during the 1799 crackdown. It contains references to 'Mr Emmet', Doyle, Maguire, Lawson, Dixon, Moore of Thomas Street, Verschoyle, O'Hara, Cummins, Quinn and others bearing the surnames of post-Rebellion United Irishmen. n.d., NA, Rebellion Papers, 620/12/148/18.

102 Information of Thomas Wright, 1 May 1799, PRO London, Home Office Papers, 100/86/301. See also Ó Broin, *Unfortunate*, pp. 40–41 and Pollock to [Cooke?], 28 April 1799, NA, Rebellion Papers, 620/7/74/27.

103 McGucken, 3 May 1799, NA, Rebellion Papers, 620/7/74/30.

104 Information of Thomas Wright, 1 May 1799, PRO London, Home Office Papers, 100/86/301. See also Wickham to Castlereagh, 1 May 1799, PRO London, Home Office Papers, 100/86/302 and Landreth, *Pursuit*, pp. 109–10.

105 'Belfast' [McGucken] to Anon., 24 Sept. 1800, NA, Rebellion Papers, 620/49/54. See also [McGucken] to Marsden, 4 June 1803 in MacDonagh (ed.), *Viceroy's post bag*, p. 275; Smith to Anon., 15 May 1797, NA, Rebellion Papers, 620/30/80; McGucken, 31 May 1803, British Library (BL), Hardwicke Papers, MS 35739/131; 2 July 1803, BL, Hardwicke Papers, MS 35740/14.

106 Madden, *United*, II, pp. 581–3 and Castlereagh to Wickham, 22 Oct. 1798, PRO London, Home Office Papers, 100/79/57.

107 King to Portland, 13 Sept. 1798, PRO London, Home Office Papers, 100/79/328. See also Cooke to Castlereagh, 11 Dec. 1798 and Wickham to Castlereagh, 10 Jan. 1799 in Londonderry (ed.), *Castlereagh Correspondence*, II, pp. 40–1, 86–7 and Martin Burke, 'Piecing together a shattered past: the historical writings of the United Irish exiles in America' in Dickson, Keogh and Whelan (eds), *United Irishmen*, p. 303.

108 Richard Annesley to Downshire, 19 Mar. 1799, PRO Northern Ireland, D. 607/G/127. See also Cornwallis to Portland, 12 Nov. 1798, PRO London, Home Office Papers, 100/82/277; 6 March 1799, PRO London, Home Office Papers, 100/88/175; Dickson, *Revolt in the North*, p. 187.

109 Dr Robert Emmet to Anon., 12 Feb. 1799 in Ó Broin, *Unfortunate*, p. 36.

110 Addis Emmet to Cornwallis, 18 March 1799, NA, Rebellion Papers, 620/15/2/17.

111 Madden, *United*, III, p. 91.

112 Dickson, *Narrative*, pp. 106–7.

113 Alexander Marsden to Castlereagh, 11 Dec. 1798, PRO London, Home Office Papers,100/82/328; 25 Dec. 1798, PRO London, Home Office Papers, 100/82/333; Elliott, *Partners*, pp. 278–80; Carroll, *Russell*, pp. 153–4; Emmet, *Memoir*, I, p. 273.

114 Drennan to McTier, 8 June 1799 in Agnew (ed.), *Drennan-McTier Letters*, II, p. 512.

115 Drennan to McTier, 24 June 1799 in ibid., p. 514.

116 McTier to Drennan, 11 Mar. 1800 in ibid., p. 583.

117 Cornwallis to Portland, 4 Mar. 1799, PRO London, Home Office Papers, 100/86/19. See also 25 Mar. 1799, PRO London, Home Office Papers, 100/86/195; 25 Mar. 1799, PRO London, Home Office Papers, 100/86/228; 31 Mar. 1799, PRO London, Home Office Papers, 100/86/239; Information of Joseph Holt, 27 Feb. 1799 in Ross (ed.), *Cornwallis Correspondence*, II, pp. 186–7.

118 See E. H. Jones, 'Mutiny in Bantry Bay', *Irish Sword*, I, 3, 1951–2, pp. 202–9; Nicholas Tracy (ed.), *The Naval Chronicle, the contemporary record of the Royal Navy at war, volume II, 1799–1804* (London, 1998), pp. 35–6; Evan Nepean to Castlereagh, 1 May 1799 in Londonderry (ed.), *Castlereagh Correspondence*, II, p. 295.

119 Buckingham to Grenville, 11 Mar. 1798 in Fortescue, *Fortescue*, IV, p. 497.

120 Examination of Samuel Hume, 26 Jan. 1800 in Fitzpatrick, *Sham Squire*, p. 345.

121 Hudson to Charlemont, 8 April 1799 in Charlemont, *The manuscripts and correspondence of James, First Earl of Charlemont*, 2 vols (London, 1891–4), II, pp. 348–9. See also Hudson to Charlemont, 22 Mar. 1799 in ibid., p. 347.

122 Castlereagh to Portland, 29 June 1799, PRO London, Home Office Papers, 100/87/31. See also Nugent, 10 May 1799, PRO London, Home Office Papers, 100/88/340 and Wickham to Castlereagh, 26 May 1799, PRO London, Home Office Papers, 100/86/434.

123 See O'Donnell, 'Marked for Botany Bay' and McDowell, *Imperialism and Revolution*, pp. 667–8.

124 Price Journal, 8 Oct. 1799, BL, MS 13,880, p. 45; 8 Oct. 1799, Londonderry (ed.), *Castlereagh Correspondence*, II, pp. 417–18; Wickham to Cooke, 5 Sept. 1799, PRO London, Home Office Papers, 100/89/177; John Mannion, 'Transatlantic disaffection: Wexford and Newfoundland, 1798–1800', *Journal of the Wexford Historical Society* (1998–99), p. 56.

125 Report of Major-General Trench, 30 Mar. 1799, PRO London, Home Office Papers, 100/86/248. See also McGucken, 2 Feb. 1799, NA, Rebellion Papers, 620/7/74/6.

126 Sheila Molloy, 'General James Joseph MacDonnell (1763–1848)', *Co. Roscommon Historical and Archaeological Society Journal*, pp. 73–6 and Hayes, *The last invasion of Ireland*, pp. 277–8. Emmet's associates looked to Francis Blake to lead 4,000 Connacht men when the French landed. He stayed at 118 Capel Street when in Dublin but hailed from the Galway/Mayo border. McGucken, 3 Jan. 1799, NA, Rebellion Papers, 620/7/74/2.

127 See Anon., n.d., TCD, Sirr Papers, MS 869/8, fo. 92 and Anon., n.d., TCD, Sirr Paper, MS 869/8, fo. 153. The Cherry Tree was owned by Patrick Power who had been denounced as a United Irishman by Higgins in June 1798. Power's brother John, a publican at 109 Thomas Street, was subsequently knighted and founded Power's Distillers. See Bartlett (ed.), *Higgins*, pp. 440–41.

128 See O'Donnell, *Aftermath*, pp. 16–18, 41–6 and John Caldwell senior, Nov. 1798, PRO Northern Ireland, T/3541/6/2. The apprehension of Genoud cost £234 by 31 Jan. 1801 and Dwyer's bounty was never paid. *An account of the expenditure of the different sums granted for apprehending public offenders in Ireland* in House of Commons, 1805, VI, p. 499.

129 Littlehales to Castlereagh, 29 Oct. 1799 in Londonderry (ed.), *Castlereagh Correspondence*, II, p. 437. See also Marsden to Castlereagh, 28 Sept. 1798 in ibid., p. 407.

130 11 Oct. 1799, NA, Rebellion Papers, 620/6/19/13 and Ruan O'Donnell, 'Philip Cunningham: Clonmel's insurgent leader of 1798', *Tipperary Historical Journal* (1998), pp. 150–7.

131 T. F. Culhane, 'Traditions of Glin and its neighbourhood', *Journal of the Kerry Archaeology and History Society* (1969), pp. 74–101 and Madden, *Hope*, 29.

132 John Bagwell to Anon., 7 Sept. 1799, PRO London, Home Office Papers, 100/89/187. See also John King to Anon., 7 Sept. 1799, PRO London, Home Office Papers, 100/89/185 and Lake to Anon., 14 Sept. 1799, PRO London, Home Office Papers, 100/89/214.

133 'Information', n.d. [Sept. 1799] in Londonderry (ed.), *Castlereagh Correspondence*, II, p. 395. See also Cooke to Castlereagh, 18 Sept. 1799 in ibid., p. 403; Thomas Lane to Downshire, 12 Oct. 1799, PRO Northern Ireland, D. 607/G/200; *Freeman's Journal*, 9 Nov. 1799; Allan Marsden to Alexander Marsden, 16 Oct. 1799, NA, State of the Country Papers, 1018/34.

CHAPTER FIVE

1 *Hibernian Telegraph*, 24 Jan. 1800. See also ibid., 30 Jan. and *Saunder's Newsletter*, 2 and 6 Jan. 1800.

2 Castlereagh to John King, 8 Jan. 1800, PRO London, Home Office Papers, 100/93/3 and [McGucken] to Cooke, 9 Mar. 1800, NA, Rebellion Papers, 620/49/11.

3 General Sir James Duff to Lake, 14 Mar. 1800, PRO London, Home Office Papers, 100/93/206. See also Information of Thomas P[. . .], 14 Mar. 1800, PRO London, Home Office Papers, 100/93/204 and *Saunder's Newsletter*, 19 March 1800. Limerick man James Kennedy was given '500 lashes & Transportation for life' for 'tendering oaths & whip[pin]g people' on 19 April 1800, while in Tipperary Maurice Cuddihey was sentenced to seven years transportation in Clonmel on 17 May 1800 for 'delivering a threatening letter'. Kilmainham Papers, NLI, MS 1198.

4 Cornwallis to Portland, 17 Mar. 1800, PRO London, Home Office Papers, 100/93/188. See also *Saunder's Newsletter*, 23 May 1800.

5 Mrs Leslie to Mrs Stewart, 22 Mar. 1800, PRO Northern Ireland, D.3167/3/C/1. The Ballymena courts martial convened by General Drummond

were amongst the most severe in Ireland between 1798 and 1803. On 10 February 1800 Alexander Stewart was sentenced to 'death & [to be] buryed [sic] und[er the] Gall[ow]s' for robbery of firearms, while William Stewart, almost certainly a relation, was transported for life arising from his conviction on the 21st for being a 'rebel'. Stewart's co-defendant, John Martin, was then ordered to endure 200 lashes for 'perjury', i.e. refusing to repeat on oath in court information which he had previously given in a deposition. The same punishment was inflicted on James Moore on 3 March for 'reb[ellio]n & consp[irac]y to murd[er]' and also upon Thomas Sloan for being a United Irishman. Mere 'treas[onabl]e express[ion]s' earned John Sheils a sentence of general service abroad (conscription into a regiment posted overseas) on the 4th. He was fortunate in comparison to Samuel Ballantine who was capitally convicted that day for the same charge as Moore. The notorious Thomas Archer was tried on 5 March at which time his alias was erroneously given as 'Gen[era]l Holt', the *nom de guerre* used by Dickey/Dickson who led a different Antrim faction. Charged with 'murder', Archer was sentenced to 'death, dissection and [the] gibbet'. Mathew Boyd was also condemned on the 5th for being a 'rebel & admin[istrin]g [illegal] oaths'. Dennis Murphy had the misfortune to appear in Ballymena on 6 March to answer allegations of prosecuting rebellion and robbery but escaped with a sentence of general service from the panel which hanged Samuel Dunlop for identical crimes on the same day. Two days later William Scullion and Thomas Stewart received capital convictions for being 'rebel[s] in arms' and Alexander Sheerer was transported for life along with Hugh Dowdle, another perjury offender. United Irishman William McCann was sentenced to general service on 10 March bringing to an end the first batch of Drummond's trials. They recommenced on 9 April when James Griffin was sentenced to death for being a 'rebel' while John McConnell and Hugh McErlane were earmarked for 'flogging' and transportation for life. On the following day Arthur Lavery, an alleged 'rebel . . . endeav[ourin]g to overt[hro]w Gov[ernmen]t', received sentence of '500 lashes and transport[atio]n' but the corporal punishment was remitted upon review. Neil McCarry was transported on the 21st for being a 'rebel' and 'drink[in]g Treas[onable] Toasts', while rebellion and robbery were deemed to warrant death for Samuel Hume (aka Humes) on the 22nd. Drummond agreed to commute Hume's sentence four days later and he was transported to New South Wales where he acted as joint leader of the most serious convict revolt in Australian history in March 1804. Archer and Hume were men of stature within the Ulster United Irishmen, as was the lesser known William Craig, 'a rebel colonel', sentenced to death in Ballymena on 4 July 1800. The military proved at Ballymena in the spring and summer of 1800 that the special treatment meted out to Presbyterian republicans by General Nugent in 1798 was a thing of the past. Kilmainham Papers, NLI, MSS 1197–8.

6 John Devereux, a Wexford 'rebel leader' in 1798, was sentenced to seven years transportation by a Cork court martial on 27 November 1799. Kilmainham Papers, NLI, MS 1197. Devereux was not active in 1799 unlike fellow insurgent officers John Morris and Patrick McHale. Morris was ordered by a Wexford town panel on 5 July 1800 to be transported for life for being a 'Rebel capt[ai]n & aid[in]g murder' and McHale's Castlebar court martial on 29 December 1799 specified 'service for life' for being a 'Rebel leader levy[in]g money' in Mayo. If the sentence was not commuted or set aside upon review, those destined for military service were generally sent to either the Isle of Wight or Chatham Barracks, London for induction. Those sentenced to transportation were held in Irish military depots such as New Geneva Barracks, Waterford, where the Inspector General of Recruits frequently conscripted men who would otherwise

be sent to New South Wales. Ibid., MS 1198. See also O'Donnell, 'Marked for
   Botany Bay', Chapter Seven.
7 Steele to Marsden, 18 Sept. 1800, NA, Rebellion Papers, 620/49/59.
8 28 Jan. 1801, NA, Rebellion Papers, 620/10/113/2.
9 Madden, *United*, III, p. 341.
10 Drennan to McTier, 8 July 1800 in Agnew (ed.), *Drennan-McTier Letters*,
   pp. 609–10. See also Drennan to McTier, n.d. [c. Mar. 1800], in ibid., II, p. 585.
11 [MacNally], 17 Sept. 1800, NA, Rebellion Papers, 620/10/121/128. Higgins also
   attempted to locate Carolan and his contacts in Dublin. These allegedly included
   Bernard Coile. See [Higgins] to [Marsden], 12 Sept. 1800 in Bartlett (ed.),
   Higgins, pp. 495–6. A John Carolan of Carrickmacross, Monaghan, an apothecary, had joined the United Irishmen in late 1792. He was evidently a relation of
   the 1800 emissary and joined at the same session as Robert Emmet's Dublin and
   Paris associate Hampden Evans. McDowell (ed.), *Proceedings*, p. 55.
12 [Higgins] to [Marsden], 29 Sept. 1800, NA, Rebellion Papers, 620/18/14. Cox
   was named as part of a group which met in Eades Tavern in Hoey's Court, in
   May 1801. Another participant, Thomas Wilkinson, was a printer and publisher
   at 30 Winetavern Street. [Higgins] to [Marsden?] in Bartlett (ed.), *Higgins*,
   p. 555. See also 'Suspect list', n.d., NA, Rebellion Papers, 620/12/217.
13 [Higgins] to [Marsden], 18 May 1801 in Bartlett (ed.), *Higgins*, pp. 544–5.
   Higgins claimed the Dubliners sent Mrs Sharkey to London with £172 for their
   'brethren suffering in the cause' and corresponded with allies in Manchester and
   Edinburgh. Troy of Trinity Street was also named, a clerk and seller of the
   Dublin Evening Post who was one of the first men arrested in the aftermath of
   the Rising of 1803. Ibid.
14 Emmet/Delaney Memorial, 15 Sept. 1800, Archives des Affaires Étrangères, Vol.
   593, ff 288–9, translated by S. Kleinman.
15 Thomas Addis Emmet to Lord Hope, 14 Dec. 1801 cited in Madden, *United*,
   III, p. 289. See also ibid., III, p. 33 and Emmet, *Memoir*, I, p. 273.
16 Mrs Emmet to Thomas Addis Emmet, 14 July 1800 in Madden, *Robert Emmet*,
   p. 9. See also Emmet, *Memoir*, I, p. 274.
17 Drennan to McTier, 4 June 1800 in Agnew (ed.), *Drennan-McTier Letters*, II,
   p. 599; Madden, *Literary remains*, p. 284; Emmet, *Memoir*, I, pp. 282–310,
   327. Russell wrote to his brother about the 'delightful' Emmet family. Thomas
   Russell to John Russell, 10 Dec. 1803 in Madden, *United*, IV, pp. 85–6.
18 Dickson had sight of Home Office instructions sent to the Governor of Fort
   George. Portland described Jane Emmet has 'having imbibed' the principles. The
   report stated: 'she shall not be the means of communication between him
   [Thomas Addis Emmet] and the disaffected in Ireland. She is only to see him in
   the presence of a proper person, and you are to take such steps as that she may
   not carry any letters or papers in or out of the fort.' Dickson, *Narrative*, p. 140.
   See also ibid., pp. 156–7.
19 Madden, *United*, III, p. 288. A Dublin United Irishman named McCormick was
   arrested in High Street in early August 1800 and found to be in possession of a
   green ribbon 'which had a device wrought upon it two hands fraternally united
   by a grip which, he said, was the badge of a new (it is supposed Erin-go-Bragh)
   order'. *Freeman's Journal*, 12 Aug. 1800.
20 Madden, *Robert Emmet*, p. 8. See also Wickham Report, 5 Dec. 1803, BL,
   Hardwicke Papers, MS 35740/202; Emmet, *Memoir*, II, p. 23; Ó Broin,
   Unfortunate, pp. 41–2.
21 2 Oct. 1803, NA, Rebellion Papers, 620/11/130/43.
22 Quoted in William John Fitzpatrick, *The Secret Service under Pitt* (London,
   1892), 2nd edn, p. 193. See also Emmet, *Memoir*, II, p. 25; Elliott, *Partners*,

pp. 272–5; Weber, *Road to Rebellion*, pp. 150–3; 25 Nov. 1803, NA, Rebellion Papers, 620/12/142/14.

23 2 Oct. 1803, NA, Rebellion Papers, 620/11/130/43. John Palmer junior died in strange circumstances in Holland having unmasked one Bureand in Hamburg as a British spy. Palmer evidently ran foul of another agent, Turner, and was obliged through poverty to enlist in the Dutch army, which was then allied to France. He reputedly drowned in the Scheldt when bathing with other recruits. See Newsinger (ed.), *James Hope*, p. 68. Hope, who knew Palmer, recalled that his christian name was John, although he has also been referred to as George. See Elliott, *Partners*, p. 248.

24 31 Aug. 1803, NA, Rebellion Papers, 620/11/130/26. This source claimed: 'Malachy Delaney & Robert Emmett [sic] arrived in Hamburg the former as Embassador [sic] from a then existing Executive here the latter as his Secretary . . . [General Augureau] considered the mission of so much consequence as to induce him to quit his command and escort them to Paris where he introduced them to the first Consul. Several conferences took place between the First Consul & the Ambassador and several memorials were prepared by E[mmet] drawn up in the usual language of the [United Irish] party . . . The Executive here [in Dublin] had proposed to supply D[elaney] with the annual salary of 150 pounds as Embassador [sic] to the Court of France.' Ibid. Elements of the Dublin United Irishmen were informed in May 1801 that 'an army of 130,000' was massed 'on the shores of France' to campaign in Ireland, Guernsey, Jersey and Cornwall. [Higgins] to [Marsden], 18 May 1801, NA, Rebellion Papers, 620/18/14.

25 Emmet/Delaney Memorial, 15 Sept. 1800, AAE, 593, ff 288–9, translated by S. Kleinman.

26 Anon. to Swan, n.d. [late 1803], NA, Rebellion Papers, 620/64/121. Cox claimed: 'M'Nevin [sic] assured him in Kilmainham that Tallyrand had sold the country (the Irish Union) to Mr Pitt for the Lord Chancellor [Clare] had read to him a paper which he had himself delivered into the hand of the French minister and he suspected Tallyrand of treachery, from the character he had heard of him.' Ibid.

27 Elliott, *Partners*, pp. 276–7 and Weber, *Road to Rebellion*, pp. 151–3.

28 [Higgins] to [Cooke], 4 Mar. 1801, NA, Rebellion Papers, 620/10/118/9.

29 Robert Emmet to Marquise de Fontenay, 19 Dec. 1801 quoted in Emmet, *Memoir*, II, p. 27.

30 Thomas Addis Emmet to MacNeven, n.d. [early Oct. 1802], in Madden, *Robert Emmet*, pp. 20–1. See also ibid., pp. 12–13.

31 Emmet, *Memoir*, II, p. 26. Emmet's departure from Paris led some to believe that he was headed for Belfast. [Higgins], 4 Mar. 1801, NA, Rebellion Papers, 620/10/118/9.

32 31 Aug. 1803, NA, Rebellion Papers, 620/11/130/26. Gallagher reputedly had 'very great intimacy with E[mmet]'. Ibid. See also Madden, *Robert Emmet*, p. 23; William Ridgeway, *A report of the trial of Robert Emmet, upon an indictment for high treason* (Dublin, 1803), p. 61; John Hennig, 'Note on Robert Emmet's military studies', *Irish Sword*, I, no. 2, 1950–51, pp. 148–50.

33 Emmet to De Fontenay, 19 Dec. 1801 in Emmet, *Memoir*, II, p. 27. See also Robert Hunter, 5 Nov. 1801 in MacDonagh (ed.), *Viceroy's post bag*, p. 259. A suspected informer named Burke, once a tailor in Rosemary Lane, Dublin, came to Paris from Hamburg in Dec. 1801. He was regarded as 'maniacal', being 'grossly ignorant & of no address'. 31 Aug. 1803, NA, Rebellion Papers, 620/11/130/26.

34 [Higgins] to [Marsden], 15 Nov. 1801 in Bartlett (ed.), *Higgins*, p. 579.

35 The ballad was 'Green on my cape', forerunner to 'The Wearing of the Green' in which the Emmet character is replaced by Napper Tandy. The original

Dundalk line was 'In Brest I met E—T'. It was apparently written by James
Garland of Lurgan, Armagh, a much persecuted ballad singer and probable
United Irishman. See Zimmerman, *Songs of Irish Rebellion*, pp. 20, 167–8.

36   Emmet to De Fontenay, 19 Dec. 1801 in Emmet, *Memoir*, II, p. 27. See also
Irish Magazine, Feb. 1809, p. 85.

37   Madden, *United*, III, p. 345 and Ó Broin, *Unfortunate*, p. 179. Fulton returned
to America in 1806 and in August 1807 launched the *Clermont* on New York's
Hudson River, thereby inaugurating the world's first steamboat service. See
Norman Longmate, *Island Fortress, The defence of Great Britain 1603–1945*
(London, 1993), pp. 265–6. For Fitzgerald and rocketry see Hamilton, *Impartial
Enquiry*, p. 7.

38   Quoted in Emmet, *Memoir*, II, p. 7. See also *Irish Book Lover*, XI, March 1920,
p. 85 and Landreth, *Pursuit*, pp. 118–20.

39   *Annual Register*, 1803, p. 434.

40   Emmet to De Fontenay, 24 April 1802 in Emmet, *Memoir*, II, p. 27. Valentine
Lawless reputedly chaired a meeting of United Irishmen at the Temple in which
an address to Lord Moira was proposed by him and seconded by Robert
Emmet's friend Richard Curran. [MacNally], n.d. [1798], NA, Rebellion Papers,
620/10/121/150.

41   Wickham to John King, 18 Oct. 1803, PRO London, Home Office Papers,
100/114/85.

42   Emmet to De Fontenay, 24 April 1802 in Emmet, *Memoir*, II, p. 27. See also
Hugh Ware to his father, 3 Dec. 1802, BL, Hardwicke Papers, MS 35737/127;
Wilson's Dublin Directory . . . 1794, p. 139; Byrne, *Memoirs*, III, p. 33. A spy
claimed that 'there was in Paris a low young man of the name of [Edward]
Carolan particularly intimate with Emmet'. 6 Oct. 1803, NA, Rebellion Papers,
620/11/130/45. He was the United Irish emissary who in February 1801,
according to British sources in Hamburg, was 'shortly to return to the continent
from Ireland by way of England'. Sir James Crauford to Anon., 17 Feb. 1801,
PRO London, Home Office Papers, 100/100/132.

43   30 Nov. 1803, NA, Rebellion Papers, 620/11/130/60.

44   3 Sept. 1803, NA, Rebellion Papers, 620/11/130/30.

45   Castlereagh notes, Aug. 1798 in Londonderry (ed.), *Castlereagh Correspondence*,
I, p. 326.

46   31 Aug. 1801, NA, Rebellion Papers, 620/11/130/26. See also 3 Sept. 1803, NA,
Rebellion Papers, 620/11/130/32. Bolton, like 'Jones', had moved from Dublin
to England, Hamburg and Paris but had not attended Trinity or taken part in
the *Anacreon* expedition in Sept. 1798. Michael Farrell, in common with 'Jones',
had been arrested in England in 1800, released to the Continent and was later
in the British army. Farrell, however, had been expelled from Trinity and was not
on the *Anacreon*. It is unlikely, therefore, that either Bolton or Farrell could be
'Jones', although their information may be contained in his reports. William
Corbett had been in Trinity and was on the *Anacreon* but did not join the British
military. See Wickham to King, 3 Nov. 1803, PRO London, Home Office
Papers, 100/114/151.

47   Sadlier (ed.), *Irish Peer*, pp. 41, 48–9, 56, 70. For Egan see also Walsh, *Ireland
sixty years ago*, pp. 158–9.

48   Quoted in Sadlier (ed.), *Irish Peer*, p. 41.

49   Catherine Wilmot, *An Irish Peer on the Continent, 1801–1803* (London, 1923)
cited in Ó Broin, *Unfortunate*, p. 48. See also 31 Aug. 1803, NA, Rebellion
Papers, 620/11/130/26.

50   This was the view of the informer 'F', who had known Temple and Addis
Emmet. He was in Paris in 1801–2 and sent a letter concerning Robert Emmet

to the Castle the following year marked 'Secret information [James or Abraham?] Fullar'. 2 Oct. 1803, NA, Rebellion Papers, 620/11/130/43.

51 Louisa Penrose was the daughter of Robert Uniacke Fitzgerald, MP for Cork. The Mount Cashells departed for Italy on 15 Sept. 1802 but left the children at Nîmes in the care of Egan, where he was detained as a subject of an enemy power on the outbreak of war. Sadlier (ed.), *Irish Peer*, pp. 70, 78. Lady Moira deemed Egan a 'vulgar & absurd' man with 'conceited airs'. Moira to Scully, 15 Feb. 1803 in MacDermot (ed.), *Papers of Denys Scully*, p. 63. See also ibid., pp. 64–5. Philip Long, when questioned in captivity by Lord Redesdale, denied being acquainted 'with any man of the name of Egan'. Redesdale, therefore, suspected that Egan had access to the Emmet/Long circle or wished to convey that message to his uncooperative prisoner. Long, 18 Aug. 1803, NA, Rebellion Papers, 620/11/138/4.

52 Emmet to De Fontenay, 24 April 1802 in Emmet, *Memoir*, II, p. 27.

53 Ibid. See also Macartney to Hardwicke, 3 July 1802, BL, Hardwicke Papers, MS 35735/96.

54 'List of prisoners remaining in the New Jail [Cork]', 29 Oct. 1803, NA, Rebellion Papers, 620/12/142/9.

55 Thomas Addis Emmet, Arthur O'Connor and William MacNeven, *Memoire, or detailed statement of the origin and progress of the Irish Union: delivered to the Government . . . before the Secret Committee of the Houses of Lords and Commons, in the summer of 1798* (London, 1802).

56 Thomas Addis Emmet to MacNeven, n.d. [early Oct. 1802], in Madden, *Robert Emmet*, pp. 20–22, Emmet, *Memoir*, I, pp. 328–9 and Carroll, *Russell*, p. 163.

57 28 Nov. 1803, NA, Rebellion Papers, 620/11/130/59. Higgins reported the movements of two Irish officers in the Spanish military in Dublin in late 1800. He claimed: 'There is a Lieutenant Colonel Clinch in the Spanish service who has been here about three months, is not only an avowed rebel in language, but most nearly related to several in the city who are open abettors. This person is frequently with Ambrose Moore, a violent republican, with [John] Fitzsimmons, a wine merchant in [187] Abbey St[reet], who was also in the Spanish service and is the relative of Clinch.' [Higgins] to [Marsden?], 19 Sept. 1800 in Bartlett (ed.) *Higgins*, p. 502.

58 Long, 18. Aug. 1803, NA, Rebellion Papers, 620/11/138/4.

59 For Portugal see MacNeven et al., *Pieces of Irish History*, p. x and 30 Nov. 1803, NA, Rebellion Papers, 620/11/130/60.

60 30 Nov. 1803, NA, Rebellion Papers, 620/11/130/60. Farrell, regarded as possessing 'very extraordinary talents and address', had been arrested in London in 1800 but released due to lack of evidence of sedition. Surgeon Lawless trained him in medicine in Paris and he eventually joined the Fourth Dragoons in England as a surgeon. 3 Nov. 1803, PRO London, Home Office Papers, 100/114/149.

61 Wickham to King, 3 Nov. 1803, PRO London, Home Office Papers, 100/114/149–51; Madden, *Robert Emmet*, p. 8; *Saunder's Newsletter*, 16–17 April 1798; *Finn's Leinster Journal*, 29 May and 28 Aug. 1798.

62 Robert Emmet to John Patten, 7 Aug. 1802 in Landreth, *Pursuit*, pp. 121–2. For Wilson see *Report of the Committee of Secrecy*, pp. 123–5.

63 Thomas Addis Emmet to MacNeven, n.d. [early Oct. 1802], in Madden, *Robert Emmet*, p. 21.

64 Thomas Russell to John Russell, 17 [September] 1802, NA, Rebellion Papers, 620/12/145/16.

65 Madden, *United*, III, pp. 245–6 and Davis, 'MacNeven' in Jackson (ed.), *Science*, pp. 9–11. See also William James MacNeven, *A ramble through Swisserland in the summer and autumn of 1802* (Dublin, 1803).

66 Madden, *Robert Emmet*, pp. 22–4 and Byrne, *Memoirs*, II, pp. 213–17. Russell did not trust Tallyrand and claimed that he had 'sold every expedition that was ever planned against Ireland to the English government'. Information of James Farrell, 24 Oct. 1803, PRO London, Home Office Papers, 100/114/123. James Farrell 'was deeply implicated in the late Rebellion' and worked in London in 1802. A spy reported that he had an 'intimacy' with Russell which Farrell's own recollections confirmed. Farrell reputedly wore a locket inscribed 'Remember Wolfe Tone and Teeling' when working as a clerk 'in the counting house' of Gordon & Murphy, 30 Broad Street Buildings, London. Edward Burton to William Bower, 14 Sept. 1803, NA, Rebellion Papers, 620/11/130/39. Farrell and Patrick Finnerty organised ticket-only benefit dinners in London for United Irishmen in reduced circumstances and were acquainted with one McCarthy and others arrested in England in 1802. Finnerty to Farrell, n.d., 1802, NA, Rebellion Papers, 620/12/145/16.

67 James Quinn, *Soul on fire, A life of Thomas Russell* (Dublin, 2002), p. 234. O'Connor's accounts of his dealings with the Emmet brothers were inconsistent and geared towards self-exculpation. Having dealt closely with their agent, William Putnam McCabe in June 1803, O'Connor falsely claimed to have first learned of the inner workings of the conspiracy some months later when conversing in Paris with John Allen. See Hames, *O'Connor*, p. 225. O'Connor remained close to John Stockdale and left his 'natural charge' in his care after 1807. 'Supect list', NA, Rebellion Papers, 620/12/217.

68 Madden, *United*, III, p. 314. See also Madden, *Robert Emmet*, p. 55 and Ó Broin, *Unfortunate* p. 80. Emmet reputedly told Revd Thomas Gamble in Sept. 1803 that 'Buonaparte' was 'the most savage unprincipled Tyrant by whom the earth was ever disgraced. His ambition has involved Belgium and Switzerland in the most abject slavery.' n.d. [late Sept. 1803], NA, Rebellion Papers, 620/11/133.

69 Madden, *Robert Emmet*, p. 55.

70 Lawless, *Life and Times*, pp. 163–4. Higgins suspected that 'the government authorized Dunn to *wink* at the escape of [William] Corbett' which implies that the authorities did not wish to prolong the diplomatic row with France or, perhaps, that they expected him to be of assistance. [Higgins] to [Cooke], 27 Feb. 1801 in Bartlett (ed.), *Higgins*, pp. 530–1. Dunn was reputedly bribed and sent a relative to Dixon of Kilmainham to collect 90 guineas. Same to Same, 4 Mar. 1801, ibid., p. 534. Stafford was also involved in springing the Corkman. Corbett joined the French army's Irish Legion at Morlaix in 1803 and survived the Napoleonic wars in its ranks and those of the 70th Regiment. His brother Thomas died at Lesneven in 1804 after a notably vicious duel with John Sweeney, another captain in the Irish Legion. Hampden Evans, formerly of South Great George's Street, Dublin, was probably a colonel in the city organisation until his arrest in July 1798. See Byrne, *Memoirs*, II, pp. 37–9; Liam Swords (ed.), *The Green Cockade, The Irish in the French Revolution, 1789–1815* (Dublin, 1989), pp. 145–6, 171; TCD, MSS 5966–7. For Tandy see 31 Oct. 1803, PRO London, Home Office Papers, 100/114/232–4.

71 MacNally described James Tandy in May 1798 as 'having born[e] a[n army] commission . . . He served long in India; was, I understand, an excellent officer and considered a martinet. He is, perhaps the best shot with a musket, fusee or pistol in Europe. Tandy is a good son, yet I believe [the] last man in Europe he wishes to see is his father.' [MacNally], n.d. [May 1798], NA, Rebellion Papers, 620/10/121/155.

72 31 Aug. 1803, NA, Rebellion Papers, 620/11/130/26. See also 20 Aug. 1803, NA, Rebellion Papers, 620/11/130/18 and 1 Sept. 1803, NA, Rebellion Papers, 620/11/130/29.

73 McCormick, Keogh and McLaughlin were close associates in Dublin during the late 1790s. Keogh and McCormick were reputedly irritated with the rise to prominence of Fitzgerald and Arthur O'Connor and 'the manner in which they treated Keogh in committee' in January 1798. [Higgins] to [Cooke], 1 Feb. 1798 in Bartlett (ed.), *Higgins*, pp. 375–6.
74 Lady Moira to Lady Granard, 13 Oct. 1800, PRO Northern Ireland, T/3765/J/9/2/8.
75 Information of Michael Quigley, 13 Oct. 1803, PRO London, Home Office Papers, 100/114/56. When McCormick returned to Ireland in 1814 he told John Patten that he 'was cognizant of the projected revolt of 1803 but did not approve of it or take part in it'. Emmet apparently refused to disclose the full details of what was planned as McCormick would not first agree to commit himself to involvement. Madden, *United*, III, p. 335.
76 In 1803 Philip Long was questioned as to whether Robert Emmet had introduced him to Neilson. The two were actually acquainted from the mid-1790s whereas Long and the younger Emmet apparently first collaborated in 1798. Long, 18 Aug. 1803, NA, Rebellion Papers, 620/11/138/4.
77 Byrne, *Memoirs*, I, pp. 340–1.
78 Madden, *United*, III, p. 328. See Ó Broin, *Unfortunate*, pp. 41–2.
79 Thomas Addis Emmet to MacNeven, 8 Nov. 1802 in Madden, *Robert Emmet*, p. 19.
80 John Russell to James Farrell, 4 Nov. 1802, NA, Rebellion Papers, 620/12/145/16. Thomas Russell occasionally wrote to his brother John from Paris in letters addressed to Farrell and, as such, it is often impossible to identify with certainty the intended recipient of the information. William St John, part of their circle, furthermore, arranged to receive letters from Ireland at this time 'under the name of James Sinclair'. Hamilton and one 'Delany', presumably Malachy Delaney, were mentioned in the same communication. R. Wilson to Farrell, 28 [. . .], 1802, ibid.
81 [Russell to Farrell], n.d. [c. Oct. 1802], NA, Rebellion Papers, 620/12/145/16.
82 [Russell] to Farrell, n.d. [1802], NA, Rebellion Papers, 620/12/145/16.
83 [Malachy?] D[elaney] to William St John, 19 Sept. 1803, NA, Rebellion Papers, 620/12/143/17. St John had 'transmitted' a 'proposal' to which Delaney acceded. Ibid.
84 William St John to William Dowdall, n.d., 1802, NA, 620/12/143/8. Delaney lived in Paris and was evidently in correspondence with United Irishmen based in Britain. Ibid.
85 Philip Long to 'Mr O'Donoughue', 4 Sept. 1802, NA, 620/12/143/16.
86 Philip Long to William Dowdall, 27 July 1802, NA, 620/12/143/13.
87 For Hope and Dowdall see Madden, *Hope*, p. 28.
88 Long, 18 Aug. 1803, NA, Rebellion Papers, 620/11/138/4.
89 Madden, *Hope*, p. 28. See also Clifford D. Conner, *Colonel Despard, the life and times of an Anglo-Irish rebel* (Pennsylvania, 2000); Madden, *Robert Emmet*, pp. 22, 28–35; Fitzpatrick, *Secret Service*, p. 354.
90 20 Aug. 1803, NA, Rebellion Papers, 620/11/130/18. The informer claimed that McCann told him one Burgess, 'nephew to Dixon of Kilmainham' had gone from Paris to Dublin in the spring of 1803. Ibid. Dixon was probably the Kilmainham tanner James Dixon who helped Corbett escape to France. *Wilson's Dublin Directory . . . 1803*, p. 39.
91 McCann to William Dowdall, 13 Jan. 1803, NA, Rebellion Papers, 620/12/143/19. Long had interceded on McCann's behalf with his wealthy uncle John Roach. McCann believed that Hervey Mountmorency Morres was in Ireland in January 1803. 25 Nov. 1803, NA, Rebellion Papers, 620/12/42/14.

Ridgeway was thirty in 1803 and deemed to be a 'sea faring man' of 'no fixed place of abode'. Ibid.

92 Madden, *United*, IV, p. 152.

93 25 Nov. 1803, NA, Rebellion Papers, 620/12/142/14. Teeling had moved to 20 North Anne Street in 1803 and was in partnership with one Moore. Ibid. and *Wilson's Dublin Directory . . . 1803*, p. 99.

94 Barrington, *Recollections*, pp. 190–1. Barrington and Musgrave believed that Coile also owned a whiskey distillery in Dublin. Ibid. See also Musgrave to Lindsay, 1 Aug. 1803 in MacDonagh (ed.), *Viceroy's post bag*, p. 313; *Times*, 31 Aug. 1803; *Wilson's Dublin Directory . . . 1803*, p. 32. For Coile's political activities in the 1790s see Smyth, *Men of no property*, pp. 47, 119, 152–3 and Curtin, *United Irishmen*, p. 164. A government document listed him as 'violent bigot crazy'. 'Suspect list', n.d., NA, Rebellion Papers, 620/12/217.

95 20 Aug. 1803, NA, Rebellion Papers, 620/11/130/18. For Ridgeway and Neilson's emigration see Weber, *Road to Rebellion*, pp. 172–3.

96 Quoted in Madden, *United*, IV, p. 152.

97 Newsinger (ed.), *James Hope*, pp. 89–90.

98 Ibid. and 'Supect list', n.d., NA, Rebellion Papers, 620/12/217.

99 Madden, *United*, IV, p. 153.

100 K[ennedy] to Anon., 23 May 1803, NA, Rebellion Papers, 620/65/126. One of Kennedy's informants was president of the New Light Lodge of Masons which met on Wednesday nights in Parker's of Duke Street. Byrne of Stephen's Street, an unlisted calenderer and printer, allegedly distributed a 'nonsensical ballad' to mark the re-commencement of the war against France. Ibid. The printer was probably bookseller Arabella Parker of 72 Grafton Street, off Duke Street. *Wilson's Dublin Directory . . . 1803*, p. 84.

101 Madden, *United*, IV, p. 154.

102 MacNeven memoir quoted in Madden, *United*, III, pp. 316–17. See also Fitzpatrick, *Secret Service*, p. 194 and Wickham Report, 5 Dec. 1803, BL, Hardwicke Papers, MS 35740/202–3. Countess d'Haussonsville, who knew Emmet in Paris, believed that MacNeven gave the Dubliner 'a proclamation calling on the Irish people to revolt'. This was probably the document prepared by MacNeven in 1804 when a French invasion of Ireland was planned. See Emmet, *Memoir*, II, p. 29.

103 See NA, Rebellion Papers, 620/12/155/2–7.

104 [McGucken], 4 June 1803 in MacDonagh (ed.), *Viceroy's post bag*, p. 275. See also 'Suspect list', n.d., NA, Rebellion Papers, 620/12/217.

105 [McGucken] to Marsden, 8 July 1803 in MacDonagh (ed.), *Viceroy's post bag*, p. 277.

106 30 July 1801, NA, Rebellion Papers, 620/49/111. Rourke had returned to live in Rathcoole in 1801. *Faulkner's Dublin Journal*, 15 Sept. 1803.

107 Anon. to Swan, n.d. [late July 1803], NA, Rebellion Papers, 620/64/121.

108 Nagle, 19 Dec. 1803, NA, Rebellion Papers, 620/11/138/48.

109 Thomas Bernard to Anon., 2 Sept. 1801, PRO London, Home Office Papers, 100/104/96. See also Dundas to Anon., 1 Oct. 1801, PRO London, Home Office Papers, 100/104/179 and 'Secret', 25 Sept. 1801, NA, Rebellion Papers, 620/49/133.

110 Day Diary, 23 Aug. 1802, RIA (Royal Irish Academy), MS 12. W. 11.

111 Sirr to Marsden, 20 July 1800 in Hammond, 'Sirr, part one', p. 25. O'Brien was helping Sirr in a raid upon a May 1800 football match in Kilmainham when, in a near psychotic fit of rage, he stabbed John Hoey to death. Madden, *United*, I, p. 471.

112 Byrne, *Memoirs*, I, p. 331.

113 Thomas King to Lieutenant Colonel George Stewart, 12 Dec. 1802 in Dickson, *Dwyer*, p. 208. Bryan Early and James Cullen, arrested by Major Sirr in Jan. 1801 in Dublin's Francis Street, were found in possession of 300 recently cast bullets, which were probably intended for the Wicklow rebels. Early assumed 'many names' when living in Dublin. *Finn's Leinster Journal*, 17 Jan. 1801.

114 See Zimmerman, *Songs of Irish Rebellion*, pp. 38–9. Earlier editions were printed in 1796 in Philadelphia and in 1798 in New York. Ibid.

115 'Citizens of Dublin', NA, Rebellion Papers, 620/12/155/5.

116 'Suspect list', n.d., NA, Rebellion Papers, 620/12/217. Roche was evidently '(John Roche & Co.), Merch[ant]'at 9 Lower Ormond Quay and 9 Great Sackville Street. *Wilson's Dublin Directory . . . 1803*, p. 90.

117 4 July 1805, NA, Rebellion Papers, 620/14/187/12.

118 Information of James Tandy, 31 Oct. 1803, PRO London, Home Office Papers, 100/114/232.

119 Long to Dowdall, 4 Sept. 1802, NA, Rebellion Papers, 620/12/143/16. See also McCann to Dowdall, 13 Jan. 1803, NA, Rebellion Papers, 620/12/143/19. McCann addressed the letter to 'Mr William Dowdall at Mr Philip Long's Crow Street'. It was seized with Dowdall's papers by Major Sirr in July 1803. Ibid.

120 Ryan was known in the Castle as a 'Merchant [who] was implicated in 98 and strong presumption of his guilt in 1803 by his connection with Emmet'. 'Suspect list', n.d., NA, Rebellion Papers, 620/12/217.

121 Madden, *United*, III, pp. 370, 555–6, Information of Thomas Wright, 1 May 1799, PRO London, Home Office Papers, 100/86/301–2 and Information of David Fitzgerald, 23 Nov. 1803, NA, Rebellion Papers, 620/11/138/43.

122 For the conspiracy theory see Landreth, *Pursuit*, pp. 124–8.

123 Information of Michael Quigley, PRO London, Home Office Papers, 100/115/37; Wickham Report, 5 Dec. 1803, BL, Hardwicke Papers, MS 35740/203–208; Carroll, *Russell*, pp. 165–7; *Annual Register*, 1803, p. 58. John Russell understood that McCabe 'got the money from the [French] Government . . . perhaps Smith and Long were too hasty quitting him'. Russell to Farrell, n.d. [1802], NA, Rebellion Papers, 620/12/145/16. The procurement and storage of large numbers of firearms in the complex is proof that normal business concerns were not uppermost in McCabe's mind in 1802–3.

124 *Faulkner's Dublin Journal*, 23 Nov. 1802.

125 Madden, *United*, III, pp. 297–300; Roger Wells, *Insurrection, the British Experience 1795–1803* (Gloucester, 1986), p. 244; *Faulkner's Dublin Journal*, 17 and 26 Nov. 1802. Dowling's brother, Lord Blandford's gardener, was suspected of harbouring him in England in 1803. Wickham to King, 31 Oct. 1803, PRO London, Home Office Papers, 100/114/141.

126 Madden, *United*, I, p. 515 and Wells, *Insurrection*, p. 166. Benjamin Binns wrote 'The burning of Scullabogue barn' which blamed the atrocity on 'two agents' sent by 'the subtle Cooke – the Castle scribe'. This absurd allegation testified to the extent to which the United Irishmen deemed themselves vulnerable to Castle propaganda once deprived of legal and effective means to defend their perspective. See anon. *Emmet song book* (Dublin, 1903), p. 22.

127 Madden, *United*, III, p. 356. See also ibid., p. 293; Wells, *Insurrection*, p. 242; Wickham to John King, 24 Oct. 1803, PRO London, Home Office Papers, 100/114/113–6. Cloney, famous for his heroism at the Battle of New Ross (5 June 1798), had been released from twenty-one months' imprisonment in Wexford and Waterford on 12 Feb. 1801. Although subject to £2,000 bail and barred from Ireland for two years, Cloney spent five months living secretly in Dublin before going to Liverpool. See John Joyce, *General Thomas Cloney, Wexford Rebel of 1798* (Dublin, 1988), p. 41.

128 See information on James Woulfe in 'Suspect list', n.d., NA, Rebellion Papers, 620/12/217. Woulfe was clearly the source of the Castle's file on Norris after 1803. He claimed: 'Norris was born in Co. Limerick & was educated in Cork for a Priest, that he was obliged to leave that city in 98 on account of his principles, that the year following he became acquainted with Counsellor Holmes who introduced him to John Patten whose partner he became in the Tanning business' in Dolphin's Barn. Ibid.

129 Wickham Report, 5 Dec. 1803, BL, Hardwicke Papers, MS 35740/206; Information of Edward Condon, 3 Nov. 1803, NA, Rebellion Papers, 620/11/138/36; Byrne, *Memoirs*, I, p. 332; Seán Ó Coindealbháin, 'The United Irishmen in Cork County, VII, Corkmen in Emmet's Rising', *Cork Historical and Archaeological Journal*, LVIII, 187 (1953), pp. 91–2. A man named Norris, then in Guernsey, had come to the attention of General Myers in early 1799 as it was believed he could confirm or deny information obtained from Cork committeeman Timothy Conway. Myers to Castlereagh, 6 May 1799, NA, Rebellion Papers, 620/7/74/31.

130 'Suspect list', n.d., NA, Rebellion Papers, 62012/217.

131 Robert Harney to Marsden, 19 April 1803, NA, State of the Country Papers, 1025/8. See also 20 Aug. 1803, NA, Rebellion Papers, 620/11/130/18.

132 Byrne, *Memoirs*, I, p. 348.

133 Madden, *United*, III, pp. 338–9; Ó Broin, *Unfortunate*, p. 67; Thomas Jones Howell (ed.), *A complete collection of state trials*, XXVIII, p. 1130; Memorial of Assistant Town Major William Bellingham Swan, 13 July 1802, NA, Rebellion Papers, 620/63/41. Swan was described by Watty Cox as 'about 5 feet 6 inches high, woman's face, in knee'd, occasioned by carrying a drum in his infancy, to which business he was reared, lives in G[rea]t George's Street, North, in as Inspector of Licenses, and a Justice of the Peace, is notorious for boasting of killing several poor unarmed people, by shooting and stabbing them. Alas! poor Irishmen, this infamous wretch is taken from the dregs of society, and rewarded with his Majesty's commission, for inhumanity.' *Union Star*, n.d., 1797. Swan's dedication to his work was obsessive and he reputedly took just one holiday in nineteen years. Hammond, 'Sirr, part one', p. 21. He was stabbed by Fitzgerald in May 1798, 'met an unlucky accident' in March 1801 and was almost beaten to death by a republican mob in July 1802. [Higgins] to [Cooke], 4 Mar. 1801, NA, Rebellion Papers, 620/10/118/9.

134 Drennan to Martha McTier, 14 Dec. 1802 in Agnew (ed.), *Drennan-McTier Letters*, III, p. 87. See also Anne Fitzgerald to La Touche, 31 July 1803 in MacDonagh (ed.), *Viceroy's post bag*, pp. 333–4 and Madden, *United*, III, pp. 12–13, 342–3. The author of a short memoir of the Emmet family in 1803 was evidently unaware that Dr Emmet had passed away. *Annual Register*, 1803, p. 433.

135 Drennan to Martha McTier, 14 Dec. 1802 in Agnew (ed.), *Drennan-McTier Letters*, III, p. 87. See also Drennan to Martha McTier, n.d. [c. June/July] 1803 in ibid., III, p. 124; Howell (ed.), *State trials*, XXVIII, p. 1130; Madden, *United*, III, p. 338.

136 Emmet, 'Account', BL, Hardwicke Papers, MS 35740/199. Allen lived prior to the Rebellion at 80 Francis Street and served his apprenticeship with the firm of O'Brien, 2 Francis Street. Madden, *United*, I, p. 493.

137 Anon. to Swan, n.d. [late 1802], NA, Rebellion Papers, 620/64/121.

138 Thomas King to Anon., 12 Dec. 1802 in Dickson, *Dwyer*, p. 205.

139 King to Sirr, 17 Jan. 1803 quoted in Dickson, *Dwyer*, p. 212.

140 Hardwicke Report, BL, Hardwicke Papers, MS 35736/216. See also Madden, *United*, III, p. 590; Anon. to Major-General Edward Morrison to Wickham, 1

and 2 Nov. 1802, NA, Rebellion Papers, 620/49/156; Standish O'Grady to Marsden, 8 Nov. 1802, NA, Rebellion Papers, 620/49/146; Hardwicke to Addington, 14 Jan. 1803, BL, Hardwicke Papers, MS 35737/264.

141 Payne to Marsden, 3 June 1803, BL, Hardwicke Papers, MS 35738/182. See also Payne to Marsden, 1 March 1803, BL, Hardwicke Papers, MS 35738/117–18 and 35736/216. Crown Solicitor for the Munster circuit, Samuel Prendergast, noted that the 1802 city and county spring assizes of Limerick cost £314, compared with £131 in the summer of 1802 and £570 for the spring assizes of 1803. The combined total of £1,005 contrasts with those of £170 for Kerry and £344 for Cork in the same period. *Accounts presented to the House of Commons of the expenditure . . . for criminal prosecutions in the years 1801, 1802 and 1804* [sic] in *House of Commons*, 1805, VI, p. 513.

142 Anon., Nov. 1803, PRO London, Home Office Papers, 100/114/201.

143 Madden, *United*, III, pp. 330, 356, 370; Elliott, *Partners*, p. 302; Landreth, *Pursuit*, pp. 133–4. Madden claimed that 'Barrett . . . is said to have been a liberal contributor to the objects of the men of 1798 and 1803'. Madden, *United*, III, p. 374. See 'Supect list', NA, Rebellion Papers, 620/12/217. Barrett's name appeared on the same Dowdall account as leading United Irishmen Marlay, Cox, Moore ('bookseller'), Ryan and Dunn. 'Money received since Mr Dowdall left Ireland and how disposed of', n.d., NA, Rebellion Papers, 620/12/143/40. The compiler wrote: 'Being necessitated to absent myself from Dublin twice in consequence of search being made for me and on account of the disturbed state of Carlow, from which place I used to receive small annuity . . . had Mr D[owdall] or Mr [Arthur] O'C[onnor] been in Ireland [I] should have made [sic] no doubt but either would have assisted me when suffering in a Cause they were so strenuous in.' Ibid.

144 Elliott, *Partners*, pp. 302–3; Madden, *United*, III, pp. 317–18; 20 Aug. 1803, NA, Rebellion Papers, 620/11/130/18. Addis Emmet claimed in March that his daughters teething and minor illness made him indisposed to cross the Atlantic. Addis Emmet to John [Patten], 31 March 1803, NA, Rebellion Papers, 620/15/2/20. Russell would have been highly pleased by reports that long-standing United Irish leaders in Ulster, not least Revd William Steel Dickson, William Tennent and Frank McCracken, were keen to fight again. See Quinn, *Soul on fire*, p. 248.

Index

The following abbreviations have been used:

RE   Robert Emmet
UI   United Irishmen

Act of Union 11, 51, 107, 111,
    122–3, 149, 159, 160–1,
    171, 181, 193, 199, 241
    UI and 124–7, 146–7, 152
Adams, John (US President) 121,
    153, 241
agrarian unrest 11, 146–9, 158,
    159–60, 162–3
Ahanagran 160
Alexander, William 56–9, 69, 225
Allen, Bog of 97, 235
Allen, John
    before Rebellion 52, 53, 74,
        133, 139–40, 178, 218,
        260
    after Rebellion 132–3, 178–9,
        180, 195, 200, 256
Allen, Wood of 19
Alleyburn, James 133
Amiens 172, 177, 180, 186, 191,
    193
amnesty 10–19, 102, 104, 107,
    110–12, 115, 120, 137–40,
    159, 172, 214, 233, 239
Amnesty Act 108, 157, 159, 163,
    172
Amsterdam 178, 180
Anacreon expedition 118, 213, 254
Ancient Britons 37, 227
Andemar 184, 198
Anderson, Henry 137
Anglo-French War 142, 158,
    175, 179
    'Brest ruse' 158, 170, 202
    effect on France's Irish policy
        39, 40, 119, 155–6, 158,
        170–2, 177, 180, 182–6,
        191, 193
    effects in Ireland (1793–96) 19,
        20, 21, 30
    and exile of state prisoners
        121, 153, 154, 171
    'Louisiana incident' 186, 196,
        202
    negotiations and peace 169–70,
        171, 172, 177, 180, 186
Annamoe 138
Antrim 13, 37, 39, 49, 73, 92,
    130, 131, 134, 157
    Rebellion in 95, 96, 97, 135
    disturbances post-Rebellion
        145, 147, 150, 156, 158,
        162–3
Arbour Hill 47, 84, 103, 130
Archer, Revd Foster 148
Archer, Thomas 150, 156, 163,
    251
Ardagh, Arthur 48
Ardee 106
Ards 150

Ariadne, HMS 178
Arklow 92, 94–6, 105, 139, 157,
    219, 246
Armagh 13, 25, 34, 37, 53, 73,
    102, 130, 134, 135, 145,
    188, 198
Armagh town 134
arms 40, 42, 60, 67, 69, 72, 75,
    76, 78–9, 82, 98, 102–3,
    111, 115, 119, 138, 156,
    158, 159
    pikes 42, 60, 68–9, 70, 72, 74,
        75, 76, 78–9, 83, 85, 102
Armstrong, Captain John
    Warneford 74, 107
Armstrong, Lieutenant George
    1231
army 20, 30, 37, 39, 40
    Ancient Britons 37, 102
    5th Royal Irish Dragoons 102,
        116
    reinforcements from Britain 97,
        117, 197–8
    see also militia; yeomanry
Artane 25, 79
Athlone 210
Athy 60, 162
Augereau, General P.F.C. 168,
    169, 181, 253
Australia 157, 160
    see also New South Wales
Austria 152, 154, 155, 168, 225
Avoca 138, 201
Aylmer, William 97, 98, 105,
    132, 148

Babington, Dr 9
Bacon, Eliza (wife of Thomas
    Bacon) 93
Bacon, Thomas 14, 84, 88, 92,
    93, 158, 208, 209, 212, 229,
    232
Baggott, James 160
Bagwell, John 160
Baird, Henry 88, 93, 113, 119,
    127–8, 131–2, 133, 151
Balbriggan 78
Ballie, Major J.H. 165
Ballinamuck 113, 117–18, 130,
    158
Ballinascorney 90, 95
Ballingarry 160
Ballitore 60, 152
Ballyboden 83, 138
Ballyboghill 84, 106
Ballybrack 103
Ballycanew 95
Ballyellis 102, 143
Ballygullen 102
Ballylow 120

Ballymahon 225
Ballymanus 73, 95, 97, 131, 141,
    143, 148, 225
Ballymena 156, 163, 250–1
Ballymoney 64
Ballymore-Eustace 83
Ballynahinch 37, 70, 97, 135
Ballynahowa 104
Baltinglass 159
Banishment Act (1798) 153, 177,
    178, 187, 203, 228, 239
Bank of Ireland 3, 12, 89, 231
Bantry Bay 30, 31, 34–5, 37, 156
Barber, Colonel Lucius 49
Baris Moore 49
Barlow, Joel 173
Barnwell, Lieutenant Christopher
    231
Barrack Division (UI) *see* Dublin
Barrett, Fr John 142, 143
Barrett, James (innkeeper) 139
Barrett, James (lace merchant)
    202, 261
Barrington, Jonah 7, 83, 188, 258
Barry, Edmund 222
Barry, Patrick 142
Bath 148
Beggs, William 137
Behan's (Bath St.) 94
Belfast 3, 6, 27, 29, 37, 41, 48,
    66, 78, 86, 97, 108, 154,
    170, 222
    and UI 11, 13, 31, 39, 44, 49,
        92, 131, 162, 189, 203
Belgium 178, 181, 183, 185, 187,
    202
Bell, Justice John 25
Bellamont, Earl of 37
Bennett, Thomas 45, 222
Berehaven 156
Beresford, John 56, 73, 86, 103,
    126, 226–7, 235
Beresford, John Claudius 235
Beresford, Marcus 49
Beresford's Riding School 98
Bernadotte, General Jean 169
Bernard, Thomas 193
Berthier, General Louis-
    Alexandre 175, 184
Binns, Benjamin Pemberton 197,
    215, 259
Binns, John 53, 74, 132, 149,
    180, 197, 215, 218
Birchgrove 202
Bird, John 33, 212, 216, 218,
    236, 244
Birr 193
Blacker, William 48, 63, 65
Blackmore Hill 72, 79, 87, 89,
    91, 92, 94

Blackrock 79, 86, 101, 104
Blake, Francis 250
Blaris Camp 38
Blessington 79, 87, 88, 98, 101, 106, 116
Blue Bells 152
Board of Ordnance 82
Bohernabreena 90
Bolton, Lyndon 93, 118, 174–5, 176, 183, 187, 200, 240, 254
Bompard, Admiral 118, 119
Bonaparte, Napoleon 40, 56, 85, 119, 166, 169–71, 173, 175, 180–2, 184, 195, 202, 253
Bond, Oliver 121, 232
    early 1790 16, 31, 32, 45, 116, 180, 212, 215
    1797–March 1798 36, 38, 42, 51, 74, 80, 92, 121, 218, 220
    arrests at his house 55–6, 59, 61, 67, 107, 131, 212, 219
    prisoner and death 104, 107, 108–9, 121
Bonham (London Corresponding Society) 215
Booterstown 101
Bordeaux 121, 172, 179, 182, 188
Boston 5
Botany Bay see transportation
Boyle 22, 210
Boyle, Thomas 53, 77, 218, 246
Brannigan, Thomas 179
Braughall, Thomas 15, 46, 83, 84, 85, 228–9, 230
Bray 60, 67, 110, 139, 142, 197
Brazen Head pub 55
Brennan, John 94
Brest 116, 148, 155, 156, 162, 172, 182
'Brest ruse'158 169, 170
Brett family 70
Bridewell (Dublin) 109, 231
Bridport, Alexander Hood, 1st Viscount 119, 155–6, 158
Bristol 148
Britain
    republicanism in 108, 175, 184, 197
    United Britons 132, 133, 149
    UI in
        1798–9 43, 51, 102, 115, 132, 148–9, 179, 213
        1800–3 133, 157, 165, 178–81, 183, 185, 188, 254, 259
    conspiring in 132, 148–9, 172, 175, 178–81, 186–7, 194, 197–8, 202
    see also Coigley; Despard; O'Connor
    RE in 161, 164–7, 170, 180, 183, 184–5, 200
    see also Scotland; Wales
Broderick, Charles (Bishop of Kilmore) 110–11, 117, 237
Browne, G.J. 208
Browne, John 66, 222
Bruff 162, 218
Bruix, Admiral 155
Brussels 178, 181, 183, 185, 202

Bryan, Michael 145
Buckingham, George Temple, 1st Marquis of 2, 7, 9, 10, 106, 117, 147, 238, 242
Buncrana 118
Bunting, Edward 44
Burdett, Sir Francis 175, 187
Burke 111, 120
Burke, Edmund 12, 215
Burke, John 215
Burke, Martin 227
Burrowes, Peter 16, 41
Burrowes, Peter 29
Bushe, Charles Kendall 41
Butler, Simon 17, 45, 211
Butterfield, John 139
Byrne, Edward ('Ned') 131, 141, 143
Byrne family (Mullinahack) 102, 235
Byrne, Garret 73, 97, 100, 105, 106, 132, 143, 148, 167, 225, 245
Byrne, Hugh 'Vesty' 143
Byrne, James 78, 85
Byrne, John 102, 208, 212, 235
Byrne, John (Dundalk) 236
Byrne, Michael 129
Byrne, Miles xii, 45, 82, 104, 106, 114, 141–3, 181, 184, 192–3, 194
Byrne, Patrick 15, 74, 208, 214, 225
Byrne, Walter 14, 138
Byrne, William ('Billy') 95, 97, 141, 142
Byrne, William Michael 107, 108, 109, 158, 233, 245

Cadiz 155, 178, 179
Cahir 162
Caldwell, John 45, 159, 221
Caldwell, Richard 45, 64, 159, 221
Camden, John Jeffreys Pratt, 2nd Earl 24–5, 37, 51, 57, 60, 61, 62, 69, 83, 94, 100, 106, 123, 224, 227, 235
Campbell, Captain P. 178
Campbell, Patrick 98
Campbell (Scotland) 184
Campbell, William 7
Camperdown, Battle of 30
Cape St Vincent, Battle of 30
Cappagh 162
Cappawhite 1
Carey, William 24
Carhampton, Lieutenant-General Luttrell, Earl of 25, 34, 50, 51, 55, 219
Carleton, Oliver 56, 220
Carlow 39, 60, 136, 144, 159, 161, 162, 163, 193, 220, 261
    Rebellion 87, 94, 114, 135, 219
Carlow town 86, 144
Carnew 60, 83
Carolan, Edward 164, 166, 185–6, 202, 241, 252, 254
Carolan, John 252
Carrick-on-Suir 17, 160
Carrickfergus 150
Carrickmacross 164

Carroll, Daniel 58–9
Carroll (Fingal) 84, 227, 229
Carroll, John 222
Carty, Robert 202
Cary, Patrick 34
Cashel 145, 161
Castle Otway 159
Castlebar 113, 158, 243, 251
Castlebellingham 21
Castlecomer 102
Castledermot 143
Castlehaytown 94
Castlekelly 104
Castlereagh, Robert Stewart, Viscount 24, 60, 83, 110, 112, 125, 137, 146, 151, 156, 175, 208, 217, 224, 237, 241
Castletown 233, 235
casualties 135
Catholic Committee 15, 16, 19, 24, 31, 44, 116, 122, 236
    Catholic Convention 15–16, 18, 19–20, 143, 212, 223
Catholics 7, 11, 13, 16, 19–20, 24–7, 62, 71, 96, 123, 139, 146, 159, 170, 183, 189, 195, 208, 229
    Catholic Emancipation 16, 45
    in Trinity College 19, 35, 36, 44, 62
    see also Catholic Committee
Cavan 21, 81, 86, 102
Celbridge 235
Chamberlain, Judge 41, 50–1
Chambers, John 8, 45, 75, 80, 81, 214, 228
Chapelizod 34, 74
Charlemont, James Caulfield, 1st Earl of 37
Cherry Tree Inn 93, 158, 250
Chester 102
Church of Ireland 5, 13, 104
Churchtown 86
Clane 144
Clara 138, 215
Clare 48, 146, 148, 159, 162
Clare, 1st Earl of see Fitzgibbon
Clinch, John (Coombe) 137
Clinch, John (Rathcoole) 85, 229
Clohogue 96
Clonard 105, 236
Cloncurry, Lord see Valentine Lawless
Clondalkin 78, 83, 89
Clone Hill 116
Clonee bridge 231
Cloney, Thomas xii, 94, 100, 179, 193, 197, 198, 259
Clonmel 12, 17, 159, 160, 250
Clonsilla 231
Clonskeagh 38, 66, 214
Clontarf 67, 76, 79
Cloone 113
Clotworthy, John 137
Cobh 146, 157, 211
Cody, James 144
Coffey, Edward 137, 138
Coffey, William 212
Coigley family 188
Coigley, Fr James 30, 53, 56, 74, 109, 132, 133, 188, 212, 213

Coile, Bernard 130, 188, 189, 198, 200, 252, 258
Colclough, John 94
Cole, William 42, 114, 164, 225
Coleraine 108
College Green *see* Irish Parliament
College of Physicians (Dublin) 2, 10
Colligan, Barney 143
Collins, Thomas 17, 23, 24, 35, 90, 208, 210, 223, 229, 239
Collooney 136
Colville family 36
Colville, Sarah 11
Colville, William 12
Condon, Edward ('Ned') 198
Connacht 26, 34
  UI 39, 73, 134, 149, 158, 250
  Rebellion 82, 106, 112–13, 114, 117, 118, 124, 135, 136, 147
Connagh 162
Connelly, Bartholomew (informer) 236
Connelly, Lady Louisa 220, 224
Connor's (pub, Thos. St) 140
Conway, Timothy 18, 43
Cooke, Edward 53, 60, 104, 108, 110, 111, 139, 149, 170, 214, 229, 243, 259
Coolgreany 116
Coolock 25, 67, 73
Coolrain 186
Coombs, Robert 43
Cope, William 55
Corbally, Joseph 18, 209, 211
Corbett, Thomas 35, 36, 45, 182, 222, 256
Corbett, William 35, 36, 44, 45, 117–18, 182, 222, 240, 254, 256, 257
Corcoran, James 136, 144, 163
Cork
  and Emmet family 8, 41, 47
  pre-Rebellion 20, 21, 23, 30, 47, 48, 160, 222
  Rebellion 84, 99, 135, 217
  post-Rebellion 123, 145, 147, 148, 177, 219, 251, 261
Cork city 1, 2, 29, 40, 60, 134, 155, 179, 193
Cork Gazette 20
Corke Abbey 197
Cormick, John 71, 75, 88, 226
Cornwallis, Charles 1st Marquis of (Viceroy 1798–1801) 99, 101, 102, 104, 107–8, 112, 116, 123, 147–8, 154, 172, 177, 237, 242
Corofin 145
Court of King's Bench 49, 53, 92
courts martial 38, 52, 83, 85, 99, 108, 111, 139, 141, 157, 250–1, 251
Cox, Walter ('Watty') 33–4, 214, 219, 228
  and pre-Rebellion UI 53, 124, 218, 224, 228, 261
  adviser to Fitzgerald 42, 53, 55, 76, 164, 219, 225
  and Rebellion 82–3, 169, 193, 218

post-Rebellion UI 164, 252
  and Rising of *1803* 42, 126, 164, 193, 200, 214
  and Dublin Castle 55, 82–3, 169, 219
  selective information to 55, 214–15
  and *Union Star* 40, 50, 173, 214
  as a source on the period xii, 76, 81, 137, 169, 260
Craig, Lieutenant-General Sir Peter 52–3, 116, 239
Craig, William 251
Crauford, Colonel Sir James 118
Creeve 67, 134, 189, 190
Cremorne 67, 189
Croghan Mountain 114
Crone, Luke 137, 234
Crook, Hugh 218
Croppy's Acre 83, 84
Crosbie, Sir Edward 5
Crosbie, W. A. 146
Crow Street Theatre 4
Crowe, Thomas 146, 247
Crumlin 78, 81, 89
Cullinane, Daniel 145, 161
Cummins, George 231
Cunningham, Phil 159–60, 161
Curragh 87
Curran, John Philpot 8, 22, 24, 41, 43, 49, 50, 177, 191
Curran, Richard 43, 132, 149, 254
Curran, Sarah x, xi, 43, 177
Cusack, John 61, 113

Dalkey 79
Dalton, Michael 144
Daly, Michael 139, 246
Darcy, William 99
David, Jacques Louis 175
Dawson, High Constable W. H. 89
Day, Judge Robert 147, 193, 209, 217, 242
Defenders 22, 26, 31, 33, 34, 40, 53, 74, 139, 143, 162, 188, 210, 211, 212, 214, 218, 233, 235
  and UI 17, 18, 21–2, 25–7, 38, 130, 135, 156, 233
Delahyde, Charles 233
Delaney, Malachy 46, 82, 152, 164–5, 167–9, 174–6, 181, 183, 186, 187, 192, 225, 253, 257
Denmark 154
Denniston, Alexander 118
Denniston, Hans 118
Derry 24, 37, 38, 73, 97, 119, 156
Derrylossary 96
Despard, Colonel Edward Marcus 132, 175, 186, 187, 188, 191, 196–7, 202
Devlin, Anne xii
Dickson, James 'Holt' 150, 156, 251
Dickson, Revd William Steel 11, 13, 134, 166, 208, 217, 252, 261
Dillon, Patrick 89–90, 91, 93, 158, 225, 232
Dillon, Richard 116, 131, 208, 212, 229, 236

Dillon, Robert 14, 232
Dillon, Thomas 212
Dillon's (White Bull Inn, Thos. St.) 140
Dissenters 12, 13, 27
Dixon, James 33, 53, 75, 85, 143, 164, 170, 200, 212, 225, 233, 256, 257
Dixon, Sam 234
Dobbs, Francis 108, 109, 110, 111
Dolphin's Barn 69, 76, 84, 88, 99, 103, 198, 236
Donaghadee 166
Donard 101, 139
Donegal 38, 73, 92, 117–18, 119, 145
Donnellan, Mathew 144
Donnybrook 89, 91, 101, 116, 158, 199, 225, 232
Donnybrook Hurlers 33, 40, 52, 114, 133, 232
Doorley, John 141, 144, 246
Doorley, Michael 144, 193
Douglas, Archibald 5
Dowdall, William xii, 40, 50, 59, 109, 132, 133, 152, 175, 179, 180, 186–7, 188, 189, 190, 195, 196, 202, 217, 259, 261
Dowling, Mathew 4, 14, 16, 17, 31, 33, 50, 88, 178, 190, 209, 212, 218, 225, 233, 246, 259
Down 21, 37, 45, 64, 70, 73, 134, 145, 156–7, 162, 166, 208, 221, 246
  Rebellion 95, 96, 97, 135
Downne, Henry 142
Downshire, Lord 146
Doyle, John 88, 91, 95, 129, 140, 141
Doyle, Luke 99
Doyle, Mathew 42, 82, 97, 246
Doyle, Michael 132, 149
Doyle, Thomas 132, 149
Drennan family 66
Drennan, Martha (later McTier) 11, 154–5
Drennan, Mary (wife of William) 166
Drennan, William xii, 10, 42, 123, 126, 163, 164
  and Emmet family 10, 11, 12, 14, 17, 23, 101, 123, 217
    after Rebellion 154–5, 163–4, 166, 208
  and UI 11, 12, 16, 17, 23, 24, 31, 40, 50, 183, 210
Driscoll, Denis 20, 21, 209
Drogheda 188
Dromard 17
Dromore 37
Drummond, Brigadier General 162, 250–1
Drury, Justice Frederick 70–1, 72, 86
Dry, Richard 30, 31, 33, 38, 212, 214
Dry, Thomas 38, 212
Duagh 160

Dublin 210–11
  UI early *1790s* 11, 14, 16–17,
    20, 24–7, 29, 31, 139,
    209, 212
  1797 33–4, 38–9, 42–3, 140
  1798 (Jan–May) 42–5, 50–4,
    56–62, 64, 66–9, 127–8,
    136, 140–1, 189–90, 219,
    220
  1798 (May–July) 80–103, 136,
    191, 198
  1798 (July–Dec) 103–6, 108,
    111–17, 119–20, 135,
    137–42, 201, 228, 238
  1799 127–34, 138–54, 156,
    158, 184, 198, 201
  1800–1 140, 149, 162, 164,
    167, 170–2, 183–8, 192,
    252, 253
  1802–3 49, 183–8, 191–200
    see also Rising of *1803*
  UI Divisions
    Barrack 39, 61, 68, 115, 116
    Rotunda 39, 61, 68, 76, 100,
      115, 128
    St Stephen's Green 39, 44,
      61, 68, 76, 81, 84,
      89–91, 114, 115, 140
    Workhouse 39, 61, 81, 89,
      92–3, 115
    see also prisons; Trinity College
Dublin Castle 7, 10, 20–1, 24
  intelligence 14, 19, 57, 59, 93,
    94, 114, 128, 131, 137–8,
    155, 214, 217
    from *1800* 131, 176, 183,
      184, 189, 192, 193, 260
    on RE 150–3, 175, 196,
      198–9
    see also informers
  and UI 13–14, 17, 30, 42,
    53–4, 115–16, 128, 142,
    149, 158–9, 161, 163,
    177, 192, 198–9, 259
  and Rebellion 76–7, 78, 83,
    94, 98–9
  and state prisoners 57, 61, 70,
    99, 106, 108–13, 153
Dublin Evening Post 24
Duff, Major-General Sir James
  87, 231
Duggan, Bernard 105–6, 174,
  193
Duigenan, Dr Patrick 48, 62, 63,
  65, 74, 109, 174, 222
Duigenan, Miles 33–4, 38, 42,
  58, 76, 85, 88, 105, 200,
  212, 218, 225
Dunboyne 104, 162, 218, 231
Duncan, Admiral Adam 39
Dundalk 38, 102, 105, 111, 172,
  202, 236
Dundas, General Sir Ralph 55,
  111, 239
Dundrum 69, 86, 240
Dungarvan 160
Dunlavin 60, 83
Dunn, Edward 33, 38, 256
Dunn, James 34
Dunne (of Thomas Court) 116,
  246
Dunne, Thomas 138, 245

Dunshaughlin 78, 86, 231
Dwyer, Michael 141, 143
  and Rebellion 82, 141, 144,
    200
  and amnesty 110, 111, 159
  in Wicklow post Rebellion 104,
    120, 136, 138, 141, 144,
    159, 163, 164, 200, 227,
    250
  and preparation for Rising of
    1803 82, 104, 144–5, 163,
    193–4, 200
Dwyer's (Sth. Earl St.) 119, 140

Eadestown 163
Edgeworth family 177
Edinburgh University 8–9, 11,
  15, 165
Edwards brothers (school) 4
Edwards, George 144, 247
Edwards, John 144, 247
Egan, John 35, 44, 45, 63, 65,
  175–6, 213, 216, 221, 222,
  254, 255
Egan, Sylvester 35
Elliott, Marianne 118–19, 170
Ellis, Thomas 125–6
Elrington, Revd Thomas 47
Emigration Bill 237
Emly 162
Emmet, Anne Western (wife of
  Christopher Temple Emmet,
  née Temple) 8, 207
Emmet, Catherine (daughter of
  Christopher Temple Emmet)
  8, 199–200, 206
Emmet, Christopher Temple
  (brother of RE) 3, 6, 8, 9,
  11, 22, 23, 28–9, 65, 173,
  207, 215
Emmet, Elizabeth (daughter of
  Thomas Addis Emmet) 166
Emmet, Elizabeth (wife of Dr
  Robert Emmet, née Mason)
  1, 5, 66, 125–6, 165, 166,
  173, 177, 199
Emmet family
  ancestry and relations 1–6, 8,
    9, 12, 17, 22, 29, 65, 147,
    199, 205
  property and finances 2, 3, 12,
    35, 172–3, 199–200, 202,
    208, 216, 222
  homes 151
    Molesworth St 2–3, 206
      St Stephen's Green 3, 5,
        6, 8, 11–14, 25, 41–2,
        43, 47, 56, 58, 62, 66,
        80, 124, 151, 163, 173,
        207–99
    Casino House, Milltown 42,
      63, 66, 80, 122, 125,
      127, 150, 151, 155,
      163–4, 166, 171, 188,
      195, 199, 200, 215
    Bloomfield House 143, 199
  political views 6, 7, 11, 14, 41,
    46–7, 103, 122–3, 171,
    199
  circle and connections 2, 5–7,
    9, 36, 41, 47, 48, 50, 60,
    122–4, 127, 177, 215

republican 12, 14, 18, 31, 51,
  124, 189, 198, 208, 252
effects of sons' political
  involvement 58, 65, 127,
  154–5, 163–4, 170–1,
  178, 199
and expectations for children 9,
  22, 29, 65
graves 3, 8, 199, 206
Emmet, Henry (brother of RE) 4
Emmet, Jane (wife of Thomas
  Addis Emmet, née Patten) 3,
  11, 12, 57, 58, 123, 124,
  166, 172, 220, 252
Emmet, Margaret (daughter of
  Thomas Addis Emmet) 166
Emmet, Mary Anne (sister of RE,
  later wife of Robert Holmes)
  see Mary Anne Holmes
Emmet, Rebecca (wife of
  Christopher Emmett, née
  Temple) 1, 5, 206
Emmet, Robert 2, 36, 47, 173–4,
  176
  birth and childhood 3–5, 8,
    10–12, 14–15
  education 4–5, 14–15, 22, 28,
    62
    see also Trinity College
    Dublin
  early political influences 41, 46,
    123, 164
  and UI 27, 31, 58, 65–6, 68,
    80, 90, 110, 113, 114,
    124, 205
  leadership in
    1798 24, 25, 26, 31, 34,
      42–5, 51, 59, 67,
      81–2
    1799–1801 113–14, 121,
      124, 127–9, 131,
      136, 146, 148–52,
      154–5, 163–7, 184,
      188
    see also Dublin Castle;
      Rising of *1803*; state
      prisoners; T. A. Emmet;
      Trinity College; Wright
  and Rebellion 80–2, 84,
    90–1, 93, 98, 101–2,
    114, 119, 121, 124,
    127–8, 135, 136
  and state prisoners 107,
    109–10, 114
  and Act of Union 122, 126,
    146, 152
  in Britain 161, 165–7, 170,
    183, 184–5
  return to Ireland *1802* 170,
    182–5, 198
  burial 3
  artistic skills 42, 215
  reading 36–7, 123, 164, 171
  sources on, and biographies
    x, xi, xii
  writings by x, 10–11, 14, 29,
    41, 47, 48, 58–9, 80,
    84, 130, 152
    see also Emmet family; Sarah
    Curran
Emmet, Robert, Dr (father of
  RE) 11, 42, 173

death, burial and will 199–200, 202, 260
medical career 1, 2, 3, 6, 7, 10, 11, 172
political views 3, 6, 7, 10, 41
political connections 2, 5, 7, 9
and sons' political activities 41, 65, 66, 154, 155, 164, 166, 171, 172–3
see also Emmet family
Emmet, Robert (son of Thomas Addis Emmet) 9, 12, 166
Emmet, Thomas Addis
family and homes 26, 43, 172, 178, 215
see also Emmet family
education 8–9, 10, 11
legal career 12, 16–17, 20–2, 24, 26, 46, 49–51, 58, 92, 132
political activities 11–12, 16–17, 37, 41, 49–50, 151, 215
and Catholic Committee 15–16, 19, 31
and UI 124, 147
to 1796 12, 14, 16–18, 20–7, 31–2, 90, 183, 213
from 1797 32, 39, 41–2, 46, 50–1, 56–7, 172, 180, 211, 212, 214, 217, 220
and France 19, 27, 32–3, 53, 80, 136, 147, 167, 171, 180, 182–4, 202
and RE's involvement in xi, xii, 35–6, 45, 49, 127, 180, 190–1
state prisoner 38, 56–8, 65, 107–10, 112, 121, 125, 127, 129, 153–4, 237
in Fort George 165–7, 171, 172, 178, 182, 197, 252
associates of 6, 16, 31, 41, 62, 67, 83, 90, 174, 177, 179
and Arthur O'Connor 31, 41, 53, 256
disagreements on French role in Rising 32, 166–7, 182, 183–4, 190, 202
and Tone 9–12, 14, 16, 18, 25–7, 31, 121, 174, 241
writings 11, 40–1, 51, 112, 178, 214
Emmet, Thomas (uncle of RE) 1, 3
Emmett, Christopher (grandfather of RE) 1
England *see* Britain
Ennis 145, 146
Ennis, Patrick 138, 245
Enniscorthy 60, 87, 96, 100, 245
Enniskerry 23, 69, 101
Enniskillen 202
Ennistymon 145
Esmonde, Dr John 24, 84, 229
Esmonde, Sir Thomas 229
Eustace, General 229
Evans, Hampden 88, 182, 212, 252, 256
Exshaw, John 10, 66, 69

Farranshane 37
Farrell, Edward 73

Farrell family 19
Farrell, James 110, 129, 131, 149, 150, 179, 180, 185–6, 197, 239, 243, 256, 257
Farrell, John 215
Farrell, Martin 45, 222
Farrell, Michael 36, 45, 225
Trinity College 35, 36, 45, 63, 64–5, 216, 221, 222, 225, 254
and Rebellion 80–1, 93, 102, 115, 118, 179, 235
after Rebellion 124, 180, 197
in England 115, 179–80, 197, 254, 255
in France 174, 179–80, 195, 254, 255
Farrell, Richard 71, 72, 75, 83, 223, 226, 228, 230
Farren, Charles 59
Faulkner's Dublin Journal 112, 196
Fermanagh 21, 222
Fethard 160
Fingal 86, 105, 229, 231
Finglas 69, 86
Finlay, Lieutenant-Colonel John 84
Finn, Edward 152
Finn, John James 177
Finnerty, Patrick 256
Finnerty, Peter 47, 219, 220
Finney (banker) 85, 230
Finney, Patrick 50, 51, 132, 197, 218
Fishpond (Louth) 102
Fitton, William 62
Fitzgerald, Lord Henry (brother of Lord Edward) 10, 16, 26
Fitzgerald, David 133, 208, 259
Fitzgerald, Edward (Newpark) 95, 97, 100, 105, 106, 132, 148, 167, 245
Fitzgerald, Gerald 160
Fitzgerald, Lady Anne 41, 199
Fitzgerald, Lady Pamela 70, 124, 220
Fitzgerald, Lady Sophia 224
Fitzgerald, Lord Edward 184
and Emmet family 25–6, 31, 41, 124
and UI
to 1798 2, 25, 31, 32, 34, 40, 42
1798 51–4, 57, 68, 128, 164, 183, 212, 220, 226, 257
associates in 76, 91–2, 97, 105, 114, 124, 127, 128–9, 131, 133, 160, 164, 225
plans for rising 54–5, 56, 67, 72–3, 80, 82, 135, 173, 191, 218–19, 231
in hiding, arrest and death 56, 69–73, 80, 82, 92, 96, 223–4, 243, 260
Moore's biography of xi, 28, 43
Fitzgerald, Robert Uniacke 255
Fitzgerald (silversmith, Skinner's Row) 100, 235
Fitzgibbon, John, 1st Earl of Clare 44, 48, 62–5, 109, 110, 174, 222, 237, 253

Fitzsimmons, Hugh 170
Fitzwilliam, William Wentworth, 2nd Earl of (Viceroy 1794–5) 24, 26, 59, 215
Flannery, Patrick 137
Fleming, Thomas 81, 82–3, 85, 89, 96, 246
Flinn, John Thomas 36, 44, 45, 216, 222
Flood, Henry 6
Fontenay, Marquise de 171, 173
Foote, Lundy 61
Fort George 126, 127, 153–4, 165–8, 170–2, 178, 182, 183–4, 190, 195, 197, 252
Foster, John 106, 126, 237
Foundling Hospital (Dublin) 7
Fourcroy, Antoine 180
Fox, Charles James 2–3
Fox and Geese common 78, 83, 89
Fox, Lieutenant-General Henry Edward xi
France and Ireland 6, 13
and Defenders 21, 25
French Revolution 10, 11, 12, 55, 123, 147, 164, 166, 197
Irish exiles in
pre-1800 92–3, 129, 153–4, 209, 226, 239–40
after 1800 36, 169, 172, 174–8, 179–82, 185–7, 252, 254
see also Rising of 1803
in French army 111, 153, 158, 225, 238, 256
and pre-Rebellion UI 13, 20, 22, 25, 27, 31–3, 37–8, 40, 42, 53–4, 112
French in Bantry Bay (1796) 30, 31, 34–5, 37
and planning for Rebellion 32, 54, 67–8, 80, 183–4
and Rebellion 80, 98, 102–3, 106–7, 117, 119–21, 135
Killala landing (Aug 1798) 112–19, 128, 130, 136, 142, 145, 158, 179, 181, 240
Donegal landing (Oct 1798) 118–19, 121, 153
1799 127–8, 134, 136, 144–6, 148–50, 155–6, 158–9, 247
see also Anglo-French War; Rising of 1803
Franklin, Benjamin 173
Freeman's Journal 18, 70, 85
freemasonry 33, 70, 133, 209, 210, 258
Fry, Oliver 22, 210
Fugitive Act (1798) 153
Fuller, Abraham 23, 210, 254–5
Fuller, James 23, 210, 254–5
Fulton, Robert 173, 254
Fyan, Robert 208, 212, 233

Gaffney, Peter 99
Gallagher, John 97
Gallagher, Patrick 69, 70, 72, 88, 92, 97, 98, 129, 130, 172, 174, 175, 176, 200, 223, 234, 243, 253

Galway 41, 146, 147, 148, 158, 162, 192, 250
Galway city 148
Gamble, Revd Thomas 256
Genoud, William 159, 250
George, Denis (judge) 41
George III 7, 10, 19, 112
Geraghty, James 46
Germany 9, 121
Gibbet Rath 87, 231
Giffard, Ambrose Harding 23
Giffard, John 220, 231
Giffard, Lieutenant William 231
Gilligan, John 234
Gilligan, Thomas 234
Glendalough 104
Glendalough road 96
Glenmalure 104, 116, 143, 144
Glin 160
Glin, John Fitzgerald, 23rd Knight of 160
Glindon, James 99, 235
Godfrey, Capt. J. 99
Godwin, William 37, 123, 164
Gorey 60, 139
Gowan, Hunter 142
Granard family 127, 177
Granard, George Forbes, 6th Earl of 122, 241
Granard, Lady Selina Frances (née Rawdon, wife of 6th Earl) 122, 125
Grange 43, 138, 227
Grattan, Henry 6, 10, 191, 215, 229
Graves, Rev Richard 6, 22, 63, 64, 65
Gray, John 175, 183
Gray, Jonathan 51, 232
Gray, Nicholas 82, 88, 91, 94, 141, 143, 164–5, 193, 232, 246
Gray, Robert 183
Green Division *see* St Stephen's Green Division
Greenan 116
Gregg, Tresham 47, 75–6
Grey, George 118, 240
Grose, Brigadier-General Francis 98
Guernsey 119, 157, 260
Guinness, Arthur 220
Guiry, Roger 160
Guy's Hospital (London) 9

habeas corpus 49, 107, 167, 177, 185, 199
Hacketstown 86, 91, 100–1, 105, 141, 158
Halpin and Hannan (distillers) 131, 144, 247
Halpin, James (distiller) 75, 144, 247
Halpin, Thomas (informer) 227
Hamburg
  UI in 175, 190, 235, 254
  1797–9 20, 118, 130, 143, 148, 235
  Tandy affair (1798) 118, 153, 182
  1800–1 67–9, 164–5, 254
  1802–3 178, 179, 180, 183, 184, 187–8, 189, 198, 253

RE in 164–5, 167–9, 170, 183, 184, 189, 190, 202
informers in 187–8, 198
Turner 164, 167, 169, 240, 253
Hamilton, Dacre 44, 64, 222
Hamilton, Joseph 225, 226
Hamilton, Surgeon Robert 241
Hamilton, William 118, 182, 185–6, 196, 202, 240, 257
Hammond family 47
Hapsburg, Empress Maria Theresa 181
Hardwicke, Philip Yorke, Earl (Viceroy) xi, 123, 201
Hardy, Brigadier General Joseph 239
Harold, Fr James 229
Harold's Cross 44, 68–9, 79, 88
Harp of Erin 40
Hartigan, William 103
Harvey, Beauchamp Bagenal 23, 83, 94, 96, 134, 141, 212, 215
Hausonville, Comtesse de 173, 258
Hawkins, Thomas (informer) 232
Hay, Edward 245
Healy, John 138
Henderson, John 134
Henry, Robert 134
Heron, Isaac 20
Hibernian Journal 112
Hibernian Telegraph 50
Higgins, Francis 70, 95
  information from
    to 1797 214, 215, 217
    early 1798 70, 75, 77, 220, 224, 226, 233
    Rebellion 10, 120, 137, 229, 238, 241, 250
    after 1798 139, 164, 170, 212, 247, 252, 255, 256
Hillsborough 37
Hinchey, David 144
Hoche 118
Hoche, General Lazare 30, 35, 241
Hodgestown 106
Holland 39, 150, 153, 154, 168, 178, 180, 183, 184, 188, 253
Holmes, Mary Anne (wife of Robert Holmes, née Emmet) 3, 11, 14, 101, 122, 123, 124, 126–7, 152, 154, 163, 166, 175, 217
Holmes, Robert 11, 101, 122–3, 125–7, 152, 163, 166, 198, 260
Holt, Joseph 90, 95, 96, 98, 100, 104, 105, 110, 111, 114, 116, 120–1, 127, 137, 138, 141, 142–3, 201, 240, 245
Holt, Thomas 90
Holt, William 201
Holycross 60
Honfleur 185
Hope, James xii, 30–1, 39, 42, 92, 130, 134, 136, 137, 149, 152, 187, 189, 197, 223, 236, 253

Hope, Lord (Lord Advocate of Scotland) 165
Horish, William (Master Sweep) 10, 99, 137, 141, 235
house burnings 68, 75, 139, 159
Houston, Thomas 92, 95, 229
Howth 67, 87, 238
Hudson, Edward 44, 59
Hudson, Revd Edward 156
Hughes, James 144
Hughes, John 107, 226
Humbert, General Jean Joseph 113, 115–18, 128, 136, 142, 153, 181, 196, 202
Hume, Samuel 156, 160, 249, 251
Hunter, Robert 73, 172
Hussey, James 137
Hutchinson, Robert 148
Hynes (rebel, Dublin) 111, 237–8

Imaal 110, 163
Inch 95, 208
Indemnity Act (1796) 29
Indomptable 30
informers 9, 49, 93, 155
  pre-Rebellion 18, 23, 31, 39, 43, 48, 61, 63, 65, 69, 75, 77, 93, 210, 226, 233–4
  during Rebellion 89, 90, 103, 107, 112, 116, 224, 232
  post-Rebellion 93, 131, 149, 160–1, 172, 174–6, 187–8, 189, 217, 227, 253, 260
  see also Bird; Boyle; Collins; Cox; Egan; Higgins; Hume; McGucken; MacNally, L.; Magan; Neil; Reynolds, T.; Sproule; Trinity College; Turner, S.; Wright
Insurrection Act 29, 30, 37, 40, 71, 147
Irish executive *see* Dublin Castle; Privy Council
Irish Parliament (College Green)
  Constitution of 1782 14
  House of Commons 6, 17, 19, 112, 124
  House of Lords 19, 59, 123, 124
    Secret Committee of 26, 109, 112
  see also parliamentary reform; Westminster
'Irish Republic' 168, 170
Irishtown 190
Italy 9
Ivers, Peter 219

Jackson family 66, 67, 189
Jackson, Henry 31, 32, 38, 45, 51, 56, 67, 74, 189–90, 209, 212, 214, 220, 225, 229
Jackson, Hugh (brother of Henry) 189–90
Jackson, Hugh (son of Henry) 190
Jackson, John (brother of Henry) 189
Jackson, Revd William 22, 24, 26
Jamaica 157

James, William 106, 220, 230
Jeffrey, John Fitzpatrick 91
Jenkins, Alderman 101
Johnson, Robert (judge) 145
Johnson, Thomas 183
'Jones' *see* John Egan
Jones, William Todd 6–7, 13, 14, 15, 130, 179, 189, 198, 242
and rising of *1803* 7, 14, 179, 189, 198
Joseph, François 142
Judd, Samuel 138

Kane, William 57
Kavanagh, James 138
Kavanagh, Morgan 141
Keadeen 116
Keady 134
Keane, Edward 208, 212
Kearney, Andrew 88
Keelogue 138
Keely, David 78
Kells 230
Kelly (loyalist) 52, 218
Kemmis, Thomas 53
Kenmare, Thomas Browne, 4th Viscount 15
Kennedy, Dr Henry 71, 223
Kennedy, Edward ('Ned') 45–6, 142, 143
Kennedy, Samuel 190, 196, 258
Keogh, Edward 78, 83
Keogh family 19, 191
Keogh, George 44, 222
Keogh, John 15, 31, 44, 70, 83, 170, 183, 184, 189, 195, 236, 257
and Rising of *1803* 44, 170, 184, 195
Keogh, John (junior) 44, 222
Kerr's school 8
Kerry 1–2, 8, 15, 21, 28, 147, 159–60, 201, 222, 240, 261
Kiernan, Dr Robert 241
Kilbeggan 70, 98, 102
Kilbride 95
Kilcock 106
Kilcullen 82, 111
Kildare 1, 144, 186, 194–5
pre-Rebellion UI 39, 54, 60, 73, 220, 225
Rebellion 135, 174
June/July 96, 97–8, 104–6, 115, 246
May 79, 82, 84, 86, 87, 152, 158, 231
late *1798* 91, 94, 114, 115, 116, 238, 239
UI *1799* 132, 136, 140, 141, 158–9, 161
UI *1800–03* 162, 163, 193, 201
Kildea, Hugh 145
Kilgobbin 86, 103
Kilkenny 61, 100, 106, 135, 145, 220
Killala 113, 117, 118, 192
Killarney 2
Killincarraig 120
Kilmacthomas 160
Kilmainham 53, 85, 225, 257, 258
Kilmainham agreement 180
Kilmainham prison *see* prisons

Kiloughter 138
Kilternan 138
Kilwarden, Arthur Wolfe, Lord 123
Kilworth 123
King, Margaret (later Lady Mount Cashell) 123
King, Rufus 153
King, Thomas 194, 200, 209
King's County 87, 96, 98, 135, 144, 158, 161, 193, 215, 220, 246
see also militia
Kingston, Edward King, 1st Earl of 210
Kingston, Robert King, 2nd Earl of 225
Kinnegad 105
Kirwan, Owen 51
Kirwan, Revd Walter Blake 41
Knightstown Bog 106
Knockderig 105
Knox, George 9, 207
Kogh, Mathew 83
Koskiusko, General 175
Kyan, Esmonde 244–5

La Touche, Captain George 103
La Touche, David 43, 78, 218, 227–8
La Touche family 3
La Touche, John 227
Lacey, John 139, 141
Lake, Lieutenant-General Gerard 37, 49, 83, 100, 101, 159, 247
Lamphier, John Pennyfather 222
Langan, James 137
Langan, Thomas 160
Lansdowne family 3
Laois *see* Queen's County
Lavoisier, Antoine 180
Lawless family 36, 131
Lawless, John 36, 44, 67, 90, 110, 124, 174
Lawless, Philip 132, 144
Lawless, Valentine (later Lord Cloncurry) xii, 16, 36, 40, 43, 53, 67, 132, 149, 152, 174, 176–7, 182, 187, 190, 212, 213, 214, 222, 254
Lawless, William 67, 71, 72, 74, 75, 132, 144, 174, 175, 179, 180, 181, 182, 185, 196, 226, 255
Lawson, Edward 131–2, 151, 152, 192, 244, 248
Ledwich, Fr 96
Ledwich (Rathfarnham) 78, 83
Leech, Peter 93, 233–4
Lees, John 77, 93
Leesons 212
Lefroy, Thomas Langlois 46, 216
Lehaunstown camp 67, 95, 112, 116, 234
Lehaunstown conspiracy 67, 74, 81
Leinster 52, 138–9, 159, 188
martial law 67, 75, 191
UI 38–9, 42, 60, 67, 73, 92, 119, 137, 138–9, 144, 152, 163

Leinster Directory *see* United Irishmen
Rebellion 81–2, 85–8, 93–100, 102, 105–7, 114–16, 118, 124, 127, 132, 191, 219, 244–5
see also Dublin; Kildare; Meath; Wexford; Wicklow
Leinster, Earl of 37
Leinster House 54, 55, 56, 219
Leinster, James Fitzgerald, 1st Duke of 2, 37
Leinster, William Robert Fitzgerald, 2nd Duke of 10
Leitrim 25, 135, 145
Leoben 170, 172
Leonard, Bill 160
Leonard, Michael 200
Lewins, Edward 45–6, 167, 168, 212
Liberties 74, 193, 226
Limerick 1, 21, 22, 60, 84, 87, 122, 145, 146, 159, 160, 162, 198, 201, 218, 222, 250, 261
Lindsay, Colin 171
Lisbon 179
Lisburn 6, 130
Listowel 160
Liverpool 115, 117, 170, 179, 186, 198
Locke, John 36–7, 213
London 9–10, 12, 166
see also Britain
London Corresponding Society 215
Long, Philip 114, 133, 179, 194, 208, 225, 239
to *1799* 42, 114–15, 124, 133, 164, 212, 225, 232, 239, 257, 7490
and Rising of *1803* xii, 42, 74, 90, 152, 164, 212, 233
address of *1803* 48, 55, 194
financial support for 114, 133, 194–5, 202
planning and preparation for 56, 133, 179, 180, 186–8, 191, 194–6, 200, 259
statement after Rising 114, 239, 255, 257
Longford 36, 45, 64–5, 80–1, 102, 115, 118, 135, 136, 174, 179, 222, 225, 235
Loughlinstown 103
Loughlinstown Camp 34, 81, 218
Louisiana 186, 196, 202
Louth 17, 21, 37, 73, 86, 88, 102, 106, 135, 145
Lowe, Fr Christopher 96
Lowry, Alexander 38, 130
Lucan 78, 87, 99, 142, 231
Lullymore 144, 193
Lumm, Colonel 73, 182, 225
Lurgan 13, 188, 189
Lusk 79, 86, 101, 234
Luttrellstown 34
Lyon 178
Lyons, Nicholas 100, 111
Lysaght, Francis 145, 146

Macartney family 48
Macartney, Revd Dr Arthur
    Chichester 46, 48, 65, 216
Macartney, Sir John 77
McCabe, Patrick 51, 82, 92, 131,
    138, 139–40, 200, 233, 245,
    246
    and Rising of 1803 51, 82, 92,
        131, 140, 200
McCabe, William Putnam 162
    in pre-Rebellion UI 30, 39, 42,
        56, 70, 72, 137, 223
    after Rebellion 110, 114, 116,
        129, 150
    preparations for Rising of 1803
        42, 192
    new leadership 116, 129,
        161, 192
    in Ulster 149–50, 152, 162
    in Britain 129, 131, 150,
        165, 187
    in France 129, 168, 169,
        179, 186, 196, 256, 259
McCann, Anthony 117, 182,
    188, 189, 195, 198, 202,
    235, 257
McCann, John 38–9, 56, 68, 107,
    108, 127, 189, 220, 236
McCarroll, John 189
MacCarthy, Timothy 148
McClaren, Sergeant Archibald 230
McClune, Southwell 76, 81, 88,
    94, 101, 104, 111, 115, 137,
    141, 158, 228, 234, 241
McCormick, Richard 15, 31, 32,
    51, 56, 63, 74, 75, 91, 130,
    169, 175, 183–4, 189, 190,
    212, 220, 235, 236, 257
McCracken family 44, 188
McCracken, Francis 261
McCracken, Henry Joy 27, 30,
    31, 73, 95, 97, 108, 135
McCracken, Mary Anne 47, 217
McDermott, Bryan 105–6
McDermott, Major Anthony
    James 105, 164, 225
MacDonnell, James Joseph 158,
    174, 196
McGucken, James 128, 131, 134,
    149–53, 192, 196, 242, 244,
    247, 248, 258
McKenna, Theobald 15
McKeown, Anthony 102
Mackintosh, Sir James 9
McLaughlin, Con 128, 129, 131,
    195, 257
McLaughlin family 19, 70
McLaughlin, Peter 44, 118, 222,
    257
McMahon, C.M. 89
McMahon family 232
McMahon, Francis 76, 78, 88,
    89–91, 93, 94, 95, 98, 100,
    104, 111, 114, 115, 116,
    117, 119–20, 129, 141, 158,
    201, 232
McMahon, James 90
McManus, John 70, 98, 99, 102,
    232
McNally, James 86, 230, 231
MacNally, Leonard
    barrister 17, 49, 167

informer 17, 35
    before Rebellion 17, 50, 57,
        208, 211, 212, 214, 220
    Rebellion and trials 78, 79,
        86, 230
    post Rebellion 67, 148, 149,
        164, 196, 248
    and James Tandy 183,
        244, 256
MacNamara, John 132
MacNeven, William 191, 208
    and UI to 1797 14, 32, 36, 41,
        45, 183, 228
    1798 80, 136, 169, 183, 212,
        214, 220
    and Catholic Committee 16,
        24, 31
    state prisoner 56, 109–10
    writings 112, 153, 178, 180
    abroad 178, 180–1, 185
    and Rising of 1803 xii, 14,
        182, 184–5, 190–2, 202,
        258
Macroom 148
MacSorley, Revd J.J. 199
McTier family 11
McTier, Martha (née Drennan)
    11, 199
Madden, John 133
Madden, Richard Robert 5, 9,
    32, 34, 46, 122, 126, 167,
    171, 181, 182, 187, 200
Madden's (Lr. Bridge St.) 140
Magan, Francis 52, 69–70, 72,
    73, 77, 224, 226
Magauran, Thomas 138, 141, 246
Maguire, Bryan 52
Maguire, Daniel 143
Maguire, Simon 27
Mahon's (Merchant Quay) 120,
    132, 241
Maidstone 53, 74, 109, 133, 178
Manchester 132, 148, 175
Margate 53
Markey, Thomas 102, 105, 111,
    236, 238
Marlay/Marley, Patrick 261
Marley Estate 43, 78
Marsden, Alexander
    (Undersecretary) x–xi, 125,
    159, 192, 241
martial law 29–30, 33, 37,
    39–40, 49, 51–2, 60–1, 67,
    71, 83, 99, 136, 141, 147–8,
    160, 163, 191, 224
Martin, Fr John 92, 95–6, 233
Mason, Elizabeth (later Emmet) 1
Mason, St John 5, 44, 165, 169,
    243
Masterson, Michael 99, 235
Mathews, John 91, 100, 141
Maynooth 142
Mayo 25, 75, 112–13, 118, 135,
    142, 145, 146, 158, 222,
    250, 251
Meath 21, 39, 60, 73, 130, 139,
    162, 212, 218, 220
    Rebellion in 38, 79, 82, 86–7,
        95–6, 98, 102, 104, 105,
        106, 114, 116, 135, 139,
        210, 230, 231, 246
Meath, Earl of 3

Medlicott, Captain J. 77
Meighan, Michael 133
Mernagh, John 144
Metcalf, William 39, 152, 162
Meyrick, Brigadier General 146
Middleton family 110
Militia 20, 21, 30
    in action 40, 52, 60–1, 69, 141
        in Rebellion 84, 87, 101
    disaffection in 37–8, 52, 67,
        81, 104, 143, 156
    Fermanagh Militia 52, 61, 84,
        101, 141
    King's Co. Militia 52, 81, 104,
        143
Militia Act (1793) 21
Millar, Revd George 29
Milltown 69, 101, 103, 214
    see also Emmet family
Milltown (Antrim) 48
Milltown Malbay 145
Minchin, Humphey 219, 227
Miness, William 39
Mitchel, Patrick 156
Moira family 122, 127, 177, 241
Moira, Francis Rawdon, 2nd Earl
    of 37, 70, 189, 254
Moira House 70, 124, 125, 241
Moira, Lady (wife of 2nd Earl)
    183, 221, 255
Monaghan 37, 67, 87, 102, 114,
    134, 135, 164, 190, 202
Monaseed 45, 114, 142, 143
Monck, Lord Charles Stanley 69
Moneyduff 156
Moneyhore 94
Moore, Ambrose 143, 164, 212,
    225, 255
Moore, Edward (of Mooresfort)
    6, 18, 215
Moore, James 14, 65, 69, 71, 92,
    96, 212, 223, 229, 233, 248
Moore, Major-General Sir John
    110
Moore, Miss (Thomas St.) 70, 71
Moore, Patrick 137
Moore, Thomas xi, xii, 5, 28, 34,
    43, 44, 46, 47, 48, 59, 62,
    63, 64, 66, 205, 213, 215,
    216, 217, 220, 222
Moore, Thomas (Mayo) 75
Mooresfort 18, 215
Moran, Fr Peter 75, 220
Morres, Hervey Mountmorency
    73, 136, 225, 244–5, 257
Morrison, Major-General
    Edward 201
Mount Cashell family 122, 124,
    125, 175, 176, 177
Mount Cashell, Lady Margaret
    (née King) 123, 124, 175,
    255
Mount Cashell, Stephen Moore,
    2nd Earl 123, 241, 255
Mount Jerome 44, 70, 191, 195
Mount Merrion 101
Mount Pelier Hill 101
Mount Venus 138
Mucklagh Hill 116
Muley, Daniel 138, 208
Mullinahack 208, 235
Mullinaveigue 90

Mullingar 211
Munich 160
Munro, Henry 95, 97, 135
Munster 11, 20, 41, 75, 87
   UI 17, 39, 60, 73, 156, 160,
      198, 201
   Rebellion 82, 84, 87, 99,
      106, 135, 136, 217
   after Rebellion 145, 189, 201
Munster Circuit 8, 12, 20, 21
Murphy, Fr John 100, 106
Murphy, Fr Michael 95
Murphy (killed March '98) 52,
   218
Murphy, Nicholas 71, 72, 85, 96,
   114, 223, 224, 233
Murphy, Revd John 123, 124
Murphy, William 9, 207
Murray, Earl of 165
Musgrave, Sir Richard 78, 258
Myers, Major-General William
   101, 155, 260
Myler, William 120, 132, 238, 241

Naas 60, 61, 87, 106, 115, 116,
   140, 162
Napier, Lady Sarah 235
Naples 55
National Guard 16, 18, 209
Naul, the 18, 130, 152, 187, 189
Navan 106
Needham, Major-General Sir
   Francis 95, 100
Neil, John 116, 120, 142, 239
Neilson, Revd (Dunshaughlin)
   231
Neilson, Samuel 92, 184
   and UI, before 1798 11, 12
   in Ulster 11, 13, 27, 31,
      38–9, 188, 189, 208
      Northern Star 40, 217
   and UI in Dublin, 1798 56, 67,
      71–2, 223, 225, 257
   strategist for Rebellion 72–3,
      76, 80, 82, 91, 92, 135,
      183, 184
   arrest and imprisonment 75–7,
      92, 107–9, 112, 172, 226
   and Rising of 1803 184,
      187–90, 192
   exile and death 190, 258
Nelson, Horatio 119, 186
Nenagh 17
Netherlands *see* Holland
New Geneva Barracks
   (Waterford) 251
New Ross 94, 141, 219, 259
New South Wales 26, 94, 141, 160
   see also transportation
New York 9, 158, 159, 190
Newcastle 95, 138, 162
Newell, Edward John 69
Newenham, Sir Edward 7–8, 13,
   41
Newfoundland 119, 157
Newgate *see* prisons
Newmarket 77
Newpark 95, 97, 148
Newry 167, 236, 239
Newtownmountkennedy 60, 87,
   139, 230
Nihils, Laurence 144, 247

Norbury, John Toler (judge) 17,
   53
Norris, William 198, 200, 260
Northern Star 40, 48, 59
Northern Whig Club 189
Northland, Lord 9
Norway 118, 154
Nugent, Captain (baker) 91, 95
Nugent, Major-General George
   97, 156, 251

oath of allegiance 86, 102, 107,
   115
   see also amnesty
O'Brien, Jemmy 50, 193, 218,
   223, 258
O'Connell, Daniel 195
O'Connell, Mr 20
O'Connor, Arthur
   and UI before Rebellion 25, 40,
      56, 214
   leadership in 32, 34, 42, 45,
      80, 130, 212, 214, 220,
      225, 257
   in England with Coigley
      52–3, 74, 109, 218
   state prisoner 108–10, 112,
      125–6, 127, 153, 242
   in Fort George 154, 165,
      166–7, 178, 183–4
   and Thomas Addis Emmet 31,
      41, 53, 256
   and French role in Rising 32,
      166–7, 182, 183–4, 190,
      202
O'Connor, Roger 40, 109, 180
O'Finn, John 179
O'Flaherty, Francis 134, 158
Ogle, George 188
O'Gorman, Nicholas Purcell
   48–9
O'Hanlon family 188
O'Hanlon, Hugh 93, 100, 113,
   116, 128–9, 131, 133,
   150–1, 153, 169, 201, 239
O'Hara, Charles (junior) 241
O'Hara, Charles (senior) 91–2,
   119, 120, 131, 139–40, 152,
   184, 190, 192, 195, 201,
   212, 225, 233, 238, 241
O'Hara, Henry 192, 233, 241
O'Leary, Jeremiah 53, 74
O Longáin (Langan), Thomas
   160
O Longáin, Micheál Og 160
O'Neil, Denis 127
Oporto 179
Orange Order 25, 59, 63, 72,
   116, 125, 139, 142, 156,
   199, 209, 210, 240
   and yeomanry and militia 30,
      138, 159
Orr, George 213
Orr, John 94
Orr, William 37, 47, 48, 92, 216,
   242
Oswald's school 4
Oulart Hill 87
Ovidstown 98, 102, 105

Paine, Tom 12, 18, 37, 175
Painstown 148

Palmer family 130, 131
Palmer, John (junior) 42, 70, 92,
   124, 129, 150, 165, 168,
   175, 179, 223, 243, 253
Palmer, John (senior) 190
Palmerstown 103, 140
pardons *see* amnesty
Paris *see* France
Parliament, Irish (College Green)
   3, 6, 7, 13–14, 19, 89, 99,
   108–9, 112, 122–4, 152
parliamentary reform 6, 7, 10,
   13–14, 15, 18, 19, 24, 25,
   31, 122
Parnell, Sir John 177
Parsons, Sir Laurence 37
Passmore, Nicholas 141
Patriots 5, 6, 20, 41, 122
Patten, Jane (later Emmet) *see*
   Jane Emmet
Patten, John 5, 15, 16, 41, 65,
   90, 115, 122, 123, 152, 165,
   166, 180, 181, 194, 198,
   257, 260
Patten, Rev John 12
Payne, John (Rear Admiral) 201
Payne, Major-General Sir
   William 198, 201
Peep Of Day Boys 25
Pelham, Thomas (Chief
   Secretary) 38, 49
Pennefather, Colonel Richard 6,
   60
Pennefather family 6, 7, 41, 60
Penrose, James 177
Penrose, Louisa 177, 255
Perrot, Joseph 174
Perry, Anthony 14, 95, 96, 100,
   106, 208, 246
Pheonix Park 38, 136
Philadelphia 27, 157
Phipps, Robert 59, 63, 65
Pigeon House 113, 117
Pigeon House hotel 89
Pitt, William 235, 253
Pluck, William 144
Plunket, William Conyngham 9
Plunkett, Major James 45, 73,
   132, 136, 148, 208, 225
Poland 13, 164, 175
Pollock, John 49, 50, 149, 151,
   167, 210, 217
Portland, William Bentinck, 2nd
   Duke of 24, 112, 166, 252
Portugal 154, 179
Post Office 93, 155
Power, David 48, 217
Power family (Kerry) 1
Power, John 91–2, 93, 158, 250
Power, Patrick 92, 93, 158, 250
Powerscourt 69, 101, 233
Powerscourt, Richard Wingfield,
   4th Viscount 120
Poynings' Law, repeal of (1782)
   6, 18
Prague 178, 181
Presbyterians 12, 13, 19, 24, 134,
   251
Press 40, 41, 47, 48, 49, 51, 59,
   62, 80, 216, 217
press 112, 117, 145, 214

prison tenders 30, 37, 99–100, 119, 129, 138, 157
prisons 231
 Kilmainham prison 18, 38, 56
  and Rebellion 74–5, 83, 169, 226, 231
  see also state prisoners
 Newgate prison 38, 47, 74, 75, 85, 107, 109, 121, 127, 129, 154, 165, 208, 221, 231, 237
 Provost prison 84, 98, 121, 138, 231, 246
Privy Council 17, 75, 158
Prosperous 84
Protestants 5, 12, 13, 14, 27, 104, 134, 189, 240
 Protestant Ascendancy 11, 19, 24, 122, 188, 199
Providence 188
Provost prison *see* prisons
Prussia 157
Puleston, Lieutenant Colonel Richard 227

Quakers 134
Queen's County 50, 60, 100, 105, 106, 135, 186
Quigley, Michael 82, 105–6, 174, 183–4, 190, 195, 239, 257, 259
Quinn 76, 91, 129
Quinstown 90

Raheen 104
Randalstown 156
Rathangan 87
Rathcoffey 105, 174
Rathcoole 79, 85, 140, 227, 229, 232
Rathdown 233
Rathdrum 95, 97, 101, 120, 138, 139, 194, 200–1, 209
Rathfarnham 26, 43, 59, 61, 78–9, 81, 83, 85, 87, 88, 89–90, 95, 96, 97, 100–1, 103, 138, 218, 227, 245
Rathgar 94
Rathlin Island 117
Rathmichael 103
Rathmines 58, 71, 94
Ratoath 104, 106, 231
Rattigan, Edward 68, 72, 74–5, 88, 91, 93, 100, 104, 105, 111, 137, 141, 158, 223, 226, 232, 238
Rawlins, Joseph 200
Raymond, Private (yeomanry) 84, 229
Rebellion of 1798
 casualties 135
 see also Connacht; Leinster; Munster; Ulster; arms; army; Dublin Castle; France; informers; militia; RE; yeomanry
Rebellion Act (1799) 157
Redesdale, Lord 14–15, 255
Redmond, Denis Lambert 118
Redmond, James 138
Reilly (Cavan) 102, 235
Reilly, James 134, 244

Relief Act (1792) 15
Relief Act (1793) 19, 20
Relief Bill (1778) 6
Repeal Association of New York 9
Revenue Commissioners 33–4, 56, 228
Revenue Officers 7, 53
Revolutionary Wars *see* Anglo-French War
Reynolds, Michael 75, 141, 158
Reynolds, Thomas 6, 14, 24, 54, 55, 57, 107, 218, 220, 221, 222, 226
Richard, Thomas 213
Ridgeway, Thomas 187, 188, 258
Rightboys 11, 18, 159, 242
Ringsend 79, 117, 129, 190
Rising of *1803* xi, xii, 21, 22, 48, 71, 74, 84, 89, 90, 120, 125, 130, 135, 181, 184, 187–8, 190–2, 198
 and informers 35, 63, 126, 141, 176, 180, 184, 190, 192, 196, 224, 254–5, 258
  see also Walter Cox
 people involved in 4, 14, 42, 51, 52, 53, 81–2, 89–91, 94, 98–9, 103, 104, 105–6, 113, 114–15, 118–19, 132–3, 138, 139, 140–1, 143, 144, 152, 158, 160, 162, 164, 170, 174, 184, 189, 190–8, 200–3, 215, 232
  see also Dwyer,M.; Emmet, T. A.; Jones, W. T.; Keogh, J.; Long, P.; McCabe, P.; McCabe, W. P.
 planning of 33–4, 40, 44, 56, 80, 135, 150, 156–7, 163, 171, 177, 188, 190–203, 257
 arms 76–7, 173, 196
 reorganisation of UI 26, 117–18, 129, 140–1, 150, 156–7, 161, 163, 189, 192, 200
 strategy 34, 56, 76–7, 80, 81, 84, 106, 118, 136, 191–2
 RE abroad *1801–2* 168, 178–80, 181, 183
  see also Britain; Hamburg; RE in France (below)
 and France 46, 156–7, 162–7, 169, 174–5, 181–7, 190–3, 195–8, 201–3, 257, 259
  RE in France 46, 63, 118, 125, 129, 148, 158, 161, 172–7, 179–81, 192, 258
  negotiations 164–5, 167–72, 177, 180–2, 184–5, 191, 194–5, 253, 256
 RE returns from France *1802* xi, 153, 170, 177, 182–8, 189–91, 195, 198
 trial of RE 9, 17, 28, 130, 164, 200, 207

Roach, John 194, 257
Robinson, Dr Robert 2
Robinson, Robert 134
Roche, Revd Philip 96
Roden, Lord 83, 227
Roe, Nicholas 71
Roebuck 66, 209
Rooney, Walter 78, 227
Roscommon 21, 22, 25, 136, 148, 225
Rose, Alderman 238
Rose, James 73
Ross, Major-General Sir Charles 155
Ross, Robert 115
Rotterdam 178
Rotunda Division (UI) *see* Dublin
Rouen 186, 196
Roundwood 90, 95, 96, 101, 138
Rourke brothers 140, 233
Rourke, Bryan 140, 246
Rourke, Charles 91, 111
Rourke, Felix 72–3, 82, 91, 94, 100, 104, 105, 111, 115, 137, 141, 192, 229, 232, 236, 238, 258
Rourke, Mary (sister of Felix) 115
Rowan, Archibald Hamilton 16, 17, 18, 20, 22, 23, 24, 31, 211, 229
Rowan, William 24
Royal Barracks 83, 121
Royal College of Surgeons in Ireland 3, 90, 103, 174
Royal Irish Academy 22
Royal Navy 26, 30, 82, 118, 120, 155, 173, 179
 mutiny 156
 see also transportation
Rush 104, 212, 230
Russell, John 132, 143, 185–6, 187, 197, 202, 237, 252, 257, 259
Russell, Thomas 12, 41, 44, 132, 166
 and UI 10, 12, 26–7, 27, 40, 44, 127
 state prisoner 127, 129, 166, 178, 181, 184
 and Rising of *1803* xii, 138, 157, 160, 181, 182, 184, 185–6, 190, 191, 192, 196, 202–3
Rutland, Charles Manners, 4th Duke of 7
Ryan, Benjamin (pub, Thos. St.) 140
Ryan, Captain Thomas 69, 71–2, 224
Ryan, James 'Duke of Marlborough' 195, 259, 261
Ryder, James 144

Sadlier, Richard 12, 208
Saggart 78, 229
St John, William 186, 243, 257
St Patrick's Hospital (Dublin) 2, 7
St Patrick's Society 8
St Peter's Church (Aungier Street) 1, 3, 8, 41, 90, 206
St Stephen's Green Division (UI) *see* Dublin

Saintfield 135
Sallins 106
Sampson, William 26, 36, 40, 49, 51, 56, 63, 67, 109, 179, 211, 212, 220, 228
Sandes, Nicholas 160
Sandymount 77, 86
Sandys, John 237
Sandys, Major William 85, 141, 246
Sankey, Henry Gore 10
Santry 78
Saunder's Newsletter 112
Saurin, William 146, 199
Savary, Commodore 118
Scotland 12, 64, 97, 126, 153–4, 166–7, 172, 184, 197–8
see also Edinburgh University; Fort George
Scully, Denys 122, 123, 125, 127, 242
Scully (student informer) 48, 65, 125
Seafield 145
Seagrave, Thomas (Greek St.) 75, 76, 88, 91–2, 116, 158, 233, 240
Seagrave, Thomas (Kevin St.) 240
Secret Committee (1798) 26
Shannon, Richard Boyle, 2nd Earl of 61, 62, 78, 94
Shaw, John 134
Shaw, Zachariah 106, 120
Shea, David 222
Sheares, Henry 31, 47, 49, 67, 73–4, 81, 107–8, 208, 211, 212, 215, 220, 248
Sheares, John 29, 31, 38, 40, 47–8, 67, 73–4, 81, 107–8, 135, 208, 211, 212, 215, 248
Sheehy, Manus 160
Sheffield, Lord 106
Shelley, Mary 123
Sheridan, Richard Brinsley 4
Shirley, William 5
Short, Edward 138
Simms family 11, 136
Simms, Robert 135, 203
Simms, William 135
Simpson, John 90
Sirr, Joseph 227
Sirr, Major Henry Charles 4, 27, 219, 245
 agents 50, 120, 142, 193
 searches and arrests
  pre-Rebellion 55–6, 61, 68–9, 74
  Lord Edward Fitzgerald 69–70, 71–2, 224
  Rebellion 111, 129, 140, 227, 237, 243
  1799–1803 1, 142, 149, 195, 246, 258, 259
  and RE 4, 196, 199, 248
  pardons 115, 137, 233, 239
Skerret, John 157
Sligo 21, 25, 135, 145
Smith, James 186, 259
Smithfield 39, 77, 207
Sorrell Hill 103
Southey, Robert 151
Spain 153, 154, 155, 178–9, 180
Special Commissions 201
Spring-Rice family 1

Sproule, Samuel 77, 93, 94, 104, 119, 120, 233–4
Staël, Madame Anne-Louise de 173, 176
Stafford, Nicholas 138, 245
state prisoners 74–6, 104, 113, 121, 124, 131, 142, 182
 arrests, trials and executions 38, 49, 56–7, 107–8
 exile 108–9, 110, 121, 127, 153–4, 189, 237
 give information on conspircy 107–8, 109, 112, 127, 129, 237
 and new UI leadership 128, 131, 134, 148, 154, 155
 pact 107–10, 112–13, 114, 129
 RE and 107, 109–10, 114
 after Rising of *1803* 188, 195
 see also Fort George; T. A. Emmet
Stawell, Revd 134
Stepaside 101
Stewart, Alexander (father of Robert) 217
Stewart, Robert *see* Castlereagh
Stewart, Sir James 87
Stillorgan 101
Stockdale, John 59, 181, 208, 215, 225, 256
Stokes, Whitley 16, 36, 43, 45, 62, 63
Storey, John 108
Story, Admiral 155
Stradbally 50
Stratford-on-Slaney 92
Stringer 69
Stuart, Lieutenant Colonel 165
Swan, Major William Bellingham 61, 69, 71–2, 113, 115, 119, 137, 140, 199, 223–4, 239, 260
Sweeney, John 182, 196, 256
Sweetman, John 41, 56, 57, 69, 178, 215, 220, 225, 236
Swift, Dean Jonathan 2
Switzerland 9, 154, 171, 181
Swords 78, 227

Taker (Lr. Fitzwilliam St.) 77, 227
Tallaght 79, 85, 89, 91, 103, 141, 246
Tallyrand, Charles 169, 170, 171, 175, 180, 182, 185, 253, 256
Tandy, James 4, 92, 182–3, 195, 202, 208, 229, 243–4, 256
Tandy, Napper 4, 10, 13, 16–17, 18, 20, 21–2, 92, 102, 117–18, 153, 182, 194, 196, 209, 213, 229, 243, 253–4
Tara Hill 73, 79, 84, 86, 89, 95, 105, 231
Teeling, Bartholomew 30–1, 38, 39, 84, 130, 153, 220, 235, 236, 243, 256
Teeling, Charles 27, 30–1, 130, 189, 233
Teeling, Dr Christopher 130
Teeling family 130, 131, 188
Teeling, George 30–1, 128, 130, 150, 188, 189, 192, 258
Temple, Anne Western (wife of Christopher Temple Emmet) 8, 207

Temple family 5–6, 8, 166
Temple, George Grenville Nugent, 2nd Earl *see* Buckingham, 1st Marquis of
Temple, Harriet (née Shirley) 5
Temple, John 8
Temple, Rebecca (later Emmett, wife of Christopher) 1
Temple, Robert 5
Temple, Sir John 5, 42
Temple, Sir Thomas (father of Rebecca Emmet) 1
Templepatrick 39, 130
Tennant, William 261
Thompson, Anthony 104, 113, 236
Thompson, Joseph 232
Tighe, Laurence 224, 229
Timahoe 97, 105, 235
Tipperary 1, 6, 8, 12, 17–18, 41, 60, 122, 135, 145, 159, 160, 162, 208, 222, 250
Tipperary town 1
Toler, John (Attorney-General, later Judge Norbury) 17, 53
Tone, Mathew 84, 153
Tone, Matilda (widow of Wolfe Tone) 174, 176
Tone, Theobald Wolfe 9, 14, 29
 and Dublin radicalism, *1790–1* 10–12
 and UI 12, 13, 21, 27, 29, 211
  programme for 12–14, 18, 22, 27, 31
 and Catholic Committee 15–16
 indictment and leaves for US *1794–5* 23, 24, 26–7, 29
 French expeditions 30, 118, 153
 trial and death 121
 associates of 41, 62, 168, 180
 and T. A. Emmet 9–12, 14, 16, 25–7, 31, 41, 241
torture 60, 68, 74, 75, 78, 85, 99
Tralee 20, 147
transportation 18, 37, 40, 68, 119, 148, 160, 163, 251
 New South Wales 26, 94, 108, 120, 129, 139, 146, 157, 165, 211, 219, 251
 to the Fleet 25, 26, 29–30, 61, 100, 156, 157
Traynor, Thomas 56, 61, 75, 219, 220
Tremlett 175
Trench, Major-General 158
Trim 211
Trinity College Dublin 3, 8, 12, 29, 71, 77, 89, 207, 213, 215, 216
 Catholics in 19, 35, 36, 44, 62
 informers in 23, 35, 44–5, 48, 63, 174–6, 210, 213, 221, 254
 RE at xii, 4, 5, 19, 22, 28–9, 59, 80, 117, 118, 159, 164, 179
  and Historical Society 28, 29, 35, 41, 46
  and UI at 34–6, 42, 43–9, 59, 67, 80, 114, 196, 216, 217, 225
  and the Visitation 62–6, 109, 133, 175–6, 221, 222, 240
  departure from xii, 63–5, 90, 110, 222

Troy (Trinity St) 252
Truelock, Thomas 86
Tubber Pond 99
Tubberadora 60
Tubberneering 94
Turner, Richard 104, 137, 236
Turner, Samuel 35, 50, 107, 149, 196
  in Hamburg 164, 167, 169, 240, 253
Tyrone 37, 73, 134, 156, 174
Tyrrell's house (Clonard) 105

Ulster 21, 134, 188
  dragooning of (1797) 37–8, 40, 60, 67, 83, 92
  UI 12–13, 24, 32, 38–9, 59–60, 92, 103, 113, 130, 134, 149–50, 152, 156, 251
  Ulster Directory *see* United Irishmen
  Rebellion 73, 81, 82, 86–7, 95–7, 102, 103–4, 114, 117–19, 135, 136
  after rebellion 18, 154, 156–7, 159, 203
Union and Freedom 62
Union Star 40, 50, 173, 214
United Britons 132, 133, 149
United Irishmen, Society of
  foundation, aims and strategy 13–14, 33, 42–3, 54–5, 56, 58, 60, 73, 81, 96, 106, 112, 134–5, 136, 150, 219
  leadership of 2, 80, 91, 112, 211, 217
  after Rebellion 121, 128, 131, 133–4, 148, 150, 154, 155, 165, 168, 170, 190, 196, 200
  Executive Directory
    1791–98 25, 32, 33, 35, 38, 41, 42, 53, 67, 70, 220
    1799 127–9, 131, 132, 135, 139, 147–8, 149, 156, 158, 160
    1800–02 165, 167–8, 169, 190, 192, 195, 200
  Leinster Directory 39, 45, 55–6, 68, 88, 127, 214
  Ulster Directory 30, 34, 39, 128, 134, 135, 214, 244
  Dublin Executive Committees 34, 39, 70, 93, 113, 143, 164, 220
  Military Committee 42–3, 92, 97, 164, 165, 184, 225
  and Act of Union 124–7, 146–7, 152
  and Catholic Committee 15, 19, 24, 27, 31, 143, 208
  and Defenders 17, 18, 21, 25, 27, 38, 130, 135, 156, 233
  see also under provinces and counties; Rising of *1803*; Trinity College

United States of America 13, 108, 164, 173, 175, 176
  American War of Independence 5, 6, 20, 32, 90, 164, 168, 173, 175, 182
  and Emmet family 4, 5–6, 8, 9, 171, 202

and exile of state prisoners 109, 111, 121, 153
  'Louisiana incident' 186, 196, 202
  RE meets Americans in Paris 173, 175
  UI exiles in 157, 158, 159, 171, 190, 191, 209
    Thomas Addis Emmet 4, 9, 202
  Wolfe Tone 23, 27

Vauquelin, Louis-Nicolas 173, 180
Vinegar Hill 96, 97, 100, 106
Voltaire 37
Volunteers 6, 10, 13, 16, 18, 20, 69, 209

Wade (yeomanry infiltrator) 78, 83
Wales 37, 97, 171, 198
Walpole, Colonel 94
Ware, Hugh 105–6, 174, 182, 196
Warren, Thomas 33, 102
Washington, George 7
Waterford 1, 39, 84, 145, 159–60, 222, 229, 251, 259
Waterford Gazette 20
West Indies 119, 157
Westmeath 40, 61, 70, 81, 86–7, 98, 99, 102, 118, 134, 135, 136, 215, 220, 225, 235
Westminster 4, 6, 14, 19, 30, 185
Westmoreland, John Fane, 10th Earl of (Viceroy 1790–5) 17
Westphalstown House 84, 105, 227
Westport 158
Wexford 21, 61
  UI 39, 54, 55–6, 246
  Rebellion 23, 81, 87, 91, 94–5, 96–7, 99, 100, 101, 102, 106, 114, 134, 135, 136, 141, 145, 197, 244, 259
  after Rebellion 20, 132, 134, 139, 144, 158–9, 163, 201, 251, 259
  in Dublin 138, 141, 142, 143, 164, 235
Wexford town 87
Whaley, Thomas 'Buck' 3
Whelan, Kevin 36
Whelp rock (Blessington) 98, 103, 104
Whigs (Britain) 24, 185
Whigs (Irish) 13, 41
  Whig Club 12, 59
  Northern Whig Club 189
White Bull Inn (Dillon's, Thomas St.) 140
White, John 221
White, Luke 233
White, Robert 216
Whitehall 83
Whyte, Samuel 4, 5, 22
Whyte's Academy 4, 5, 22, 62
Wickham, William xi, 147–8, 167, 174, 177, 195, 201, 214

Wicklow 162, 194
  UI before *1798* 23, 39, 137, 162, 212, 214, 233
  1798
    Jan–May 60, 73, 78, 79, 220, 225
    May–July 72, 81–2, 86–97, 100–1, 103–6, 135, 141, 157
    Aug–Dec 110, 111, 114, 116, 117, 119–20, 135, 138–9, 142, 240
  post-Rebellion UI
    1799 132, 136, 139, 143–4, 158–9
    1800–02 139, 144, 162, 163, 177, 194, 197, 200–1, 227, 259
  UI from in Dublin 138–9, 141–4, 240
Wicklow town 139, 141, 143
Wilford, Major-General Richard 105, 106
Wilkinson, George 129, 243
Wilmot, Catherine 175–6
Wilmot, Robert 176
Wilson, Hugh 180, 182
Wilson, James 137
Wilson, Revd (Monaghan) 134
Winder, Justice John 86
Winslow, Lieutenant Blaney 61, 221
Wollstonecraft, Mary 123, 164
Workhouse Division (UI) *see* Dublin
Worthington, Sir William 124
Wright, Thomas 24
  and pre-Rebellion UI 24, 38, 45, 90, 92, 212
  and RE 24, 90, 93, 98, 110, 113–14, 115, 151–2, 200
  and Rebellion 24, 90, 91–2, 93, 98, 113, 115, 119–20, 194, 201
  and UI leadership *1799–03* 128, 131–2, 151, 152, 164, 192, 208, 212, 232, 244
  warrant and arrest (1799) 150–1
  information of 24, 113, 151–2, 192, 195, 200, 233, 238, 242, 243–4, 248

Yellow Bottle pub 91, 140
yeomanry 50, 78, 209
  before Rebellion 30, 36, 40, 48, 52, 60, 61
  preparation for Rebellion 69, 72, 74–5, 77, 140
  Rebellion 78–9, 82, 84, 85, 97, 98, 101, 103, 111, 116
  after Rebellion 138–9, 142, 156, 159
  and Act of Union 124–5, 146, 199
  Lawyers corps 77, 101, 122, 199, 207
  Liberty Rangers 124–5, 174
Young, Bishop 63

Robert Emmet and the Rising of 1803

Ruán O'Donnell, University of Limerick

*'the most closely contextualised, accurate and archivally
dense biography of Robert Emmet yet produced'*
Professor Kevin Whelan
Keogh-Notre Dame Centre, Dublin

Robert Emmet is one of the best known but least understood figures in Irish history. As the premier popular hero of the nineteenth century, his dramatic speech from the dock challenged successors to vindicate his deeds by ensuring that Ireland took its place 'amongst the nations of the Earth'. The Rising of 1803, of which Emmet was the main strategist, was the first attempt of the republican United Irishmen to sever the Act of Union between Britain and Ireland by armed force and was regarded with the utmost seriousness in Dublin and London in consequence.

Emmet, arrested on 25 August 1803 and executed on 20 September, passed immediately into the ranks of Irish republican heroes. His stoicism, idealism and revolutionary acumen were all admired by contemporaries, even if the appealing lyrics of Thomas Moore represented him as a romantic figure. Emmet's stirring speech from the dock, however, ensured his iconic status with the physical force tradition whose leaders acknowledged him in 1867 during the Fenian Rising and, more importantly, during the Rising of Easter 1916. For this reason Emmet's name will be associated with the final resolution of the National Question in Ireland which the current Peace Process may yet address.

This second book in Ruán O'Donnell's contextualised two-volume biography draws on significant new research to re-evaluate Robert Emmet's revolutionary career and legacy.

368 pages illus 2003
0 7165 2786 3 €49.50 / £39.50 / $55.00 (cloth)
0 7165 2787 1 €27.50 / £20.00 / $27.50 (paper)

IRISH ACADEMIC PRESS
44 Northumberland Road, Ballsbridge, Dublin 4, Ireland
Tel: +353 (0)1 6688244 **Fax:** +353(0)1 6601610
Email: info@iap.ie **Website:** www.iap.ie

Soul On Fire
A Life of Thomas Russell, 1767–1803

James Quinn

Thomas Russell, the United Irishman and close friend of Wolfe Tone, had an eventful and varied life. He fought in India as an armed officer, was a journalist with the radical *Northern Star,* librarian with the Linen Hall Library, and one of the most important radical political activists of the 1790s. Russell played a key role in the founding of the United Irishmen, and in transforming the constitutional society into a revolutionary conspiracy. He is also accepted as the most socially radical of all the United Irish leaders, and was a fervent opponent of the slave trade and industrial exploitation. He was seen by the government as perhaps the most dangerous of the United Irishmen, and as a result he spent six years in prison without a trial. He emerged from prison in 1802 still intent on revolt, and is unique in being the only founder of the United Irishmen to participate in the society's last stand – the Emmet revolt of 1803. To assist Emmet's efforts in Dublin, he attempted to raise Ulster, but failed and was hanged in Downpatrick.

There was, however, much more to his life than politics. He participated fully in the intellectual ferment of the late eighteenth century, and had wide-ranging interests in philosophy, politics, science, literature and Gaelic culture. On a personal level, he was a fascinating man, his dark striking looks and engaging personality winning him the admiration of both men and women. Yet he was an enigmatic and tortured soul, his heavy drinking and sexual promiscuity sitting uneasily with his deeply-held Christian beliefs. Born a Protestant, he was a deeply religious man, sympathetic to all forms of Christianity, and his religious views, most notably his belief in the advent of a Christian utopia or 'millennium', offer the key to understanding his life.

336 pages illus 2002
0 7165 2732 4 €49.50/£39.50/$57.50

IRISH ACADEMIC PRESS
44 Northumberland Road, Ballsbridge, Dublin 4, Ireland
Tel: +353 (0)1 6688244 **Fax:** +353(0)1 6601610
Email: info@iap.ie **Website:** www.iap.ie